D0849821

Also by Sean Kelly and Rosemary Rogers

Saints Preserve Us!
Everything You Need to Know About Every Saint You'll Ever Need

How to Be Irish (Even If You Already Are)

Who in Hell...A Guide to the Whole Damned Bunch

The Birthday Book of Saints

Villard ⓥ New York

The Birthday Book of Saints

Your Powerful Personal Patrons of Every Blessed Day of the Year

✤· Sean Kelly and Rosemary Rogers ·✤

VILLARD BOOKS is a registered trademark of Random House, Inc.
Colophon is a trademark of Random House, Inc.

Library of Congress Cataloging-in-Publication Data

Kelly, Sean.
The birthday book of saints: your powerful personal patrons of every blessed day
of the year / Sean Kelly and Rosemary Rogers.
p. cm.
ISBN 0-375-75776-7
1. Christian saints—Calendar.   I. Rogers, Rosemary.   II. Title.

BX4655.3 .K64 2001
263'.98—dc21   2001025834

Book design by Mercedes Everett

Villard Books website address: www.villard.com

Printed in the United States of America on acid-free paper

24689753

First Edition

For Rose Rogers and Bridie Duignan,
presently having tea with Saint Anne,
and for Father James Flood,
expected shortly;
he stopped in for a short one
with Saint Brendan around the corner.

Acknowledgments

Father Francis X. Aracil, SDB
Adé Bethune
Ralf Bode and Christine Ernst Bode
Susan Brown
Moya Campbell rsj
Robert Downey, Jr.
Mercedes Everett, Random House
Bonnie Erickson
Wally Faye
Sallie Ann Glassman
Wayde Harrison
Sister Margaret Kapusnak, OSBM
Mac Kelly
Howard and Ron Mandlebaum, Photofest
Sister Marie Teresa OP, Dominican Sisters of Hawthorne
Kathleen McKeever
The McKenna family, Emyvale Co. Monaghan
Brian McLendon, Random House
Stephanie Morris, Ph.D., C.A., Sisters of the Blessed Sacrament
Kathy Pappas
Beth Pearson, Random House
Phil Runkel, Marquette University Archives
Jane Sammon, *The Catholic Worker*
The Sisters Gift Shop of Graymoor, Garrison, New York
The Sisters of St. Joseph
The Sisters of St. Basil the Great, Uniontown, Pennsylvania
Steve "Steverino" Scholem
Bruce Tracy, Villard Books
Karen Watts, Lark Productions
Katie Zug, Villard Books

Introduction

It is a truth universally acknowledged that One's Birthday is of terrific importance and consuming interest—to One.

Even the most skeptical among us cannot resist a glimpse at a horoscope—and the sign we check out first is invariably our own. Most of us can name our birthstone, many know the lucky number that numerologists assign to us based on our date of birth, and some of us can even name several celebrities with whom we happen to share a Birthday. But all of that—entertaining though it may be—is just the stuff of superstition and coincidence.

What we have here is . . . the True Significance of Birthdays!

Each and every day of the calendar year is the Feast Day of several—often of a great many—genuine, certified, canonized Christian Saints. (The date is usually that of the Saint's "Heavenly Birthday"—that is, the day on which he or she died, smiling, and became a Saint.)

That means that you were born on a day dedicated to a person or persons who are absolutely guaranteed to be in Heaven, with influential access to the Almighty. The Saint—or Saints—whose Feast Day your Higher Power chose for your birthday is therefore your Powerful Personal Patron, certain to take an abiding, benevolent interest in your affairs.

It goes without saying that anyone born on February 14—the Feast of Saint Valentine, Patron Saint of Lovers—will be of a romantic nature. Persons born on July 25—the Feast of Saint Christopher—tend to fasten their seat belts. And those born on March 17—Saint Patrick's Day—are likely to have a bit of blarney about them, or at least a way with snakes. Ah! you may object, but I know a fellow born on Saint Paddy's Day who is of a dour and sober disposition. Of course, we reply; for March 17 is also the Feast of Saint Joseph of Arimathea, the Patron of Undertakers!

In our research we have pored over many ancient books—and not a few websites—to assemble the identities and stories of these Citizens of Paradise. The dates of their Feasts are those assigned to them by the latest Roman Catholic liturgical calendar—but we have taken the liberty of retaining some of the more fabulous figures, such as Eustace and Barbara, whose commemorations were unfortunately suppressed in 1969, by the Vatican, in a fit of ill-advised "modernization."

Whenever possible we have listed the causes, places, or activities with which the various Saints have traditionally been concerned—for example, it is widely known that Saint Anthony of Padua (June 13) is of great assistance in finding lost objects; Saint Jude (October 28) handles desperate cases; Saint George (April 23) looks with favor upon people of English descent; Saint Swithin (July 15) brings rain; and Saint Uncumber (July 20) disposes of troublesome husbands.

Whenever possible we also indicate the Saint's emblem or attribute—a symbolic object with which he or she is frequently pictured, for purposes of identification. Saint Lawrence, who was roasted to death, is usually shown holding a gridiron. Those born on his Feast Day (August 10) are of a culinary inclination, for he is the Patron Saint of chefs.

We urge you—having first purchased the book, of course—to look yourself up. You will doubtless discover your Birthday to be the Feast of either your predestined role model or your secret identity: a ruthless, heretic-slaying crusader, say . . . or a misanthropic, miracle-working hermit . . . even a beautiful virgin martyr.

The Birthday Book of Saints

❧ January ❧

1. THE FEAST OF THE CIRCUMCISION

Since he was born of observant Jews, the newborn Christ Child was, "after eight days," according to the Gospel of Saint Luke, genitally mutilated. Saints Jerome and Bernard concur that the surgery was performed by none other than His Virgin Mother Mary, and that this ritual bloodshed was the first of her Seven Sorrows. In after years the Divine Foreskin was a much-prized relic, once bestowed by Angels upon the Emperor Charlemagne; a reliquary jar said to contain it still is venerated at a parish church in Calcata, Italy.

THE FEAST OF SAINT CLARUS

Obscure French prelate, 660

Patron of the shortsighted; invoked against myopia • (emblem: abbot appeasing a flooded river)

This humble French monk was so holy that he was appointed spiritual director of the convent in which his own widowed mother was a nun. Despite the many miracles attributed to Clarus, it is because of his name, which in Latin means "clear," that his heavenly aid is sought by those whose vision isn't.

THE FEAST OF SAINT ODILO

Homely but zealous abbot of Cluny, 1049

Invoked against jaundice • (emblem: monk, a skull at his feet)

An authority both spiritual and temporal, Odilo instituted the Feast of All Souls—a sort of Unknown Saints' Day—as well as the Truce of God, by which local warlords were obliged to refrain from hostilities on weekends. Odilo was especially devoted to the Blessed Virgin, through whose intercession he had, as an infant, been cured of an excess of the bile pigment bilirubin.

Also: The Feast of Saint Peter of Atroa, among whose gifts was the ability to make himself invisible, 837; and Saint Telemachus, who leapt into the arena and put an end to gladiatorial contests, c. 400.

SAINT TELEMACHUS
PEACE MAKER

2. THE FEAST OF SAINT ADELARD

Retired French politician-abbot, 827

Patron of gardeners • (emblem: spade)

Like his cousin Charlemagne, the monk Adelard (aka Adalhard) was a grandson of Charles "the Hammer of God" Martel—that is, a member of proto-French royalty. Renowned for his learning—he wrote in Latin, French, and German—he was often summoned to the Carolingian court as an adviser, and invariably banished for the advice he gave. His final exile was to Corbie, in far-off Normandy, where he enthusiastically took up horticulture.

OUR HOLY FATHER AMONG THE SAINTS
BASIL the GREAT

THE FEAST OF SAINT BASIL THE GREAT

Patriarch, Doctor of the Church, 379

Patron of hospital administrators, Russia • (emblem: a heavenly hand offering him a pen)

Born in present-day Turkey into a very religious family—both his parents, two of his brothers, and a sister are canonized Catholic Saints—Basil studied in Athens, where he was a classmate of the future infamous emperor Julian the Apostate. As bishop of Caesarea, Basil was a fearless foe of imperial heresy and a tireless

CEO, establishing and administering a vast complex of churches, hospitals, and orphanages known as Basiliad. The rule he created for monastic living is followed to this day in the Eastern (Russian and Greek Orthodox) Church, and he is still highly revered in Russia; his personality—generous, eloquent, shrewd, and pigheaded—appeals to the Russian soul.

THE FEAST OF SAINT GREGORY OF NAZIANZEN
Son of a bishop, Doctor of the Church, 390

Patron of fruitfulness, poets • (emblem: book)

An eloquent preacher and brilliant theologian, Gregory was a most reluctant administrator, and prone to nervous breakdowns. Of a shy and retiring nature—he wanted to be a monk—he was constantly conscripted by his boyhood friend Saint Basil into the battle against the Arian heresy. In retirement he composed a long and tedious autobiography in verse.

THE FEAST OF SAINT MACARIUS THE YOUNGER
Ex-confectioner, desert hermit, 408

Patron of pastry cooks • (emblem: monk, hyena and its young beside him)

A cake maker and sugar-plum merchant in Alexandria, Macarius suffered a midlife crisis in 335 and fled to the desert, there to spend the next sixty years in penitential basket weaving. His diet consisted only of uncooked beans—except during the fast days of Lent, when it was reduced to a few cabbage leaves. Racked with guilt over killing a fly, he permitted insects to bite him unmolested. Macarius considered nursing in hospitals to be grandstanding in the guise of charity, but once went to the trouble of curing a blind hyena.

Also: The Feast of Saint Abel, whom his brother Cain killed; and Saint Munchin, Patron of Limerick, Ireland, 7th century.

3. THE FEAST OF SAINT GENEVIEVE
Severe but patriotic virgin, 500

Patron of makers of wall coverings, milliners, Paris, women's army corps; invoked against drought, fever, flood, misfortune, plague • (emblem: a Devil blowing out her candle, an Angel relighting it)

In 429, while visiting the little town of Nanterre, Bishop Saint Germain (for whom the Parisian boulevard is named) "discovered" the seven-year-old Genevieve and predicted great things for her, so long as she remained "clean and untouched." At fifteen she arrived in Paris to receive from his hands the veil of a dedicated virgin. The new nun proceeded to declaim visionary prophesies of doom upon the sinful city, which made her unpopular, especially because Paris was at the time under siege by the barbaric Franks. Then, much to everyone's surprise, the gloomy prophetess personally ran the blockade, returning with boatloads of wheat to feed the starving populace. (She herself subsisted on two meals a week of barley and beans.) In 451, when Attila the Hun and his savage hordes bypassed the city, it was obvious to all that Genevieve's prayers had saved them. Since her death Genevieve has continued to protect her city. In 1129, when an epidemic of ergot poisoning raged in Paris, her holy relics were disinterred and paraded through the streets, which ended the plague, and in 1206 her intercession caused the flooding Seine to subside. The splendid church once dedicated to her was transformed, by godless French revolutionaries, into the Panthéon.

Also: The Feast of Saint Daniel of Padua, a 1st-century Jewish deacon of that city, invoked by women whose husbands are away at war.

4. THE FEAST OF SAINT ANGELA OF FOLIGNO
Formerly lusty nun, 1309

Patron of widows • (emblem: holding a Devil chained)

She married young, for money, and bore several children while conducting a series of quite scandalous extramarital affairs, but after her husband's death Angela repented and become a Franciscan recluse, renowned for her piety and penances. She wrote a passionate spiritual autobiography, *The Book of the Divine Consolation,* in which she describes in detail her mystical marriage to Christ—upon which occasion her Bridegroom endowed her with the Stigmata. Angela is sometimes referred to as the Mistress of Theologians. They wish.

THE FEAST OF SAINT PHARAÏLDIS

Poultry-resurrecting widow, 740

Patron of the unhappily married; invoked against childhood illnesses • (emblem: gosling)

This Flemish maiden (who is the official Patroness of the city of Ghent) was the niece of Saint Gertrude of Nivelles. Obliged against her will to marry, Pharaïldis was abused by her brute of a husband. Famously compassionate, she once caused a miraculous fountain to spring from the earth for the thirsty people of Braug. It is there to this day, and its waters continue to be wonderfully effective against a host of childhood illnesses. In art Pharaïldis is pictured holding a goose, in honor of the famous occasion when she—for reasons unknown—restored a roasted fowl not only to life but with its original plumage.

Also: The Feast of Saint Elizabeth "Mother" Seton, daughter of a Staten Island doctor, convert from Anglicanism, founder of the Sisters of Charity, and the first American-born Saint, 1821.

5. THE FEAST OF SAINT EDWARD "THE CONFESSOR"

Chaste English monarch, 1066

Invoked against scrofula • (emblem: five martlets)

alf Anglo-Saxon and half Norman, this listless and ineffectual king had a reputation for sanctity, based on the rumors that his touch could cure tuberculosis (then known as the king's evil) and that his marriage was unconsummated. Certainly it was without issue, and after six years of it his wife, Edith, went home to mother. In the Anglican Church, Edward's Feast is celebrated on October 13, the date his body was enshrined in Westminster Abbey.

THE FEAST OF SAINT GERLAC

Reformed outlaw who went back to nature, 1170

Patron of animals • (emblem: hermit in a tree)

Dutch soldier of fortune, Gerlac repented of his marauding ways upon being widowed and made a pilgrimage to Rome, where he confessed his many sins of pillage to Pope Eugenius III. After doing penance for seven years, he made his home in a hollow tree. Curiously, this eccentric hermit became a great friend of the estimable Saint Hildegard.

THE FEAST OF SAINT SIMEON STYLITES

Popular pillar-sitting anchorite, 459

Patron of shepherds • (emblem: pillar)

he most famous of the desert hermits known as anchorites was the son of a Syrian shepherd. He entered a local monastery at the age of thirteen but was expelled because of the extreme mortifications he performed (such as winding his body with chains until his flesh was raw and delicately replacing maggots when they emerged from his wounds for a breath of air). He became a solitary hermit on a mountaintop, but his flamboyant holiness (he dressed in wild beast

skins and performed prodigious feats of fasting) inspired crowds to seek him out for their edification—or, perhaps, entertainment. To escape their unwanted attentions he took up residence on top of a ten-foot-high pillar. Curiously enough, this attracted even greater crowds, and for the remaining thirty-five years of his life Simeon lived on a series of ever-higher pillars. His final earthly home was a six-foot-square platform on a pillar sixty feet high.

Also: The Feast of Saint John Neumann, German-born bishop of Philadelphia, 1860.

6. THE FEAST OF THE EPIPHANY

The Magi, three Kings, aka Wise Men, 1st century

Patrons of travelers • (emblem: three kings bearing gifts)

In the Eastern Empire it was on this date that Christ's nativity was originally commemorated—indeed, it still is in the Armenian Church. Western Christendom, sometime in the fourth century, began to celebrate "Christmas" on December 25—presumably to coincide with and supersede the rowdy pagan New Year festivals of Saturnalia and Yule—and the sixth of January became the "Twelfth Day of Christmas" or "Little Christmas." After Christ's birth, according to the Gospel of Matthew (2:1–12), an unspecified number of "wise men from the East" arrived in Jerusalem to worship and present gifts to the newborn "King of the Jews." By ancient tradition they were three, all of them kings: Caspar, who brought gold, Balthasar with frankincense, and Melchior with myrrh. Matthew says the Wise Men afterward "departed into their own country," but legend has it that the Apostle Saint Thomas encountered the trio on his mission to India and consecrated them as bishops. Three centuries later their corpses were miraculously discovered by Saint Helena, in Constantinople. They are now enshrined in the cathedral in Cologne.

THE FEAST OF SAINT MACRA

Mutilated virgin martyr, 387

Invoked against diseases of the breast • (emblem: breasts on a book)

A maiden convert in Rheims, France (Gaul to the Romans of the time), Macra refused to renounce either her Faith or her chastity and was subjected to fiendish tortures, not the least of which was the shearing off of her—by all account substantial mammaries. It seems that Macra was something of a schol-ar, for in art she is depicted carrying her breasts on an open book.

7. THE FEAST OF SAINT ALDRIC

German forger-bishop, 856

Invoked against asthma • (emblem: as a cowherd)

This Saint was, in his youth, a member of Charlemagne's imperial court and attained the bishopric of Le Mans. He served as "guide of conscience" to Charlemagne's successor, Louis the Pious, but later upheld the claims of his rival, Louis the Bald. The documents supporting Aldric's personal territorial claims proved, even in his lifetime, to be forgeries, and he has lately been accused of concocting that scandalously fraudulent document the Donation of Constantine. The connection, if any, between his career as a con man and his heavenly Patronage of asthma sufferers is unexplained.

THE FEAST OF SAINT RAYMOND OF PEÑAFORT

Windsurfing canon lawyer, 1275

Patron of law schools and lawyers • (emblem: using his cloak for a sail)

This Catalan nobleman was already a celebrated professor of law when, at the age of forty-seven, he joined the Dominican Order. In 1230 he was summoned to Rome, where Pope Gregory IX was in the planning stages of the Inquisition and needed help researching ten centuries of contradictory Papal Decrees—the Eternal Immutable Laws that the Inquisitors were to enforce. These Decretals, as assembled and published by Raymond, form the basis of Catholic Canon Law. Made an archbishop for his troubles, he returned to Catalonia, where he spent the rest of his life (he lived to be one hundred) making things plenty hot for local heretics, Moors, and Jews. Invited by the king to the island of Majorca, Our Saint was shocked to discover that His Majesty was keeping company with a woman not his wife. The outraged Man of God insisted on returning to the mainland, but the sinful monarch denied him use of a ship—whereupon Raymond spread his cloak on the surface of the Mediterranean, tied a corner of it to his crozier, stepped aboard, and windsurfed home.

THE FEAST OF SAINT REINOLD

Busybody monk, martyr, 960

Patron of stonemasons • (emblem: stonemason's hammer)

A young Benedictine of Cologne, Reinold supervised a building project with such zeal that the stonemasons murdered him with their hammers.

8. THE FEAST OF SAINT GUDULA

Well-connected Belgian maiden, 712

Patron of Brussels; invoked against toothache • (emblem: nun carrying a lantern)

The daughter of a count of Flanders, this maiden spent her days performing devotions and charitable works. Once, on her way to church at night, her lantern went out—and was miraculously relit as a result of her prayers! A great church in Brussels is dedicated to her, and enshrined within it are all her teeth. Before this holy relic the dentally distressed assemble to beg for relief.

THE FEAST OF SAINT SEVERINUS OF NORICUM

Wonder-working abbot, c. 550

Invoked for the fertility of vineyards • (emblem: oil pitcher)

A hermit in the East before becoming a missionary to Hun-infested Austria, Severinus established several churches, in one of which he personally distributed olive oil to the starving natives. The barbarian king Odoacer asked for and received Severinus's blessing before marching off to sack Rome.

Also: The Feast of Saint Abo, Baghdad-born perfumer, converted from Islam, beheaded, 786.

9. THE FEAST OF SAINT BASILISSA

Happily married virgin martyr, 296

Invoked against breast-feeding difficulties, chilblains • (emblem: Angel pointing to a book)

There are eight Saints by this name, all exceedingly beautiful. This Basilissa married a man named Julian. On their wedding night she persuaded him to join her in a vow of perpetual virginity. As they prayed together to "overcome the wiles of the old serpent," as one hagiographer put it, their nuptial chamber was filled with unearthly light and the odor of lilies. Thereafter they lived together as brother and sister, in perfect chastity, which accounts for the chilblains but hardly the breast feeding.

Also: The Feast of Saint Adrian of Canterbury, African-born missionary to England, 710; and Saint Philip of Moscow, bishop and sanitary engineer, martyred by the command of Czar Ivan the Terrible, 1569.

10. The Feast of Saints Agatho, the first Pope to declare his own infallibility, 681; Benincasa, abbot of La Cava, near Salerno, 1194; Evagrius Ponticus, who, tempted by a friend's wife, fled to the desert, 399; Gonzalvo, Portuguese fisherman-hermit, 1560; Gregory X, Sicilian elected to the papacy while on a Crusade, 1276; John Camillus Bonus, heresy-opposing bishop of Milan, 600; Marcian of Constantinople, a Greek priest who once gave his clothes to a beggar and said Mass in the nude, 471; Nicanor, a Jewish deacon, one of the seven chosen by the Apostles, 76; Peter Urseleno, Venetian nobleman and admiral turned recluse, 987; Petronius of Avignon, distinguished Roman French bishop, 463; Sethrida, retiring Anglo-Saxon princess, 660; Thomian of Armagh, feisty Irish archbishop, 660; and William of Bourges, reluctant French abbot, 1209.

11. THE FEAST OF SAINT BALTHASAR

The African "Magus," 1st century

Patron of manufacturers of playing cards, saw men; invoked against epilepsy • (emblem: black king bearing a gift)

By a tradition at least twelve centuries old, one of the three Wise Men who followed the star to visit the infant Christ was a Negro—presumably the "king of Saba," whose arrival was foretold in the Psalms. If the Wise Men were indeed Magi, they were priests of Zoroaster and came from Persia—or, as we would say, Iran.

Also: The Feast of Saint Vitalis of Gaza, who employed unorthodox methods to save the harlots of Alexandria, 625.

12. THE FEAST OF SAINT BENET BISCOP

Culture-promoting English abbot, 690

Patron of architects, artists, glaziers, musicians • (emblem: by a river, two monasteries near him)

Born in semipagan Northumbria, Biscop Baducing adopted the name Benet (the anglicized version of Benedict) when he became a Benedictine monk. A scholar and founder of abbeys and churches, he traveled often to the Continent, always returning to his primitive homeland with collections of paintings and manuscripts. He also imported sophisticated builders—glaziers and masons—and introduced the Roman style of chant to English choristers.

Also: The Feast of Saint Arcadius of Mauritania, who continued to praise the Lord while his limbs were hacked off joint by joint, 304; and Saints Marina and Tatinia, both of whom lived, disguised as boys, in separate cloistered monasteries, until accused of fathering children, date unknown.

13. THE FEAST OF SAINT HILARY OF POITIERS

Happily married French bishop, 367

Patron of backward children, lawyers; invoked against insanity, snakebite • (emblem: child in cradle)

Born into a wealthy pagan family of Roman Gaul, Hilary was thirty-five years old and a married man with a daughter when he converted to Christianity and—much against his will—was proclaimed a bishop. His politically incorrect but theologically sound objections to the then-popular Arian heresy resulted in his exile to Phrygia, where he exterminated the serpent population. His bed has a place of honor in the cathedral of Poitiers.

14. THE FEAST OF SAINT FELIX OF NOLA

Popularly elected bishop, 260

Invoked against perjury • (emblem: priest in cave, cobweb across entrance)

One of sixty Saints named Felix, this son of a Syrian soldier was assistant to Bishop Maximus of Nola at the time of Emperor Decius's persecutions. The old bishop went into hiding; the police arrested and tortured Felix, but he escaped and successfully eluded his pursuers by hiding in a cave, across the entrance to which a spider obligingly spun a web. All this we know from a poem written by a later bishop of Nola, Saint Paulinus, who assures us that in Heaven Felix has a special sympathy for the falsely accused.

THE FEAST OF SAINT MUNGO (AKA KENTIGERN)

Missionary to the pagan Scots, 603

Patron of Glasgow • (emblem: fish with a ring in its mouth)

The first bishop of the Strathclyde Britons—that is, the Lowland Scots—was not especially popular with his flock, suggesting that his nickname, Mungo, meaning "darling," was bestowed in irony. He died while taking a bath.

THE FEAST OF SAINT SAVA THE ENLIGHTENER

Prince, patriot, bishop, 1235

Patron of Yugoslavia

Until the twelfth century—when a certain Stephen told them that he was their king—the Serbs thought of themselves as just another tribe of nomadic Slavs. King Stephen had three sons, the youngest of whom, Rastho, entered the austere Greek monastery of Mount Athos, where he took the name of Sava. Half a century later the old king abdicated, and his elder sons went to war for the throne—thereby establishing the tradition of balkanization. Sava dutifully returned to Serbia, settled the civil war (he persuaded the Pope to recognize one brother as king), and united the nation by translating Holy Scripture into Serbian. He also, according to folklore, invented windows. Sava's alliance with Eastern Orthodox, rather than Roman, Christendom has had long and unfortunate consequences.

15. THE FEAST OF SAINT MAURUS

Chilly, damp young monk, 584

Invoked against colds • (emblem: walking on water)

At the age of twelve Maurus entered Saint Benedict's abbey at Subiaco. He soon became Benedict's personal assistant, and eventually succeeded him as abbot. As an old man Maurus is believed to have crossed the Alps to found his own monastery, Saint-Maur, on the Loire. But his most wonderful miracle took place when he was yet a lad. On a cold winter's day a fellow student, Placidus, was sent to fetch wood, tumbled into a lake, and began drifting away from shore. Thinking fast, Benedict sent Maurus—who could not swim—to the rescue. Honoring Holy Obedience above all, Maurus ran fearlessly across the surface of the water, seized young Placidus by the hair, and hauled him back to shore. In the reformed Benedictine calendar, Saint Maurus's Feast Day has been moved to October, but it seems more proper to celebrate it here in mid-January, at the height of the flu season.

THE FEAST OF SAINT PAUL THE HERMIT

Naked, hairy solitary, 3421

Patron of weavers • (emblem: old man clad only in palm leaves)

When his brother-in-law threatened to expose him as a Christian, twenty-three-year-old Paul fled Thebes for the wilderness and took up residence in a cave convenient to a spring and a palm tree, where he lived for ninety years. His diet of figs was supplemented by half a loaf of bread a day, which was delivered by a raven. His only visitor was Saint Anthony, who was led to Paul's hermitage (as we learn from Saint Jerome) by a centaur. On that occasion the raven brought an entire loaf of bread for them to share. Upon Paul's death, writes Jerome, a passing pair of lions obligingly helped Anthony to bury the ancient anchorite.

Also: The Feast of Saint Ita, aka Deirdre, Irish beauty, wonder worker, and schoolteacher, 570.

16. THE FEAST OF SAINT PRISCILLA

Well-to-do matron, 98

Patron of widows

The usefulness to the clergy of wealthy widows—especially in a sect's early stages—can scarcely be exaggerated. After the death of her noble husband, Mancius Glabrio, Priscilla allowed Saint Peter to use her stately home on the Via Salaria as his headquarters—the first Vatican, if you will.

Also: The Feast of Saint Fursey, missionary Irish monk whose detailed vision of Hell allegedly inspired Dante, 648; and Saint Marcellus, a Pope who was allegedly obliged to clean stables, 309.

17. THE FEAST OF SAINT ANTHONY THE GREAT

Ferociously tempted abbot, 356

Patron of basket makers, brush makers, butchers, domestic animals, gravediggers, herdsmen, pets, swine; invoked against eczema, ergotism, skin diseases • (emblems: T-shaped cross, bell, pig)

Certain that the end of the world was at hand, young Anthony fled to the desert from his native Memphis, there to await the Last Judgment. He spent twenty years in a tomb, doing noisy and constant battle with the Devil, who unsuccessfully tempted him by assuming such terrifying forms such as a naked nubile wench and a Negro. His biographer Saint Athanasius informs us that Anthony "fasted always, wore an outer garment of sackcloth over a hair shirt, and never washed his body or his feet." Naturally he attracted quite a crowd of wanna-bes, who became the first Christian monks, squatting about the wilderness, resisting impure thoughts. At Anthony's suggestion they all took up hobbies such as mat weaving and broom making—for he, if anyone, knew what work the Devil finds for idle hands. Despite—or perhaps because of—a regimen of privation, starvation, and exposure to the elements, Anthony lived to the age of 105. In Christian iconography he is—for reasons we need not explain—represented by a pig. The runt of a litter is called the tantony pig in his honor.

THE FEAST OF SAINT DEVOTA

Martyred, seagoing maiden, 303

Patron of Corsica, Monaco • (emblem: dove above a maiden in a boat)

A Christian maiden of Corsica, the aptly named Devota was cruelly tortured—with her feet tied she was dragged over rough ground, then stretched on the rack. Still she would not deny her Lord. When she expired a white dove was seen fluttering above her corpse. A priest and a friendly boatman placed her remains in a skiff, which followed the dove across the Mediterranean to Monaco, where her tomb may be visited still.

Also: The Feast of Saint Roseline, the mind-reading prioress of Provence. When she was exhumed in 1334, four years after her death, her body was perfectly incorrupt. The astonished cleric in charge was so impressed by the beauty of her eyes that he scooped them out and took them home.

18. THE FEAST OF SAINT MARGARET OF HUNGARY

Excessively self-mortifying princess, 1270

Invoked against floods • (emblem: in a coat covered with stars)

The headstrong daughter of King Bela IV of Hungary, Margaret was convinced of her vocation to "self-crucifixion" as a very young girl and insisted on entering a convent, which she refused to leave, even to marry the king of Bohemia. (She threatened to cut off her nose and lips.) Her self-imposed penances—such as

refusing ever to wash herself—were many, and at the ripe age of twenty-eight she expired of them.

Also: The Feast of Saint Beatrix d'Este, distantly related to the Hanoverian family yet reigning over England, 1262; and Saint Volusian, bishop of Tours, who feared his shrewish wife more than he did the invading Goths, 496.

19. THE FEAST OF SAINT CANUTE

England-invading Viking, martyr, 1086

Patron of Denmark • (emblem: barefoot king, his hair in a fillet)

A descendant of the English king Canute, who tried bossing the tide, this illegitimate son of the Danish monarch Sweyn II rigorously enforced the Faith among his subjects and neighbors. But when his 1075 invasion of England failed, his disgruntled Danish subjects rose in rebellion. Canute died at the hand of his royal brother Olaf.

THE FEAST OF SAINT FILLAN

Eccentric Scottish hermit, 8th century

Invoked against insanity

It is said of this learned man that he could study all night by the light of his glowing left hand. In the company of his mother, Saint Kentigerna, he left

Ireland for Scotland and there resided beside the lake henceforth known as Strathfillian. His presence while living had a miraculously calming effect upon the mentally ill, and until recently the most obviously mad of the Scots were bound hand and foot and conducted to that site, where they were obliged to spend the night. If their bonds were loosened by morning, they were considered cured.

THE FEAST OF SAINT HENRY OF UPPSALA

Militant missionary martyr, 1157

Patron of Finland • (emblem: bishop treading on his murderer)

An English missionary, Henry accompanied the Swedish Saint-king Eric to Finland on a highly successful expedition of conquest and conversion. It was Henry's task to instruct in the Faith such Finns as survived Eric's progress among them. Henry was cruelly murdered by a Finn he had baptized and subsequently excommunicated.

THE FEAST OF SAINT WULFSTAN

Last Saxon bishop, 1095

Patron of peasants • (emblem: holding a cathedral)

Although he referred to the conquering Normans as "the scourge of God," and never did learn to speak French, Bishop Wulfstan of Worcester somehow survived the episcopal purge that followed the Battle of Hastings. Among his many good works he put an end to the lucrative trade in Irish slaves and once boxed the ears of a prattling, titled Norman dame.

20. THE FEAST OF SAINT FABIAN

Pigeon-picked Pope, martyr, 250

Patron of lead founders, potters • (emblem: kneeling at the block)

The twentieth Pope was a layman, elected to the Chair of Peter because a dove happened to land on his head. After an undistinguished fourteen years in office, he was martyred.

THE FEAST OF SAINT SEBASTIAN

Pincushion pinup martyr, 288

Patron of archers, athletes, doctors, hardware workers, lace makers, the military, pin makers, police officers, potters; invoked against gout, plague • (emblem: youth at the pillar, pierced by arrows)

It was a popular subject of art (rendered by Botticelli, Bernini, and El Greco, among others): a handsome youth, all but naked, bound to a stake, his body pierced by arrows, his eyes lifted in almost erotic ecstasy—the Martyrdom of Saint Sebastian. Actually, he was beaten to death with sticks. According to his legend, Sebastian was born in Gaul but grew up in Milan. A Christian, and thus a pacifist, he joined the Roman army as a sort of secret agent. Little did the wicked emperor Diocletian know that an officer in his elite Praetorian Guard was, on the sly, miraculously curing gout (his specialty) and baptizing his fellow soldiers. As the persecution of the Christians intensified, it was Sebastian who arranged for the Pope (Caius) to be hidden in the safest place in Rome—an apartment in the imperial palace. Eventually, Sebastian was betrayed to the authorities and sentenced to death by a bow-and-arrow firing squad. A pious Christian widow sent to collect his body discovered that he was still alive and nursed him back to health. But no sooner had Sebastian recovered than he returned to the palace, there to confront Diocletian and dissuade him from further atrocities. The emperor, astonished to encounter a man he believed to be dead, briefly considered reformation. On second thought, he ordered Sebastian clubbed to death and thrown in a sewer.

21. THE FEAST OF SAINT AGNES

Famously pulchritudinous virgin martyr, 304

Patron of Girl Scouts, virgins • (emblem: lamb)

In 304, when she was thirteen years old, this beautiful, blue-eyed, blond Roman maiden rejected all her ardent suitors, among them Eutropis, the governor's son. Spurning his costly love gifts, she declared, "I have chosen a Spouse who cannot be seen with mortal eyes, whose mouth drips with milk and honey." (All dialogue according to one official biographer, Saint Augustine, who wasn't there.) Understandably jealous, her pagan swain waxed ill for love, and his father summoned the maiden, offering honors and estates if she would marry his son—and threatening her if she did not. Agnes was unmoved when exposed to the cruel instruments of torture. "You will learn that my God is a God of purity. He will bring your wicked purpose to naught," said she. The governor ordered that she be stripped naked and paraded through the streets to a den of iniquity. Miraculously, her golden hair suddenly grew in great profusion and entirely concealed her shame. At the brothel the only customer bold enough to approach her lewdly was Eutropis himself—whereupon he was immediately struck blind or dead (accounts differ). Agnes, out of kindness, cured (or resurrected) him, whereupon she was charged with witchcraft and sentenced to the stake. Saint Ambrose (who wasn't there either) assures us that Agnes "went to the place of execution more cheerfully than others go to their weddings." Legend has it that unmarried girls dream of their future husbands on the eve of her Feast Day, but only if they have fasted for twenty-four hours and eaten an egg with salt just before bedtime. Because the name Agnes sounds like *agnus*—which is Latin for lamb—on her Feast Day the Pope with great ceremony used to bless a pair of sheep and send their wool to his archbishops.

Also: The Feast of Saint Inez, a demon-tormented Spanish nun, 1696; and Saint Lawdog, 6th-century Welsh abbot.

22. THE FEAST OF SAINT BLEASILLA

Saint Paula's daughter, widowed young, 383

Patron of brides, widows

Albeit a confirmed misogynist, Saint Jerome enjoyed the company of women. His household in Rome included Saint Paula and her teenage daughters, one of whom was the recently bereaved Bleasilla. Despite her hymenless condition, Jerome took her as his protégée, convinced, in his words, that "the loss of her virginity [had] caused her more pain than the loss of her husband." Following Jerome's penitential program of fasting and bodily mortification, Bleasilla died at twenty. At her funeral outraged Romans protested the girl's untimely death, which they blamed on the machinations of "a detestable mob of monks."

THE FEAST OF SAINT LAURA VICUÑA

Abused child, 1904

Patron of Argentina, incest victims

When a civil war broke out in Chile, little Laura's mother escaped with her babies across the Andes to Argentina. There she commenced living in sin with an amorous gaucho named Manuel Mora, while Laura was packed off to a fine Catholic boarding school, where she learned to be mortified by her mother's lifestyle. To make matters worse, when Laura went home for the holidays the lascivious Señor Mora made advances to her! Laura made a deal with God to die, if her mother might see the error of her shameful ways. God agreed; at age thirteen Laura expired smiling while at her bedside her mother tearfully repented.

THE FEAST OF SAINT VINCENT OF SARAGOSSA

Grotesquely tortured martyr, 304

Patron of roofers, schoolgirls, vinegar makers, vintners • (emblem: broken pottery)

till a boy when he was ordained a deacon by Bishop Valerius of Valencia, Vincent was arrested with his mentor by order of Dacian, the cruel governor of Spain. Because the elderly bishop stammered, it was up to young Vincent to argue their defense in court, and he was fearless in declaring his readiness to suffer for the Faith. Much impressed, Dacian dismissed all charges against old Valerius but prescribed for Vincent a course of tortures unequaled in the anals of martyrdom. (Both the poet Prudentius and Saint Augustine describe them in wonderful detail.) Vincent was stretched on the rack and torn with iron hooks, then forced upon a bed of spikes over a fire. Salt was rubbed into his wounds. He was finally rolled in broken pottery, then locked up and left to starve. The faithful would visit his cell and dip cloths in his blood—many of which precious relics are yet venerated in the churches of Valencia. In France, Vincent was taken as the Patron of vintners because his name begins with *vin.* Really.

Also: The Feast of Saint Dominic of Sora, a curiously political hermit and founder of many Benedictine monasteries in the kingdom of Naples. He is invoked against fever and snakes, 1031.

23. THE FEAST OF SAINT EMERENTIANA

Saint Agnes's stepsister, virgin martyr, 304

Invoked against stomachache • (emblem: maiden holding a stone)

hen the relics of a martyr named Emerentiana were discovered near the shrine of Saint Agnes, the faithful conjectured that the two were related. As the legend evolved, Emerentiana was said to be not yet a Christian but was "baptized in blood" when she was stoned to death by a pagan mob, who caught her praying at Agnes's grave.

THE FEAST OF SAINT JOHN THE ALMSGIVER

Entirely admirable administrator, 619

Patron of beggars, boatmen, merchants • (emblem: purse)

fifty-year-old layman of Cyprus, married with children, John was elected patriarch of Alexandria. By taxing the clergy he created the financial resources to assist worthy mercantile enterprises but also to indulge in charity to the poor—whom he called his lords and masters. He established maternity hospitals and shelters for the homeless and infirm. In his will he boasted that he had "found the church treasury full and left it empty." Then, from the grave, he granted absolution to a penitent courtesan.

Also: The Feast of Saint Ildefonsus, bishop of Toledo, much devoted to celebrating in verse and prose Our Lady's miraculous virginal pregnancy. The grateful Mother of God eventually appeared to him and personally presented him with a splendid handmade chasuble, 667.

24. THE FEAST OF SAINT FRANCIS DE SALES

Prolifically literate bishop, Doctor of the Church, 1622

Patron of editors, journalists, writers; invoked against deafness • (emblem: heart crowned with thorns)

The militantly Catholic duke of Savoy had a problem: the majority of his subjects along the shores of Lake Geneva had, by 1593, become militantly Protestant. Furthermore, the wily Calvinists, taking shameless advantage of an outbreak of literacy, were distributing copies of the Bible, translated into French—although the Vatican had forbidden the publishing of the Good Book in any language but Latin. After a papally approved attempt to bribe the Protestant clergy failed, the duke sent for Francis de Sales. Our Saint was a local boy, and by all accounts a gentleman and a scholar. Francis began wandering among the heretical Savoyards, passing out not copies of the Bible—that obscure and dangerous text—but of his own *Introduction to the Devout Life*—an early classic of self-help literature. Surviving the odd assassination attempt, Francis succeeded in bringing most Savoyards back into the fold and was made bishop of Geneva.

Also: The Feast of Saint Zamma, the first bishop of Bologna, 268.

25. THE FEAST OF SAINT DWYN

Winsome Welsh virgin, 460

Patron of lovers; invoked against sickness in animals

Although this Welsh maiden was the daughter of parents both noble and devout, she nevertheless fell passionately in love with a young man named Maelon Mafrodril, and he with her. It was a stormy relationship, and once, following a spat, Dwyn asked the Lord up above, "Why must I be a teenager in love?" An Angel immediately appeared and offered a heavenly potion to cure her heartache. She drank it—and its immediate effect was to turn Maelon to stone. Appalled, Dwyn requested, and was granted, three wishes. Her first, naturally, was that Maelon be restored to life. The second was that all true lovers who invoked her name would either achieve their hearts' desire or recover quickly from their disappointment . . . and finally she asked that she herself never marry, nor wish to do so. So Dwyn became a nun, serving as abbess of the convent at a place that still bears her name, Llanddwyn. There can be found a miraculous spring wherein, from the movements of the fish, an adept can tell the future. Its waters also work wonders with sick beasts.

Also: The Feast of three Saints whose names are not often assumed by the faithful these days: Conan, 648; Poppo, 1048; and Prix, 395.

26. THE FEAST OF SAINT PAULA

The money and brains behind Saint Jerome, 404

Patron of widows • (emblem: scourge)

This aristocratic Roman matron (descended from both the Scipios and the Graccis) suffered, in her thirty-second year, the deaths of both her husband and her eldest daughter, and endured what might be called a nervous breakdown. Then the great Saint Jerome entered her life. He persuaded the wealthy widow to accompany him to the Holy Land, give him all her money, and see to his daily needs—such as cooking and laundry—which he was far too holy to be bothered with. Jerome was about to undertake his life's work—his translation of the Bible from Greek into Latin—and since he knew very little Greek, a language in which Paula was fluent, there has been speculation that she may have been of some small assistance to him.

THE FEAST OF SAINT TIMOTHY

Self-medicating Apostle, 97

Invoked against stomachache • (emblems: club, stones)

On this day—which follows the Feast of Saint Paul's conversion—we celebrate the heavenly birthday of his long-time companion, Timothy. The son of a Greek father and a Jewish mother, Timothy was instructed in the Faith by Paul, who personally circumcised him— for complicated theological reasons. In an epistle to him, Paul advised his disciple to "use a little wine for thy stomach's sake" (1 Timothy 5:23)—hence Our Saint's traditional Patronage of those who suffer from digestive distress. In his old age, as bishop of Ephesus, Timothy took strong exception to the lewd dancing in the streets honoring the pagan goddess Diana; he was beaten to death with sticks by the pagan merrymakers.

THE FEAST OF SAINT TITUS

Proudly uncircumcised bishop, 97

Patron of Crete; invoked against freethinking • (emblem: bishop with a radiant face bearing a palm)

aint Paul, at the Council of Jerusalem, insisted first that his friend, disciple, and personal secretary Titus be permitted to retain his foreskin (Galatians 2:3) and then that he be appointed bishop of Crete, the natives of which Paul characterized as "all liars, evil beasts, slow-bellies" (Titus 1:12). The Cretans decapitated Titus. His head is enshrined in Saint Mark's Cathedral, Venice.

27. THE FEAST OF SAINT AVITUS

Dubious martyr, date unknown

Patron of the Canary Islands • (emblem: raising a monk to life)

he *Roman Martyrology* suggests that on this day a missionary bishop by this name died in Africa.

Also: The Feast of Saint Angela Merici, visionary, vegetarian, and founder of the Ursuline Sisters, the first teaching order of nuns, 1540; and Saint Julian of Le Mans, rumored to be none other than Simon the Leper, whose home in Bethany Jesus visited (Matthew 26:6). He is supposed to have sailed to France and there converted the Druids, 250.

28. THE FEAST OF SAINT CHARLEMAGNE

(Un)Holy (Un)Roman Emperor, 814

Patron of the University of Paris • (emblem: fleur-de-lis)

espite his less than edifying personal life, the bellicose, lusty, and illiterate king of the Franks was canonized in 1165 by an antipope, Pascal III; his afterlife status was downgraded to "blessed" by Pope Benedict XIV.

THE FEAST OF SAINT THOMAS AQUINAS

Rotund "Angelic" Doctor of the Church, 1274

Patron of pencil makers, students, theologians, universities; invoked against sudden death, thunderstorms • (emblems: Angels bringing him a girdle, a star on his breast)

Known to posterity as the Light of the Church, and to his fellow students as the Dumb Ox, Saint Thomas remains to this day the most influential Roman Catholic philosopher. In his two great works, the *Summa theologica* and the *Summa contra gentiles,* he "cast greater light within the Church than all the other Doctors together," according to Pope John XXII, who canonized him in 1323. Thomas's closely argued case against abortion, and indeed any form of birth control, is still the granite cornerstone of Catholic ethics. He was a strong advocate of chastity—including marital chastity, asserting in the *Summa theologica* that "nothing drags the mind of a man down from its elevation so much as the caresses of a woman and the bodily contacts without which a man cannot possess his wife." It must be admitted that

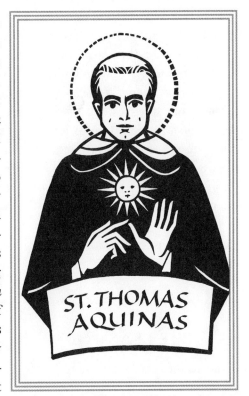

ST. THOMAS AQUINAS

Thomas personally took a dim view not only of sex but of the Fair Sex, observing, "Because there is a higher water content in women, they are more easily seduced by sexual pleasure." But he had his reasons. When he was a bookish seventeen-year-old, Thomas informed his aristocratic family that he intended to become a monk. His mother (Countess Theodora) locked him in the tower of the family castle, and his brothers (both military men) sent a naked prostitute up to his room. The young Saint had the presence of mind to seize a firebrand and drive the shameless hussy from his chamber—whereafter he had a vision. Two Angels appeared, bearing a golden girdle wherewith they wrapped his loins—and never after was he troubled with temptations against purity. (All this Thomas revealed to his confessor, Father Reynolds, thirty years after the event.)

29. THE FEAST OF SAINT GILDAS THE WISE

Grouchy British historian-hermit, 570

Invoked against dog bites, rabies • (emblem: snarling dog)

This wholly admirable monk was born in the year 500 in Britain—which was then a Celtic Christian nation, abandoned by the Roman army of occupation. When it was invaded by the Anglo-Saxons, Gildas fled his debauched homeland, as did many of the best Britons, for the Continent, settling in the area subsequently named Brittany. There he wrote an eyewitness history of his times—*Concerning the Ruin and Conquest of Britain*—which is the only firsthand account of the era that survives. In it he describes King Arthur's heroic stand against the Saxon foe at the Battle of Bredon Hill, and otherwise excoriates the cowardice of his contemporaries and their shameful collaboration with the square-headed, barbaric Saxons. In sacred art Gildas is represented by a snarling dog in tribute to his vitriolic literary style. By reason of this his protection is invoked against attacks by man's best friend.

Also: The Feast of Saint Dallan Forgaill, a blind Irish poet-monk murdered by pirates, 598.

30. THE FEAST OF SAINT ADELELM

Most aristocratic bishop, 1097

Patron of menservants

A French nobleman and soldier, Adelelm returned from a pilgrimage to Rome and became a priest much favored by the queen of Old Castile. One night on the road to Lyons, he was surprised by a sudden tempest. Father Adelelm instructed his manservant to light a lantern—and despite the wind and the rain, it remained lighted until they found shelter.

THE FEAST OF SAINT ALDEGUND

Snow White–story abbess, 684

Invoked against cancer, childhood illnesses, eye disease, fever, sudden death, wounds • (emblem: walking on water)

The biography of this beautiful Frankish noblewoman reads like a fairy tale. Her parents, Walbert and Bertila, were Saints, as was her sister Waudru, but Aldegund's wicked stepmother ordered this dedicated virgin to marry. Aldegund escaped to the forest (crossing, dry-shod, a raging river) and was granted the gift of invisibility whenever her stepmother or jilted fiancé came searching for her. In true Disney style her pet, a fish, was once attacked by a naughty raven but rescued by a ferocious lamb. Aldegund settled in a hermitage near Maubeuge, in the wilds of Flanders, in a spot that afterward became a Benedictine convent. Although she soon died of breast cancer, she did so, we are told, "in an ecstasy of serene joy."

THE FEAST OF SAINT BATHILDE

Cinderella-story queen, 680

Patron of children • (emblem: children climbing a ladder)

Bathilde, born in England, was carried off by pirates and sold as a kitchen slave to the mayor of the palace of the Frankish king Clovis II. The mayor immediately took a fancy to her, but the chaste Bathilde smeared her lovely face with soot and clad her comely body in filthy rags in order to discourage his advances. By all accounts she was a model servant and soon rose in the domestic ranks to wait on the king's own table. Clovis—a bit of a rogue, if the truth be told—fell passionately in love with the modest maiden and made her his queen. She bore him three sons in as many years, whereupon he died; for the next eight years, as regent for her son Prince Clotaire, this Saxon woman ruled the Western Franks. (Rumors that during her reign she arranged for the assassination of ten difficult bishops are doubtless exaggerated.) In 665, Bathilde was ousted in a palace coup, and she lived out her days in an abbey she had founded. Her emblem in art, as befits her upstairs-downstairs story, is a ladder.

THE FEAST OF SAINT MARTINA

New mother, martyr, 228

Patron of breast feeding, Rome • (emblem: tongs)

Pope Urban VIII is best remembered for forcing his friend Galileo to deny the movement of the earth around the sun. But that pontiff was also a vigorous promoter of the cult of the maiden Martina, an entirely mythical Saint under whose Patronage he placed the city of Rome, and in whose honor he constructed a great basilica at the Roman Forum. According to her legend, Martina was, in sequence, flogged with iron hooks, drenched in boiling oil, thrown to the lions, and burned at the stake—none of which prevented her from singing God's praises.

When she was beheaded, not blood but a fountain of milk sprang from her severed neck, hence her traditional Patronage of nursing mothers.

Also: The Feast of Saint Hyacinth of Mariscotti, a most reluctant nun, 1640.

31. THE FEAST OF SAINT JOHN BOSCO

Known and honored as Don, 1888

Patron of apprentices, editors, young people • (emblem: surrounded by young people)

Father Giovanni Bosco was, by any definition of the word, a Saint. His mission was to the urban poor of his native Turin, especially to children, particularly to boys. As was his English contemporary Charles Dickens, the don was deeply moved by the plight of the recently created class of exploited and expendable street urchins; rather than write tearjerkers about them, he provided them with food and shelter, education and recreation. For the boys' amusement he performed magic tricks. For their welfare he performed miracles. Although the Salesians, the teaching order he founded, spread across Europe and around the world, the don himself never left Italy. But once, in a dream, he flew over a great city and the next day described it in detail to an American visitor, who was astonished to realize the don had been granted a vision of Boston.

THE FEAST OF SAINT TRYPHAENA

Matron, martyr, date unknown

Patron of nursing mothers • (emblem: bull)

In the town of Cyzicus on the Hellespont, Tryphaena's captors tore her newborn infant from this virtuous Christian matron's arms before subjecting her to unspeakable torments in the arena; finally she was gored to death by a wild bull. Where she fell the customary miraculous fountain of milk sprang up.

Also: The Feast of four other married women Saints: Marcella, 410; Louise degli Albertoni, 1474–1533; Mary Cristina, 1813–1836, queen of the two Sicilys; and Paula Gambra-Costa, 1473–1515.

⁂ February ⁂

1. THE FEAST OF SAINT BRIGID

Goddesslike Celtic abbess, 525

Patron of fugitives, Ireland, milkmaids, newborns, New Zealand, nuns, poultry raisers; invoked against fire • (emblems: cow, barn)

The illegitimate daughter of a pagan chieftain and a Christian slave girl, Brigid—Patron of all things lactose, with a miraculous ability to multiply butter—was born while her mother was on her way back from the dairy. After her mother's death the girl was claimed by her royal father, and she grew up to be outstandingly beautiful. She hated her beauty, of course, for it attracted numerous suitors, despite her well-known vow of chastity. Finally, her constant prayers to become ugly were answered—God made one of her eyes disappear and the other grotesquely huge—and her father consented to her becoming a nun. It is said that during the ceremony Angels appeared and shoved aside the attending priest to present her with the veil, whereupon the wooden steps on which she knelt burst into leaf and flower and her good looks were restored. Known as the Mary of the Gaels, Brigid was a force in early Irish Christianity, founding many churches, convents, and monasteries. But since she was born shortly before the death of Saint Patrick, reports of their great friendship seem exaggerated. Nor is it necessarily true that the holy bishop Saint Mel, while drunk, consecrated her a full-fledged bishop herself. Of some facts we may be sure. Her bathwater was often transformed into beer for the sake of thirsty visitors; she could hang her damp cloak on a sunbeam to dry; she taught a fox to dance; she made armies invisible to each other; and her tomb at Downpatrick was looted by English troops in the reign of Henry VII. It is a happy coincidence that her Feast falls on Imbolg, the Feast of a Celtic goddess also named Brigid.

THE FEAST OF SAINT SEVERUS OF AVRANCHES
Garment-spurning bishop, 389

Patron of drapers, hatters, milliners, silk makers, weavers, wool workers • (emblem: weaver's loom)

The child of poor peasants, Severus was hired by a rich pagan farmer to tend his mares. When Severus returned naked from his first trip to town, having given away all his clothes, his employer banished him to the barn, where the mares' breath kept the boy warm. The sight of this caused the farmer to convert. Severus went on to become a priest and then a bishop. According to one mystifying legend, one of his flock went to the baths, departed without paying, and dropped dead. The proprietor of the baths demanded a vast sum from the grieving widow, who sought the bishop's aid. Severus led an expedition to the grave and demanded of the deceased how much he owed. The corpse sat up and replied, "One egg," which apparently settled the matter. What any of this has to do with hatters is anybody's guess.

2. THE FEAST OF THE PRESENTATION OF OUR LORD AND OF THE PURIFICATION OF THE BLESSED VIRGIN (CANDLEMAS)

On this day, the fortieth after Christmas, we commemorate the occasion when, obedient to Mosaic law, His parents brought Jesus to the Temple in Jerusalem and paid the requisite five shekels to the High Priest. Today in Catholic churches, all the year's candles are consecrated. In the benighted Middle Ages, in Poland, it was believed that one particular candle, Mary's Thunder Candle, kept wolves at bay; throughout Europe it was once understood that winter was only half over if on Candlemas the weather was fair. We moderns prefer to consult a groundhog.

THE FEAST OF SAINT ADALBALD OF OSTREVANT
Long-suffering layman, 650

Patron of parents of large families

A Frankish courtier whose marriage to the daughter of Gascon nobility was bitterly opposed by her family, Adalbald, with his wife, Rictude, managed to produce four offspring before he was murdered by his in-laws. In the fullness of time, husband, wife, and all four children were sainted.

THE FEAST OF SAINT CORNELIUS THE CENTURION
The first Gentile Christian, 1st century

Patron of the military

A Roman army officer stationed in Caesarea, Palestine, Cornelius was baptized by Saint Peter (Acts 10), thereby becoming the first non-Jewish follower of Christ.

Also: The Feast of Saint Joan de Lestonac, who founded the teaching order the Congregation of Norte Dame, 1640.

3. THE FEAST OF SAINT ANSKAR
The Apostle of the North, 865

Patron of Denmark, Germany, Iceland • (emblem: wearing a fur pelisse)

A nskar was continually dispatched, over a period of thirty years, by Pope Gregory IV, King Louis the Pious, and King Louis the German, to baptize and otherwise civilize the Norsemen, whose Viking raids were an ongoing irritant to Christendom. Anskar eventually succeeded in converting the kings of Sweden and Denmark, but after his death Sweden relapsed into its naturally barbaric condition.

THE FEAST OF SAINT BLAISE
Medical-miracle-working bishop, martyr, 316

Patron of builders, carvers, sick cattle, the sugar harvest, windmill owners, wind musicians, wool workers; invoked against coughs, goiter, sore necks, throat disease, wild animals • (emblem: wool comb)

Blaise was both a bishop and a physician in Armenia. Fleeing persecution, he took refuge in a cave in the woods, to which many wild beasts would repair for sanctuary and medical assistance, until he was reported, by irate hunters, to the authorities. On his way to prison Blaise encountered a woman whose pig had just been carried off by a wolf. He reasoned with the savage beast, who contritely returned the pig. In gratitude the woman brought candles to Blaise's dark jail cell. Among his miracles while imprisoned was the removal of a fish bone from the gullet of a choking child. Blaise was eventually beheaded, but first he was tortured with wool carders' steel combs. To this day on his Feast—which occurs at the height of the flu season—Saint Blaise's candles are applied, in church, to the throats of the faithful. And water blessed on this day does wonders for ailing livestock.

Also: The Feast of Our Lady of Supya. This small statue of the Virgin Mary, discovered in 1747, has been venerated by the native Indians ever since and was officially declared Honduras's Patron in 1953.

4. THE FEAST OF SAINT ANDREW CORSINI

Reformed juvenile delinquent, bishop, 1373

Invoked against quarrels, sudden death • (emblem: wolf and lamb)

While expecting little Andrew, his mother dreamed she gave birth to a wolf that entered a Carmelite church and turned into a lamb. Sure enough, after a violent and dissipated youth, her son joined the Carmelite Order and turned into a bishop who was instrumental in resolving feuds.

THE FEAST OF SAINT JOHN DE BRITO

Portuguese missionary to India, martyr, 1693

Patron of Portugal • (emblem: in Swami attire)

Born into a noble Portuguese family, young John was a favorite of Prince Don Pedro. When eight years old he fell gravely ill, and his mother prayed for his recovery to Saint Francis Xavier, the Apostle of India, promising to dedicate her son to him. Upon his recovery she began dressing the boy in priest's vestments, making him something of a curiosity at court. At sixteen John entered the Jesuits. In 1673 Don Pedro, now King Pedro, found himself at odds with the Pope and the Dutch over trading rights in southern India. He sent his boyhood friend to Goa, ostensibly to preach to the natives and possibly to solidify his territorial claims. John ingratiated himself with the natives, even joining the Brahman caste, and succeeded in converting the local ruler to the Faith. But when he persuaded the newly baptized raja to divest himself of his youngest wife, John went too far. The lady complained to the Hindu clergy, who beheaded him. His head was returned to Portugal, where King Pedro ordered a Mass of Thanksgiving to be celebrated. John's mother attended, wearing a festive gown.

Also: The Feast of Saint Joan of France, the hunchbacked daughter of King Louis XI, 1505.

5. THE FEAST OF SAINT AGATHA

Mammarily mutilated virgin martyr, 251

Patron of bell makers, bell ringers, jewelers, Malta, nurses, wet nurses; invoked against breast disease, fire, volcanoes • (emblem: holding her breasts on a platter)

When this noble Sicilian virgin rejected the suit of a Roman senator, he spitefully but correctly accused her of being a Christian and ordered her breasts—said to be her best feature—cut off. According to pious legend, Saint Peter himself appeared in Agatha's prison cell and, through the application of a "celestial ointment," restored her assets. In sacred art Agatha is invariably depicted carrying her severed breasts on a dish. In the Middle Ages the faithful mistook those mysterious objects for bells and made her the Patroness of bell founders; or for buns, for which reason small loaves are blessed in churches on her Feast Day. Back in Sicily, Agatha survived, intact, a court-ordered stint in a house of shame operated by the bawd Aphrodesia. Next, an attempt to burn her at the stake failed (hence she is invoked against fire) when interrupted by volcanic eruptions (against which she is likewise petitioned). So they cut off her head.

THE FEAST OF SAINT BERTULF

Priest of Flanders, 705

Invoked against rain • (emblem: with eagle on his arm)

A convert from paganism, priest and protégé of Count Wambert, Bertulf is said to have once employed an eagle as an umbrella and is still believed to rattle the walls of his tomb whenever his beloved city of Ghent is in danger.

Also: The Feast of Saint Jacob, the wily biblical patriarch, 2000 B.C.

6. THE FEAST OF SAINT AMAND

Most hospitable bishop, 679

Patron of brewers, hotel workers, beer and wine merchants • (emblem: dragon on the end of a crozier)

A wandering bishop, Amand preached the Gospel with great zeal but not much success to the Slavs, the Franks, and the pagans of Flanders. He founded a religious community in Ghent, where he died at the age of ninety. His traditional Patronage of the hotel and beverage trade is doubtless a tribute to his renowned hospitality.

THE FEAST OF SAINT DOROTHY

Irresistible flower-loving virgin martyr, 320

Patron of brides, florists, gardeners, newlyweds; invoked against fire, lightning, thieves • (emblem: basket of apples and roses)

A beautiful Christian maiden of Caesarea, Dorothy rejected the marriage proposal of the pagan provost Fabricus. He sent his two sisters to plead his case, but Dorothy converted them to the Faith. So she was imprisoned (and fed by Angels), thrown into boiling oil (which turned to soothing balm), then stretched out on an iron bed over fire (on which she smiled). As she was being led to the place of her beheading, a sarcastic bystander named Theophilus asked her to send him fruit and flowers from her "heavenly garden." After Dorothy's death a child (actually, an Angel) appeared before Theophilus bearing apples and roses—in February, remember!—and told him that Dorothy awaited him in her garden. After tasting one of the apples, he was converted, executed, cut into pieces, and fed to the birds.

THE FEAST OF SAINTS PAUL MIKI AND PETER BAPTIST

Crucified missionary martyrs, 1597

Patrons of Japan • (emblem: three Jesuits on the cross)

Peter was a Spanish Franciscan, Paul a Japanese-born Jesuit. Together with twenty-four others—including a Korean lay brother (Saint Leo Karasum) and thirteen of their Japanese converts, including three altar boys—they were crucified on the orders of the xenophobic Shogun Toyotomi Hideyoshi.

Also: The Feast of Saint Mel, an Irish bishop who once caught a fish in a plowed field in order to prove he hadn't committed incest with his aunt, 488.

7. THE FEAST OF SAINT MOSES
Nomadic desert hermit, 389

Patron of Saracens

An Arab monk of Mount Sinai and bishop to a wandering flock, Moses served as a peacemaker between the hostile Syrians and Egyptians at the personal request of Maoria, queen of the Saracens.

Also: The Feast of Saint James Sales, a French Jesuit shot by Huguenots whom he had defeated in a theological debate, 1592; Saint Luke the Wonder Worker, a levitating Greek lad, 946; Saint Romuald, who turned to religion after he saw his father kill a man in a duel, and founded several monasteries around France, from each of which he was expelled, 1027; Saint Thomas Sherwood of London, who for the crime of attending Mass was condemned "to be dragged through the streets, hung, then cut down, to have his bowels drawn out, his head cut off, his body quartered and the pieces exposed in such places as the Queen shall designate," 1578.

8. THE FEAST OF SAINT CUTHMAN
Poor boy who took care of his mother, 900

Patron of shepherds • (emblem: bearded, holding a church in both hands)

A simple shepherd who answered the Call, Cuthman wheeled his ancient mother about in a wheelbarrow while founding churches and otherwise doing good. His memory is much venerated in his native Sussex, England.

THE FEAST OF SAINT JEROME EMILIANI

Escaped POW, creator of the catechism, 1537

Patron of orphans • (emblem: broken chain)

After a carefree, not to say dissolute, youth, Jerome joined the Venetian army in the war of the Italian city-states and was taken prisoner. Held captive in a dungeon, wearing a ball and chain, he repented of his former ways and prayed fervently to the Blessed Virgin. At length Our Lady appeared to him bearing a key. She unbound the captive and led him from prison in a disguise she thoughtfully provided. Jerome proceeded directly to her shrine at Treviso, hung his fetters upon the wall of her chapel, and entered the priesthood. He devoted himself especially to the care of abandoned children and is credited with having invented the question-and-answer form of catechism for their enlightenment.

THE FEAST OF SAINT MEINGOLD

Pious French aristocrat, 892

Patron of bakers, bankers, millers, miners

This Belgian nobleman incurred the enmity of his brother-in-law, a certain Duke Albrecht. In the course of their feud Meingold's castle was sacked, and the duke died. Convinced of the vanity of vanities, Meingold abandoned his wife and estate to become a wandering beggar. Nevertheless he was sought out by enemies and murdered. His Patronage of gold diggers and moneymen is probably a pun on his name. His Patronage of millers is a mystery, as is, for that matter, his claim to Sainthood. It has been suggested that his devotees confused him with a slightly later Belgian holy man of the same name.

Also: The Feast of Saint Jacqueline, a Roman matron called Brother by Saint Francis of Assisi. He gave her a pet lamb, which served her as an alarm clock, 1273.

9. THE FEAST OF SAINT APOLLONIA

Dentally tortured martyr, 249

Patron of dentists; invoked against toothache • (emblem: pincers holding a tooth)

The home of this wealthy spinster of Alexandria was a refuge for her fellow Christians until Apollonia got on the wrong side of a sorcerer and was attacked by a pagan mob. In the course of her martyrdom her teeth were extracted. Rather than deny her faith, Apollonia leapt into the fire—Saint Augustine went to considerable lengths to prove that this was not an act of suicide. Teeth of this holy woman can be found in Antwerp, Brussels, Naples, Liège, and Cologne.

Also: The Feast of Saint Sisebutus, Spanish abbot immortalized in the epic *El Cid* as Abbot Sancho, 1082.

10. THE FEAST OF SAINT SCHOLASTICA

St. Benedict's sensible sister, 543

Patron of nuns; invoked for rain, against convulsions in children • (emblem: dove ascending)

Scholastica was the beloved twin sister of the founder of Western monasticism, Saint Benedict. It was her lifelong conviction that sanctity is a matter of willpower. With her brother's help she founded a convent some five miles from his own monastery at Monte Cassino. In his *Dialogues* Saint Gregory the Great tells us that Benedict visited his sister one day a year, and on the last occasion—she knew that she was about to die—Scholastica begged him to stay a while longer. When he declined she began to pray, flooding the table between them with her tears, and a mighty thunderstorm blew up. "God forgive you, sister," said Benedict. "What have you done?" She replied, drying her tears, "I asked a favor of you and you refused it. I asked it of God, and he granted it." And thus they spent the night together, talking of holy things. Three days later she died—and Benedict, from his distant cell, saw his willful sister's soul rise to Heaven in the form of a white dove. The grave of Benedict and Scholastica—they were buried together—was discovered in 1946, in the bombed-out rubble of Monte Cassino.

Also: The Feast of Saint Clare of Rimini, a once worldly widow who subjected herself to extravagant penances, such as being dragged through town with a rope around her neck to celebrate each Good Friday, 1346.

11. THE FEAST OF OUR LADY OF LOURDES

Apparition, 1858

Patron of the Philippines, Portugal

St. Bernadette

On this occasion, the first of eighteen appearances to Saint Bernadette, the Mother of God, with considerable theological subtlety, proclaimed herself the Immaculate Conception.

THE FEAST OF SAINT CAEDMON

Original Anglo-Saxon versifier, 680

Patron of poets • (emblem: sleeping cowherd, Angel with a harp near him)

A Saxon cowherd, Caedmon lived on lands belonging to the abbess Hilda of Whitby. He could neither read nor write and was so tone-deaf that he departed from Feasts when the singing began and fled the very sight of a harp. Then one night in the stable he was awakened by a Voice commanding him to sing, which he commenced to do. His lyrics were, understandably, of a religious nature. The astonished abbess became his Patron and, since Caedmon was the first English-language poet, she is considered the founder of English literature. The only example of Caedmon's work survives in Saint Bede's *History of the English Church and People*—although Bede modestly apologizes for the inadequacy of his translation from the Anglo-Saxon into Latin.

Also: The Feast of Saint Theodora, ferocious Byzantine empress, mother of the emperor Michael the Drunk, 867.

12. THE FEAST OF SAINT JULIAN THE HOSPITALER

Ferry boatman, parracide, matricide, date unknown

Patron of boatmen, circus performers, epicures, fiddlers, innkeepers, travelers • (emblem: killing his parents in bed)

When a stag he was hunting warned him that he would someday murder his own parents, Julian moved to a distant country, where he married a rich widow. Years later he surprised a couple in his marriage bed, assumed the worst, and slew them—only to discover that they were his parents come for a visit. (His wholly innocent wife had welcomed them and gone off to Mass.) Overcome with remorse, Julian resolved to abandon the good life and establish a hospice for poor pilgrims. One dark and stormy night he gave shelter to a leper, who turned out to be an Angel and assured Julian that he had been divinely forgiven. Because of his hospitality he is prayed to by all travelers—but especially itinerant entertainers.

Also: The Feast of Saint Marina, a girl who became a monk, was accused of fathering a child by an innkeeper's daughter, and was banished from the monastery. She became the child's guardian, and eventually the pair were readmitted to the monastery. Only after Marina's death was her gender revealed; date unknown.

13. THE FEAST OF SAINT AGABUS

Seer mentioned in Acts of the Apostles, 1st century

Patron of fortune-tellers • (emblem: dressed as a Carmelite, holding model of a church)

Every trade and craft—including the theologically questionable profession of fortune-telling—once had a Patron Saint. We are told in Acts 11:28–29 that Agabus, a Jewish convert, correctly predicted a dreadful famine as well as Saint Paul's capture and imprisonment and his own martyrdom. Medieval seers and soothsayers invoked Agabus against their inevitable persecution by civil and religious authorities—distress that they (who better?) could foresee.

THE FEAST OF SAINT EUSTOCIUM OF PADUA

The Cinderella of the Cloister, 1469

Patron of the mentally ill

The illegitimate daughter of a nun who had strayed, Lucrezia Bellini herself joined a convent at the age of seventeen. She was gentle and pious but suffered chronic fits of violent hysteria. Believing her to be diabolically possessed, her superiors had her variously exorcised, starved, and imprisoned. When she died, at the age of twenty-six, the name of Jesus was discovered burned into her breast.

THE FEAST OF SAINT MODOMNOC

Irish apiarist-hermit, 550

Patron of bees

A member of Ireland's royal O'Neil clan, Modomnoc sailed to Wales to study under Saint David. Among his duties there was beekeeping, and when it came time for him to return to Ireland, a swarm of bees insisted on accompanying his ship, becoming, as the legend has it, the ancestors of "the gifted race of Ireland's bees."

Also: The Feast of Saint Catherine dei Ricci, Florentine prioress, visionary, and reformer who every Friday was granted the Stigmata and frequently held long chats with Saint Philip Neri in Rome without leaving her convent in Prato, 150 miles away, 1590; and Saint Martinian, a Palestinian recluse who fled temptation by leaping first into the fire and then into the sea, 398.

14. THE FEAST OF SAINTS CYRIL AND METHODIUS

Alphabet-creating missionaries, 869, 884

Patrons of Europe, the Slavs • (emblem: eastern bishop and monk holding a church)

The Cyrillic alphabet, in which the Russian, Ukrainian, and Slavonic languages are written, was allegedly devised by these two missionary brothers. When not preaching or translating the Scriptures, they quarreled with the German ("Latin") prelates over liturgical rights to all the territories east of the Danube. In 1980 Pope John Paul II, himself a Slav, declared them Patrons of Europe.

THE FEAST OF SAINT VALENTINE

Any one of three martyrs by this name, 269

Patron of lovers • (emblem: heart)

The martyrdoms of several Saints named Valentine are celebrated on this day; in various Roman churches eight complete bodies and one head of Saint Valentine are venerated. The association of this date with courtship may arise from the mid-February fertility festival of Lupercal, or from the medieval belief that the birds chose their mates on this day. "Valentines" were originally cards inscribed with girls' names, which boys drew by lot. Saint Francis de Sales once attempted to improve this custom by substituting cards with the names of Saints to be emulated, but they didn't catch on.

15. THE FEAST OF SAINT EUSEUS

Syrian ex-cobbler hermit, 550

Patron of shoemakers • (emblem: shoemaker's tools)

This immigrant hermit of Piedmont worked at the cobbler's trade.

THE FEAST OF SAINT SIGFRID

English missionary bishop, 765

Patron of Sweden • (emblem: three heads in his hand)

An Englishman, Sigfrid was sent by King Ethelbert at the request of the Swedes to renew Christianity among them. Arriving in the company of three nephews, Sigfrid immediately converted and baptized Olaf, the Swedish king, and was given the use of a palace. Sometime thereafter his nephews were murdered, dismembered, and thrown in a well. King Olaf offered to execute the killers, but Uncle Sigfrid forgave them. In art he is shown holding his nephews' heads, which looked like loaves of bread; thus Sigfrid is invoked by Scandinavians in time of famine.

Also: The Feast of Saint Georgette, a pious French maiden whose funeral, according to Saint Gregory of Tours, was attended by a flock of Angels thinly disguised as white doves, early 6th century; and Saint Severus of Valeria, a priest whose tears restored a dead parishioner to life, 530.

16. THE FEAST OF SAINT GILBERT OF SEMPRINGHAM

Unfortunate Englishman, 1189

Patron of cripples

Son of a Norman knight, Gilbert gave away his wealth and founded the Gilbertines. Famously charitable, he earned the wages of virtue—he was briefly imprisoned on a false charge of treason, then slandered by his lay brothers and censured by the Pope before becoming blind.

THE FEAST OF SAINT JULIANA

Virgin who wrestled the Devil, 305

Invoked against sickness, temptation • (emblem: maiden leading a Devil in chains)

In the tradition of Beautiful Virtuous Roman Christian Virgin Martyrs, Juliana's troubles began when she refused to marry, citing her vow of perpetual chastity. The rejected suitor in this case was Eliusus, the provost of Nicodemia. Suspecting her of Christianity, Juliana's pagan father beat her savagely and turned her over to the authorities—that is, the provost, the recently rebuffed Eliusus! He commenced his investigation by ordering that his beloved be stretched between pillars and doused with molten lead. The undaunted maiden was then thrown into a dungeon, where she took part in a series of debates and wrestling matches with a Devil, self-identified as the Son of Beelzebub. Juliana got the better of him, pinning him to the ground and binding his hands and feet, but the demon escaped—only to reappear (disguised as an Angel) as a surprise witness against her at her trial, after which she was beheaded. Her head, as it happens, is now property of the Metropolitan Museum, New York.

Also: The Feast of Saint Viridiana, a Tuscan recluse who shared her tiny cell with two large serpents, 1242.

17. THE FEAST OF SAINT FORKERNUS OF TRIM

Irish prince and bishop, 5th century

Patron of bell makers

Saint Patrick was accompanied to Ireland by Saint Loman, the son of his sister Tigris. Patrick proceeded to Tara, leaving Loman back in Meath, on the banks of the Boyne River. There Loman managed to convert the local king as well as his son Forkernus, who eventually succeeded him as bishop of Trim. Our Saint is invariably pictured in the company of bell makers, for which reason he is reckoned their Patron.

Also: The Feast of Saints Evermond, missionary bishop to the Wends of Ratzburg, who could break chains by sprinkling them with holy water, 1178; Fintan of Cloneenagh, strictly vegetarian abbot, 603; Marianne, sister of the apostle Saint Philip, who accompanied him to Phrygia; and Silvinus, who on the eve of his wedding fled for the Holy Land and returned as a bishop to work among the pagan Belgians, 720.

18. THE FEAST OF SAINT THEOTONIUS

Fearless exposer of royal vice, 1166

Henry of Portugal was not an especially effective ruler, but he was generous to the clergy. When he died his widowed Queen Teresa began to carry on quite scandalously with the Galacian count Ferdinand. Theotonius rebuked her from the pulpit. Shamed, Teresa fled into exile, and her son Alfonso became count of Portugal. He was likewise generous to the clergy—going so far as to place his entire realm under the protection of the Holy See, to which he paid annual tribute, while Theotonius, his work done, retired to a monastery.

Also: The Feast of Saints Agatha Lin, a schoolteacher, and Andrew Nam-Thung, a mayor, Chinese martyrs for the Faith in the 1850s; and Saint Constance, daughter of the emperor Constantine, former leper and adamant virgin, c. 354.

19. THE FEAST OF SAINT CONRAD OF PIACENZA

Reformed arsonist, abbot, 1351

Invoked against famine, hernia • (emblem: birds perched on a cross)

A nobleman who accidentally caused a fire, Conrad at first thought to let a local ruffian take the blame but eventually confessed his guilt and was subjected to a severe fine. He and his wife surrendered all their possessions and, with nothing to lose, joined the Franciscans and Poor Clares, respectively. Conrad became famous for his piety and miracles—once, during a famine, he produced a number of freshly baked buns. Whenever he made his confession, birds flocked around him. For centuries hernia sufferers have sought relief at his tomb.

Also: The Feast of Saint Boniface of Lausanne, against whom the students at the University of Paris went on strike, 1260; and Saint Mesrop the Teacher, creator of the Armenian alphabet, 441.

20. The Feast of Saint Amata of Assisi, Saint Clare's formerly dissipated niece, 1250; Saint Colgan, surnamed the Wise and known as the Chief Scribe of the Scots, 796; Saint Eleutherius of Byzantium, martyred by heretics for preaching orthodoxy, 532; Saint Eucherius, Frankish bishop who dared oppose King Charles Martel, 743; Saint Falco, a holy Benedictine; Saint Leo of Catania, Sicilian priest and wonder worker, 787; Saint Shadhost, murdered with 128 other Persian Christians for refusing to worship the sun, 345; and Saint Wulfric of Haselbury, English hermit who could cut chain mail with ordinary scissors, 1154.

21. THE FEAST OF SAINT PETER DAMIAN

Militantly celibate cardinal, 1072

Invoked against headache • (emblem: holding birch, book)

Born to wealthy parents Peter was orphaned at a tender age and placed in the care of a nasty elder brother, who made him tend swine. He was soon adopted by a couple of passing monks and became deeply religious—praying for long periods of time with his arms outstretched and throwing himself into a thorn bush at the onset of impure thoughts. Not content with having attained perfect personal purity, Peter became a zealous reformer of his fellow clergymen. He published *The Book of Gomorrah,* in which he exposed and condemned practitioners of "the unnatural vice," that is, married priests. This brought him to the attention of Pope Leo IX, who made Peter a cardinal and sent him to Mainz, to dissuade Emperor Henry IV from divorcing his wife. When not operating as the chief of the Pope's fun police, Peter passed the time scourging himself and making wooden spoons.

Also: The Feast of Saint Noel Pinot, a parish priest driven underground during the godless French Revolution, captured and guillotined while still dressed for Mass, 1794.

22. THE FEAST OF SAINT MARGARET OF CORTONA

Most penitent after a career of sex and violence, 1297

Patron of fallen women • (emblem: with dog, skull at her feet)

*A*t the age of twelve, while Margaret was still living with her farmer father and wicked stepmother, she was seduced by a passing cavalier and went to live with him in his castle, without benefit of clergy. For nine years she was his mistress, parading shamelessly through the streets of Cortona, flaunting her finery, even bearing him a son. Then one day her dog led her to the spot where lay the decomposed body of her murdered lover. Realizing instantly that his death was the result of her beauty and her sin, she took her little son and retired to a Franciscan friary, there to begin her career as a penitent. She undertook a regime of extreme mortifications—although her confessor, Fra Giunta, persuaded her not to cut off her nose and lips—until Jesus himself (speaking from a crucifix before which she was praying) released her from her penance. The two then undertook a series of conversations on a wide range of topics. Twice the figure of Jesus gave Margaret messages of an admonitory nature to deliver to a local bishop, which she did, but the proud prelate paid her no mind—and after her second visit he dropped dead. Margaret's unsavory past was not forgotten by the locals—tongues began to wag about her relationship with her holy confessor, resulting in his transfer to Siena—but in the end she won the town over by her obvious sanctity and her many acts of charity, so that the people of Cortona to this day venerate the Magdalene of the Franciscans.

Also: The Feast of Saint Elvis, Irish missionary to Cornwall, 6th century.

23. THE FEAST OF SAINT MILDBURGA

Nature-loving abbess, 715

Patron of birds • (emblem: geese at her feet)

Of pious English stock—her aunt, mother, and two sisters are all Saints—Mildburga served as abbess of Wenlock in Shropshire, performing many wonders, not the least of which were levitation and restoring the dead to life. During a drought one blow from her horse's hoof caused a spring to flow from a rock—and its waters had miraculous properties. At Mildburga's request the birds of the neighborhood would go easy on the crops until after the harvest. Her grave was discovered in the eleventh century when some boys tumbled into a hole containing sweet-smelling bones. Wonderful cures took place at the site—including the regurgitation by one pilgrim of the longest tapeworm on record.

THE FEAST OF SAINT POLYCARP

First martyr whose relics were collected, 156

Invoked against dysentery, earache • (emblem: holding a book)

Polycarp was ordained bishop of Smyrna by the Apostle Saint John himself and governed his flock in peace until, under Marcus Aurelius, the persecutions began. The account of his death, written by a contemporary, is the first record of a martyrdom. At the age of eighty-six, Bishop Polycarp was arrested and tried before the Roman proconsul in the amphitheater. When he would not deny his Faith, he was condemned to the stake. But the flames would not touch the old man, "forming themselves like the sails of a ship in the wind" around him. He was then stabbed with a spear—whereupon "such a quantity of blood came forth as to quench the fire." The Faithful gathered Polycarp's bones, "more precious than costly stones," and buried them where they resolved to "gather together to celebrate the day of his martyrdom as his birthday." This is the first historical evidence of the keeping of an annual Saint's Feast.

THE FEAST OF SAINT WILLIGIS

Bishop, proud son of a teamster, 1011

Patron of carters • (emblem: wagon wheel)

When Willigis became archbishop of Mainz, he asked that the emblem on his banner be a cartwheel, in memory of his cart-driving peasant father—and the coat of arms of the city of Mainz bears a cartwheel to this day. Willigis was a statesman, chaplain to Emperor Otto II, and regent to the boy emperor Otto III, upon whose death Our Saint contrived to have his cousin Henry assume the throne.

24. THE FEAST OF SAINT PRIX

Controversial martyr, 676

Prix, the bishop of Clermont, was also known as Praejectus, Prest, and Preils, and several quite different stories explain his martyrdom. In one version the bishop complains to King Childeric about a certain Hector, who had illegally seized an estate. The king has Hector executed, and in revenge two of the thief's henchmen bash in the bishop's head. In a more convoluted scenario Prix blesses the marriage of Childeric's son Merovaeus to his aunt Brunhilde, sister of the king's poisoned first wife, thereby incurring the wrath of the king's second wife, who hires an assassin to stab Our Saint in the armpit. But all authorities agree these events transpired at Volvic in the Vosges.

Also: The Feast of Saint Adela, youngest daughter of William the Conqueror and dominating mother of the ill-fated, reputedly gay king Stephen of England, 1137.

25. THE FEAST OF SAINT WALBURGA

White witch and abbess, 779

Patron of crops, orchards, pets; invoked against coughs, frenzy, plague •
(emblems: three ears of corn, flask of oil)

An English-born nun, Walburga joined her uncle Saint Boniface on his mission to heathen Germany. At Heidenheim, in 761, she established an ecclesiastical precedent, taking charge of a coed establishment, an abbey housing both monks and nuns. Walburga was a Woman of Power—an herbalist, skilled in the healing, not to say magical, arts. (She once cured a girl possessed of a ravenous appetite by feeding her three ears of grain.) At Eichstätt miraculous cures are to this day ascribed to a liquid flowing from a rock near her relics, and on the eve of her Feast, Walpurgisnacht, covens of witches hold their revels on the Blocksberg in the Harz Mountains. Possibly these misguided souls have confused Our Saint with an ancient Teutonic goddess named, by sheer coincidence, Walburga.

Also: The Feast of Saints Avertanus and Romeo, a pair of French pilgrim-monks who brought the plague with them to Italy, 1380.

26. THE FEAST OF SAINT PHOTINA

Samaritan woman, 1st century

In Greek tradition Photina is the name given to the woman Jesus scandalized the pious by speaking to when they met at a well (John 4). She is alleged to have been martyred later in, of all places, Rome.

THE FEAST OF SAINT PORPHYRY

Politically connected pilgrim, 420

In ill health Porphyry traveled from his native Macedonia to Jerusalem, where, upon Mount Calvary, he was cured by a vision of Saint Dismas, the Good Thief.

Consecrated bishop, he befriended the empress of Byzantium, and at his request she ordered the destruction of many pagan temples. A statue of Aphrodite—blasphemously prayed to by young women in search of love—once destroyed *itself* when Porphyry strolled past it.

27. THE FEAST OF SAINT GABRIEL POSSENTI

Pistol-packing priest, 1862

Patron of college students, handgun owners • (kneeling before a statue of the Virgin)

Gabriel's father was a lawyer and a leading Catholic layman of Assisi, begetting thirteen children of his wife before she died of it. Orphaned at four, the boy was raised by Jesuits, who nicknamed him Il Damerino—the little ladies' man. As an adolescent he postponed joining the priesthood until explicitly instructed to do so by a Holy Picture of Our Lady of Sorrows. Until his death of tuberculosis he was a model novice, humble, obedient, and always wrapped in studded chains in order to mortify his potentially sinful flesh—so it is small wonder that at the time of his canonization, the Sacred Congregation of Rites recommended him as Patron of college students. But Our Saint has recently been adopted—by a Gabriel Possenti Society of Arlington, Virginia—as the Patron Saint of handgun owners. It seems that in 1859 or '60, the village of Isola, where he lived, was threatened by Goblins—that is, a gang of Garibaldi's rebels. They were apparently subdued when the slender, cassock-wearing Gabriel appeared before them brandishing a pair of pistols and, to prove he meant business, blew away a passing lizard.

THE FEAST OF SAINT GALMIER

Handyman-monk, 650

Patron of locksmiths • (emblems: pincers, hammer, anvil)

A locksmith in Lyons, Galmier—who is also known as Baldomerus—lived a life of great austerity and gave everything—even his tools—to the poor. His holiness inspired a monastery to give him a cell to live in and the birds to eat out of his hands. Although there is no record of his having been a drinking man, in France a very large wine bottle is called *un Saint-Galmier.*

Also: The Feast of Saint Anne Line, crippled widow of Merrie England, hanged for attending Mass, 1601.

28. THE FEAST OF SAINT HONORINA

Virgin martyr of Normandy, date unknown

Patron of boatmen • (emblem: oar)

One of the early martyrs of Gaul, Honorina is highly revered by the fisherfolk of Normandy, but nothing historical is known about her.

THE FEAST OF SAINT ROMANUS

Relatively liberal abbot, 460

Invoked against drowning, insanity • (emblem: monk carrying food, bell)

Strongly affected by reading about the early Desert Fathers, Romanus fled the monastery in Lyons and took to the hills—specifically, the cold Alpine slopes of the Jura. There he prayed continuously, his only shelter a large fir tree. He was soon joined by his brother Lupicinus and their sister, whose name history does not record. All clad themselves in the skins of beasts and wore wooden shoes. Of the brothers, Lupicinus was the stricter with regard to diet, eschewing not only meat and eggs but milk.

29. THE FEAST OF SAINT OSWALD OF WORCESTER

Leap-year-baby bishop, 992

Patron of reapers • (emblem: driving off the Devil with a stone)

In the 1930s this Saint's Feast was moved to February 28, but during the preceding centuries it was celebrated only in leap years. Of Danish descent, Oswald was both a monk and a bishop (of York, for twenty years) and apparently a man of political savvy as well as personal piety. The vast tracts of land granted to him by King Edgar served as a buffer zone between His (Danish) Majesty's realm and the fractious Saxons to the north and Welsh to the west. Saint Oswald's lasting achievement was the founding of the great Benedictine abbey of Ramsgate.

❧ · March · ❧

1. THE FEAST OF SAINT DAVID

Abstemious Welsh abbot, known as the Water Man, 589

Patron of doves, poets, Wales • (emblem: daffodil)

David—whose real name was Dewi—was of royal descent, Welsh style. He was begotten when Sant, a fierce Celtic chieftain, raped the pure and pious nun Saint Non. Through this connection, as the historian Geoffrey of Monmouth observed, David was descended from King Arthur himself. As a young man David traveled to the Isle of Wight to study under Saint Paulinus and upon his arrival cured the ancient monk of his blindness, which had been caused by excessive weeping. When he returned to Wales, David began vigorously establishing monasteries—the ruins of which may be seen at every crossroads west of Herefordshire. Pelegianism, a dreadful heresy (of the typically English, "anything goes" school of thought) was then popular in Britain. David would have none of it; his life and his rule were severe. He was a strict teetotaler, and his diet consisted of nothing but bread, salt, and that most Welsh of vegetables, the leek.

THE FEAST OF SAINT SWITHBERT

Missionary to the Frisians, 715

Invoked against angina • (emblem: bishop with a star in his crozier)

One of the dozen English Benedictine missionary monks who crossed the Channel to preach the Gospel to the heathen Dutch, Swithbert is by tradition Patron of chest pain sufferers, but no one knows why.

Also: The Feast of Saint Albinus, a French bishop whose breath could kill, 554.

2. THE FEAST OF SAINT CHAD

Watery English bishop, 672

Patron of medicinal springs • (emblem: vine)

When it was explained to him that he had been improperly consecrated bishop of York, Chad humbly returned to Lichfield, where his prayers to calm the wind and recitation of the Psalms against thunder were much valued by his parishioners. After his death a pinch of dust removed from a convenient hole in Chad's coffin long served as an all-purpose nostrum. Because the New River, which was London's main water supply, had its source in Chad's Well Springs, a chic spa in Georgian London was known as Saint Chad's Well.

THE FEAST OF SAINT CHARLES THE GOOD

Noble knight, 1127

Patron of Crusaders

The son of King (and Saint) Canute of Denmark, Charles fought in the Second Crusade and returned to become count of Flanders. Because he invariably took the side of the poor, he was hailed by his subjects as "the Good." Charles walked barefoot to Mass every day—and one morning a gang of thugs in the pay of his wealthy enemies murdered him right there in church.

Also: The Feast of Saint Ferona, surnamed the White, who succeeded Saint Columcille as abbot of Iona, 637.

3. THE FEAST OF SAINT ARTHELAIS

Much lusted-after virgin, 560

Patron of victims of kidnapping

This lovely and virtuous maiden of Constantinople caught the eye of the randy emperor Justinian, so her parents packed her off to live with her uncle

Narses Patricius in Benevento, Italy. On her way there she was kidnapped by miscreants but miraculously escaped their clutches.

THE FEAST OF SAINT CUNEGUND

Married empress, certified virgin, 1033

Patron of Lithuania, Luxembourg • (emblem: walking on a hot plowshare)

A princess of Luxembourg, Cunegund was wooed and won by the Bavarian duke (later, Emperor and still later Saint) Henry II. As man and wife they lived sinlessly—respecting each other's vows of chastity. So, when he surprised his bride sharing her bed with a handsome young man, Henry was upset. He was relieved to have her alibi—that it was only the Devil—established when she proved her innocence by walking barefoot on a bed of hot plowshares. After Henry's death the empress happily took the veil, eventually becoming an abbess. According to an edifying legend, she once slapped an unruly novice in the face, leaving the marks of her fingers on the grateful nun's face until her dying day. In 1715, Pope Clement XI named Cunegund Patron of Lithuania, a nation that did not exist during her lifetime but is, geographically speaking, territory her husband stole.

THE FEAST OF SAINT GUIGNOLE

Allegedly most virile abbot, 530

Invoked against impotence, infertility • (emblem: fish and bell)

I n England, where many churches are dedicated to him and most of his relics rest, this Saint is called Winnol, Winwaloe, or Gwenno. In France, he is Guignole. He was a typical Celtic monk of the sixth century, much given to mortifications; he is said to have carried a bell, which he rang to attract the fish he ate. In a church in the city of Brest there is an unusual statue of him—its most prominent feature being a protruding, rigid male member. For centuries the faithful of both sexes, eager for charms against inadequacies, have been whittling bits off it—yet Guignole's prowess remains miraculously undiminished. So great was his

fame in medieval times that he became, slapstick at the ready, a character in a rather risqué puppet show. Thus, since the nineteenth century a Parisian theater specializing in the lewdly grotesque has called itself le Grand Guignole.

Also: The Feast of Saint Katharine Drexel, a Philadelphia heiress who labored tirelessly on behalf of the poor, African Americans, and Native Americans until her death in 1955. On October 1, 2000, she became the second American-born woman to be canonized.

4. THE FEAST OF SAINT CASIMIR OF POLAND

Reluctant prince, 1484

Patron of bachelors, Lithuania • (emblem: kneeling in ecstasy, holding a lily)

Casimir was a great disappointment to his father, King Casimir IV, because he refused to lead an army into Hungary—preferring to stay home clad in a hair shirt, repeating aloud the long Latin prayer "Daily, Daily Sing to Mary," which is now known as Casimir's Hymn. Neither would he marry the daughter of the German emperor, having sworn himself to perpetual chastity. He died, aged twenty-six, of tuberculosis. Miracles occur with astonishing frequency at his tomb in Vilna.

Also: The Feast of Saint Humbert, who married four times, 1189; and Saint Leonard, muscular ruffian turned bishop, 614.

5. THE FEAST OF SAINT PHOCAS OF ANTIOCH
Nontoxic Syrian martyr, 320

Invoked against snakebite • (emblem: serpents twined around him)

It is flatly asserted in the *Roman Martyrology* that anyone bitten by a deadly serpent need only touch the doors of the Roman basilica dedicated to Phocas to be immediately cured.

THE FEAST OF SAINT PIRAN
Legendary Cornish hermit, 480

Patron of Cornwall, miners

The tin miners of both Cornwall and Brittany have long invoked the aid of this holy hermit, who is also known as Perran and Pyran. He is not to be confused with Saint Kieran, a holy hermit whose Feast Day this is as well.

Also: The Feast of Saints Gerasimus, a Palestinian monk inseparable from his pet lion, 475; and John Joseph of the Cross, a mind-reading, levitating Neapolitan hunger artist, 1734.

6. THE FEAST OF SAINT FRIDOLIN
Relic-finding hermit, 650

Patron of optometrists; invoked for fruitful weather • (emblem: leading a skeleton by the hand) icknamed the Traveler, this Irish monk made his way through darkest Europe as far as the Rhine. At Poitiers, which had recently been sacked by Vandals, he was granted a sort of miraculous X-ray vision, which enabled him to discover the holy relics of Saint Hilary in the rubble. In pursuit of justice Fridolin once brought a dead man (named Urso) into court to testify on a legal matter.

Also: The Feast of Saint Colette, relentless reformer of other nuns, who could converse with birds, 1447.

7. THE FEAST OF SAINT DRAUSIUS

Whose tomb Crusaders venerated, 576

Patron of champions; invoked against the machinations of enemies

he magnificent sarcophagus of Drausius is now an exhibit in the Louvre. (It is empty of his holy relics, which were desecrated and scattered by Liberals during the French Revolution.) For centuries, while it was in the cathedral of Notre Dame de Soissons, Drausius's tomb was the site of all-night vigils by French, English, and German warriors who believed that Drausius could make them invulnerable. The Saint himself had led an austere life of zealous church building and flagellation.

THE FEAST OF SAINTS PERPETUA AND FELICITY

African matron and slave, killed by a crazed cow, 203

Patrons of cows, mothers • (emblem: cow)

n Carthage, in the bad old days, the nobly born Perpetua and her pregnant slave Felicity were arrested for the crime of Christianity. According to their *Acts,* a journal of their captivity written by Perpetua herself, both women were eager to suffer for the Faith but feared the authorities would spare Felicity because of her delicate condition. Their prayers were answered when Felicity gave birth prematurely, so that they could both take part in the games celebrating the emperor's son's birthday in the local amphitheater. As the audience cheered, the two Christian women, wrapped in nets, were exposed to a herd of wild cattle. Saint Augustine, although not present at the event, assures us that even as they were being tossed on the horns of the beasts, both ladies were careful to keep their skirts down.

Also: The Feast of Saint Paul the Simple, a cuckolded farmer who became a desert hermit, 339.

8. THE FEAST OF SAINT JOHN OF GOD

Ex–book peddler, nursing order founder, 1550

Patron of booksellers, hospitals, nurses, printers, the sick and dying; invoked against alcoholism, heart disease • (emblem: pomegranate inscribed with a cross)

By the time he was forty, this Portuguese soldier of fortune had done it all—fought the French in Spain and the Turks in Hungary and sold slaves in Morocco. In Granada, where he ran a little bookshop, John one day chanced to hear a stirring sermon by John of Ávila and went suddenly, spectacularly mad, right there in church. Visiting him in the asylum, the preacher recognized the symptoms of lunacy as a form of penance and urged the guilt-crazed bookseller to undertake a life of charitable works. Upon his release John opened a hospice for the sick and destitute, on whose behalf he labored for the next fifteen years with astonishing zeal, despite a debilitating heart condition. Because a rehab hospital in Dublin is named for him, John is also considered a Patron of alcoholics.

THE FEAST OF SAINT PHILOMEN

Egyptian entertainer, martyr, 305

Patron of dancers

A popular dancer and flute player in Alexandria, Philomen was converted by Saint Apollonius and refused to dance before a pagan idol. The two of them were sewn in sacks and flung into the river.

9. THE FEAST OF SAINT CATHERINE OF BOLOGNA

Book-illustrating virgin, 1463

Patron of artists • (emblem: nun with book and Christ child)

In her youth this pious virgin was tormented by diabolic visions that caused her to doubt the Real Presence of Christ in the Eucharist. But she got over it and joined the Poor Clares. One Christmas Eve, after reciting a thousand decades of the rosary, she was visited by Our Lady and permitted, briefly, to baby-sit the Christ Child. Some years after her death Catherine's tomb was opened and her body was found to be sweet-smelling and incorrupt. It was placed in a glass case in the convent chapel, where it remains on display to this day—somewhat (alas) the worse for wear. Exhibited nearby is a little book, which the Saint herself illuminated with considerable artistic skill.

THE FEAST OF SAINT DOMINIC SAVIO

Teenage protégé of Don Bosco, 1857

Patron of choirboys, juvenile delinquents

Dominic, who died at the age of fifteen, holds the record as the youngest (nonmartyr) Saint ever officially canonized. It is thanks to the influence of Saint John Don Bosco, his kindly mentor (and biographer), that this teenage mystic from Turin was prevented from becoming an altogether insufferable little prig. Although Dominic enjoyed confiscating and destroying his schoolmates' dirty magazines and inserting a crucifix between playground combatants, he was, the don assures us, no tattletale.

THE FEAST OF SAINT FRANCES OF ROME

Glowing-Angel-guided widow, 1440

Patron of motorists, widows • (emblem: nun led by a glowing Angel)

Had there been society pages in Rome in 1397, they would have banner-headlined the nuptials of the beautiful and aristocratic Francesca dei Roffredeschi, aged thirteen, and the dashing Lorenzo, heir to the vast Ponziano estates. In truth the marriage got off to a rocky start, and the bride, who would have preferred to become a nun, waxed pale and sickly. Only after Saint Alexis appeared to her in a dream did she resign herself to the married state, recover, and in due time give birth to three children. But those were the days of the Great Schism, and when the wicked antipope attacked Rome, the Ponziano family castle was sacked and razed. The once wealthy family wore rags and begged for scraps. After two of her children succumbed to plague, an Angel appeared to Francesca. (She described him as blond, with very clean feet.) Thereafter this being's unearthly radiance—visible only to her—enabled Our Saint to see in the dark, which accounts for her Vatican-approved Patronage of motorists. With the Angel to guide her, she bravely endured her husband's death and her surviving son's unfortunate marriage. She eventually retired to a convent, wherein she experienced—and described in entertaining detail—several visions of Hell.

10. THE FEAST OF SAINT KESSOG

Pious Irish prince, 560

Patron of Scotland • (emblem: bent bow, arrow)

efore Saint Andrew became their Patron Saint, it was Kessog (aka Mackessog) whose name the Highland clans invoked before battle. He was an Irish prince who as a boy lost two friends in a swimming mishap. Then, to appease their parents, he restored them to life. Ordained a priest, he set out to convert the Scots, establishing himself on what is still known as Monks' Island in Loch Lomond. Thence he wandered the bonny banks and braes, preaching and working miracles. The town of Luss takes its (Gaelic) name from the herbs in which Kessog's body was embalmed, and the bell he carried remains a tourist attraction in the town of Lennox.

Also: The Feast of Saint Anastasia the Patrician, cross-dressing desert hermit, formerly lady-in-waiting to the empress Theodora, 597; and Saint John Ogilvie, Glasgow-born priest and martyr, 1615.

11. THE FEAST OF SAINT EULOGIUS OF CÓRDOBA
Moor-opposing Spanish martyr, 859

Patron of carpenters, coppersmiths • (emblem: sword and lance)

scholar-priest in Moor-occupied Spain, Eulogius was betrayed by a treacherous bishop and taken prisoner by the infidels. In his cell he composed the moving *Exhortation to Martyrdom*, which inspired his fellow prisoners to die bravely. Eulogius himself was released, then rearrested for sheltering a Muslim convert. At his trial he offered to convert the *kadi*, the presiding magistrate. But he was beheaded instead.

Also: The Feast of Saint Oengus, Irish monk and author, who preferred to say his prayers while immersed in a tub of icy water, 824.

12. THE FEAST OF SAINT FINA
Rat-infested sickly virgin, 1253

Patron of spinners • (emblem: rat)

She was christened Seraphina, but everyone in the little town of San Geminiano, Tuscany, knew her as Fina, the shy and beautiful daughter of a poor but pious widow. At the age of six Fina got sick. She immediately asked to be removed from her cot and to lie on a hard board, in emulation of Jesus on the cross. Nor did she utter a word of complaint when rodents nibbled on her sores—for the ghost of Pope Gregory the Great had appeared to her in a vision and promised her a happy death on his Feast Day, which used to be celebrated on this very date. And so it came to pass. And when the neighbors came to bury Fina, they discovered that the board on which her little body lay was covered not with scabs and pus but with sweet-smelling violets.

Also: The Feast of Saint Maximilian, beheaded for his refusal to serve in the Roman army, 295.

13. THE FEAST OF SAINT ANSOVINUS
Wine-bibbing bishop, 840
Patron of harvests • (emblem: hood full of wine)

This Italian bishop worked many wonders. In times of famine, for example, the granaries he opened to the poor miraculously refilled themselves (which accounts for his Patronage of harvests). But Ansovinus performed his most famous miracle in a tavern. While on the road from his native Umbria to Rome, he and his companions stopped at an inn at Narni and ordered wine. The surly host served them a bottle of the local vintage that had been watered down to a criminal degree. Nor would he provide the company with cups to drink from, saying his customers were expected to bring their own. The bishop removed his cloak and ordered the insolent innkeeper to pour the wine into the garment's hood. When he did the water drained out, leaving pure wine for the merry company to enjoy.

14. THE FEAST OF SAINT MATILDA
Rich but sorrowful widow, 968
Patron of those with disappointing children

atilda married King Henry "the Fowler" of Germany and gave him two sons, Otto the Great and Henry the Quarrelsome. The king died, and Otto, the elder, succeeded him, but Henry contested the throne on the grounds that his mother had always liked him better—which was true but hardly the point. After a brief civil war the boys patched it up and jointly went after their mother, for squandering the royal treasury. She got her to a nunnery.

THE FEAST OF SAINT LUBIN

Water-tortured bishop, 557

Invoked against rheumatism • (emblem: dying, receiving extreme unction)

A peasant boy of Burgundy, Lubin was a day laborer at a monastery, in which he studied by night and eventually was received into the order. When a looting and pillaging army of pagan Franks overran the countryside, they captured Lubin, tied his feet together, and lowered him into a river, demanding to know the whereabouts of the monastery's treasure. The Franks got nothing, and Lubin got rheumatism. He ended his days as bishop of Chartres.

15. THE FEAST OF SAINT CLEMENT MARY HOFBAUER

Persistent Redemptorist, 1820

Patron of Vienna

The son of a Czech butcher who had changed his name from Dvorak, Clement became a baker in Vienna, then a hermit, then made his way to Rome, joined the missionary Redemptorist Order, and returned to his native city. There he established churches and schools before being arrested and expelled by the anticlerical Austro-Hungarian emperor Joseph II. He proceeded to Warsaw and undertook further good works until he was expelled again, this time by the anticlerical French emperor Napoleon. Returning to Vienna, Clement strove mightily against the anticlerical congress there.

THE FEAST OF SAINT LONGINUS

Roman soldier whose spear pierced Christ's side, 1st century

Invoked against injustice • (emblem: lance)

Tradition merges the soldier whose spear pierced the side of the crucified Jesus (John 19:34) with the centurion who later acknowledged him to be the Son of God (Matthew 27:54). According to his legend, Longinus was either struck blind or cured of blindness on Calvary, was then baptized by the Apostles, and eventually died, a martyred bishop, in Cappadocia.

THE FEAST OF SAINT LOUISE DE MARILLAC

Hands-on activist widow, 1660

Patron of orphans, social workers, widows • (emblem: with child in her arms)

In Paris in 1625, Mme. Louise Le Gras (née Marillac), age thirty-five, became a wealthy widow. She might have founded a glittering salon or, being of a religious nature, joined a cloistered nunnery. Fortunately, her friend and spiritual adviser was Saint Vincent de Paul. Customarily for "Monsieur Vincent," rich and devout widows were merely financial resources. But in Mme. Le Gras, delicate as she appeared, he sensed real possibilities. Under his direction she began to do actual work among the poor, the sick, and the destitute. Eventually she founded the Daughters of Charity, an altogether new sort of order, "whose convent is the sickroom and whose cloister is the streets." The sisters took no vows. Louise and the women who gathered around her—not all of them aristocrats—founded and staffed orphanages, schools, and shelters for abandoned women throughout France. Their operation of the great Hôtel-Dieu hospital in Paris was to be an acknowledged inspiration to Florence Nightingale. When in 1934 the Vatican pronounced Louise de Marillac a Saint, the act was entirely superfluous.

THE FEAST OF SAINT MATRONA

Queasy virgin, date unknown

Invoked against dysentery

A Portuguese princess, Matrona was advised in a vision to travel to Capua, Italy, in order to be cured of the complaint against which she is invoked. She expired of it there, where her memory is much revered.

16. THE FEAST OF SAINT HERIBERT

Weather-controlling hermit, 1022

Invoked for rain • (emblem: bishop calling down rain)

This German cleric served as chancellor to Emperor Otto III but did not get along with that monarch's successor, Saint Henry (husband, in name only, to Saint Cunegund). In the year 1000 a terrible drought was assumed by all to signal the end of the world—but Heribert's prayers brought rain.

Also: The Feast of Saint Papa, who was forced to walk in shoes filled with nails, then tied to a dead tree, which flowered at his death, 300.

17. THE FEAST OF SAINT GERTRUDE OF NIVELLES

Highly hospitable abbess, 659

Patron of cats, gardeners, travelers; invoked against mice

In sacred art Gertrude is portrayed so rapt in prayer that she is unaware of a mouse scampering up her pastoral staff. Therefore, in her native Belgium this kindly nun is still invoked against infestations of rodents, and cakes baked in her convent's kitchen are believed to repel vermin. In her lifetime she was celebrated for her hospitality—Belgians still call a drink for the road Saint Gertrude's cup, and some believe that the souls of the departed spend their first night of the afterlife in Saint Gertrude's care.

THE FEAST OF SAINT JOSEPH OF ARIMATHEA

He lent Christ his tomb, 1st century

Patron of cemetery keepers, pallbearers, tin miners • (emblem: flowering staff)

In all four Gospels it is related that Jesus was buried in the tomb of this wealthy disciple. According to one pious legend, Joseph was Jesus' uncle and a tin miner. After his nephew's Resurrection and Ascension, Joseph accompanied Mary Magdalene to France. Then, alone, he made his way to Britain, bringing with him the chalice drunk from at the Last Supper, which became an ornament of the church he established at Glastonbury, Somerset. And that is how the Holy Grail ended up in England, and why King Arthur, who built his own castle at Glastonbury, was so concerned with it. For a millennium and a half it was believed that Joseph of Arimathea's staff, which had grown into a large hawthorn tree, flowered every Christmas Eve. This was the sort of papist superstition the Puritans scorned—but, just to be on the safe side, they cut it down.

THE FEAST OF SAINT PATRICK

Remarkably successful Apostle to the Irish, 461

Patron of Ireland, Nigeria; invoked against snakes • (emblem: shamrock)

He wasn't Irish, he was Welsh Italian. His given name wasn't Patrick, it was Succat. He wasn't the first Christian missionary to Ireland—that was Saint Palladius. And there were never any snakes in Ireland to begin with. Aside from that, everything you know about him is true. In Benin, Saint Patrick is identified with the serpent-god Da because of his close association with snakes. In April 1961 the Sacred Congregation of Rites declared him the Patron Saint of Nigeria.

18. THE FEAST OF SAINT FRA ANGELICO

Maker of masterpieces, monk, 1455

Patron of artists

Guido di Pietro, a Dominican friar, first painted frescoes for the monastery at San Marco in Florence, then decorated the Vatican at the direction of various Popes. Although venerated as "Blessed" by his contemporaries, he was not officially made a Saint until 1984, when, over the objections of the bureaucrats in the Congregation for the Causes of Saints, John Paul II unilaterally declared Fra Angelico the Patron of artists. Art historians in general agree with the poet Browning, "Brother Angelico's the man, you'll find."

Also: The Feast of Saint Edward the Martyr, an English king done in by his stepmother, 978; and Saint Frigidian, an Irish pilgrim to Rome who settled in Lucca and became its bishop, 588.

19. THE FEAST OF SAINT JOSEPH

Foster father of Our Lord, 1st century

Patron of Austria, Belgium, Canada, carpenters, fathers, Mexico, Peru, Vietnam, workers; invoked when house hunting, for a happy death, against Communism and doubt • (emblem: carpenter's square)

In many parts of the world, including the United States, small statues of Saint Joseph are buried in the lawns of homes for sale when the real estate market is slow. This is because Joseph, a carpenter and a "just man," according to the

Scriptures, was the provider of shelter for Jesus and his mother. An elaborate account of his genealogy is given by Luke the Evangelist, establishing his descent from King David, from whose lineage the Messiah was prophesied—but since Joseph was not Our Lord's biological father, the point seems moot. When his chaste fiancée announced her pregnancy, Joseph was understandably upset, until a visiting Angel explained matters to him and the nuptials took place as scheduled. That Joseph and his wife, Mary, remained celibate throughout their married life is a cornerstone of the Catholic Faith—and nothing contradicts this doctrine except the Gospel of Saint Mark, chapter 6, wherein Jesus' four brothers are listed by name. In the Middle Ages, Joseph was portrayed as a feeble old man—eighty-nine years old at the time of his marriage, according to the learned Saint Epiphanus (315–403). Among his emblems in art is a crutch, which symbolizes his supposed impotence, and he was a slightly comic figure, sometimes known as the Divine Cuckold. But Joseph became a more positive role model in response to the crisis of the Reformation. Mary of Agred, a fifteenth-century nun, was favored with a vision that inspired her to write the true biography of Saint Joseph. In her *Mystical City of God,* we learn that he was thirty-three at the time of Jesus' birth and sometimes ate meat—unlike his wife, who was a strict vegetarian. During his final illness he was constantly attended by his wife, and "if she withdrew for a moment, it was only to serve her Divine Son." Thus, it is assumed that Joseph enjoyed a happy death. His current image as a red-blooded, blue-collar kind of guy was underscored by Pope Pius XI, who in 1933 proclaimed him "Patron of those who combat atheistic Communism," and by Pope Pius XII's institution of the Feast of Saint Joseph the Worker, to be celebrated on the first of May, as a sort of counterdemonstration to the socialists' godless May Day.

20. THE FEAST OF SAINT CUTHBERT

Rustic English bishop-hermit, 687

Patron of sailors; invoked to withstand cold • (emblems: otters, swan)

A strapping shepherd lad from the north of England, Cuthbert became a monk (according to Bede's *History*) in response to a vision. It was Cuthbert's custom to pray naked, winter and summer, immersed to his neck in the chilly North Sea. Witnesses claimed that seals (or otters—accounts vary) would snuggle up to him for warmth. Although he preferred a life of solitude on a barren island, he consented to serve as bishop of Lindisfarne from 685 to 687. Of his episcopal zeal the noted hagiographer Sabine Baring-Gould writes, "No saint of his time or country had more frequent or affectionate intercourse than Cuthbert with the nuns." Among his miracles were restoring dead children to life and verbal communication with aquatic fowl.

THE FEAST OF SAINT MARTIN OF BRAGA

Hungarian missionary to northern Spain, 580

Patron of Portugal, (Spanish) Galicia

Martin was a monk in Palestine when he met two pilgrims from the Iberian Peninsula who convinced him their homeland needed him. At Braga (which is now in Portugal), he first founded a monastery. Appointed bishop, he brought multitudes of local heretics back to the Faith. His writings record his interest in the area's quaint superstitions.

21. THE FEAST OF SAINT NICHOLAS VON FLÜE

Wise, Alps-dwelling hermit, 1487

Patron of counselors, Switzerland • (emblem: hermit in a mountain landscape)

A prosperous fifty-year-old farmer with ten children, Nicholas up and left one day to wander the countryside in prayer. Fortunately, he was stricken on the way with a stomachache, as a result of which he had no need of earthly food for the remaining thirty years of his life. He settled in a hut on a mountaintop, and word soon spread around the canton that a wise and holy old geezer in the Alps was living on air. The locals flocked to his hermitage to seek the advice of "Bruder Klaus." He was a man of few words and often grouchy, but they always descended from his mountain feeling better about things. In 1481, when Switzerland was threatened with civil war, both sides were persuaded to seek his counsel, and although history does not relate what he told the would-be combatants, they settled things peacefully.

22. The Feast of Saint Avitus, Visigoth warrior turned hermit, 516; Saint Isnardo of Chiampa, a remarkably fat Dominican friar, 1244; Saint Lea of Rome, much praised by Saint Jerome for wearing no makeup, 383; Saint Nicholas Owen, Jesuit lay brother torn to pieces for his alleged treason to the British Crown, 1606; and Saint Paul of Narbonne, baptized by Saint James, with whom he intended to travel to Spain, but was left behind in France, 250.

23. THE FEAST OF THE BLESSED SIBYLLINA BISCOSSI
Blind foundling raised by nuns, 1367

Patron of illegitimate children

She was orphaned at five, put out to work, and blind by the age of twelve. Nevertheless, Sibyllina longed to join a Dominican convent, for she was certain that Saint Dominic would give her back her sight. On his Feast Day he did, indeed, appear to her and answer her prayer. The answer was no. Sibyllina then received permission to live walled up in a cell of her own, where she was exceedingly uncomfortable, as she wished to be. Despite her sightless condition she could sense the presence of the Blessed Sacrament. Once a priest on a sick call passed the little window of her hermitage, and she called out to him that the host he was carrying was not consecrated. He checked—and, by golly, she was right!

THE FEAST OF SAINT TORIBIO

Reforming missionary archbishop, 1606

Patron of Peru • (emblem: kneeling at altar, surrounded by Angels)

By 1580, forty-five years after Pizarro claimed Peru for the Spanish Crown, the place was a mess. Negligent of their duties as emissaries of Christendom, the conquistadors were warring among themselves while enslaving and slaughtering the natives. Back in Granada, Toribio Alfonso de Magoveja was a devout, middle-aged layman when he was summarily ordained a priest, consecrated a bishop, and dispatched to Lima to straighten things out. His new parish consisted of eighteen thousand square miles of jungles, mountains, greedy Spanish landowners, savage Spanish soldiers of fortune, and countless pagan souls. Toribio personally baptized half a million of those last and labored to vitiate the worst excesses of his fellow Europeans. He even—at the risk of being accused of "liberation theology"—attempted to learn the language of the natives.

Also: The Feast of Saint Gwinear, a Cornish hermit at whose grave many miracles occurred: King Alfred was cured there of something serious, and a pair of lovers locked in an embrace were carried thence to be disentangled, date unknown.

24. THE FEAST OF SAINT CATHERINE OF SWEDEN

Married queen turned nun, 1381

Invoked against abortion, miscarriage • (emblem: abbess with a hind)

The fourth of eight children born to Saint Bridget of Sweden, Catherine Ulfsdotter demonstrated her devotion to holy chastity early in life. As an infant she would refuse her mother's breast "as if it were absinthe" after those occasions when her mother had been obliged to endure carnal relations with her husband. Catherine herself was married at fourteen but persuaded her husband (however reluctantly, for she was fabulously beautiful) to respect her treasured virginity. After five years she left, over his objections, to join her mother on a pilgrimage to Rome, and soon thereafter he conveniently died. In later years many noble Romans attempted to woo—or even rape—the lovely widow. Many of them testified at her canonization hearings that their wicked stratagems were invariably foiled by the sudden and distracting appearance at her side of a shining white doe.

THE FEAST OF SAINT GABRIEL

Archangel who first uttered "Hail Mary," 4 B.C.

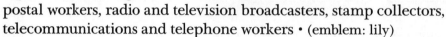

Patron of childbirth, diplomats, messengers, postal workers, radio and television broadcasters, stamp collectors, telecommunications and telephone workers • (emblem: lily)

After the Archangel Michael, Gabriel is the most glorious of the Heavenly Host. Throughout history he has acted as God's envoy to mankind. It was he who explained the meaning of his visions to the imprisoned Hebrew prophet Daniel, who advised the father of Saint John the Baptist that his ancient wife was with child, and who announced to the Blessed Virgin Mary that she was in the Holy Family Way—coining, at the same time, what must be the most repeated phrase in history, "Hail Mary." By tradition it was Gabriel who conducted the choir of Herald Angels who proclaimed Christ's birth to certain shepherds. Muslims call him Gibrail and believe that he dictated the Koran. Pope Pius XII, in 1952, declared him Patron of everyone employed in the communications industries. Paul VI put mail carriers—and, by extension, stamp collectors—under his protection.

Also: The Feast of Saint William of Norwich, the first Christian child to have his murder blamed on the Jews, 1144. This Feast was abolished in 1965.

25. THE FEAST OF THE ANNUNCIATION

The Virgin Mary as Patron of news dealers, ribbon makers

Today is Lady Day, when Mary of Nazareth was visited by the Angel Gabriel and agreed to an offer she couldn't refuse from the Godfather of them all, God the Father. (It is exactly nine months until Christmas.)

THE FEAST OF SAINT DISMAS

"The Good Thief," 33

Patron of criminals, thieves, undertakers • (emblem: Angels receiving his soul)

According to Scripture, Jesus was cruci-fied between two criminals, to one of whom He promised Paradise. Pious legend ascribes to the Savior's fellow victims of capital punishment the names Gestas and Dismas, and further relates that they had all three met before, when the Baby Jesus and His parents were on their flight into Egypt. On that occasion as well young Gestas behaved like a cad, but Dismas was a perfect little gentleman.

THE FEAST OF SAINT MARGARET CLITHEROW

Partner in her husband's butcher shop, martyred 1586

Patron of businesswomen • (emblem: door)

At the age of fifteen Margaret Middleton, the child of well-to-do Protestants, married John Clitherow, a butcher in the city of York, England. She became his business partner, bore him three children—and somehow found time to convert to the recently outlawed religion of Roman Catholicism. Imprisoned for refusing to attend Anglican services, Margaret learned to read and upon her release began teaching school. Rearrested for giving shelter to priests (one of her small sons was terrified into testifying against her), she was found guilty and was slowly crushed to death beneath an eight-hundred-pound weight.

26. THE FEAST OF SAINT LUDGER

Charlemagne-defying bishop, 809

Patron of Saxons • (emblem: swan)

Educated and ordained a priest in England, Ludger returned to the Continent on a mission to his fellow Frisians, where he kindly shared with the emperor Charlemagne the loot from sacked pagan temples. Driven out by the invading Saxons, Ludger toured the empire before returning as a missionary to those very Saxons. A changed man, he began distributing the booty to the needy. Charlemagne was outraged and demanded an audience with the bishop, but Ludger kept him waiting while he completed his devotions—much to the emperor's edification. The German city of Münster is named for the monastery Ludger founded there.

27. THE FEAST OF SAINT ALKELDA

Strangled virgin, 10th century

Invoked against eye troubles • (emblem: strangled by two women with a napkin)

The neck of this Anglo-Saxon princess was wrung by female Danish pirates. A church dedicated to Alkelda's memory still stands in the Yorkshire village of Giggleswick. Near it is a holy well, from which the Faithful obtain eyewash.

THE FEAST OF SAINT PELLEGRINO

Beloved friar of Saint Francis, 1253

Invoked against toothache

hile still a student this noble youth heard Saint Francis preaching in Bologna and begged to join his company. Francis accepted him, exhorting him to "keep the way of humility." Thus the learned Pellegrino never took Holy Orders but remained a simple lay brother. "Consumed with the thirst for martyrdom," he once visited the Holy Land but returned unscathed to Italy, where he died.

28. THE FEAST OF SAINT GONTRAN

Reformed homicidal despot, 593

Patron of murderers • (emblem: monk in a cave full of money)

Burgundian king, Gontran married the sickly Austrechild, tried to kill her doctors, then divorced her and married Mercatrude. At an advanced age he repented, as was evident from his generosity to the local clergy's building fund.

Also: The Feast of Saint Tutilo, shy Swiss poet, painter, and musician, 915.

29. THE FEAST OF SAINT ARMOGASTES

Martyred pauper, 455

Patron of poverty • (emblem: as a cowherd)

rmogastes was an official in the court of Genseric, king of the Vandals (the *Roman Martyrology* rather cryptically identifies him as a "count, and president of the theater") at Mascula, in North Africa. When the king became an Arian, Armogastes declined to join him in his heresy and was hung upside down in chains, then banished to work in the mines—quite a comedown.

THE FEAST OF SAINT RUPERT

Who developed the salt mines at Salzburg, 710

Patron of salt miners; invoked against "red rain" • (emblem: salt bucket)

Of French (say the French) or Irish (say the Irish) descent, Rupert was bishop of Worms before setting out to bring the Word to southern Germany. There he baptized the duke of Bavaria, who gave him a ruined Roman castle—which became a monastery, which became the city of Salzburg. Saint Rupert is sometimes given credit for developing the nearby mines for which the city is named.

Also: The Feast of Saint Cyril the Deacon, martyred in Lebanon by heathens who ate his liver, 362.

30. THE FEAST OF SAINT QUIRINUS

Nonexistent Roman knight and martyr, 117

Patron of cattle, horses; invoked against earache, gout, hemorrhoids, the pox • (emblem: his tongue thrown to a falcon)

According to the entertaining but unfortunately fake *Acts of Pope Alexander,* Quirinus was a Roman tribune and the Pontiff's jailer. Converted by him to the Faith, he himself was soon cruelly martyred by dismemberment—his tongue thrown to a passing falcon, who refused it. Quirinus's holy relics are the pride of the cathedral in Neuss, Germany, where he is known, for some reason, as Saint Grein and invoked for the healing of fistulas. The last resort of Neuss's desperate-to-marry women is to climb the cathedral dome and scratch the back of Quirinus's copper statue up there.

Also: The Feast of Saint Dodo, remarkably self-mortifying hermit of Frisia, 1231.

31. THE FEAST OF SAINT BALBINA

Fictitious virgin martyr, 130

Invoked against lymph gland disease, scrofula • (emblem: maiden kissing chains)

Balbina was the virgin daughter of yesterday's mythical Saint Quirinus, likewise baptized by His Holiness Pope Alexander, who also cured her of a bad complexion by advising her to locate and kiss Saint Peter's chains. There is a

Balbina Cemetery in Rome, on the Appian Way, which perhaps accounts for her invention.

THE FEAST OF SAINT GUY OF POMPOSA
Political intriguer and abbot, 1046
Patron of spies

A vain young man of Ravenna, Guy was inspired one day to tear off his finery and set off in beggars' rags for Rome. He returned a tonsured monk, joined the monastery at Pomposa, and rose to the rank of abbot. His reputation for sanctity seems to have irritated Heribert, archbishop of Ravenna, who resolved to undertake a secret inspection of the abbey. But in a vision Guy was notified of the archbishop's impending arrival, for which he made appropriate preparations, and thus became Patron of the intelligence community.

Also: The Feast of Saint Amos, Old Testament prophet, 8th century B.C.; and Saint Benjamin, who refused to stop preaching to the pagan Iranians and was burned at the stake, 422.

❧·April·☙

1. THE FEAST OF SAINT HUGH OF GRENOBLE

Self-denying bishop, 1132

Invoked against headaches • (emblem: three flowers in his hand)

A reluctant but efficient bishop, Hugh once resigned his post and retired to a monastery but was ordered back to his duties by Pope Gregory VII. Hugh was constantly tempted by, and sometimes succumbed to, the sin of blasphemy. But he was renowned for his charity (he sold his rings to feed the poor), for his chastity (he could not recognize any woman by sight), and for his relentless fasting (which resulted in his chronic headaches). At the end of his life he lost his memory for everything except the Lord's Prayer, which he recited over and over.

2. THE FEAST OF SAINT FRANCIS OF PAOLA

Priest devoted to mariners, 1508

Patron of maritime pilots, naval officers, sailors, seafarers • (emblem: ass and forge)

At age thirteen Francis became a friar, at fifteen a solitary hermit in a cave by the sea, and at nineteen the founder of an order, the Minims (the lowest ones), who specialized in feats of fasting. Although he never wore shoes, bathed, or changed his clothes, everyone Francis met commented on his peculiar heavenly odor. Francis was renowned as a miracle worker, mind reader, and adviser to the succeeding French kings Louis the Spider and Charles the Affable. Always short of funds, he was once berated by a blacksmith for nonpayment and commanded his horse to kick off its new shoes—which it did. Stranded in Sicily without money for his fare, Francis spread his cloak on the waves, stepped aboard, and floated home. For this miracle his aid is invoked by all who sail; in 1943 Pope Pius XII officially declared him the sailors' Patron.

THE FEAST OF SAINT MARY OF EGYPT

Penitent ex-harlot, 430

Patron of fallen women •
(emblem: covered with long white hair)

At the age of twelve Mary left home to become a whore in Alexandria and plied her trade there for seventeen years. So perverse was she that she embarked for the Holy Land with a party of Libyan pilgrims with the intention of seducing them all on the way. But once in Jerusalem she experienced a mystical vision of the Blessed Virgin, who advised her to repent her ways and retire to the desert on the far side of Jordan. This she did, and in the wilderness subsisted on a diet of roots and herbs for forty-seven years; her clothes rotted, but her long hair covered her nakedness. All this we know because Mary confessed to the wandering holy hermit Saint Zosimus (whose cloak she first borrowed to cover herself). When she died Zosimus himself buried her, with the assistance of a passing lion. Her legend, for obvious reasons, was long a favorite topic of sermons.

THE FEAST OF SAINT URBAN OF LANGRES

Popular bishop, 450

Patron of barrel makers, drunkards, vintners; invoked against fainting •
(emblem: book with wine vessel)

The ancient cathedral city of Langres in Burgundy is not far from the great wine-producing areas of the Côte d'Or and Champagne, but it is farther to the north, and its vineyards are threatened by cold Swiss weather. Thus the protection of Saint Urban is annually invoked by everyone engaged in the wine industry of the Haute-Marne.

3. THE FEAST OF SAINT IRENE

Martyr to literacy, 304

Patron of Macedonia, peace • (emblem: near a horse)

Once upon a time in Thessalonica, Irene and her sisters Agape and Chionia were arrested for refusing to eat food that had been offered in sacrifice to the gods, and for illegal possession of Holy Scriptures. One night the drunken governor, who lusted after all three, groped his way into their dark prison cell and was tricked by the chaste but mischievous trio into kissing kitchen utensils. Agape, Chionia, and the sacred books were burned—the beautiful Irene was chained naked in a brothel, then executed by an arrow through the throat. In New York City an icon of this Patroness of Peace is said to weep real tears in time of war.

THE FEAST OF SAINT RICHARD OF CHICHESTER

Chancellor of Oxford, 1253

Patron of coachmen • (emblem: chalice at his feet)

Richard de Wyse showed early promise as a farmer but chose instead to become a scholar, first at Oxford, then in Paris and Bologna. He returned to England in 1215 to serve as chancellor of his alma mater. Consecrated bishop of Chichester—over King Henry III's objections—Richard became renowned for his clerical reforms and his knack for cultivating figs. Because he drove a farm cart as a boy, the coachmen's guild of Milan adopted this quintessentially English Saint as their heavenly Patron.

4. THE FEAST OF SAINT BENEDICT THE BLACK

Son of slaves, sometime abbot, 1589

Patron of African Americans, Palermo • (emblem: Negro in Dominican habit)

orn on a farm in Sicily, this son of African slaves was granted his freedom by a kindly master at the age of eighteen. Benedict first displayed a commendable entrepreneurial spirit, purchasing a team of oxen and laboring as a plowman. He endured many racist taunts, like Big Black Ben, but his piety and honesty soon earned him another nickname, il Santo Moro, that is, the Holy Negro. At the urging of a passing hermit, Benedict sold his team and retired to the woods, where he dressed only in palm leaves. When the Pope (Pius IV) commanded that all solitary hermits join organized religious communities, Benedict joined the Franciscans, where he was employed as a cook. Although he could neither read nor write, Benedict was eventually elected superior—but he soon returned gladly to the kitchen. His culinary skills—enhanced by his belief that eating is a sinless pleasure—included the miraculous ability to multiply food. Despite his cloistered humility, he acquired a popular reputation for sanctity, in part owing to the heavenly light that surrounded him while praying.

THE FEAST OF SAINT ISIDORE OF SEVILLE

"The Schoolmaster of the Middle Ages," 636

Patron of Spain, proposed Patron of computer users, the Internet •
(emblem: aged bishop holding a pen and a book)

he last of the Latin Fathers, Isidore was a bishop and scholar, the prolific author of books on theology, astronomy, and geography as well as a history of the world, a history of the Goths, and a twenty-volume encyclopedia. He was an enterprising converter of heretics and Jews, employing methods no longer politically correct, although Dante puts him in Paradise. Because of his wideranging interests, he has been proposed as Patron of the Internet. Here is an example of his knowledge—taken at random from his database: "After touching menstrual blood, fruits do not sprout, blossoms fade, iron rusts."

5. THE FEAST OF SAINT VINCENT FERRER

Fiery preacher, 1419

Patron of brick makers, builders, lead casters, pavement workers, plumbers • (emblem: trumpet)

Born in Valencia of noble parents, Vincent joined the Dominican Order to study philosophy, but in a vision he was implored by Saints Francis *and* Dominic—a pair who hardly ever agreed—to employ his gift of eloquence to preach salvation. It was his custom to prepare for a sermon by staring at a crucifix for hours; when he hit the pulpit his remarkable good looks and powerful baritone voice often caused his female listeners to swoon. His career, as he toured western Europe, was not uneventful. Although he spoke only Spanish, Vincent's words were understood by people of all nations, and he converted 8,000 Moors and 25,000 Jews, including a rabbi who later became a bishop. When one audience doubted Vincent's claim to be "the Angel of Judgment," he was obliged to halt a passing funeral cortege and restore to life the recently deceased. Vincent's theology was not always strictly orthodox, and he was placed

on the Inquisition's black list until his good friend Benedict XIII—at the time one of three claimants to the Chair of Peter—had Vincent's dossier burned. Our Saint, somewhat ungratefully, then withdrew his support for Benedict's papacy, which forced Benedict to resign, thus bringing about (God's ways are not our ways) the reunification of Holy Mother Church.

Also: The Feast of Saint Derfel Gadarn, a Welsh soldier who fought alongside King Arthur in his last battle before becoming a holy hermit, 5th century.

6. THE FEAST OF SAINT NOTKER BALBULBUS

Speech-impaired musician-monk, 912

Invoked against stammering • (emblem: striking Devil with a broken rod)

Balbulbus, this Swiss monk's nickname, means "the stutterer." Notker overcame his handicap through his talent for music and poetry; he was a pioneer of the singing style known as Gregorian chant. With his best friends and fellow monks Tutilo and Radbert—the "three inseparables" shared a love of music and practical jokes—he came to the attention of Emperor Charles the Fat, likewise a musician. Notker composed his hymn "Sancti Spiritus Adsit Nobis Gratia" to the rhythm of the monastery mill wheel and sent it to Charles, who composed a hymn of his own and sent it back by the same messenger. The Alpine monastery of Saint Gall soon surpassed Rome itself as the preeminent school of chant, but Notker stayed humble. To his hymn to Saint Stephen he appended this inscription: "Sick and stammering and full of evil, I, Notker the unworthy, have sung the triumphs of Stephen with my polluted mouth."

7. THE FEAST OF SAINT HERMAN JOSEPH

Hymnist mystically married to the BVM, 1241

Patron of mothers, children, watchmakers

Outstandingly devout even as a child, Herman Joseph once offered an apple to a statue of the Virgin and Child and later described how Mary (who spoke excellent German) accepted the gift and briefly gave him Baby Jesus as a play-mate. He entered a monastery at the age of twelve and throughout his life com-posed passionate hymns to Our Lady—until, in a mystical vision, he married her, with Angels as attendants. He suffered from chronic headaches on liturgical Feast Days, which occasioned a witty remark—a pun in Latin that need not concern us here.

THE FEAST OF SAINT JOHN BAPTIST DE LA SALLE

Founder of the Christian Brothers, 1719

Patron of teachers • (emblem: with pen and book, students near him)

Born into a wealthy family of Rheims, John Baptist entered the religious life at eleven and at sixteen was granted the prestigious and lucrative office of canon of the cathedral of that city. Touched by the plight of the many poor and ignorant children, he resolved to devote his life and his considerable fortune to their education. His pedagogical innovations were many, including the training of teachers, lessons taught in the vernacular (rather than Latin), and classes divided into grades. The teaching order he founded, the Brothers of the Christian Schools, weathered lawsuits and even riots, but in the end John Baptist prevailed. Thanks to him, untold thousands of Christian Brothers have since terrorized and/or educated untold millions of Catholic boys in parochial schools around the world.

8. THE FEAST OF SAINT WALTER OF PONTOISE

Escape-artist abbot, 1099

Patron of vintners; invoked for the deliverance of prisoners • (emblem: bishop with corn and grapes)

When he came to the defense of a peasant who had been locked up in the monastery brig for some wrongdoing, Walter's fellow monks beat him up. Later they made him abbot. Saint Walter seems to have been something of a manic-depressive. At his investiture he knocked away King Philip's hand, declaring, "It's not from you but from God that I accept governance of this abbey." But he repeatedly fled the abbey and his office, to be retrieved from the nearby forest by his monks. Walter was considered sanctimonious by some; his denouncing of easy living among the clergy caused one recently married bishop to spit in his face.

9. THE FEAST OF SAINT CASILDA

Comely daughter of a Moorish king, 1007

Invoked against bad luck, sterility • (emblem: Saracen maiden with roses)

Casilda was a Moorish princess whose father, the king of Toledo, persecuted his Christian subjects and kept many of them captive in his castle. Casilda enjoyed visiting the prisoners, bringing them food and wine, and in time they converted her. Once her father confronted her on a mission of mercy and demanded to know what she was carrying under her cloak. Casilda answered, "Roses," and, in the tradition of Saints Margaret of Hungary and Zita, the food was transformed into flowers. Casilda was miraculously cured of a terrible illness by bathing in the waters of Lake Saint Vincent, beside which she built a hermitage in which she died, at the age of one hundred. Her memory is yet revered in Toledo.

Also: The Feast of Saint Mary Cleophas, the Blessed Virgin's stepsister and mother of the Apostle James the Less, 1st century; and Saint Waldetrudis, Patron of the city of Mons, Belgium, whose parents, sister, husband, and children are all canonized Saints. Annually, on Trinity Sunday, her head is conducted in procession through the streets of Mons, 688.

10. THE FEAST OF SAINT MACARIUS OF GHENT
Widely traveled archbishop, 1012

Invoked against plague • (emblem: three arrowheads)

A native of Antioch, Macarius became bishop of Constantinople, was driven out by the Saracens, and journeyed west to Belgium, where he died of the plague. Perhaps he is the Sainte-Macaire whose name is given to those great Bordeaux wines.

Also: The Feast of Saint Ezekiel, Hebrew prophet and surrealist, 6th century B.C.; Saint Fulbert of Chartres, poet and scholar, 1029; the Blessed Madelena of Canossa, founder of the Daughters of Charity, who when young was much fancied by Napoleon for her "angelic" beauty, 1833.

11. THE FEAST OF SAINT GEMMA GALGANI
Visionary invalid virgin, 1903

Patron of pharmacists

The turn of the last century featured a flurry of flamboyantly holy female mystics, such as the Fatima children, Louise Lateau, and Therese Neumann, but Gemma Galgani was the only one to be canonized—in 1940—and not without considerable opposition within the Church. Her popularity, especially in Italy, is still immense, but the Vatican remains embarrassed by the supernatural phenomena surrounding her. Born in Tuscany, the daughter of a pharmacist, Gemma avidly sought and for the most part enjoyed a life of God-given pain. As a child she suffered from ill health (spinal tuberculosis and deafness) as well as temptations against holy chastity, but she was miraculously cured of both after making a novena to Saint Gabriel Possenti. Orphaned at nineteen, Gemma entered domestic service, having been rejected from a convent because of her ill health. The nuns, however, had been kind enough to give her a pamphlet, "An Hour with Jesus Agonizing on the Cross." No sooner had Gemma read it than the Blessed Virgin Mary, accompanied by an Angel, appeared to her and bestowed upon her the Stigmata. Every Friday for eighteen months Gemma's hands, feet, and side gushed blood. She was also blessed with the wounds of the Crown of Thorns. For the most part she endured her suffering meekly, and her occasional outbursts of rage—howling, breaking a rosary, spitting on a crucifix—we may safely attribute to diabolical possession. At the age of twenty-five she died, her arms outstretched as if on the cross. The inscription on her tomb assures us that "this most pure virgin" is now "in the bosom of her Celestial Spouse."

THE FEAST OF SAINT GODEBERTA

Frankish court virgin, 6th century

Invoked against drought, plague • (emblem: abbess with a ring)

Godeberta's noble parents brought her to court to find a suitable husband, but there a bishop—Saint Eloy—intervened. He slipped his own episcopal ring on the little maiden's finger and declared her the bride of Christ. King Clotaire of the Franks officially recognized the marriage and bestowed upon Godeberta a convent, where she and twelve companions lived a life of austerity and meditation. Godeberta's prayers once halted an outbreak of the plague, and on another occasion she quenched a fire by making the Sign of the Cross at it.

THE FEAST OF SAINT STANISLAUS

Royally butchered bishop, 1079

Patron of Poland • (emblem: hacked to pieces at the altar)

King Boleslaus II of Poland was not a good man—he ordered peasant mothers to nurse his dogs instead of their children. But he met his nemesis in Archbishop Stan Szczepanovsky. When the king staked a claim to some real estate that a certain Peter had willed to the Church, the bishop summoned the deceased himself as a witness. Peter, moldering and malodorous, duly appeared in court to testify on the bishop's behalf. Foiled, Boleslaus stormed into the cathedral where Stanislaus was saying Mass, chased the prelate out into the streets of Crakow, and hacked him to pieces. From Heaven three eagles descended to defend the holy relics; Pope Gregory VII placed Poland under interdict, and Boleslaus went into exile.

12. THE FEAST OF SAINT ZENO

African Italian fisherman-bishop, 371

Patron of anglers, babies, Verona • (emblem: fish dangling from a crozier)

It is said that soon after his birth—in North Africa—Zeno was stolen by Devils, who placed a goblin in his cradle. The imp suckled for eighteen years but never grew; Zeno, meanwhile, had been raised by some kindly monks. Summoned to his long-lost mother's side, he obliged the changeling goblin to vomit all the milk it had consumed into a large vat. As bishop of Verona, Zeno was a reformer, campaigning against the abuses of love feasts and loud lamenting during funeral Masses, but he found time to indulge his passion for fishing in the river Adige.

Two hundred years after his death, when this river overflowed its banks, people sought refuge in his church, into which the flood waters refused to enter, although the doors and windows were open. A grateful survivor testified, "It was as though the thin liquid element had been transformed into a solid wall."

13. THE FEAST OF SAINT HERMENEGILD

Martyred by heretical relatives, 586

Patron of converts, Seville • (emblem: king bearing an ax)

A prince of the Spanish Visigoths, raised by his father, King Leovigild, in the Arian heresy, Hermenegild married a Roman Catholic and converted to Orthodoxy, much to his father's displeasure. A yearlong civil war followed in which the prince's vastly outnumbered forces were besieged in Seville; after a brief reconciliation, Leovigild's wicked second wife proposed that the prince consent to take Holy Communion from an Arian priest. Hermenegild's adamant refusal was the last straw. His father ordered him beheaded.

THE FEAST OF SAINT MARGARET OF CASTELL

Misbegotten maiden, 1320

Patron of the right to life movement

A blind, lame, deformed dwarf, Margaret was hidden away by her parents—walled up in a chapel—at the age of six. When she was fourteen her desperate parents brought her to the Dominican convent of Città-di-Castello in hopes of a miraculous cure. Disappointed, they abandoned her there to the custody of the nuns, who adopted the creature and put her in charge of their day-care facility, where she became not only useful but beloved by the townsfolk.

Also: The Feast of Saint Ursus, the son of a Sicilian gangster who became bishop of Ravenna and revived the custom of keeping Saints' Feast Days. He is invoked against faintness and kidney disease, 398.

14. THE FEAST OF SAINT BÉNEZET

Shepherd-engineer, 1184

Patron of Avignon, bridge builders • (emblem: boy carrying a stone on his shoulder)

As a pious lad keeping the family flock in the hills of Savoy, little Bénezet watched with pity the travelers below, in peril as they attempted to wade across the raging river Rhone. Then one day, during a solar eclipse, he heard a Voice three times command him to go to the town of Avignon and build a bridge there. Without hesitation he obeyed. At first the bishop of Avignon was unimpressed by the diminutive shepherd's proposed project, but a miracle or two changed his mind and he gave the go-ahead. Bénezet directed the building operations for seven years, and when he died he was buried under his bridge.

THE FEAST OF THE BLESSED KATERI TEKAKWITHA

"The Lily of the Mohawks," 1680

Patron of ecologists, the environment, exiles

Tekakwitha was born in what is now upper New York State, the daughter of a captive Algonquin woman and a Mohawk chief of the Turtle clan. Shortly after smallpox and Christianity were introduced to the New World, this Indian maiden contracted both. Disfigured and nearly blind from the former, she was instructed in the latter by a Jesuit missionary. Mocked and abused by the Mohawks, she trekked two hundred miles north through the wilderness to the village of Caughnawaga, near Montreal. Baptized there and christened Kateri, she resolved to emulate the mortifications practiced by European Saints—sleeping on a bed of thorns, sprinkling ashes in her gruel, even making a quite superfluous vow of chastity. She died at the age of twenty-four, and it is said that shortly thereafter her skin cleared up.

THE FEAST OF THE BLESSED LYDWINA

Accident-prone virgin, 1433

Patron of skaters • (emblem: ice skates)

Her name means "friend of suffering," and Lydwina lived up to it. Like many a physically attractive female Saint, she prayed to become less beautiful, and her prayers were answered. This Dutch maiden fell while skating and broke a rib, which pierced the flesh, resulting in an abscess that never healed and led to a series of unique symptoms—a fissure extruded from her brow to her nose, and her lower lip fell off her chin. She offered up her suffering for the sins of humanity, added to her misery by wearing a horsehair girdle, and took to her bed for the next thirty-three years, applying eel fat to her wounds. She once asked a visitor for the fat from one of his chickens. When he refused she shouted, "Well, I hope the mice get your chickens." And they did, that very night. Although a band of curiosity seekers once broke into Lydwina's room to marvel at her sores, her only constant companion was her Guardian Angel, who escorted her to Paradise and introduced her to various Saints. Once in church, a Communion wafer descended from Heaven and headed in her direction. When the parish priest refused to serve it to her, he incurred the wrath of the townsfolk, who chased him into the cemetery. Before she died, choking on her own phlegm, God saw fit to add to Lydwina's afflictions—headache, toothache, bedsores, and blindness—the Stigmata.

THE FEAST OF SAINT PETER GONZALES

Seamen's friend, 1246

Patron of sailors • (emblem: Dominican lying on hot coals)

When Peter first entered the clergy his politically connected uncle had him simultaneously raised to the exalted posts of deacon and canon. But when Peter arrived in full regalia for his investiture ceremony, his horse bucked him off into a dunghill—thereby setting him on a lifelong course of poverty and humility. His zeal as a reformer brought him to King Ferdinand's court, where the debauched nobles determined to corrupt him; they hired a professional courtesan to seduce him in the confessional. But Peter foiled them by jumping into a fire and inviting the woman to join him there. Until his death Our Saint had a special devotion to sailors, waiting in ports for their return, frequently boarding ships to minister to their needs. Portuguese mariners believe that the eerie light that appears around ships' masts in storms, elsewhere called Saint Elmo's fire, is Peter's work. Thus they know him as Saint Telmo.

15. THE FEAST OF THE VENERABLE FATHER DAMIEN

Priest, leper, 1880

Joseph de Veuster, the son of a Belgian (Flemish) farm family, joined the Fathers of the Sacred Hearts of Jesus and Mary and was sent as a missionary to the Hawaiian Islands, where he was ordained priest in Honolulu in 1864. After serving nine years in that earthly Paradise, he volunteered to go to Hell—that is, to the leper colony on the island of Molokai, where eight hundred men, women, and children were abandoned to decompose on a barren cliff side. Father Damien labored among them for eleven years, building homes and chapels, hearing confessions, bandaging wounds, digging graves, until one Sunday he began a sermon with the words "We lepers . . ." He was slandered during his lifetime and after his death as "coarse, dirty, headstrong," and despite a ringing defense of his compassionate sanctity by Robert Louis Stevenson (in 1905), Father Damien's canonization proceedings have gone slowly.

THE FEAST OF SAINT HUNNA

Royal washerwoman, 679

Patron of laundresses • (emblem: queen doing laundry)

Although she was the daughter of an Alsatian duke and the wife of Count Huno of Strasbourg, Hunna (or, as she was sometimes known, Huva) took in washing for her needy neighbors, who dubbed her the Holy Washerwoman. She was not officially canonized until 1520, apparently as a papal favor to the duke of Württemberg.

16. THE FEAST OF SAINT BENEDICT LABRE

Disheveled wandering eccentric, 1783

Patron of beggars, the homeless, pilgrims • (emblems: beggar's bowl, three-cornered hat)

Born in France at the dawn of the "Age of Reason," Benedict Joseph Labre did the most irrational thing: he took the Gospel literally. Of course, this rendered him unfit for membership in any religious order. After being rejected by the Trappists, Carthusians, and Cistercians, he undertook a barefoot four-year pilgrimage to all the shrines of Christendom. This holy hobo was careful to practice absolute poverty, which left him emaciated and disheveled, not to mention verminous. Arriving at last in Rome, he spent seven years camping out in the Colosseum by night and praying fervently in various churches by day. Citizens and tourists took to calling him the Beggar of Rome and the new Saint Francis, among other things.

THE FEAST OF SAINT BERNADETTE

Who saw Our Lady at Lourdes, 1879

Patron of shepherds •
(emblem: kneeling, blessed
Virgin above her in grotto)

Outside the mountain town of Lourdes in southwestern France, in 1858, the Mother of God appeared to a fourteen-year-old, asthmatic, undersized, backward shepherd girl named Bernadette Soubirous, who was out gathering firewood. Our Lady was praying the rosary— reciting, presumably, "Hail me, full of grace, the Lord is with me. Blessed am I among women, et cetera." On seventeen occasions thereafter the Blessed Virgin appeared to Bernadette, requesting that she eat grass to atone for the sins of mankind and pointing out the hidden source of a spring of water. Today twenty-seven thousand gallons of miraculously curative Lourdes water pour from that spring per week. Three million pilgrims each year visit the site, where an underground church seats twenty thousand. Bernadette herself became a simple nun. She died at age thirty-five, having worked hard at her earthly task, which she once described as "being ill." Her visions and tribulations were the subject of a big, fat, pious, best-selling book made into a two-and-a-half-hour-long Hollywood movie, *The Song of Bernadette.*

THE FEAST OF SAINT DROGO

Repulsive hermit, 1189

Patron of coffeehouse owners, shepherds, the ugly; invoked against gravel, hernias • (emblem: Benedictine with sheep)

Drogo was a Flemish shepherd, renowned for his sanctity and self-loathing as well as for his ability to hear Mass in church while simultaneously tending his flock in the fields—hence the Flemish folk saying "Not being Saint Drogo, I can't be in two places at once." Severe misfortune befell Drogo in the form of an ulcer that emitted so foul an odor it forced him into seclusion. He built a humble hut by the side of the church, which he refused to vacate even when the church caught fire. Eventually, his bowels putrified, leading to his death. For reasons of their own, the coffeehouse owners of Flanders long ago adopted him as their Patron.

THE FEAST OF SAINT MAGNUS OF ORKNEY

Pacifist Viking, martyr, 1116

Patron of fishmongers, Norway • (emblem: battle-ax)

Although he was a true Viking, a descendant of Thorfinn Skullsplitter, Magnus refused to join in pirate raids, preferring to stay aboard ship reading psalms. This earned him the enmity of his fellow Norsemen, so Magnus escaped for a while to Scotland before returning home to claim his share of the earldom of Orkney. He was executed by order of his bloodthirsty cousin Haakon. Magnus is still much revered in Scotland—he appeared to King Robert the Bruce on the eve of the Battle of Bannockburn, in 1314.

17. THE FEAST OF SAINT JAMES DUCKETT

Elizabethan bookmaker, 1602

Patron of booksellers, publishers

orn a Protestant in Westmorland, England, James Duckett became a printer's apprentice in London. When he converted to the True Faith, he began printing Catholic books. Elizabethan censors took their work seriously. Duckett was several times imprisoned for his illegal activities and eventually sentenced to death when a jailhouse snitch accused him of having published the Jesuit poet Robert Southwell's book *Supplications*—which, ironically, he had not. Duckett forgave the stool pigeon before they were hanged together at Tyburn.

18. THE FEAST OF SAINT AYA

Whose will was contested, 707

Invoked against lawsuits

efore her demise this wealthy Belgian widow bequeathed her wealth and property to a convent at Mons. When her heirs contested the will, Aya testified against them, "in a hollow voice," from her tomb. Case dismissed.

Also: The Feast of Saint Apollonius, a Roman senator executed despite his eloquent defense of the Faith, 185; and Saint Perfecto, a priest in Moorish-occupied Córdoba who was executed for his Faith and died bravely cursing Mohammed and the Koran, 850.

19. THE FEAST OF SAINT EXPEDITUS

Useful but mythical martyr, 4th century

Invoked in emergencies, against procrastination
• (emblem: knight holding a cross inscribed HODIE)

lthough his cult is venerable and he has answered many a plea for instant gratification, Saint Expeditus might not have existed. Perhaps he was an

Armenian martyr. But a persistent rumor concerns a packing case once shipped from Rome to a Parisian convent. It contained the skeleton of a Vatican-authenticated Saint and was labeled, in Italian, "*spedito,*" or, as we would say, "special delivery." But the good sisters translated the word into Latin, *expedito,* and assumed it to be the name of the Saint whose relics were within. This tale has an envious Protestant or malevolent agnostic ring to it.

Also: The Feast of Saint Alphege, a tithe-imposing Anglo-Saxon bishop whom the Vikings pelted to death with ox bones, 1012; and Saint Emma, a wealthy widow whose generosity to the poor and the Church is symbolized by her open right hand, preserved in the abbey of Saint Ludger, Weden, 1050.

20. THE FEAST OF SAINT PETER MARTYR

Hammer of heretics, 1252

Patron of Inquisitors, new mothers; invoked against headache • (emblem: Dominican with a knife in his head)

Despite the fact that his Veronese parents and family were Cathars, subscribing to the Albigensian heresy, Peter remained orthodox and entered the Dominican Order. He soon rose to prominence as a preacher and miracle worker, becoming known as the Prince of the Inquisition. Not surprisingly, he specialized in the smiting of heresies. He dressed in white, with a red cross on his breast, and traveled on a float decorated with religious paintings. Great things happened when Peter made the Sign of the Cross. He was able to produce a black cloud, make a black horse vanish, cure a scorpion bite, and defeat heretics in battle. And he had a temper. Once, when some boys threw stones at him, he cursed them, causing a building to collapse and kill them all. When a young man confessed to Peter that he had kicked his mother, the Saint ordered him to cut his foot off, which the sinner promptly did. (Peter thoughtfully put it back on.) He was assassinated by heretics on the road to Milan and before dying, in a final, typical gesture, wrote "Credo Deum" on the ground in his own blood.

THE FEAST OF SAINT URIEL

Archangel, "the Fire of God"

One of the seven Angels who stand before the throne of God (Revelation 8), Uriel was positively identified by Pope Gregory the Great as the Angel who stands guard at the gates of Eden with a fiery sword. Milton, in *Paradise Lost,* describes Uriel "gliding on a sunbeam." He is Patron of a church in Palermo.

21. THE FEAST OF SAINT BEUNO

Head-transplanting hermit, 5th century

Invoked against diseases of cattle • (emblem: with staff in one hand, hare's head in the other)

His boyhood friend, the famous Welsh chieftain Iddon ap Ynyr Gwent, gave Beuno a tract of land, which the Saint abandoned upon hearing a neighboring Saxon calling to his hounds. "The nation of that man," he declared, "has a language which is abominable." The most famous miracle attributed to Beuno involves a bridegroom who cut off his bride's head and ran off with her gold and horses. Beuno restored the lady's head, causing a fountain to spring up where she had lain. Later the bride's vengeful brother cut off the runaway groom's head, and Beuno restored that, too—but without producing a fountain. In a variation of the tale, the wicked king Caradoc decapitates Saint Winifred for rebuffing his rude advances. Beuno replaces her head and curses the king, who dissolves into a puddle. These stories fail to explain why Beuno is the Patron of sick cattle, but for centuries the Saint's earthly representatives toured Wales, collecting money in his name to ensure the health of domestic livestock.

THE FEAST OF SAINT CONRAD OF PARZHAM

Monastery porter, 1894

Patron of doormen

A Bavarian farmer, Conrad joined the Franciscan Capuchins at the age of thirty-one and for the next forty-one years served as the friary's doorkeeper. A simple soul, he extended hospitality to all—beggars, pilgrims, travelers—and he was said to have the gift of prophesy and the ability to "read hearts."

Also: The Feast of Saint Anselm, Archbishop of Canterbury, defender of the Church against succeeding English kings, as well as a philosopher of note, 1109.

22. THE FEAST OF SAINT EPIDOSIUS

Turned in by a servant, martyred, 178

Patron of the betrayed; invoked against the machinations of enemies

A Christian bachelor of Lyons during the persecutions of Emperor Marcus Aurelius, Epidosius was tattled on by a trusted servant, imprisoned, racked, punctured, and beheaded.

THE FEAST OF SAINT THEODORE OF SYKEON

Anchorite and wonder worker, 613

Invoked for reconciling the unhappily married, for or against rain • (emblem: crocodile under his feet)

Theodore's father was a typical seventh-century Greek acrobat and trick rider—he abandoned his son at birth to be raised by his mother, aunt, and grandmother, all of whom were prostitutes. Saint George appeared to his mother, instructed her to educate Theodore, and provided her with a chef—which enabled her to convert the brothel into a restaurant. (All his life Theodore promoted the cult of Saint George.) A poor student, Our Saint learned to recite the Psalms only after tasting honey that issued from the mouth of an icon of Christ. Young Theodore became a hermit so devout that from Christmas to Palm Sunday he confined himself to a wooden cage, wearing an iron girdle. He graduated to an iron cage suspended from a cliff, his hands and feet shackled. He was a celebrated exorcist, specializing in driving unclean demons out of young women and in marriage counseling. He was also clairvoyant—able to divine that a certain chalice was in fact the former chamber pot of a harlot, and that a certain general named Maurice would become emperor. Maurice made Theodore a bishop.

Also: The Feast of Saint Opportunata, a French abbess who once scolded a flock of birds, 770.

23. THE FEAST OF SAINT ADALBERT OF PRAGUE

Determined missionary-martyr, 997

Patron of Bohemia, Poland, Prussia • (emblems: club, two lances)

Christened Voytech, Adalbert assumed the name of his mentor, an earlier missionary Saint, and entered Prague barefoot in an attempt to Christianize the Czechs. A spot of trouble arose over a noble adulteress to whom he granted sanctuary; the locals stormed the church and slew her at the altar. Adalbert returned to Rome but eventually achieved martyrdom, executed as a Polish spy by pagan Prussians.

THE FEAST OF SAINT GEORGE

Dragon-slaying knight, 303

Patron of Boy Scouts, cavalry, England, equestrians, farmers, horses, Portugal; invoked against herpes, leprosy, syphilis · (emblems: red cross, mounted knight slaying a dragon)

George was a Palestinian soldier who suffered martyrdom in the persecutions of Diocletian. His cult flourished in England during the Crusades—perhaps the Crusaders imported it from the Middle East. King Edward III declared George England's Patron, and Henry V invoked his aid before the Battle of Agincourt. The story of George and the dragon—a parable of Good versus Evil—has several variations. In the classic version he is a young knight who rescues a maiden princess from a flying reptile with bad breath. He pierces the creature with his lance, leads it through town using the princess's garter as a leash, and thereby converts thousands of pagans to Christianity. In the East, George is a demigod who endures a series of tortures, such as running in red-hot iron shoes. In the West he is a Cappadocian prince whose bravery wins even the Empress Alexandra to the Faith. There is even an ignoble George. In his *Decline and Fall of the Roman Empire,* Gibbon depicts George as a black marketeer dealing in bacon. "Riding Saint George"—that is, sexual intercourse with the woman on top—was long considered a certain way of begetting a bishop.

24. THE FEAST OF SAINT WILLIAM FIRMATUS

Agrarian solitary, 1103

Invoked against crop-destroying pests, headache · (emblem: burning his arm in a fire)

A well-to-do medical man, William received a Divine warning against avarice, gave all his possessions to the poor, and became a wandering hermit.

Also: The Feast of Saints Bova and Doda, sisters and abbesses at Rheims, 680; and Saint Ivo, much venerated in Cornwall, 8th century—all three with strangely corporate-logo-like names.

25. THE FEAST OF SAINT MARK

Evangelist, possible martyr, 1st century

Patron of cattle breeders, Egypt, lantern makers, notaries, Venice; invoked against fly bites • (emblem: winged lion)

Not one of the original twelve Apostles, Mark—aka John Mark—was a cousin of Saint Barnabas and probably a Levite. He was personally baptized by Saint Peter, who sometimes referred to him as "my son." His was the first Gospel written, and it is assumed that his primary source was the eyewitness Peter. Mark accompanied Saints Paul and Barnabas on their first missionary expedition but for some reason turned back, to the immense irritation of the irritable Paul. It is believed that Mark became the first bishop of Alexandria and was martyred there— dragged through the streets with a rope around his neck, then strangled. It is also believed that a ship on which Mark was sailing the Adriatic had once taken refuge from a storm in a lagoon—the one now called San Francesco della Vigne—where an Angel appeared to promise Mark that a great city would be built there in his honor. It is certain that in 829 merchants of Venice smuggled Mark's alleged relics out of Muslim-occupied Alexandria by covering them with pork, which the superstitious Moors would not touch. They rest now beneath the high altar of the magnificent Cathedral of San Marco.

26. THE FEAST OF THE MOTHER OF GOOD COUNSEL

Miraculous icon of the Blessed Virgin

Patron of Albania

In 1467, in a small church in Gennazzano, southeast of Rome, a small picture of the Mother of God, known as La Madona del Paradiso, was discovered to be supernaturally floating in the air. Naturally, pilgrims flocked to the site and many miracles took place. The wonders quickly won papal approval—the picture itself was crowned with gold by Pope Innocent XI in 1682. In response to persistent rumors that the marvelous image had originally been venerated at Skodra in Albania, the Sacred Congregation of Rites in 1915 declared Mary, under the title Mother of Good Counsel, the Patron of that Christian nation.

Also: The Feast of Saint Joseph the Hymnographer, a Sicilian who fled the Saracen invasion of that island, became a monk in Constantinople, and on a voyage to Rome was captured by pirates and sold as a slave to Cretans. Eventually he escaped to Rome, where he wrote many hymns, some of them with a charming sea-chantey character, 845.

27. THE FEAST OF SAINT ZITA

Downstairs help, 1278

Patron of housemaids, servants; invoked to find lost keys • (emblem: bunch of keys)

She worked as a domestic servant for two generations of the wealthy Fatinelli family, who were alternately edified and irritated by her saintly ways. Innocent and a little dotty, Zita received the constant help of Angels: when she was caught in the rain, they kept her dry beneath their wings; when she was rapt in spiritual ecstasy, they did her household chores; and when she gave her master's fur coat to a beggar, an Angel returned it to her door the following day. (In Lucca today they will show you "the Angel's door.") Even the Blessed Virgin once came to her assistance, leading her home when she got lost on a pilgrimage. The night Zita died a star shone from the window of her attic room, illuminating all of Lucca, and her body, frequently disinterred, remains incorrupt.

Also: The Feast of Saint Maughold, an Irish thief reformed by Saint Patrick himself, who sent him to evangelize the Isle of Man, where he is still much venerated, c. 498.

28. THE FEAST OF SAINT PETER MARY CHANEL

Martyred on Futuna Island, 1841

Patron of Oceania

The Faith's first ambassador to the South Pacific was a Marist father, the son of a poor French farmer. He landed on the tiny island of Fortuna in the New Hebrides in 1836. For three years he made little headway in converting the local cannibals, until he managed to baptize the son of the chief. That tattooed pagan dignitary was outraged and lost no time in sending a band of warriors armed with spears and clubs to take care of Father Chanel. The Saint's last words to them—which he spoke in the local lingo—were "It is well for me that you do this thing." Suitably impressed, his killers—indeed the entire population of the island—immediately became devout Roman Catholics.

Also: The Feast of Saint Aphrodisius, a kindly Egyptian who sheltered the Holy Family in exile; Saint Theodora, a Christian maiden condemned to a brothel; and Saint Didymus, a compassionate Roman soldier who exchanged garments with her, to the astonished chagrin of the first customer, both 304.

THE FEAST OF SAINT CATHERINE OF SIENA

Outspoken bride of Christ, 1380

Patron of Italy, laundrywomen, nurses; invoked against fire • (emblem: wearing crown of thorns, her heart at her feet)

At the age of six Catherine had her first vision—Christ appeared to her dressed in papal vestments, flanked by Saints Peter, Paul, and John. At sixteen she defied her parents by refusing to marry, cut off her long hair, and took up residence in a cramped corner of the family kitchen until she was permitted to take the veil of a Dominican nun. When she was nineteen, praying in her room while the rest of Siena was celebrating carnival, Our Lord appeared to Catherine again, this time accompanied by His Mother, who gave Her blessing to their marriage. The magnificently bejeweled wedding ring Christ slipped onto Catherine's finger was, alas, invisible to others. (On a later occasion she and her Divine Spouse exchanged their physical hearts.) At the age of twenty-four Catherine gave up food—for twenty years she ate little, swallowed less, and used a quill pen to help her vomit anything that went down. She took up nursing, caring personally for Siena's lepers and cancer victims, and once, for the sake of self-mortification, broke her dietary principles to swallow a bowl of cancerous pus. Naturally, she attracted followers—a band of disciples who called her, curiously, Mama. Although valued as a peacemaker by the feuding citizens of Siena, Catherine vigorously supported the idea of a Crusade against the Turks, which was then being urged by Pope Gregory XI. While visiting Pisa to lead a rally in favor of the Crusade, she dropped into church to pray and was granted the Stigmata—a painful affliction, but, like her wedding ring, invisible. In 1375 Catherine was sent by the Sienese authorities on a diplomatic mission to Avignon and took the opportunity to prevail upon Pope Gregory XI, then in residence there, to return to Rome. He did, thus ending the Vatican's scandalous seventy-three-year-long Babylonian Captivity. Grateful for her tireless support for his successful claim to the disputed papacy, the subsequent Pope, Urban VI, invited Catherine to Rome, where she died, wrestling (invisible) demons on her deathbed. In 1970 Catherine was declared a Doctor of the Church in honor of her writings. She dictated four treatises, known as the *Dialogue,* which describe her many mystical experiences, including a vision of Hell thronged with persons who had "sinned against the married state," that is, practiced contraception. (She herself was the youngest of twenty-five children.)

Also: The Feast of Saint Hugh of Cluny, abbot for sixty years of the largest church in Christendom, valued adviser to nine Popes and countless kings and emperors, invoked against fever, 1109.

30. THE FEAST OF SAINT ADJUTOR

Aquatic ex-Crusader, 1131

Patron of swimmers, yachtsmen; invoked against drowning • (emblem: Crusader, a broken chain near him)

In 1095 this noble Norman youth sailed off with the First Crusade, and after sixteen years of battle for the Holy Land he was captured by the Muslims and imprisoned. Then one night Saint Mary Magdelene appeared to Adjutor in his cell and struck off his chains. Back in France he eliminated a dangerous whirlpool in the river Seine by sprinkling it with holy water.

THE FEAST OF SAINT WOLFHARD

Humble German hermit, 1127

Patron of saddlers; invoked against gallstones • (emblem: in a stone coffin)

A German-born tradesman, Wolfhard arrived one day in Verona, set up shop, and began giving all his earnings to the poor—he soon became revered by the citizens as a living Saint. Embarrassed by this he retired to a hermitage on the riverbank, where a passing boatman urged him to join a nearby monastery. For the rest of his life Brother Wolfhard kept a stone coffin in his cell, maintaining that he wished to be buried in it under the church porch so that his grave would be trampled underfoot.

Also: The Feast of Saint Hildegard, Charlemagne's second wife, who bore him nine children and is a Patron of the sick, 783; and Saint Pius V, the Pope who in 1570 excommunicated Queen Elizabeth I of England, 1572.

May

1. THE FEAST OF SAINT BRIEUC

Charitable hermit of Brittany, 510

Patron of purse makers • (emblem: three purses)

Like many other sixth-century Celtic monks, Brieuc commuted frequently to the Continent, so there are towns named for him in Brittany (Saint-Brieuc) and Cornwall (Saint Briock). Because he was famous for his charity, Our Saint is always pictured—or sculpted—holding an open purse; hence purse makers took him as their Patron.

THE FEAST OF SAINT MARCULF

Hermit, friend of French royalty, 558

Invoked against scrofula • (emblem: bishop touching the chin of a supplicant)

As everyone knows, the touch of a true king cures the skin disease scrofula—hence it is known as the king's evil. In France all monarchs were endowed with this power through the intercession of Marculf, whose relics in Normandy were visited as a part of any coronation ritual until 1825.

THE FEAST OF SAINT PEREGRINE LAZIOSI

Miraculously cured priest, 1345

Invoked against cancer • (emblem: with crutch, showing his bleeding leg)

Throughout the twelfth and thirteenth centuries, two factions, the Guelphs and the Ghibellines, struggled for political power in Italy. (The poet Dante, himself a Guelph, consigned numerous Ghibellines to Hell.) Peregrine was a rowdy young Ghibelline activist in the town of Forlì. When a papal legate (the Pope was a Guelph) showed up there, he took the opportunity to punch Peregrine in the nose. Peregrine was immediately—some might say miraculously—converted to the Guelph position and, acting on the advice of a statue of the Madonna, moved to Siena to join the Servite Order. As a sign of his repentance he vowed never again to sit down—which penance became more severe when he developed a repulsive and malodorous cancer of the foot. However, the night before the putrifying extremity was to be amputated, Christ himself climbed down from a crucifix and effected a complete cure.

THE FEAST OF SAINT SIGISMUND OF BURGUNDY

King who strangled his own son, 524

Invoked against fractures, marsh fever • (emblem: imperial orb)

On the one hand, a Vandal in every sense of the word, Sigismund was briefly king of Burgundy, during which time he strangled one of his sons for talking back to his stepmother. On the other hand, he was generous to the local clergy. Defeated in battle, Sigismund disguised himself as a monk, but his enemies found him out and threw him down a well, along with his wife and surviving kids. For some reason Sigismund is venerated as a martyr.

2. THE FEAST OF SAINT ATHANASIUS OF ALEXANDRIA

Doctor of the Church, "Father of Orthodoxy," 373 • (emblem: holding an open book, standing over a defeated heretic)

The dreadful Arian heresy (to which, alas, the Unitarians and Jehovah's Witnesses of our day still subscribe) maintained that Jesus Christ was not God but a creature. Although this wacky notion was condemned by the Council of

Nicaea, in 325, the Arians persisted in their beliefs, and as bishop of Alexandria Athanasius opposed them by all means necessary, until he was deposed and exiled (by an Arian emperor) for his alleged complicity in the murder of Arsenius, a prominent Arian bishop. Athanasius was soon restored to his office by a succeeding, orthodox emperor—and, for the remainder of his life, five times deposed and reinstated, depending on the party in power.

Also: The Feast of Saints Exsuperius and Zoë, married slaves martyred by their pagan master, 140; Saint Mafalda of Portugal, who took the veil after her marriage to the king of Castile was annulled, 1252; and the Swabian Saint Wiborada, who bound books while walled up in an anchorage and was martyred by invading Hungarians, 925.

3. THE FEAST OF OUR LADY OF CZESTOCHOWA

Miraculous icon, "Queen of Poland"

Patron of Poland

This fifth-century portrait of Mary and the Infant Jesus is of mysterious origins but arrived in Poland in 1384. In the succeeding centuries thousands of sufferers have been healed while praying before it, and to it the Polish king John Casimir attributed his 1656 victory over the Swedes. (Even though he lost.)

THE FEAST OF SAINT JAMES THE LESS

Apostle, first bishop of Jerusalem, 1st century

Patron of druggists, the dying, hatters, pie makers, Uruguay • (emblem: saw)

The younger, and hence the "less," of the two Apostles named James became bishop of Jerusalem after Peter's escape to Rome. Because he knelt constantly in prayer, his knees were said to resemble those of a camel. According to pious legend, James once resolved to fast until the Second Coming, until Jesus Himself appeared to him and cooked him a nice, nourishing meal. James was flung by Pharisees from the pinnacle of the Temple but survived long enough to forgive his attackers—after which he was beaten to death with a club. In Bavaria no darning should be done on Saint James's Day.

THE FEAST OF SAINT PHILIP

Apostle, dragon slayer, 1st century

Patron of Luxembourg, Uruguay • (emblem: three loaves of bread)

A disciple of John the Baptist and a married man with two daughters, Philip was the third Apostle called by Jesus—he helped serve the miraculously multiplied loaves and fishes at the picnic following the Sermon on the Mount. After Pentecost, Philip traveled to Phrygia, where a hideous dragon with terrible breath guarded a statue of Mars. Philip performed an exorcism, in the course of which the beast breathed on the son of a local dignitary, killing him. The citizens then stoned the Apostle to death.

THE FEAST OF SAINT PHILIP OF ZELL

Rabbit-befriending hermit, 8th century

Patron of babies

W e have it on the authority of Alban Butler's *Lives of the Saints* that "soon after his death [Philip] came to be regarded as the protector of small children." But we don't know why. Philip lived in the woods near the city of Worms and was a friend of the Frankish king Pepin as well as of the wild fowl and rodents of the neighborhood.

4. THE FEAST OF SAINT FLORIAN

Conscientious objector, martyr, 304

Patron of Austria, brewers, chimney sweeps, firefighters, Poland, soap boilers; invoked against fire, flood • (emblem: pouring water from a jug on a burning house)

A n officer of the Roman army of occupation in Austria, Florian confessed his own Christianity rather than take part in the persecution of the Faithful. The skin was flayed from his body before he was tossed into the river Enns. Florian is alleged to have extinguished a fire by pouring a single pitcher of water on it—hence his Patronage of firefighters. The pitcher he holds in sacred art explains his association with brewers. His death by drowning accounts for his invocation by those in danger from water. He is a Patron of Poland because Pope Lucius III bestowed his sacred relics upon the city of Crakow. But why is he prayed to by soap boilers?

Also: The Feast of Saint Pelegia of Tarsus, who, if she indeed existed, was roasted to death for refusing to marry the son of the emperor Diocletian, c. 300.

5. THE FEAST OF SAINT AVENTINE

Quite mythical hermit, 1189

Invoked against dizziness

Aventine is a completely fictitious Englishman, to whom a church is dedicated in Tours, France.

THE FEAST OF SAINT JUDITH

Teutonic widow and hermit, 1260

Patron of Prussia

When her beloved husband lost his life on a Crusade, Judith (also known as Jutta) provided for her children and betook herself to live as a recluse in Kulmsee, Prussia.

Also: The Feast of Saint Hilary of Arles, a much beloved but imprudent bishop, twice reproved by the Holy See, 449.

6. THE FEAST OF SAINT AVA

Immigrant to Brittany, 1st century

Patron of children learning to walk

Ava (or Avoy) is believed to be the only maiden of Saint Ursula's eleven thousand martyred companions to have been spared. Taken prisoner by savage Huns, she was daily fed—through the bars of her cell—dainty buns by the Blessed Virgin. Exposed to several lions (the Huns traveled with them as mascots), Ava remained unscathed, so the heathens put her to the sword. Her mutilated body sailed away in a stone boat, which washed ashore near the town of Avray in Brittany. To this day toddlers are dipped in this vessel to help them develop strong legs.

Also: The Feast of Saint John Before the Latin Gate, upon which occasion the Evangelist, while visiting Rome, emerged unscathed from a cauldron of boiling water, 1st century.

7. THE FEAST OF SAINT DOMITIAN

Dragon-banishing bishop, 560

Invoked against fever

Shortly after he was appointed bishop of Maastricht, Domitian endeared himself to the populace by exterminating a dragon that had been poisoning the local water supply, a spring near Huy on the river Meuse. His popularity increased when, during a time of famine, he predicted a bumper crop, thereby convincing the rich to distribute the grain they had been hoarding.

Also: The Feast of Saint John of Beverly, the peace-loving bishop of York through whose intercession the British have won several wars, 721.

8. THE FEAST OF SAINT VICTOR MAURUS

African-born Roman soldier, martyr, 287

Patron of Milan • (emblem: black knight in armor)

A native of Mauritania stationed with the imperial forces in Milan, Victor Maurus is one of the martyrs whose discovered relics Saint Ambrose made a great deal of fuss about, to the immense edification of the public.

THE FEAST OF SAINT WIRO

Missionary English monk, 739

Patron of Holland • (emblem: hearing king's confession)

Missionary bishops from Northumbria, England, Wiro and his companion, Plechelm, devoted themselves to Christianizing the pagan Frisians. They were encouraged in this noble undertaking by King Pepin of the Franks, who desired to include the people of the Low Countries in his empire. Wiro was himself Pepin's favorite father confessor.

9. THE FEAST OF SAINT TUDY

Cornish-Breton hermit, 5th century

Invoked against rheumatism • (emblem: attired as Pope, a dragon at his feet)

Variously known as Tudy, Tudinus, Tegwin, and Thetgo, Tudy has a festival celebrated with much picturesque merrymaking in Landevenee, Brittany, and a parish church in Cornwall bears his name.

Also: The Feast of Saint Pachomius, a soldier turned hermit turned abbot who at the time of his death ruled over three thousand solitaries on the banks of the Nile. He permitted his sister to live as a nun on the far side of the river but, in the interest of holy chastity, would never so much as look at her, 348.

10. THE FEAST OF SAINT CATHAL

Wandering (to Italy) Irish bishop, 685

Invoked against drought, hernia, storms, ulcers

This Irish-born missionary has been the object of a cult in southern Italy since 1071, when his relics, including a bishop's crozier, were discovered in Treviso. He is especially adept at curing ulcers but is apparently no slouch in the weather department either.

THE FEAST OF SAINT JOB

Long-suffering Patriarch, date unknown

Invoked against depression, ulcers • (emblem: on a dungheap, his wife upbraiding him)

Among the many Old Testament figures venerated as Saints was this hero of a Persian fable that somehow found its way into the Holy Bible. Prosperous and pious, Job became the object of a bet between God and Satan and was subjected to a series of catastrophes, not the least being the "comfort" of his friends. In the end God made everything all right by explaining that He had created crocodiles and hippos. In the light of Job's dual Patronage, it would appear that medieval folk made a connection between depression and ulcers.

THE FEAST OF SAINT SOLANGIA (AKA SOLANGE)

Beloved French virgin martyr, 880

Patron of children, shepherds; invoked for or against rain • (emblems: sheep, distaff)

The beautiful and virtuous daughter of a worker in a local vineyard, Solange, as she is known, tended sheep in a meadow. She caught the eye of one Bernard, son of the duke of Poitiers, but she rejected his improper advances, whereupon he stabbed her to death. This crime did much to raise class consciousness among the ninth-century French peasantry, and in times of need a reliquary containing Solange's head is still paraded through the streets of Berry.

11. THE FEAST OF SAINT GENGULF

Murdered by his wife's lover, 760

Patron of the unhappily married • (emblem: a spit)

A noble knight of Burgundy and comrade-in-arms of King Pepin the Short, Gengulf was troubled by rumors that his highborn and beautiful wife was unfaithful to him. He confronted her in the garden of their castle, and she denied his allegations but, just to be sure, he asked the lady to plunge her arm into the cool water of the well. She did, and the water immediately boiled, scalding the deceitful adulteress. Rather than slay her, the pious Gengulf withdrew to another of his castles, near Avallon, where he undertook a life of quiet prayer; to his retreat his wife sent her paramour, who surprised Our Saint in his bed and hacked him to pieces. Gengulf is invoked against cuckoldry in France, Holland, and Belgium.

Also: The Feast of Saint Claudian Mamertus, bishop of Vienne and a poet of note, whose prayers were effective against earthquakes, forest fires, and wild boars, 475.

12. THE FEAST OF SAINT DOMINIC OF THE CAUSEWAY

Bridge and road builder, 1109

Patron of pilgrims • (emblem: cockerel)

Rejected from various orders, Domingo became a hermit and busied himself constructing a twenty-four-arch bridge across the river Oja on the Camino de Santiago, the pilgrims' road to Saint James's shrine at Compostela. Some time after Domingo's death a family of pilgrims stopped at a nearby inn. The publican's promiscuous daughter took a shine to the son, Hugonell by name, who spurned her advances. She took her revenge by accusing him of theft; he was hanged forthwith. But as his parents were leaving they heard Hugonell whisper from the gallows that he was still alive, supported by Domingo. They rushed to inform the local magistrate, who swore their son was no more alive than the cock and hen he was about to eat. Whereupon the cock and hen leapt up, sprouted feathers, and declared the boy's innocence. And that is why, in case you wondered, a live pair of barnyard fowl are kept in the cathedral of Santo Domingo de la Calzada.

THE FEAST OF SAINT FRANCIS PATRIZZI

Feud-resolving priest, 1328

Patron of reconciliations

member of the Mendicant Servites of Siena, Francis became a popular con-fessor. Repentant sinners from miles around came to him seeking absolution, which made some of his fellow Servites jealous. Then the Blessed Virgin appeared to Francis, advised him to "use his tongue and not his ears," and struck him stone deaf. Unable to hear confessions, he became a celebrated extemporaneous preacher, whose sermons reconciled the bitterest of enemies.

THE FEAST OF SAINT PANCRAS

Brave boy-martyr, 304

Patron of children, oaths, young seeds and flowers, treaties • (emblem: young knight trampling on a soldier)

This teenage Phrygian lad was mar-tyred for the Faith in Rome, on the site of the church that now bears his name, San Pancrazio Fuori le Mura. Saint Gregory of Tours wrote that oaths sworn over the tomb of Pancras were especially binding. Anyone swearing falsely in that holy place goes mad even before reach-ing the doorstep. The first church built in England was dedicated to Pancras, as was a church in London where the Saint Pancras railroad station now stands.

13. THE FEAST OF SAINT IMELDA

Excessively devout virgin, 1903

Patron of first communicants • (emblem: radiant host appearing to her)

As a child Imelda amused herself by building and decorating altars around the castle of her parents, Count and Countess Lambertini of Bologna. At age nine she was sent to be educated by nuns, to whom she constantly expressed her passionate desire to take Holy Communion, lisping prettily, "How can anyone receive Jesus into his heart and not die?" Yet Imelda was deemed too young for the Sacrament. After Mass on the Feast of the Ascension of her eleventh year, however, the Host was seen to fly out of the tabernacle and hover near her, which the officiating priest took as a sign. He plucked the sacred wafer from the air and placed it upon the pious maiden's tongue, whereupon she expired in rapture.

THE FEAST OF SAINT SERVAIS

Allegedly Jewish German French bishop, 384

Invoked against foot and leg troubles, frost, mice, rats, vermin, for success in any enterprise • (emblem: key in his hand, a dragon beside him)

A member of the Holy Family—he was Jesus' first cousin once removed—Servais had in his possession a silver key to the heavenly gates; he got it from either Saint Peter or an Angel. He is alleged to have died having shoes thrown at him. The grass on his grave in Maastricht is green in all seasons.

Also: The Feast of the Blessed Dame Juliana of Norwich, English mystic, author of the moving and consoling *Revelations of Divine Love,* 1423; and Saint Rolanda, a French princess who lived in Cologne in the sixth—or eleventh—century. She is invoked against colic and gravel.

14. THE FEAST OF SAINT BONIFACE OF TARSUS

Reformed party animal, martyr, 306

Patron of converts • (emblem: with reeds thrust under his nails)

By all accounts a big, good-looking fellow who liked his wine, Boniface kept company with a certain Aglaë, a naughty Roman high-society lady. She, however, got religion and sent Boniface from Rome to Tarsus to recover the bodies of certain recent martyrs, and there he was himself martyred—so it was his relics Aglaë eventually received. Talk about irony!

THE FEAST OF SAINT MATTHIAS

Apostle who replaced Judas, 1st century

Patron of carpenters, sailors; invoked against alcoholism, smallpox • (emblem: battle-ax)

According to an ancient but unreliable legend, Matthias became one of Christ's disciples to atone for having married his own mother. What is certain is that, following the suicide of Judas, a Jewish disciple named Matthias was chosen by lot to join the Apostles. His most famous mission was to Ethiopia, where he was captured and blinded by cannibals, and rescued in the nick of time by Saint Andrew, who arrived in a boat piloted by Jesus Himself. Matthias's Patronage of drunkards is venerable but unexplained.

Also: The Feast of the Blessed Giles of Portugal, who sold his soul to the Devil while a university student in Paris. For seven years he studied alchemy in a cave, after which he was terribly clever and lived a shockingly debauched life until he had a vision of demons dancing on his grave. He invoked the Virgin Mary and moved to Spain, where he joined the Dominicans. After seven years of penance he was much relieved to find, on his seat in the choir, his canceled IOU to Satan, 1265.

15. THE FEAST OF SAINT DYMPHNA

Irish virgin, victim of incest, 7th century

Patron of asylums, mental health workers; invoked against epilepsy, insanity, sleepwalking • (emblem: crowned maiden with a sword, a Devil in chains)

In Gheel, Belgium, is one of Europe's most progressive mental hospitals. It is named in honor of Dymphna (in Irish, Damhnait), the daughter of Damon, an Irish chieftain. When Damon's wife died he was inconsolable. He searched, they say, the Western world in vain for another bride so fair, until his grief-crazed gaze fell upon her living image—their own fifteen-year-old daughter. No sooner did he make his intentions known to the girl than she made her escape by sea to far-off Belgium, aided and accompanied by the court jester and an old priest, Father Gerebran. They settled in a forest hut at Gheel, east of Antwerp. Spies sent by Damon located the fugitives by following the trail of Irish coins they had paid for food or distributed to the poor along the way. Damon himself then sailed for Belgium, surprised his daughter, and restated his monstrous demands. When she refused he drew his sword and slew first the ancient priest and then, in his fury, Dymphna. At her tomb, discovered in the thirteenth century, miraculous cures of epileptics and other "lunatics" began to take place, and Dymphna has ever since been invoked by those suffering from emotional or nervous disorders, suggesting a possible connection between childhood sexual abuse and mental illness.

THE FEAST OF SAINT HALLVARD

Chivalrous Norse prince, 1043

Patron of Oslo; invoked in defense of innocence • (emblem: holding millstone)

The object of a Norwegian cult, this young prince was about to launch his boat on the river when a slave woman implored his aid. She had been falsely accused of theft, she said, and needed to escape. As she boarded Hallvard's vessel an angry mob arrived on the dock, demanding custody of the woman. Once more she pled her innocence, and the prince cast off—only to be slain by a shower of arrows from the shore.

THE FEAST OF SAINT ISIDORE THE FARMER

Angel-assisted plowman, 1130

Patron of farmers, farmworkers, Madrid, ranchers • (emblem: Angel plowing)

A Spanish favorite, Isidore was born in Madrid and spent his entire life as a hired hand, working the farm of the rich Juan de Vargas. Both Isidore and his equally holy wife, Maria, spent hours daily in prayer and church-going, so that their employer began to wonder when any farm-work was getting done. He paid a surprise visit to his fields and discovered, sure enough, Isidore was praying beneath a tree while Angels, behind a team of snow white oxen, plowed the south forty. In winter, they say, Isidore would empty sacks of grain to feed the birds—but the sacks would be miraculously refilled with better grain. In Voodoo and Santeria this unassuming Spanish tiller of the soil is the powerful god Orisaoco.

16. THE FEAST OF SAINT BRENDAN

Irish abbot who sailed to America, 577

Patron of sailors; invoked against ulcers • (emblem: monk saying mass on ship, fish crowd around)

All right, so the Irish saved civilization. But did they discover America? It is certain that Saint Brendan founded many monasteries in Ireland. There is no doubt that he visited Scotland, Wales, and Brittany (where he is invoked by those suffering from ulcers). But no one knows whether to classify the published saga of his sixth-century voyage to North America as fiction or nonfiction. The Promised Land of the Saints was the name he gave to the balmy land he found somewhere in the North Atlantic—but was it one of the Canary Islands, or the Azores? Or the

Florida Keys? Or a mirage? Could he and his crew actually have crossed the ocean in a curragh—a round, hide-covered boat, a glorified canoe? In 1976, the author-adventurer Tim Severin built such a boat to Brendan's specifications and sailed from Ireland to Newfoundland.

THE FEAST OF SAINT HONORATUS

Namesake of Paris street, bishop, 6th century

Patron of bakers, millers • (emblem: three hosts on a baker's shovel)

Rue Saint-Honoré in Paris, where the finest pastry shops abound, is named after this bishop of Arles—as is a cholesterol bomb of a French cake. His traditional Patronage of bakers might be explained by the fact that he once received the Eucharist, "the Bread of Angels," from the hand of God Himself.

THE FEAST OF SAINT JOHN NEPOMUCEN

Father confessor thrown from bridge, 1393

Patron of Bohemia, bridges, bridge builders, Czechoslovakia; invoked against detraction • (emblem: padlock on his lips)

It was long believed that this bishop of Prague died a martyr to his priestly vows and to the "seal of the confessional" because after he refused, even under torture, to reveal to King Wenceslaus IV the details of Queen Sophia's confession to him, he was flung from a bridge to his death. Certainly the king was wicked—cruel, jealous, and lascivious (his mistress was Susannah the Bathwoman). And by his command Bishop John of Nepomuk was indeed tossed into the river Vltava—a plaque on the bridge in Prague still marks the site. But modern scholarship suggests that Our Saint was deep-sixed in a political feud between the Church and the court. Be that as it may, when John's tomb was opened, in 1718, his (silent) tongue was found to be perfectly preserved.

THE FEAST OF SAINT SIMON STOCK

Creator of the scapular medal, 1265

Patron of tanners • (emblem: scapular)

Born in Aylesford, Kent, Simon lived briefly in a tree before becoming the first prior general of the English Carmelite Friars. In the vision for which he is famous, the Virgin Mary appeared to assure him that no one who wears the scapular—the brown felt, poncholike garment distinctive to the Carmelites—will burn in Hell. This afterlife insurance policy (so to speak) has had an understandable appeal to generations of sinners, and "scapular medals" are still available in Catholic church gift shops at surprisingly reasonable prices.

THE FEAST OF SAINT UBALD

Italian exorcist-bishop, 1160

Invoked against dog bites, rabies • (emblem: Devils fleeing a blessing bishop)

Although he was physically frail—his limbs had a tendency to break—as bishop of Gubbio Ubald confronted the ferocious emperor Frederick Barbarossa and talked him out of sacking the town, a persuasion much appreciated by his flock. Ubald was adamantly celibate, refusing to "pollute himself with the pleasures of women," and strongly opposed to the marriage of priests, which practice he banned in his diocese. We may assume that the many exorcisms he conducted account for his association with mad dogs—since in his day no fine distinction was made between demonic possession and hydrophobia.

17. THE FEAST OF SAINT MADERN

Therapeutic Cornish hermit, 545

Invoked against lameness • (emblem: lighted lamp)

On a desolate moor in Cornwall stand the ruins of this hermit's chapel. Within is a stone bench, Madern's bed, and nearby a well. The disabled who bathe in the well and sleep the night on the bench are certain to rise cured. The author Sabine Baring-Gould (*Lives of the Saints,* volume 5) provides a moving account of the miraculous recovery there of several injured football players c. 1640.

THE FEAST OF SAINT PASCHAL BAYLON

Devout but neglectful shepherd, 1592

Patron of chefs, Italian women, shepherds • (emblem: monstrance)

Paschal was a professional shepherd but not a very good one. While he prayed in the meadow his flock wreaked havoc with the neighboring vineyards. Somewhat reluctantly, the Franciscans allowed the semiliterate twenty-four-year-old to join their order as a cook—but they were soon impressed by his prolonged trances of devotion before the Blessed Sacrament. After his death Paschal worked many wonders and frequently made his lingering presence known to his devotees by noises called Paschal's knocks.

18. THE FEAST OF SAINT ERIC

Finn-bashing king, 1160

Patron of Sweden • (emblem: fountain springing from his blood)

Eric IX of Sweden believed that the neighboring Finns should either be baptized or die, and he saw to it that a great many of them did one or the other. An army of Danes, abetted by a few treacherous Swedes, put an end to his glorious reign by beheading him.

THE FEAST OF SAINT THEODOTUS

Highly unlikely martyr, 304

Patron of innkeepers • (emblems: sword, torch)

The romantic tale of Theodotus, an innkeeper by profession, and his pious foster mother, Thecusa, is long, elaborate, and historically worthless. It concerns the recovery of a martyr's relics, a corpse identified by a ring, a wine-selling priest getting Roman soldiers drunk, and naked Christian virgins drowned for refusing to partake in an orgy. You don't want to know.

THE FEAST OF SAINT VENANTIUS

Flung from wall, 257

Patron of leaping; invoked against falling • (emblem: young man holding a city wall)

The story of this interesting early martyr was rescued from obscurity by Michael Walsh, editor of *Butler's Lives of the Patron Saints* (1990). Venantius, a fifteen-year-old native of Camerino, not only endured the traditional tortures of scourging, burning, beating, and being fed to wild beasts but also was thrown off the city walls, only to bounce up praising the Lord—until his head was cut off.

19. THE FEAST OF SAINT CELESTINE V

Only Pope to abdicate, 1296

Patron of bookbinders • (emblem: with dove on his shoulder)

In the Year of Our Lord 1294, in the hills of Abruzzi, there lived a holy, if malodorous, eighty-four-year-old hermit named Peter, who spent his days in prayer and bookbinding. Then one day a party of cardinals arrived, knelt before him, and told him he had been elected Pope. Peter assumed the name Celestine, rode to his coronation on a donkey, moved into a small wooden cell he installed in a corner of the papal palace, and commenced to give away the Church's treasure to the poor. After four months of this, Benedetto Cardinal Caetani boldly acted to save Christendom. He bored a hole in the wall of Celestine's cell and inserted a speaking tube. For several nights, identifying himself as the Holy Ghost, Caetani urged the old man to abdicate—which he did, on December 13, full of tears and apologies. Caetani was duly elected Pope Boniface VIII. Peter/Celestine longed to return to his hermitage, but Boniface, just to be sure, had him locked up in the castle of Fumone, where he shortly died of hunger and neglect. Three Popes later, in 1313, Celestine was canonized.

THE FEAST OF SAINT DUNSTAN

Politician-artisan-archbishop, 988

Patron of armorers, blacksmiths, goldsmiths, jewelers, locksmiths •
(emblem: with tongs, holding the Devil by the nose)

In Mayfield convent, East Sussex, visitors may gaze in awe upon the blacksmith's tongs with which Saint Dunstan seized the Devil (disguised as an old woman) by the nose. As Archbishop of Canterbury, Dunstan strongly disapproved of King Edwy, whom he suspected of having sex. Banished from his see by that sinful Saxon monarch, Dunstan briefly took up the craft of a smith, and it was during this period of exile that he bested old Nick. Dunstan was restored to office and officiated at the coronation of Edwy's successor, the notoriously chaste King Edgar.

THE FEAST OF SAINT PUDENTIANA

Nonexistent virgin martyr, 160

Patron of the Philippines • (emblems: urn, sponge)

udentiana's father, Saint Pudens, was a Roman senator and a friend of Saint Peter's. Pudentiana is supposed to have died for the Faith in the year 160, at the age of sixteen. The mathematical and/or biological unlikelihood of this caused Pudentiana to be demoted in the 1750 Calendar of Saints and eliminated altogether in 1969. She is now venerated only in the magnificent cathedral dedicated to her in Rome, and in the Philippines, of which Pius XII, in 1942, confirmed her role as national Patroness. Her Latin name, by the way, means "she ought to be ashamed of herself."

THE FEAST OF SAINT YVES

Uniquely honest attorney, 1303

Patron of Brittany, judges, lawyers, notaries, orphans • (emblem: cat)

"Saint Yves was a Breton, and a lawyer as well,/But not a liar, strange to tell," goes a French nursery rhyme about this wholly admirable man. After studying the law in Paris and Orléans, he returned to practice in the courts of his native Brittany, first as a (free) advocate for the poor and oppressed and later as a just and incorruptible judge. He was always concerned with the welfare of orphans, seven of whom he supported in his family manor in Kenmartin. He is sometimes confused with Saint Ives, an Irish maiden who sailed to Cornwall on a leaf.

20. THE FEAST OF SAINT BERNARDINO OF SIENA

Logo-flaunting preacher, 1444

Patron of advertising, public relations; invoked against hoarseness, lung disease • (emblem: radiant tablet inscribed IHS)

Even as a child Bernardino (Little Bernard or Bernie) was famously handsome. There is an edifying tale of his gathering a posse of his playmates to beat up an older man who made perverted advances to the attractive lad. Bernardino became a Franciscan friar at the age of twenty, but not until his thirty-seventh year did he embark on his mission as a traveling preacher. He visited, on foot, every town and city in Italy. His open-air sermons would last for hours, and he delivered several a day. His voice, once weak and raspy, became loud and resonant as he denounced vice (games of chance), sorcery (heretics), and usury (Jews). He employed as a visual aid a large placard on which were blazoned the letters IHS. A maker of playing cards, bankrupted by Bernardino's condemnation of gambling, made a fortune selling a line of IHS cards. Competing preachers complained in vain to the Holy Office that Bernardino's methods encouraged superstition, even idolatry. His crowd-pleasing miracles were many—they included raising the dead—but he saved his best for last. At his funeral a river of his blood poured out the church doors to quell an unseemly disturbance in the streets.

THE FEAST OF SAINT ETHELBERT

Unfortunate Saxon king, 794

Invoked against thieves, to find lost articles • (emblem: two princes holding swords)

A prince of East Anglia, Ethelbert sought in marriage the hand of the princess Alfreda of the neighboring kingdom of Mercia, to which honorable end he visited the castle of her father, King Offa. He was made welcome by Offa's wicked queen, who showed him to his chamber, wherein a large and inviting armchair had been placed above a trapdoor. Ethelbert sat down and was never heard from again. King Offa, after annexing East Anglia, caused a cathedral to be raised at Hereford, which he dedicated to Ethelbert.

21. THE FEAST OF SAINT CONSTANTINE THE GREAT

Who made Christianity the state religion, 337

Patron of Greece • (emblem: cross inscribed IHS)

Constantine not only ended the persecution of the Christians but transformed them from an oppressed minority into an oppressing one. Although he styled himself the thirteenth Apostle and summoned Church councils, he postponed his own baptism until his death was imminent, since he still had some sinning to do—such as murdering his first son and second wife. Constantine is not considered a Saint in the Latin West, but in the Greek Orthodox Church he is much revered and shares this Feast Day with his mother, Saint Helena.

THE FEAST OF SAINT EUGENE DE MAZENOD
Child of divorce, troubled teen, 1861
Patron of dysfunctional families

The founder of the Oblate Order grew up in difficult circumstances. His father, Charles-Antoine, was a refined but impoverished aristocrat, his mother, Marie-Rose, the offspring of a wealthy but hopelessly bourgeois clan. The couple fought constantly. When the French Revolution broke out they fled to Italy, spatting all the way. Marie-Rose eventually returned to France, but Charles-Antoine refused to accompany her, and in 1802 they were divorced. Meanwhile, Eugene spent his neglected adolescence associating with the dissolute young nobles of Palermo until, on Good Friday, 1805, he had a mystical experience, and entered the seminary. Because of his upper-class connections the young priest was offered a cushy position, but he preferred to work among the poor of Provence, where they don't even speak proper French. Through his own efforts—as well as his staunch support of Pope Pius IX and Napoleon III—he became bishop of Marseilles and a member of the Legion of Honor. Should you wish to venerate a part of his heart, you may do so by visiting that relic in the Blessed Sacrament Chapel, San Antonio, Texas.

Also: The Feast of Saint Godric, a pirate turned hermit who kept vipers as pets and composed the first lyric poems in the English language, 1170.

22. THE FEAST OF SAINT JULIA OF CORSICA
Crucified naked virgin martyr, 5th century
Patron of Corsica, Portugal • (emblem: crowned naked maiden crucified)

A maiden of North Africa, Julia was captured and sold into slavery. Her master was a Syrian merchant mariner who was well disposed toward her because of her beauty and her manner—which was humble and obedient, as became a

Christian girl. She accompanied him on a voyage to Corsica, where he disembarked to transact some business with the island's pagan ruler, Felix, and to take part in a pagan orgy honoring the local false gods. After a few drinks Julia's master began extolling the virtues of his Christian captive. Felix offered him four slave girls in exchange for her, but the Syrian declined. The heathen governor then had Julia brought to him and made her an offer: if she would sacrifice to idols, he would grant her her freedom. Naturally, Julia refused, and after a session of torture—during which her hair was pulled out—she was crucified.

THE FEAST OF SAINT RITA OF CASCIA

Battered wife, afflicted nun, 1457

Patron of desperate cases, the unhappily married; invoked against bleeding, infertility, loneliness, tumors • (emblems: crucifix, rose, thorn)

In Italy, and in the Little Italys of the New World, devotion to this Saint rivals that to Our Blessed Mother Herself. (A major shrine to Saint Rita is in Philadelphia, Pennsylvania.) She was born at Cascia (near Spoleto) to pious, elderly parents and married, at the age of twelve, to Paul di Fernando, a local gangster. He was unfaithful to her. He beat her. He neglected her. They had two sons. After eighteen years of this, when Paul's mutilated body was dumped on her doorstep, Rita prayed fervently that her boys would not attempt to avenge the murder, and her prayers were answered when they both took sick and died. Now she was free to fulfill her childhood dream of becoming a nun. Twice the Augustine convent in Cascia rejected her, on the grounds that she was—obviously—not a virgin. But when one night she was miraculously transported into their cloistered midst, they had no choice but to accept her. She soon excelled above all in obedience—daily watering a dead twig on the orders of the mother superior. Praying before a crucifix, she longed to share the agony of Christ's Passion, and Our Lord in His mercy sent one of the thorns from his crown to pierce her brow. There it remained, and festered; the other nuns gave a wide berth to Rita and the cloud of stench in which she walked for the next fifteen years. Only after her death did her odor become that of roses—which fragrance to this day permeates the atmosphere of the convent, where her incorrupt body is on display, under glass.

23. THE FEAST OF SAINT DIDIER (AKA DESIDERIUS)

Slandered French bishop, 607

Invoked against perjury • (emblem: with a rope in his hand)

Queen Brunhilde of Burgundy (534–613) was a real character. When her sister Galswintha was murdered by her husband, Chilperic, Brunhilde urged her own husband, Sigebert, to exact revenge in the form of a vast land grab. At the end of the war Sigebert was dead and Brunhilde imprisoned. Down but not out, the plucky queen seduced and married Chilperic's son Merovech. This was too much for the bishop of Vienne, Desiderius (Didier to his friends), and he denounced her. Brunhilde then encouraged a certain woman named Jutta to accuse Our Saint of being no saint. It goes without saying that her charge was groundless—but Didier went briefly into exile. Restored to his bishopric, he was martyred by a gang of thugs acting on Brunhilde's behalf. The queen herself came to no good end when, at the age of eighty, she was dragged to death behind a horse.

THE FEAST OF SAINT WILLIAM OF ROCHESTER

Slain by his foster son, 1201

Patron of adopted children

A baker from Perth, Scotland, William set out on a pilgrimage to Canterbury accompanied by his adopted son and apprentice, David. It must have been an unusually stressful family trip, for when they reached Rochester, David murdered his foster father. No sooner had a local madwoman discovered William's body than she was immediately cured; William was proclaimed a martyr and enshrined in the cathedral.

24. THE FEAST OF OUR LADY, HELP OF CHRISTIANS

The Blessed Virgin takes sides

Patron of Australia, New York State, New Zealand

In 1656, John Casimir of Poland dedicated his army to Our Lady of Czestochowa. In 1692, Diego Vargas attributed his victory at Santa Fe to—and built a shrine to—Our Lady of Victory, La Conquistadora. In 1815, after the Battle of Waterloo, Pope Pius VII returned to Rome from exile in Savona and instituted this feast in gratitude for his deliverance from that notorious anti-Catholic Napoleon.

THE FEAST OF SAINT SARA

Mary Magdalene's dusky maid, 1st century

Patron of Gypsies • (emblem: four women in a boat, one dark-skinned)

Annually on this date Gypsies gather in Provence to celebrate the feast of their highly unofficial Patron, Saint Sara. She was the handmaiden of the Three Marys—Mary Magdalene, Mary the wife of Cleophas, and Mary Salome, mother of the Apostle James. Legend has it that they sailed—accompanied by Saints Martha and Lazarus—in a rudderless boat from Palestine to Marseilles. Sara is invariably pictured as dusky hued. The Gypsies claim her as one of their own and of Indian descent, answering to the name of Kali.

Also: The Feast of Saint Joanna, wife of King Herod's steward, one of the three women who first met the risen Christ, 1st century.

25. THE FEAST OF SAINT BEDE

Venerable English monk-historian, 735

Patron of scholars • (emblem: sun above a jug)

This Northumbrian monk was the author of the justly famous *History of the English Church and People,* a chronicle of events in Britain from Roman times to his own, meticulously researched and eminently fair—even to the Celtic clergy, with which Bede, a Saxon, had his differences. He is the only Englishman mentioned by Dante—in the *Paradiso,* of course. It was rare, in those days, for a monk to be made a priest, but Bede was ordained—hence his time-honored designation as Venerable.

THE FEAST OF SAINT URBAN I

Vinous Pope, 230

Patron of vintners; invoked against frost • (emblem: grape on a book)

The imperial persecution of Christians diminished during Urban's pontificate. Seizing the initiative, he overthrew a number of large stone idols, killing twenty-two pagan priests in the process. In Germany he has long been considered the Patron of wine makers; his Feast Day features elaborate processions through the vineyards, known as Urban's Rides, and the dipping of statues of the Saint in rivers.

Also: The Feast of Saint Gregory VII (Hildebrand), the dwarf Pope who made

Emperor Henry IV walk barefoot through the snow, 1085; and Saint Zenobius, the miracle-working bishop of Florence considered one of its Patrons, 390.

26. THE FEAST OF SAINT MARIANA DE PAREDES Y FLORES

"The Lily of Quito," 1645

Patron of the Americas

Mariana was born only ten years after the conquest of Ecuador, in its capital city of Quito, of noble Spanish lineage. Orphaned young, she demonstrated early signs of extreme piety—she made a vow of perpetual chastity at the age of ten and began calling herself Mariana of Jesus. She tried to join the Dominicans, who found her a trifle intense, so she moved in with her brother-in-law and lived as a penitential solitary, sleeping little, eating nothing at all, and otherwise mortifying the flesh in some appallingly creative ways. When a series of earthquakes began to shake the town, she rather publicly offered herself as a victim to Divine justice and expired. The earthquakes then ceased, God, presumably, having accepted the offer. It is said that a white lily sprang up immediately from her blood.

THE FEAST OF SAINT MARY MAGDALEN DEI PAZZI

Manic-depressive mystic, 1607

Patron of Florence, Naples

Even as a child Mary Magdalen was wonderfully devout; at ten she vowed her virginity to God, and at sixteen, having entered a Carmelite convent, she asked Him for, and received, five years of constant physical and spiritual suffering, which included diabolical attacks. There followed a gratifying period of mystic raptures, the details of which she dictated for posterity.

THE FEAST OF SAINT PHILIP NERI

Music-loving founder of the Oratorians, 1595

Patron of Rome • (emblem: Blessed Virgin supporting a chapel roof)

Philip Neri was one of those rare Saints (like Francis of Assisi or Thomas More) who seem to have enjoyed their faith. At the age of eighteen he arrived, penniless, in Rome. Six years earlier the Renaissance had ended with a bang. The city had been sacked by imperial troops, thousands of its citizens slaughtered, its treasures looted. The Vatican, a cesspool of vice and avarice, had begun to respond to the Reformation by banning books and burning reformers. Philip lived in a garret and to pay his rent tutored his landlord's sons. A near recluse, he studied philosophy and wrote poetry. Then one day he took to the streets. He would hail passersby, "Well, my brothers, when shall we begin doing good?" He was obviously an eccentric, but a charming one. Young men would stop and listen, and together with him they began to do actual good. They founded, built, and staffed a hospital. In the evenings Philip's growing band of disciples gathered to talk and pray and listen to music in a room they called their oratory. The sorts of songs they preferred we call, to this day, oratorios. Philip was determined to remain, with his fellow Oratorians, a layman. But in 1554, in the catacomb of Saint Sebastian, he underwent a mystical experience in which he felt a "globe of fire" enter his mouth and dilate his heart. He resolved to become a missionary priest, and his mission was to the streets of Rome. There was nothing gloomy about the sanctity he preached and practiced. Fond of jokes and laughter, he would sometimes appear in public, perfectly deadpan, wearing his clothes inside out, or sniffing a bouquet of whisk brooms. At the age of eighty, observing cheerfully, "Last of all, we must die," he did. The autopsy revealed an extraordinarily large heart.

27. THE FEAST OF SAINT AUGUSTINE OF CANTERBURY

First English archbishop, 604

Patron of England • (emblem: baptizing a king)

In 596, Pope Gregory the Great dispatched this Italian monk, with some thirty companions, to save the souls of the English. Discouraged by tales they heard among the Franks of Anglo-Saxon savagery, they returned to Rome, only to be ordered back. They landed in Kent and were greeted with all courtesy by King Ethelbert. Rather than establish his see at London, Augustine (or Austen) chose to do so at Canterbury. In person Our Saint seems to have been a rather tedious prig, which endeared him to the pagan Anglo-Saxons. He was, however, less successful in maintaining relations with the many Celtic Christians already practicing the Faith, according to their lights, in Wales and southwest England. When he preached in Dorset the local fisherfolk mocked him and pinned fish tails to the back of his robes, which is why the children of Dorset are to this day born with tails.

Also: The Feast of the Blessed Bartholomea Bagnesi, a Dominican nun of Florence possessed by devils on and off for thirty years, 1577.

28. THE FEAST OF BERNARD OF MONTJOUX
Mountain-dwelling hermit, 1081

Patron of the Alps, mountain climbers, skiers • (emblem: monk, lightning near him)

For centuries pilgrims from France and Germany on the path to Rome felt obliged to cross the Alps in winter, on foot. Bernard, a missionary in those parts, established two mountaintop hospices for those travelers, on either side of the Alpine pass that still bears his name. It was there—considerably later—that his successors bred the large shaggy dogs likewise named in his honor.

Also: The Feast of Saint Germanus, bishop of Paris, after whom the Boulevard Saint-Germain is named, 576.

29. THE FEAST OF SAINT BONA
Much-traveled Italian virgin, 1207

Patron of flight attendants • (emblem: pilgrim's staff)

In 1962, Pope John XXIII, with characteristic whimsy, placed air hostesses and flight stewards under the protection of this Saint. When Bona was only three her father sailed away to the Crusades. When she was seven she had her first vision—Christ appeared to her and told her to stop sleeping with her mother. Deeply impressed, Bona started bedding down in a manger, without blankets. When she was ten the Savior reappeared and gave her the money to buy a penitential hair shirt. Bona's religious zeal seems to have had an effect on her mother as well, for she had a vision of her own—requiring her thirteen-year-old daughter to leave Pisa for the Holy Land in quest of her father. Papa, when found, turned out to be something of a rascal, with a second wife and family. On her sorrowful return journey Bona fell in with a wandering hermit, and together they attempted to convert a passing band of Saracen pirates, who took them prisoner. Bona escaped, her virtue intact, through the miraculous intercession of Saint James the Greater, and soon after her return to Pisa organized a pilgrimage to his shrine at Compostela, in Spain—a thousand miles away. Over the next thirty years she guided nine more round-trip tours, until this indefatigable traveler died happily, in her little room, at home.

30. THE FEAST OF SAINT FERDINAND III

Spanish warrior-king, 1252

Patron of engineers, governors, magistrates, rulers • (emblem: greyhound)

For a thousand years the Iberian Peninsula was a patchwork of feuding fiefdoms, all under the yoke of African Islam. "Spain" is the work of San Fernando. He inherited the kingdom of Léon from his father and Castile from his mother. Andalusia he took for himself, city by city, siege by siege, from 1215 to 1272. At the Battle of Jerez, the climax of the *reconquista,* Saint James, Santiago himself, came down from Heaven to lead the final Spanish charge, and the Moors were routed. In peace as well as war Ferdinand was the model of a Catholic monarch. He begat, by a sequence of wives,

nine sons and three daughters. He converted mosques to churches. The Jews of his realm, provided they wore funny hats and paid large fines, were not unduly persecuted. And he was as diligent in ransoming Christian slaves from the infidels as he was in selling infidel slaves to the Christians.

THE FEAST OF SAINT JOAN OF ARC

Virgin warrior, martyred at the stake, 1431

Patron of France, the military • (emblem: fleur-de-lis)

In Heaven, in the eighty-seventh year of the Hundred Years' War, Saints Catherine and Margaret, together with the Archangel Michael, decided to intervene on the side of France—or at least on behalf of the Valois party of Charles d'Orléans—against the Burgundians and their English allies. In order to make the dauphin—to all appearances a stupid coward—king of France, they chose as their instrument a teenage farmgirl, to whom they appeared (frequently) and spoke (constantly). Thanks to innumerable books and plays and films, we all know what happened next. Jeanne d'Arc, clad in white armor, led the dauphin's army to victory at Orléans and was wounded by an arrow in the breast, while Charles, who had remained prudently in the rear, was crowned. Jeanne attacked Paris and was wounded in the thigh. Charles dallied at court. The Burgundians captured her at Compiègne and sold her to the English. The king took no interest in her plight, offering neither ransom nor rescue. Because she would not deny her Saints, inquisitors found her guilty of heresy and turned her over to the civil authorities. Because she had opposed their nation's occupation of her nation, the English magistrates concluded she was a witch and burned her at the stake. She was then almost nineteen. In 1920 the Catholic Church got around to canonizing her. Over the centuries authors as agnostic and cantakerous as Mark Twain and George Bernard Shaw have fallen madly in love with her, and we invite anyone with a word to say against her to step outside and say it.

THE FEAST OF SAINT WALSTAN

English cowherd, 1016

Patron of farmers • (emblem: scythe in his hand, cattle near him)

Walstan was a simple farmworker in Norfolk, England, but so dignified and gracious in his manner that it was rumored he was really a king, come to live among the common people. A rich landowner offered to make Walstan his heir; Our Saint demurred, asking rather for the gift of two calves. When he died, praying in a field, those very animals conveyed his body to the church in Bawburgh. On Saint Walstan's Day for centuries, the farmers and laborers of Norfolk used to gather in the church to honor one of their own, a worker with a sickle who had achieved true holiness. The Reformation put an end to such nonsense.

31. THE FEAST OF OUR LADY OF HIGH GRACE

Patron of Crete, the Dominican Republic, motorcyclists, Vermont

Italian bikers—no Hell's Angels they—have long paid homage to Our Lady of High Grace in her mountain shrine at Castellazzo, and Pius XII in 1947 affirmed her Patronage of them, while urging them to affix her image to their dangerous machines. That under this title she also has a special interest in a

Mediterranean island, half a Caribbean island, and a New England state we have on the authority of Father Michael Freze, S.F.O. (*Patron Saints,* Our Sunday Visitor Press, 1992).

THE FEAST OF SAINT PETRONILLA

Saint Peter's domestic daughter, 1st century

Patron of France; invoked against ague • (emblem: broom)

Petronilla was, according to the *Roman Martyrology,* "the virgin daughter of the Apostle Peter, who refused to wed Flaccus, a nobleman." The Carolingian kings of the Franks, who styled themselves "the sons of Peter," took their "sister" Petronilla as their Patron, and today, in Petronilla's chapel in Rome, a Mass is offered for the intentions of France. A pious legend has it that she acted as the first Pope's housekeeper until she was afflicted with paralysis. Once a group of disciples dining at Peter's home chided him for being unable to cure her. The Prince of the Apostles made the Sign of the Cross over his child, who rose up hale and hearty and served the meal. After which, at another gesture from her father, she collapsed.

June

1. THE FEAST OF SAINT GWEN

Queen with three breasts, 5th century

Patron of infants, nursing mothers; invoked against cradle cap • (emblem: queen with three breasts)

A statue in Brittany of this remarkable woman clearly shows the miraculous asset for which she is honored by nursing mothers—a third breast, which she was granted after giving birth to triplets. The heads of infants are washed in the spring near Gwen's shrine, protecting them against cradle cap, known to the French as *la mal de Sainte Gwen*.

THE FEAST OF SAINT JUSTIN

Deep-thinking, argumentative martyr, 165

Patron of philosophers • (emblem: crossed quill and sword)

The first in a long line of Christian philosophers to argue that there is no necessary conflict between Faith and Reason, Justin in his youth studied Platonism in Alexandria and there met an old man on the beach who introduced him to Christianity. Baptized at the age of thirty, he visited many lands, debating with pagans, atheists, and Jews. In Rome he defeated in public debate a Cynic named Crescens, who proved to be a sore loser, turning Justin over to the civil authorities. Our Saint was then executed on the orders of Emperor Marcus Aurelius—ironically enough, a bit of a philosopher himself.

THE FEAST OF SAINT THEOBALD OF ALBA

Self-effacing hermit, 1150

Patron of porters, shoemakers • (emblem: pilgrim with shoemaker's tools)

Born into a noble family in Piedmont, Theobald was moved by his reading of the Gospel to adopt a simple life and apprenticed himself to a cobbler. He became so skilled in the trade that his dying master begged him to marry his daughter. But Theobald was bound by a vow of chastity, so he left on a pilgrimage to Spain. On his return to Alba he sought even more menial work, hauling sacks of grain and giving his meager salary to the poor.

2. THE FEAST OF SAINT BLANDINA

Virgin martyr, gored by bull, 177

Patron of the falsely accused, girls • (emblem: maiden tossed by a bull)

In Lyons in the second century, it was widely believed that Christians practiced incest ("Brothers and sisters, love one another") and cannibalism ("Take, eat, this is my body"). One group of these perverts was arrested and condemned to the arena. It included the slave girl Blandina as well as her mistress, a bishop, and a teenage boy, Ponticus. When they were exposed to the wild beasts, Blandina "strove to comfort them like a mother," according to an eyewitness account. Lions and bears devoured the others but spared Blandina, who was then tied up in a net and gored to death by a bull.

THE FEAST OF SAINT ELMO

Whose intestines were torn out, 303

Patron of sailors, women in childbirth; invoked against colic, seasickness, stomachache • (emblem: at windlass, intestines torn out)

The original name of this enormously popular Saint might have been Erasmus. He is said to have been a Syrian bishop who fled, in a time of persecution, to a cave on Mount Lebanon, where he was fed by a raven. Captured by the pagan police, he was rolled in pitch and set alight. His experience as a human torch accounts for his association with the maritime phenomenon in which a blue light—known as Saint Elmo's fire—flickers around ships' masts in electrical storms. Elmo somehow survived his ordeal, escaped, and sailed (in a boat piloted by an Angel) to Italy, where he died of his wounds. Elmo was represented in sacred art near a ship's windlass, which, during the Middle Ages, inspired among the Faithful the notion that he had been tortured by having his intestines extracted with such a device. So he is petitioned by people in abdominal distress, by women in labor, and on behalf of babies with colic.

3. THE FEAST OF SAINT CHARLES LWANGA

Chaste Ugandan martyr, 1886

Patron of African youth

Mwanga, king of Uganda (1884–1897), maintained a stable of young men in his palace, ostensibly to serve as pages but in fact the objects of his perverted lust. One of these boys was Charles, a recently baptized Catholic. He tried to persuade his fellow pages to join his religion—one in which such activities as they were called upon to perform are expressly forbidden. Outraged, Mwanga ordered Charles and twenty-two others transported to Namugango, where they were wrapped in reed mats and burned alive. Not long after this Mwanga was deposed in a popular uprising and only restored to his throne through the tireless efforts of Christian missionaries.

THE FEAST OF SAINT CLOTILDA

Queen of the Franks, 545

Patron of adopted children, queens, widows • (emblem: Angel beside her bearing a shield with a fleur-de-lis)

A Christian princess of Burgundy, Clotilda married the pagan Clovis, king of the Franks, and persuaded him to be baptized, thereby ensuring a Catholic future for the future nation of France. Unfortunately, after Clovis died in 511, his three sons feuded over the kingdom. The eldest, Clodomir, was killed in battle in 523, and the widowed queen adopted his three sons. When two of her grandsons were murdered by their uncles Childebert and Clotaire, Clotilda left Paris sorrowing and became a nun at Tours.

THE FEAST OF SAINT KEVIN

Animal-loving, woman-hating hermit, 618

Patron of Ireland • (emblem: blackbird)

In the rolling green hills of Wicklow, Ireland, you may visit a barren cave known as Kevin's bed. Near it your native guide will point with pride to the precipice from which the Saint threw a woman who had come to tempt him from his holy vows. Since no biography of Kevin was written until five hundred years after his death, the facts of his life are scarce. But legends abound. He was terrifically good-looking. He lived to 120, fed by a pet otter who caught salmon for him. And he stood motionless until the hatching of an egg that a blackbird had laid in the palm of his hand.

THE FEAST OF SAINT MORAND

Grape-eating abbot, 1115

Patron of vintners • (emblem: grapes, pruning knife)

Although a lowly Benedictine monk, Morand had the honor of becoming a trusted counselor to Count Frederick Pferz of Alsace. Because Morand once survived all forty days of Lent on a single bunch of grapes, a cluster of that fruit became his emblem, and the vintners of Alsace-Lorraine have taken him as their Patron.

4. The Feast of Saints Adalgrin, French knight turned monk, 939; Breaca and Buriana, two Irish virgins yet venerated in Cornwall, 5th century; Clateus, bishop of Brescia martyred under Nero, 64; Cornelius MacConchailleadh, archbishop of Armagh, 1176; Francis Caracciolo, a Neapolitan nobleman whose bad skin cleared up at his ordination, 1608; Nennoc, a Welsh abbess in Brittany, 467; Optatus of Milevis, an argumentative African bishop in Numidia, 387; Petroc, Welsh-born missionary abbot to Devon and Brittany, 594; Quirinus of Croatia, drowned for affirming his Faith, 308; Saturnina of Arras, a German maiden who died in defense of her chastity, in France, date unknown.

5. THE FEAST OF SAINT BONIFACE OF MAINZ

British missionary to the Aryans, 755

Patron of brewers, Germany, tailors •
(emblem: sword piercing a book)

An Englishman baptized Winfrid, Boniface was proud of his Saxon heritage and longed to go to work among the Germans of Frisia and Saxony, "whose inhabitants," as he put it, "are of our own blood." At the age of forty he set out for Friesland but found the Saxons there too busy for religious discussions, being at war with the neighboring Franks. He returned briefly to England, then set out once more. In Hesse he made a great impression on the locals by chopping down an ancient oak tree sacred to Thor. With papal approval he changed his name to Boniface and was made bishop of Mainz. He was troubled by a gaggle of leftover Gaulish priests there (one of whom he caught selling his own fingernail clippings as "holy relics"), but in time his political influence in "Roman Germany" became considerable. (He it was who crowned Pepin "Most Catholic Emperor of All the Franks.") But at the age of seventy-five his heart turned back to his beloved and still pagan Saxons, and Boniface sailed with twenty companions down the Rhine to Dokkum, where Thor had his revenge and Boniface was murdered.

THE FEAST OF SAINT JAMES SALMONELLI

Miraculously cured priest, 1315

Invoked against cancer

Shortly after his birth James's mother abandoned him to join a convent—which might, in part, account for his lifelong devotion to Our Lady. He became a Dominican priest at Folgi, not far from Bologna, and was soon famous for the cures he effected: of blindness, gout, tuberculosis, but especially of cancer—the disease, ironically, of which he himself died. Then, in his first twenty-eight months in Heaven, he performed 338 authenticated miracles.

6. THE FEAST OF SAINT CLAUDE

Busy bishop, 7th century

Patron of linseed growers, toy makers, whistle makers; invoked against bad luck, twitching • (emblem: restoring child to life)

The abbey of Sainte-Claude in the Jura Mountains of eastern France is named for this sometime soldier who became bishop of Besançon. In art Claude is sometimes shown having his insides torn out—although there is no evidence he was martyred—or raising a child from the dead—although there is no reference to this miracle in any of his skimpy biographies. Somewhere there must be a story involving linseed oil, toys, whistles, and twitching, but we haven't been able to track it down.

THE FEAST OF SAINT NORBERT

Schism-resolving bishop, 1134

Patron of peace • (emblem: monstrance)

The son of a Rhineland count and a worldly, even cynical courtier, Norbert was out riding when a thunderbolt startled his horse. Sometime later Norbert woke up in the ditch, a new man. He undertook penance for two years, was ordained a priest, and barefoot took to the snowy roads as an itinerant preacher. Appointed bishop of Magdeburg, he enforced the rule of celibacy on the clergy with singular, punitive vigor—and survived a few assassination attempts as a consequence. He was equally zealous for the Real Presence of Christ in the Blessed Sacrament and for the papal claims, against the antipope Anacletus II, of Pope Innocent II. Norbert was with the French army that entered Rome in 1133 to place Innocent on the Chair of Peter. Curiously, in Voodoo/Santeria, this ultra-orthodox prelate is invoked as the wild and crazy god Oshosi.

SANTERÍA   10

OCHOSI

THE FEAST OF SAINT PHILIP THE DEACON

Disciple, 1st century

Patron of deacons • (emblem: baptizing an Ethiopian)

Do not, as many people do, confuse this Phil, who was a disciple, with Philip the Apostle. When assignments were handed out after Pentecost, Philip the Deacon was given responsibility for the Greek-speaking widows of Jerusalem, hardly a cabinet-level position. He is chiefly remembered for having encountered, by chance, the chief eunuch in the service of the visiting queen of Ethiopia and converting him to the Faith—then performing the first baptism of a black African.

7. THE FEAST OF THE VENERABLE MATT TALBOT

Reformed Dublin drunk, 1925

Patron of alcoholics

Although he is not yet canonized, there is no doubt in the minds of the thirty thousand members of the Matt Talbot Retreat Movement (the Catholic version of AA) that Matt is a Saint. Born into a good Catholic family (he had seven brothers and four sisters), he went to work at the age of twelve as a delivery boy for a wine merchant, and his troubles began when he sampled the merchandise.

At seventeen, already a pub-crawling drunkard, he became a bricklayer's apprentice, and although he continued to attend Mass he avoided the sacraments—much to the grief and shame of the family. He would wait outside the pub, looking for a pal to stand him a drink, until he got what could only be called the bum's rush. Then, at twenty-eight, he "took the Pledge," and never again did a drink pass his lips. He managed this by replacing one addiction with another. He became a holiness junkie. For the next forty years he attended church many times a day, ate next to nothing, slept very little and that on a barplank, and wrapped his limbs in chains. He even gave up smoking. Matt's only known amusement was reading the lives of the female Saints, whom he called "great girls."

THE FEAST OF SAINT MERIADOC

Magic scarf-wearing hermit, 6th century

Invoked against deafness

At his shrine in Brittany may be found a scarf once worn by this Saint. Applied to the head of a pilgrim, it is marvelously effective against hardness of hearing. A play about Saint Meriadoc is the sole surviving example of medieval Cornish literature.

8. THE FEAST OF SAINT MEDARD

Bishop, "Le Grand Pisseur," 560

Patron of harvests; invoked against rain, toothache • (emblem: colt)

If it rains today, say the French, it will rain for the next forty days—hence Medard's nickname, which we might render the Mighty Micturater. As bishop of Noyon, in Picardy, Medard instituted the festival of the Rose Queen, an annual ceremony crowning with roses the most virtuous girl in the parish—a custom that in later days spread throughout France.

9. THE FEAST OF SAINT COLUMBA (AKA COLUMCILLE)

Self-exiled Irish bard and abbot, 597

Patron of Ireland, poets • (emblem: celtic cross)

Columba was born in Donegal, of the royal O'Neill clan, and named Columcille (Kawlum-kill), which means "Done of the Church." An excellent student, he became, naturally, a priest. He was famous as a youth for his writing—as a scribe copying hundreds of pages in his fine hand—and as a poet as well. Once he copied a manuscript without its owner's permission, which led to Ireland's first copyright lawsuit and a trial. The high king at Tara, no friend of the O'Neills, decided against Columcille, and a civil war—the Battle of the Books, fought in County Sligo—resulted. Columcille realized that it was because of his pride and bad temper that three thousand were slain in that conflict. His self-imposed penance was banishment. He vowed "never again to gaze on the face of a man or a woman on Irish ground," and to bring as many lives to Christ as had been lost in the battle. Taking with him a few choice companions, he sailed to Scotland, establishing a monastery on the small, barren island of Iona, from which, on a (exceedingly rare) clear day, the hills of Ireland are visible. From there he set out on his mission to the savage pagans of northern Britain, the Scots and Picts, preaching and working miracles—such as driving a terrible monster from the river Ness and out into the loch. The book Columcille copied is on display in the National Library of Ireland. A standing stone in Donegal marks the site of his birth, and generations of Irish have visited it before setting out on their own exiles.

THE FEAST OF SAINT EPHRAEM

Scholar-composer, 373

Patron of Syria • (emblem: weeping hermit in a cave)

When the Persians (Iranians) invaded Mesopotamia (Iraq), Ephraem, a Christian schoolteacher, hid out in a cave, wherein he composed the many hymns that have earned him the title the Harp of the Holy Ghost. He never—we are reliably informed—laughed or smiled.

Also: The Feast of the Blessed Diana of Andolo, whose family tried to remove her from the convent; she fought back, and they broke her ribs, 1236; and Saint Pelagia of Antioch, a fifteen-year-old beauty, extolled by Saint John Chrysostom for flinging herself off a roof rather than marry, c. 311.

10. THE FEAST OF SAINT OLIVE

Maiden snatched by Saracen pirates, 9th century

Patron of Palermo

Olive lived happily in the sunny seaside town of Palermo, until Saracen pirates swooped down and carried her away to Tunis. There she took up residence in a cave, praying and working miracles—until by her holy example she began to convert infidels to the True Faith. She was arrested and cruelly tortured. Dipped in boiling oil, she emerged singing God's praises. So it was ordered that she be stretched on the rack and, basted as she was, set alight. But the very torches in the hands of her tormentors extinguished themselves. So she was beheaded, and a white dove—her soul—was seen ascending to Heaven. Were the Muslims impressed? The great mosque of Tunis is called Jama as-Zituna, that is, the Temple of Olive.

Also: The Feast of Saint Landry, bishop of Paris, who after his death returned to find the bell ringer of Saint Germain playing dice in church and gave him a sound thrashing, 656.

11. THE FEAST OF SAINT BARNABAS

Sold his field to become an Apostle, 1st century

Patron of Cyprus, Florence, harvests; invoked against hail, quarrels • (emblem: rake)

Before the 1587 reform of the calendar, this day, the Feast of Saint Barnabas, marked the summer equinox, the longest day of the year—hence the folk expression "Barnaby bright." It was thus a day on which a lot of farmwork could be done, and Our Saint is often pictured holding a hay rake. Barnabas was a Cypriot Jew (real name Joses Justus) who gets the credit—or the blame—for introducing Saint Paul to the Apostles. He invariably took Paul's side in his disagreements with Saint Peter, and the thanks he got was that Paul turned against *him.* Barnabas was stoned to death in Salamis. Bits of his skull are venerated in churches in Prague and Cremona. His entire head is in the possession of churches in Genoa, Toulouse, Naples, Bergamo, and Bavaria.

12. THE FEAST OF SAINT ONUPHRIUS

Naked, hairy hermit, 400

Patron of Munich, weavers • (emblem: hairy figure with two lions)

For sixty years this Egyptian anchorite of the desert's nakedness was covered only by his long hair and beard and a homemade apron of leaves. Medieval cloth makers—a humorous bunch—took him as their Patron.

Also: The Feast of the Blessed Guy of Cortona, a gentleman who made Saint Francis warmly welcome in his home, inspiring the Saint to his famous praise of courtesy, "the sister of charity and one of the most beautiful attributes of God, who makes his sun to shine and his rain to fall on the evil and the good," 1245.

13. THE FEAST OF SAINT ANTHONY OF PADUA

Passionate preacher, 1231

Patron of asses, harvests, horses, the illiterate, the poor, Portugal, spinsters; invoked against infertility, to find lost objects • (emblem: preaching to fish)

A novice who borrowed a book from Our Saint without his permission hastily returned it after experiencing "a fearful apparition," which accounts for Anthony's well-established Patronage of those in search of lost objects. When his name was still Ferdinand and he lived in Lisbon, he joined the Augustinians. Then he changed his name and his habit, becoming a Franciscan in order to travel to Africa and be martyred by the Moors. Ill health forced him to abandon his plans, and on his voyage home a providential wind blew his ship off course, landing him in Sicily. There he met with the great Saint Francis, who instructed him to preach against the heretics of Italy. Anthony did just that—and he was some preacher. In Rimini, when the unbelievers wouldn't listen, he went to the riverbank and preached to the fish, who stood on their tails to hear him. When, long after his death, his remains were unearthed, his tongue was discovered to be "still fresh and red." (You may venerate this holy relic in Padua's cathedral.) We are told that "severe temptations against purity afflicted Anthony during his teens," and although as an adult he was strictly anti-nooky (he once miraculously caused a newborn baby to testify to the adultery of its mother), he remained—well, *passionate.* Unmarried women who invoke his Heavenly aid in their search for husbands are advised to be careful, lest Anthony fall in love with them himself. Like all Franciscans, Anthony was mindful of the poor, and on his Feast Day charitable donations are pinned to a stole around the neck of his statue, and "Saint Anthony's bread" is distributed to the hungry.

14. THE FEAST OF SAINT DOGMAEL

Welsh hermit in Brittany, 6th century

Patron of children learning to walk

Toddlers in Brittany are placed under the protection of this monk, a native of Wales and allegedly the son of none other than Ithel ap Ceredig ap Cunedda Wledig.

Also: The Feast of the Blessed Castora Gabrielli, whose earthly cross to bear was marriage to a lawyer, 1391; and Saint Marcellinus, a Pope during the persecutions of Diocletian, who apostatized under the threat of torture and burned incense to the gods, 304. Wouldn't you?

15. THE FEAST OF SAINT GERMAINE COUSIN

Extremely ugly virgin, 1601

Patron of the unattractive • (emblem: shepherdess, flowers falling around her)

Parochial school graduates are all too familiar with the heart-wrenching tale of Little Saint Germaine—the Catholic answer to Dickens's Little Nell. A French farmer's daughter, she was born with a misshapen and paralyzed right arm and hand and a disease that caused her neck glands to swell, which did nothing for her appearance. Her wicked stepmother beat her, fed her only scraps, forced her to sleep in the stable, and sent her out to the fields to mind the sheep. But Germaine was holy—she spent her days praying with a rosary she had fashioned of knotted string and sticks, and attended daily Mass. The night she died, alone on a mat of vine leaves in the stable, some nearby monks beheld a band of Angels descend and carry her to Heaven. In 1664 they dug up her grave by accident and discovered her body not merely preserved but beautiful. A monument was soon erected, pilgrimages began, and innumerable miracles effected.

THE FEAST OF SAINT VITUS

Cauldron-boiled martyr, 4th century

Patron of comedians, coppersmiths, hens, dancers, Sicily; invoked against bed-wetting, chorea, cramps, epilepsy, lightning, oversleeping, snakebite, wild animal attacks • (emblem: rooster in a cauldron)

Rheumatic chorea, which causes spasmodic twitching, is sometimes known as Saint Vitus' dance. The cult of the Saint for which it is named is a very ancient one, but the facts of his life are few and his connection with the disease somewhat tenuous. When a mere child Vitus became a Christian, under the influence of his tutor, Modestus, and his nurse, Crescentia. His pagan father, Senator Hylas, was outraged and had them all flogged. A dancing band of Angels appeared, caused something of a distraction, and struck Hylas blind, permitting the trio to escape. They proceeded to Rome (fed along the way by an eagle), and there Vitus exorcised a demon from the son of the emperor Diocletian. For this good deed the boy and his companions were condemned to death as sorcerers. Lions refused to maul them, but immersion in a cauldron of boiling oil did the trick. A relic of Saint Vitus—his arm—found its way to Prague, where it is enshrined, and good health is assured to anyone who dances before it on his Feast Day. Because a rooster was thrown into the cooking pot with him, Vitus is traditionally pictured with such a fowl—hence he is invoked against sleeping late.

Also: The Feast of Saint Abraham. Born on the banks of the Euphrates, he was held hostage for five years by Egyptian thieves, contrived to escape, made his way to France, and there became first a hermit, then a priest and abbot. He is invoked against fever, 480. And the Feast of Saint Alice, a leprous Belgian nun, 1250.

16. THE FEAST OF SAINT BENNO

Frog-silencing bishop, 1106

Patron of drapers, fishermen, Munich, weavers; invoked for rain •
(emblem: fish with keys in its mouth)

When Benno was formally canonized, in 1523, Martin Luther threw a fit, calling this "New Idol" an "Old Devil." Devil or idol, Benno had always been politically unwise. He supported the Saxons in their ill-fated uprising against the empire. He took the unpopular side of Pope Gregory in his quarrel with Emperor Henry, and upheld the failed papal claims of the antipope Guibert. Although in life he was bishop of (now Protestant) Meissen, in Heaven he is Patron of (forever Catholic) Munich, and of its cloth-making industry. In folklore Benno is known for successfully commanding frogs to stop croaking and for recovering from the gills of a cooked fish the cathedral keys he had dropped into the river Elbe.

THE FEAST OF SAINT CYRIACUS

Precocious child martyr, 4th century

Patron of children • (emblem: naked boy riding a boar)

Cyriacus was but three years of age when his mother, Julitta, was hauled before the governor of Alexandria and accused of being a Christian. When she confessed her Faith, she was stripped and scourged before the eyes of her little son, whom the governor dandled on his knee. The tot struggled and scratched his mother's tormentor, lisping, "I'm a Twistan too!" or words to that effect. The wicked magistrate flung the child down a flight of stairs, killing him, then ordered the mother's execution. Some centuries later the child Cyriacus appeared, stark naked, to Charlemagne—in the nick of time to rescue the emperor from the tusks of a wild boar—for which reason the French military academy of Saint-Cyr is named in his honor.

THE FEAST OF SAINT JOHN FRANCIS REGIS

Tireless, compassionate Jesuit, 1640

Patron of illegitimate children, lace makers, marriage, social workers • (emblem: Jesuit in a leather cape)

Père Jean-François longed to be sent to Canada to be martyred by heathens alongside his fellow Jesuits. His superiors, however, decided that his mission would be to the heathens of southeast France. There his works of practical charity were many: he founded orphanages, improved the lot of prisoners, and established a lace-making industry so that prostitutes might have a more honorable way of earning a living. This did not endear him to the pimps. He was a popular preacher, although (or because) his sermons were full of "trivial and indelicate language, satire and savage invective." The martyrdom he had wished for in the snows of Quebec he found in the snows of the Pyrenees. Undertaking a mission in winter to La Louvesc, he died of exhaustion, pleurisy, and exposure.

THE FEAST OF SAINT LUTGARDIS

Sightless Flemish visionary, 1246

Patron of the blind

Although she was a lively and attractive child, when her father lost the money for her dowry on a poor business speculation, Lutgardis was sent to a convent at the age of twelve. She had no apparent interest in matters religious until, when she was twenty, Christ appeared to her, showed her His wounds, and asked for her love. For the next decade she was heard in frequent conversation with her Heavenly Bridegroom, e.g., "Wait here, Lord Jesus, I'll be back as soon as I finish this task." She also dripped blood from her brow from time to time and levitated. Rather than become an abbess, she left her Benedictine, German-speaking convent and joined a stricter, French-speaking one. For the last eleven years of her life she was, to her great delight, blind.

THE FEAST OF SAINT TYCHON

Cyprian grape-growing bishop, 450

Patron of vintners; invoked against insects • (emblem: grapes)

On Cyprus, where he stamped out the local cult of Aphrodite, Tychon is renowned as Tikhon the Wonder Worker. A poor man, he is said to have planted a dead vine discarded by a neighbor and prayed earnestly over it, thereby achieving a miraculously early grape crop. On present-day Cyprus his Feast is celebrated with the ceremonial drinking of a singularly nasty wine made from unripe grapes.

17. THE FEAST OF SAINT BOTOLPH

Founder of the original Hub, 680

Patron of Boston

Botolph and his brother Adolph were Anglo-Saxon Benedictines. Adolph became a bishop in Belgium, while Botolph stayed home to found many abbeys in England—including one in Lincolnshire, which became known as Botolph's town or, in abbreviated form, Boston. Four churches at the gates of the city of London are dedicated to this Saint—three of them by Christopher Wren.

THE FEAST OF SAINT HARVEY

Breton abbot with a seeing-eye wolf, 6th century

Invoked against blindness, demons, foxes, wolves • (emblem: wolf leading a blind monk)

Harvey's father was a Welsh minstrel who, on his way home from playing the Frankish court, met and married a Breton maiden. Harvey was born blind, but he too was a musician, a singer, poet, and harpist of great skill whose music charmed even wild animals. A fox who stole a chicken from him returned the fowl unharmed, and a wolf who attacked and killed Our Saint's seeing-eye dog repented and volunteered to serve as his guide and companion. Harvey is a most popular Saint in Brittany, where he is invoked for the protection of flocks and herds.

18. THE FEAST OF SAINT ALENA

Beloved Belgian virgin, 7th century

Invoked against eye disease, toothache • (emblem: princess with her arm torn off)

This Anglo-Saxon princess—the Anglo-Saxons had a surfeit of Saintly princesses—was strangled by a couple of Danish women, for reasons of their own. A church dedicated to her memory stands in an English village with the quaint name of Giggleswick. Close to it is Alkelda's Well, in the waters of which the Faithful are wont to bathe their aching eyes.

Also: The Feast of Saint Elizabeth of Schönau, the famous German mystic, often bruised in her combats with demons, whose visions and prophesies—not all of them strictly accurate—fill three big books, 1164.

19. THE FEAST OF SAINT BONIFACE OF QUERFURT

Unsuccessful missionary, martyr, 1009

Patron of Prussia

Boniface, which means "does good work," was the name of an ancient martyr and has long been a pseudonym adopted by Popes and missionaries. *This* Boniface—a German monk originally called Bruno—had some success evangelizing the Magyars of Hungary and the Pechenegs of Kiev, but he and his companions were slaughtered for attempting to bring the Word of God to the Prussians.

THE FEAST OF SAINTS GERVASE AND PROTASE

Possibly martyrs, 1st century

Patrons of haymakers; invoked for healthy urine, against rain, to catch thieves • (emblems: club, scourge, sword)

In 386, on the eve of dedicating a cathedral in Milan, Saint Ambrose was led, in a vision, to the grave of these martyrs. Ambrose concluded, on no forensic evidence, that they were twin brothers, cruelly slain for the Faith during the Neronian persecutions. Many miracles immediately occurred, which greatly increased the significance of the usually lackluster dedication ceremonies. Three centuries later the holy bones of these two lads were sent to Paris. Because their Feast Day happens to fall at the height of the grain-harvesting season, they are invoked by French farmers for good weather.

20. THE FEAST OF THE BLESSED MICHELINA

Locked up as nuts by her family, 1356

Patron of the insane • (emblem: kneeling in ecstasy, in a tempest)

The duchess of Pardi and mother of a boy child, Michelina was quite the merry widow after the duke's untimely death—much to the scandal of her wealthy in-laws. Then she was stricken with grief at the death of her little son and fell under the influence of a nun. Michelina resolved not merely to take the veil but to give away (to the Church) her entire (inherited) estate. This convinced her in-laws that she was a mental case; they had her put away. She lived a most devout, nunlike life in the asylum.

THE FEAST OF SAINT OSANNA OF MANTUA

Self-taught virgin, 1505

Patron of schoolgirls • (emblem: broken heart, crucifix springing from it)

Osanna experienced her first religious ecstasy—a vision of Heaven—when she was five. She longed to find out more about the Faith and asked her father if she might learn to read. He, being a conservative gentleman, explained his views on the rights of women. But Osanna did manage to become literate—either by eavesdropping on her brother's lessons or, as proposed by her biographer, through private tutorials conducted by the Blessed Virgin. Her favorite texts were the fire-and-brimstone sermons of the heretical reformer Savonarola. Although throughout her life Osanna wore an (invisible) wedding ring given her by Christ and suffered (invisible) Stigmata, she was an amiable enough character as female Renaissance mystics go.

21. THE FEAST OF SAINT ALBAN

Original English martyr, 209

Patron of refugees • (emblem: his head in a holly bush)

England's first martyr, Alban was a Roman soldier beheaded for harboring—and then impersonating—a fugitive priest. At his execution he asked for and was refused a drink of water, so he caused a miraculous fountain to spring up. No sooner was his head off (it rolled into a holly bush) than the executioner's eyes popped out. In the Church of England Alban's Feast is celebrated five days early, because of a misreading of the numerals on his tombstone in the Roman settlement of Verulamium, now the cathedral city of Saint Albans.

THE FEAST OF SAINT ALBINUS OF MAINZ

Displaced Albanian, 5th century

Invoked against gallstones, kidney disease, sore throat • (emblem: as a bishop, with a sword, carrying his head)

A priest in Albania—as his name implies—Albinus fled to Milan when his homeland was overrun by Arian heretics. Bishop Saint Ambrose liked the cut of his jib and sent him on a mission to the Vandals, who beheaded him near the site of the future city of Mainz.

THE FEAST OF SAINT ALOYSIUS GONZAGA

Priggish Jesuit "boy Saint," 1591

Patron of AIDS caregivers and young men • (emblem: with lily, scourge)

His father, a Venetian knight, wanted his son to pursue a military career, but little Aloysius fainted at the sound of vulgar language. Sent as a teenager to serve in the luxurious court of Philip II of Spain, he was especially wary of females—he made a point of never being alone with one, not excepting his own mother. He did, however, enjoy self-abuse of all kinds. He put chunks of wood in his bed to ward off temptations of the flesh, volunteered to carry out the slops of total strangers, and, when climbing stairs, stopped to say a Hail Mary at every step, which slowed his progress somewhat. He is said to have fled the Spanish court after refusing an order to kiss a girl's shadow. Back home his father caught his seventeen-year-old son and heir flogging himself in his room and sent him off to join the Jesuits. Aloysius died before his priestly ordination, of the plague he contracted while nursing the sick. He has always been held up as a role model to Jesuit students and recently been proposed as the Patron of AIDS caregivers.

THE FEAST OF SAINT LEUTFRIDUS

Bad-tempered abbot, 738

Invoked against flies • (emblem: dispersing a swarm of flies)

This French monk enjoyed considerable fame for his cursing. When a woman mocked his bald head, she and all her progeny became bald. When a thief insulted him, the man's teeth fell out. When Leutfridus observed farmers plowing on the Sabbath, he afflicted their fields with perpetual sterility. And when a swarm of flies interrupted his meditations, he banished the pesky insects from his house.

THE FEAST OF SAINT MÉEN

Breton hermit, friend of kings, 6th century

Invoked against skin diseases

Like his mentor Saint Samson, Méen was a Welsh hermit in Brittany. Near his former cell is a fountain. Its waters bring relief to those suffering from eczema, which is known locally as *la mal de Méen.*

22. THE FEAST OF SAINT ACACIUS

Military man crowned with thorns, 303

Invoked against headache • (emblem: Crown of Thorns)

Acacius was the utterly fictitious officer in charge of ten thousand utterly ficti-tious Roman soldiers who, after their simultaneous and utterly fictitious con-version to Christianity, were crucified en masse on the slopes of Mount Ararat in Armenia, which actually exists. The example of this legion's military valor was a particular source of inspiration to the Crusaders. Because Acacius was crowned with thorns, he is of special interest to people with headaches. The crown itself is venerated in the cathedral at Cologne, as well as the one in Prague.

THE FEAST OF SAINT PAULINUS OF NOLA

Well-beloved bishop, 431

Patron of millers • (emblem: watering can)

This much is true. Paulinus was a Roman lawyer, a provincial administrator for the empire, and a poet of note, and he was married to Therasia, a wealthy Spanish lady. In a letter to a fellow poet, he described his experience of conversion to Christianity thus: "Joy has overwhelmed me like a flood." But shortly after he and Theresia retired to her estate, their infant child died. The couple gave all their possessions to the poor and took up residence at the shrine of Saint Felix of Nola. Paulinus was elected bishop, and he continued to write poetry, all of which is beautiful and some of which is very funny. This much is legend. Moors/Vandals/Saracens kidnapped Saint Paulinus and half the population of Nola, carrying them off to Africa. But the Saint miraculously convinced the African king to send them home. To commemorate this mythical event, on the Feast of Saint Paulinus the young Italian-American men of Williamsburg, Brooklyn, dance—or attempt to dance—in the streets, bearing on their shoulders a statue of Our Saint atop the giglio—an eighty-foot-high, four-ton tower.

THE FEAST OF SAINT THOMAS MORE

Man for all seasons, martyr, 1535

Patron of civil servants, lawyers, politicians • (emblem: wearing chancellor's robe and scholar's cap)

In November 2000, Pope John Paul II officially declared Sir Thomas More the Patron Saint of politicians. If you have seen the 1966 film *A Man for All Seasons,* you are already familiar with the life of this remarkable statesman, wit, and hero. If you have not seen the film, you really should. Or better still, read More's own *Utopia.*

Also: The Feast of Saint Nicetas, poet, musician, and bishop to the Goths, who is generally assumed to have written the stirring Latin hymn "Te Deum" and is the Patron of Romania, 414.

23. THE FEAST OF SAINT AGRIPPINA

Much-tortured virgin martyr, 262

Invoked against bacterial infections, demons, leprosy, storms

A Roman maiden who was stripped, scourged, and beheaded by order of the emperor Valerian, Agrippina is venerated by both the Eastern and Western churches. Thus her entire body is enshrined simultaneously in Mineo, Sicily, and in Constantinople.

THE FEAST OF SAINT AUDREY

Necklace-spurning abbess, 679

Patron of Cambridge; invoked against neck and throat diseases • (emblem: wearing necklace)

Once upon a time there was an English princess named Etheldreda, but everyone knew her as Audrey. She was chaste and beautiful but ever so slightly vain. Although she had taken a vow of celibacy, she consented, for reasons of state, to marry a neighboring prince. In time her young husband began pestering Audrey for sexual favors. He went so far as to attempt to bribe the local bishop to release her from her vows. The bishop would have none of it, and with his help Audrey escaped the palace of her lustful consort. The passionate prince pursued her to the seaside, where a Heaven-sent high tide intervened between them. He gave up, went home, and remarried. Audrey became a nun, founding the great abbey of Ely, in which she lived with unbridled austerity. She died there, of a large and unsightly tumor on her neck—an affliction she accepted as punishment for the necklaces with which she had once adorned herself. A yearly festival, Saint Audrey's Fair, was held at Ely. The exceptional shoddiness of the merchandise vended there contributed to the English language the word *tawdry*, which is a contraction of Saint Audrey.

THE FEAST OF SAINT JOSEPH CAFASSO

Death row chaplain, 1860

Patron of prisoners

According to his biographer, John Don Bosco, Father Cafasso, although tiny and misshapen, worked tirelessly among the needy of Turin—including political activists and other criminals in its prisons. He accompanied no fewer than sixty men to the gallows. Because he had heard their confessions and granted them absolution, he referred to them as his "hanged saints."

24. THE FEAST OF SAINT JOHN THE BAPTIST

New Testament prophet

Patron of auto routes, candle makers, farriers, health spas, Jordan, leather workers, Quebec, road workers, wool workers; invoked for the protection of lambs • (emblem: a lamb)

ost Saints are commemorated on the dates of their deaths—their *natales,* or heavenly birthdays. But on Midsummer Day we celebrate the earthly birthday of Saint John the Baptist. Perhaps this holy man of the desert—preacher, baptizer, and martyr—was once Our Lord's rival for the title of Messiah. All four evangelists are at pains to pay homage to this contemporary of Jesus—Saint Luke even makes him Our Lord's cousin—before describing his humble deference to the hero of their story. John, like many a Hebrew prophet before him, had harsh words for the morals of royalty. Herod had him arrested, imprisoned, and decapitated—his severed head was awarded to the king's stepdaughter, the exotic dancer Salome. As Patron of Midsummer, John has absorbed all the pagan magic associated with the day—and the eve of the day. The bonfires to the gods became Saint John's fires. The curative herb hypericum gathered at this time became Saint John's wort. (And "High John the Conkeroo" to practitioners of Voodoo.) Because John promised to "make straight the way," he is the Patron of road builders; because he called Christ the "Lamb of God" and is invariably pictured with a lamb, he looks after the wool-working trades. And having immersed sinners in the waters of Jordan, he is Patron of health spas.

25. THE FEAST OF SAINT EUROSIA

Spanish, or Hungarian, virgin martyr, 8th century

Patron of crops; invoked against bad weather

n the Pyrenees, at this critical time in the agricultural year, Eurosia is petitioned by the farmers against drought and blight. She was a pure and holy virgin of Bayonne—although some claim she was an emigrant from Bohemia—who was martyred for spurning the advances of a Saracen pirate.

THE FEAST OF SAINT MOLAUG

Missionary bishop to the Hebrides, 572

Invoked against headache, insanity

This Irish-born monk, also known as Molloch or Lugaid, was the first Christian missionary to the Highlands of Scotland and to the even more remote Hebrides Islands, where his memory is yet held dear and he is invoked against whatever passes for madness in those parts.

26. THE FEAST OF SAINT PELAYO

Unredeemed Spanish hostage martyr, 925

Patron of the abandoned • (emblem: youth, sword in right hand, left hand cut off)

The Moors who had invaded Spain and captured Córdoba held the ancient bishop of that city for ransom. The local Christians asked for time to raise the money and offered the infidels the ten-year-old Pelayo as a hostage. The Moors agreed—and for three years Pelayo languished in prison, until he caught the eye of the emir, Abdul Rahman. Offered his freedom in exchange for an act of apostasy—and who knows what else—the boy refused. He was then hung by his wrists and disemboweled—thus adding another Saint to Heaven and not a penny to the coffers of the Moors.

27. THE FEAST OF OUR LADY OF PERPETUAL HELP

Popular painting

Patron of Haiti

This icon of the Mother and Child, painted on walnut wood in four-teenth-century Crete, is one of the world's most reproduced images. For centuries the original was a crowd pleaser in Saint Matthew's Church in Rome, and it is now in the Redemptorists' church of Saint Alphonsus de Ligouri in that city. In 1966, Pope Paul VI confirmed the picture—and/or its subject—as the official Patron of Haiti, a nation, if there ever was one, perpetually in need of help.

THE FEAST OF SAINT EMMA OF GURK

Financier, widow, 1045

Invoked against eye disease

Countess of Friesach and a near relative of Emperor (Saint) Henry II, Emma—or Hemma, or Gemma—married Wilhelm von der Sann. It was long believed that their two sons were slain by disgruntled miners in Wilhelm's employ, that he then expired of sorrow while on pilgrimage to Rome, and that she founded a convent and joined it. It has come to light that one of their sons died in battle twenty years after his father's death, which slightly spoils the story. The countess is remembered for her endowments. She was generous but no sucker. As the abbey she founded was under construction, she personally paid the workers out of a miraculous purse, which dispensed to each exactly what he had earned and not a penny more.

THE FEAST OF SAINT GOTTESCHALK

Prince and translator, 1066

Patron of linguists

hen Christian Saxons slew his father, this prince of the Wends briefly abandoned the Faith and left for England. There he married a nice Christian girl, returned to both the fold and his rightful realm, and labored mightily with both pen and sword to bring his subjects to Heaven with him.

THE FEAST OF SAINT LASZLO

Would-be Crusader-King, 1095

Patron of Hungary • (emblem: rosary and sword in his hand)

A Christian knight of Hungary, the greatest since Saint King Stephen, Laszlo—or Ladislaus, or Lancelot—annexed by force of arms both Dalmatia and Croatia to his realm and to the Faith, and made Holy War on the Poles, Russians, and Tartars. Had this mighty warrior not died on his way to lead the First Crusade, that debacle might have had a happier ending. Or perhaps not.

28. THE FEAST OF SAINT BASILDES

Compassionate jailer, martyr, 202

Patron of prison officers • (emblem: soldier and maiden near cauldron)

Potamiaena was a comely Christian slave girl in Alexandria. Her master offered to free her on certain conditions, to which no comely Christian slave girl could agree. She was then sentenced to be dipped in boiling oil. She willingly accepted her martyrdom but in the interest of modesty insisted on remaining fully clothed during the ordeal, to which condition her courteous prison guard, Basildes, agreed. Later that day Potamiaena, accompanied by the Virgin Mary, appeared to Basildes and showed him the crown awaiting him after his own beheading, which was not long in coming.

Also: The Feast of Saint Irene of Constantinople, who preferred not to marry Michael III, the emperor of Byzantium, and in the Eastern Church is on that account a much venerated Patron of girls, 804.

29. THE FEAST OF SAINT PAUL

Self-nominated 13th Apostle, epistle writer, 67

Patron of Greece, Malta, rope makers, tent makers, upholsterers • (emblem: three fountains)

Paul was a convert, and like many converts he was more Catholic than the Pope. In his case the Pope was Saint Peter, with whom he frequently disagreed. He makes his first New Testament appearance in the Acts of the Apostles and virtually takes over the rest of the book: traveling, preaching, writing, debating, organizing and reorganizing churches, surviving shipwrecks, snakebite, jailbreaks, fleeing the clutches of adoring or hostile mobs. Although he began as a Greek Jewish tent maker, he became God's own CEO, a motivator, a hands-on manager, a leader by example, a Take-Charge Guy with his eye on the Big Picture and the Bottom Line. He bought into a tiny Hebrew cult and personally transformed it into a multinational, the biggest and richest in the world. Paul and Peter were arrested together in Rome. Peter was crucified, but Paul insisted—as was his right as a Roman citizen—on being executed with a sword. Where his head bounced, three times, three fountains, the Tre Fontane, sprang up.

THE FEAST OF SAINT PETER

Prince of the Apostles, Pope, martyr, 64

Patron of boatwrights, clock makers, fishermen, net makers; invoked against fever, foot troubles, wolves • (emblem: crossed keys)

Because he is invariably pictured with a handful of keys, Peter is imagined in folklore to be the gatekeeper of Heaven. By virtue of those metaphorical "keys of the kingdom," which were given him by Our Lord, Catholics believe Peter to have been the first Pope. In the Gospels he is—except for Jesus—the most often mentioned and fully described character. His Faith allowed him to walk on water; his doubt made him sink. He bravely drew his sword to defend his Master; he denied Him thrice before cockcrow. He was a fisherman named Simon bar Jonah, but jesting Jesus nicknamed him Kephas (in Latin, Petrus) or, as we would say, Rocky. He was the acknowledged leader of the Apostles, traveling (presumably in the company of his wife and daughter) to Antioch and thence to Rome, where the chair he sat in and the chains he wore in prison are now venerated on their very own Feast Days (January 18 and August 1, respectively). It was in Rome that he was martyred, crucified upside down—at his request—near the site of the gargantuan basilica that bears his name. According to his apocryphal *Acts,* he had fled the city to escape Nero's persecution when he encountered Christ Himself on the road. Peter asked Him where He was going—"Quo Vadis?"—and the rest is movie history.

30. THE FEAST OF THE VENERABLE PIERRE TOUSSAINT

Slave of New York, 1853

Patron of hairdressers

Pierre was born in Haiti, into a family of slaves, and as a child amused his genteel Catholic owners, Jean and Marie Bernard, with his singing and dancing. Rumors of an imminent slave rebellion on the island inspired the Bernards to travel to New York City, bringing with them, among their goods and chattels, the twenty-one-year-old Pierre—whom they soon apprenticed to Mme. Bernard's hairdresser. Back in Haiti, the slaves did indeed rebel. Jean learned that his plantation, the source of the family fortune, was lost—and he dropped dead. His beautiful and sensitive widow was not only grief-stricken but broke. So for the next sixteen years the black Pierre coiffed the tresses of Manhattan society ladies to support his white owner. He didn't buy his freedom because he didn't want to upset her. After Mme. Bernard's death, Pierre married. He and his wife founded an orphanage for black children and made gifts, in secret, to white Haitian refugees. Pierre's own funeral was mobbed. In 1968, Cardinal Cooke of New York introduced Toussaint's cause for canonization, and in 1996 Pope John Paul declared him Venerable. M. Toussaint is without doubt in Heaven today, but it will be a pity—role-model-wise—if the first African American to be canonized is the white folks' favorite beautician.

THE FEAST OF THE BLESSED RAYMUND LULL

Catalan warrior, poet, martyr, 1316

Patron of Majorca

Surely one of the most admirable men of the Middle Ages, Raymund, who was born in Palma, Majorca, became a knight in the court of Aragon. He married young and had children. In addition to his military and courtly duties, he was an amateur scientist and wrote many lyric poems (in his native Catalan) and prose narratives that would have been called novels, if novels had been invented. At age thirty he experienced a series of visions and determined to bring the light of Faith to the Moors—the Arabs of North Africa. He not only learned Arabic but immersed himself in Arab culture—for a year he taught Arab philosophy at the University of Paris. Twice he sailed to Tunis to preach and was expelled. On his third mission—at the age of eighty—the Saracens stoned him and left him for dead. Rescued by Genoese sailors, he died on the voyage home, within sight of his native Majorca.

THE FEAST OF SAINT THEOBALD OF PROVENCE

Exceptionally humble hermit, 1066

Patron of belt makers, charcoal burners; invoked against coughing, fits, spells of fear • (emblem: falcon)

Theobald was born into the nobility of Champagne but, influenced by his reading of the *Lives of the Desert Fathers* (and much to the dismay of his parents), he clad himself in rags and set out for the vicinity of Luxembourg, where he lived in a hovel, supporting himself and his best friend William by working at the lowliest of tasks, such as stable mucking and charcoal burning. After some years his parents heard tell of a "holy hermit of Salingo" and made a pilgrimage to the place. Imagine their delighted surprise at being thus reunited with their long-lost son!

⋆· July ·⋆

1. THE FEAST OF SAINT JUNÍPERO SERRA

Mission man, 1784

Patron of California

Junípero Serra was the founder of the California missions and, consequently, mission furniture. When he arrived in the New World from Spain, he was bitten in the leg by a mosquito, an injury that left him a cripple for life. He is the namesake of the Serra Club, an organization formed to promote Catholic religious vocations and not to be confused with the Sierra Club. His road to sainthood has been tainted by allegations that he was less than kind—short-tempered, a "screamer"—to the Indians.

THE FEAST OF SAINT OLIVER PLUNKETT

Swashbuckling Irish bishop, 1681

Patron Saint of the Urban University in Rome

Born in Ireland to a noble and pro-British family, young Oliver distinguished himself in Rome as a scholar and priest. He returned to find his country a wasteland, devastated by Cromwell's forces, but in three years he built schools and churches and personally confirmed 48,000 of the persecuted Faithful. Then the English banned Catholic bishops (and there were only two of them). With a price on his head, Oliver Plunkett traveled about the country in rakish disguise, sporting a pistol, eye patch, and wig, and using the alias Captain Brown. In 1678 he was charged in a fictitious "popish plot" to invade England and held in a London jail, where he endured the added indignity of paying for his own shackles. At his trial a disgruntled Franciscan friar still in a pique over a property dispute falsely testified against Oliver. Our Saint received a rather extreme sentence: he was drawn, quartered, disemboweled, and beheaded. His head and pelvis were soon returned to Ireland, but his road to sainthood was unusually sluggish. He languished as Blessed Oliver Plunkett for three centuries, his invocation in times of need serving as an Irish ejaculation that rivaled "Jesus, Mary, and Joseph" in popularity. When he was finally canonized in 1975, he was the first Saint from Ireland, the land of "Saints and Scholars," in more than seven hundred years.

THE FEAST OF SAINT SERF

Wandering Arab bishop, 6th century

Patron of the Orkneys

his name belies his royal lineage: Serf, the son of an Arabian princess, rejected his Oriental kingdom and likewise pooh-poohed the papacy to preach to the pagan Scots. Once the Devil, trying to lure Serf from a hiding place, inhabited a local peasant, causing him to develop a ravenous appetite. The possessed man ate a lamb, a sheep, even a cow, but was still hungry—until Our Saint fed him a flea, causing the screaming Devil to vamoose. Although Serf never managed to visit the Orkney Islands, he remains their beloved Patron.

Also: The Feast of Saint Esther, biblical beauty whose seductive powers Jews celebrate at Purim, 5th century B.C.; and Saint Simeon Salus, an Egyptian hermit who was, as his name implies, an idiot, 588.

2. THE FEAST OF SAINTS PROCESSUS AND MARTINIAN

Jailers, martyrs, 1st century

Patrons of prison guards; invoked against demonic possession, infirmity, injury • (emblem: between them, a tree growing in a tub)

hen Nero cast Peter and Paul in prison, Processus and Martinian were their guards. They soon asked Peter to baptize them. He struck a rock, and a fountain gushed forth, creating an instant baptismal font. Later, when they were escorting a limping Peter from his cell, they beheld a foot bandage descend from Heaven. Thus inspired, they affirmed their Faith by spitting publicly on a statue of Jupiter and were promptly flogged and decapitated. A fountain still flows in the Mammertine Prison on the site of their baptism.

3. THE FEAST OF SAINT THOMAS

"Doubting" Apostle, martyr, 53

Patron of architects, builders, carpenters, construction workers, the East Indies, geometricians, India, masons, Pakistan, quantity surveyors, those about to marry; invoked against blindness, doubt • (emblem: carpenter's square, a T square)

A Jew and a Galilean, Thomas was one of the original twelve Apostles, called Didymus (the twin), since he was the twin brother of Saint James the Less. He is characterized by his incredulous nature, hence his nickname Doubting Thomas. He refused to believe in the Resurrection until he had put his fingers in the wounds of the Risen Christ, and his stunned reaction, "My Lord and my God," made its way into the canon of the Roman Mass. Thomas likewise doubted the Assumption of Mary, until she lowered Her girdle to him on Her way up to Heaven. Gnostic texts found by an Egyptian farmer near the river Nile in 1945 are attributed to him. This Gospel of Thomas is a collection of 114 sayings of Jesus, wherein Our Lord sounds like a fortune cookie or a Zen master. Some of His pithy wisdom seems addressed directly to His doubting disciple: "There is nothing hidden that will not be revealed," "Split a piece of wood, I am there," and "What you look for has come, but you do not know it." Thomas was also quite a foreign missionary. During his stay in India he started to build a palace but gave the money to the poor instead—which explains his Patronage of architects. Many Indians along the Malabar Coast region still call themselves the Christians of Saint Thomas, and the women there wear their saris in a distinctive way as a tribute to the Saint. That Saint Thomas's voyages took him as far as the New World is established by the undeniable evidence of his footprints on a rock near Bahia, Brazil, where he is sometimes confused with the plumed serpent god Topiltzin.

4. THE FEAST OF SAINT ELIZABETH OF PORTUGAL

Matriarch of a dysfunctional royal family, 1336

Patron of the falsely accused, victims of jealousy, Portugal, the Third Order of Saint Francis; invoked against difficult birth • (emblem: her apron full of roses)

The daughter of King Peter III of Aragon, Elizabeth was married at twelve to a reluctant King Denis of Portugal, who was rude enough to gripe about her oversized ears. Ignoring this and other indignities, Elizabeth became the most benevolent of monarchs, building hospitals (where she personally washed feet) and orphanages, yet still finding time to be skilled in the art of fandango dancing and an expert on the castanets. The family feuds that consumed Elizabeth's life spanned three generations: her father versus her grandfather, her son versus her husband, her son versus her grandson. When her son and husband took up arms against each other, Elizabeth rode a mule down the center of the battlefield in an attempt to make peace. Like her great-aunt and namesake, Saint Elizabeth of Hungary, she carried food for the poor in her apron, food that was turned into roses when uncovered by a niggardly royal. Her Patronage of the falsely accused derived from a castle scandal in which a filthy-minded page told King Denis that Elizabeth was having an affair with another page. The king (who himself obliged Elizabeth to raise his illegitimate children) ordered her alleged lover thrown into a lime kiln. In a happy mix-up, convincing all of Elizabeth's innocence, the evil page was thrown in instead! Elizabeth's Feast Day, Rainha Santa, is cause for great celebration in parts of Portugal.

THE FEAST OF SAINT ULRIC

The first papally canonized Saint, 973

Invoked against difficult births, dizziness, floods, mice, moles • (emblem: fish)

Ulric was the first Saint officially declared by papal canonization (in 993). Thenceforth, the power of "making Saints" was the Pope's alone. A Swiss bishop, Ulric made a practice of visiting a hospital every afternoon and washing the feet of twelve paupers. He argued against clerical celibacy on the basis of the

Bible and common sense, though shunning female company himself, explaining, "Take away the fuel and you take away the fire." In his lifetime he could heal those bitten by mad dogs, and pregnant women drank from his chalice to obtain easy labor. The earth in which Ulric is buried (at Augsburg) is a powerful rodent repellent and has often been carried off for that purpose.

SAINT ULRIC   4

AGWÉ

5. THE FEAST OF SAINT ATHANASIUS OF ATHOS

Unlucky abbot, c. 1000

Founder of the famous Greek monastery on Mount Athos, Athanasius died in the collapse of a building he was dedicating.

Also: The Feast of Saint Anthony Mary Zaccharoa, whose mother pressured him to be a doctor. After studying medicine for a while, Anthony decided he would rather heal souls. This was obviously a career move blessed in Heaven, since Angels dressed up as altar boys arrived to serve at his first Mass, 1539.

6. THE FEAST OF SAINT GOAR

Hermit accused of sorcery, 575

Patron of potters; invoked against whirlpools • (emblem: miter floating in the air)

A parish priest from Aquitaine with a reputation for holiness, Goar retreated into a solitary life, preaching, working miracles, and building up a devoted following. He had his detractors, though, who declared Goar a "humbug who ate a big breakfast before noon" and reported him to the local bishop, Rusticus. The bishop then declared Goar a sorcerer. At this point a three-day-old child was brought into the proceedings and testified that Bishop Rusticus was its father! The bishop was unfrocked, but Goar fell ill for seven years and died, his home becoming a place for pilgrimages. He is invoked against whirlpools because Gewirr, on the Rhine, is a whirlpool near his town; it might also explain his name. Like Saint Brigid, he could hang his cloak on a sunbeam.

THE FEAST OF SAINT GODELEVA

Miserably married martyr, 1070

Patron of Flanders; invoked against throat disease, for or against rain • (emblem: rope around her neck)

Godeleva was born near Boulogne, around 1045. After her marriage to the Flemish nobleman Bertulf, her new mother-in-law called her the Black Crow because of her dark hair and bushy eyebrows. The groom shared his mother's distaste for his bride, deserting her during the wedding feast and refusing to consummate the marriage. Godeleva's miserable mother-in-law gave her nothing to eat except bread that had been previously chewed by the dogs. The desperate (and hungry) Godeleva begged the local bishop for help; the bishop forced her to return to her vile husband. This time Bertulf, anxious to marry his more attractive paramour, convinced Godeleva that the cure for their marital woes was a love elixir. When the game Godeleva set off on the trail of such a potion, Bertulf's henchmen killed her by putting a thong around her neck, sticking her head in a pond, then shoving her corpse into a well. The site of her murder became famous as a place that cured sore throats. Bertulf, after fighting in the Crusades, repented and entered a monastery.

THE FEAST OF SAINT MARIA GORETTI

Died defending her virtue, 1902

Patron of teenage girls • (emblem: lily)

After her father's death Maria's mother, Assunta, was forced to go back to work, leaving Maria in charge of the family. In 1902 Maria, who looked more mature than her twelve years, attracted the most unwelcome attention of her next-door neighbor, Alexander Serenelli, who read naughty magazines. When he

found her alone Alexander attacked her, growling, allegedly, "Submit or die!" Maria, repelling his advances, replied, "Death, but not sin!" which so angered Alexander that he stabbed her. The dialogue sounds like bad subtitles, but the wound was real. Maria forgave her attacker on her deathbed, and Alexander went to prison, where Maria came to him in a vision dressed in white and gathering lilies. Maria's canonization in 1950 was held outdoors to accommodate the vast throngs. It was the first time both a Saint's mother and a Saint's murderer attended a canonization, for Alexander, now a Capuchin lay brother, was present. Pope Pius XII heralded Maria as "the Saint Agatha of the twentieth century" (which may explain the striking resemblance between the two on holy cards), and he used the occasion of her canonization to decry the lack of female modesty in the press and cinema. It has been theorized that the Pope enthused about Maria to counteract the influence of the uninhibited and predominantly Protestant American occupation troops.

THE FEAST OF SAINT MODWENNA

Virgin and hermit. Or virgin and abbess. 7th century. Or 5th century

Modwenna was one of forty-nine children of the fecund King Brychan of Wales. This may explain her opting for a hermit's life on a deserted island off the coast of England, where she was content to work her miracles alone. On the other hand, she may actually be Monenna, a sensible Irish abbess and likewise a miracle worker. At any rate, hagiographers have them hopelessly confused, and England, Scotland, and Ireland all claim her (their) relics.

7. THE FEAST OF SAINT ETHELBURGA

Retiring Anglo-Saxon princess, 664

Invoked against rheumatism • (emblem: abbess with instruments of the Passion)

Her father was a king and her sister was an abbess and her niece was a Saint befriended by Angels, but Ethelburga had a strangely quiet life. She was a nun who attempted to build a (small) church but died (peacefully) before it was completed. The most exciting thing we know about her is that when her body was exhumed years after her death, it was discovered to be in the odor of sanctity.

THE FEAST OF SAINT FERMIN

Bishop of Amiens, martyred by bulls, 304

Patron of Pamplona • (emblem: bull)

To commemorate the unusual method of Fermin's martyrdom (he was dragged through the streets by bulls), his annual Fiesta on this day features the world-famous Running of the Bulls, during which the young men of the town (and Hemingway fans from America) are gored and trampled.

THE FEAST OF SAINT PALLADIUS

Feckless missionary, 432

Patron of Scotland • (emblem: in episcopal vestments, red cope and gloves)

In the year 430 this Roman deacon was promoted to the rank of bishop and dispatched by Pope Celestine I to preach the Gospel to the natives of Ireland, who were as yet entirely innocent of the True Faith. Palladius landed (from

England) in Wicklow, where he built three churches—into which he had no luck whatsoever attracting the Celts. He left in what appears to have been a huff, sailing to Scotland, where he is remembered fondly around Aberdeen. Two years later Saint Patrick arrived in Ireland, and the rest is (glorious) history.

8. THE FEAST OF SAINT KILIAN
Hanged missionary, 689

Patron of Bavaria, hanged men, whitewashers • (emblem: crossed swords)

Kilian (whose name in Gaelic means "church") was an Irish missionary to Bavaria who succeeded in converting the local ruler, Gozbert. Unfortunately, after the baptismal formalities Our Saint was obliged to inform Gozbert that his marriage to his former sister-in-law, Geilana, was invalid in the eyes of the Church. The chief agreed in theory but nonetheless had Kilian and his two companions assassinated. A strong cult grew up around the Saint—his image appeared on local coins and seals, and he became the subject of the yearly Kilianfest in Würzburg. This happy Teutonic festival includes a play reenacting the Saint's life, in which the blame for his murder is placed squarely on the woman, Geilana.

Also: The Feast of Saint Withburga, a holy Anglo-Saxon princess and nun who died in 743. When it was disinterred in 1106, not only was her body incorrupt but, according to the historian Thomas of Ely, the limbs were flexible.

9. THE FEAST OF MARY, QUEEN OF PEACE
Patron of civilian war victims

Mary has always been invoked as Queen of Peace in her litany; an image of the Virgin in Toledo was venerated under this title in 1085, after the Spanish negotiated a treaty with the Moors. But it was only after World War I that devotion to the Queen of Peace became universally popular, and it was Pope John XXIII who formally declared her the Patron of civilian war victims. In the recent Marian apparitions in war-ravaged Medjugorje, Yugoslavia, this is how Our Lady identifies herself.

THE FEAST OF THE BLESSED ROSE HAWTHORNE

Daughter of *The Scarlet Letter*'s author, 1926

Patron of divorced people, difficult marriages, sick children, and parents who have lost a child

This candidate for sainthood distressed her father, Nathaniel Hawthorne—who had once described Catholic immigrants as "more numerous than maggots in cheese"—when she converted to the Faith. Rose survived the death of her only child and a disastrous marriage to the alcoholic editor of *The Atlantic Monthly.* She moved to a tenement in the slums of New York, taking in the cancerous poor who had been shunned by family and friends, for cancer was then considered contagious. She and an artist friend, Alice Huber, nursed and fed the incurable patients—ironically, most of them immigrants. They were soon joined by other women, and so was formed the Dominican Sisters for the Care of Incurable Cancer.

THE FEAST OF SAINT VERONICA GIULIANI

Stigmatic with crown of thorns, 1727 · (emblem: heart)

When her dying mother assigned each of her five children a wound of Christ, Veronica received the special one, the sword wound in His side, which indicated to her that her heart was one with Christ's. An irritable child and adolescent, she started having heart pains, which she carefully diagrammed. After her death an autopsy revealed the marks of an incision on her heart that corresponded to her diagram. In the convent Veronica was favored with visions, ecstasies, and a wedding ring from Christ, adorned with a raised, reddish stone.

Finally, on a Good Friday, she received the Stigmata. After her phenomena were declared genuine, she was elevated to mistress of her convent, where she improved the plumbing. She resented those who did not share her enthusiasm for strict religious disciplines until she had a vision in which she saw her heart—and it was made of steel. Her autobiography, forty-four volumes, details her many mystical experiences.

10. THE FEAST OF SAINT AMALBURGA

Emperor-resisting virgin, 770

Invoked against arm injuries, bruises • (emblem: nun holding fish, sieve)

Charlemagne maintained several wives and a rotating cast of concubines. But when he took a shine to this virtuous and beautiful German maiden, Amalburga spurned his advances, cut off her magnificent locks, and left town. The lust-crazed tyrant pursued her, found her in a church, and brutally laid hands on her, causing the bruises against which she is yet invoked. Once more she escaped, crossing the river Schelde on the back of a large and accommodating sturgeon. She died a virgin. Among her domestic skills, it is recorded, was her ability to carry water in a sieve.

11. THE FEAST OF SAINT BENEDICT

Abbot, founder of Western monasticism, 550

Patron of architects, coppersmiths, the dying, erysipelas, Europe, farmworkers, fever, gallstones, inflammatory diseases, monks, servants who break things, spelunkers; invoked against gossipmongers, kidney disease, poison, temptations of the Devil, witchcraft • (emblems: raven, broken cup)

Benedict, the founder of Western monasticism, had an immense influence on the Christianization of Europe after the fall of the Roman Empire. His "how-to" book for monks, the Rule of St. Benedict, is one of the basic documents of the Middle Ages, those centuries during which monasteries were Europe's only surviving centers of art, learning, and civilization. He was born in Nursia, Italy, early in the sixth century, of noble parents. His twin sister is Saint Scholastica. After his first miracle (he repaired, by prayer, a dish a servant had broken) he retreated to an underground cave at Subiaco, where he lived for three years dressed in animal skins, fed by—accounts vary—a magic raven or a hermit named Romanus. The Devil tormented him by assuming the form of a black bird, flying in Benedict's face to remind him of a beautiful signorina he had admired in Rome. Thinking fast, Our Saint tore off his garments and threw himself into a thorn bush, never again to be troubled by sexual desire. He and his followers formed a religious order, dedicated to the principle that "to work is to pray"—thereby opposing the foolish prejudice of those unenlightened days against manual labor. He made his way to Monte Cassino, a malarial swamp, where he transformed ruined temples of Jupiter and Apollo into oratories to John the Baptist and Martin of Tours, thereby laying the foundation for the greatest monastery in all Christendom. At Monte Cassino, Benedict healed the sick, raised the dead, and read the minds of his fellow monks, even mentally tracking them while they were on long journeys. He also had the gift of prophesy. He foretold, accurately, the imminent death of Totila the Barbarian but could, alas, also foresee the destruction of Monte Cassino. After Benedict's death his great monastery was razed to the ground by the Lombards, restored, sacked by the Saracens, rebuilt, and destroyed a final time by the Allies in World War II (who bombed it to rubble, believing it to be German headquarters). Despite his many Patronages, Benedict is today known mainly by his image as a chucklesome monk on the labels of brandy bottles.

THE FEAST OF SAINT OLGA

Vengeful Russian princess, 969

Patron of converts

A simple peasant girl, Olga married Prince Igor of Kiev and when he was assassinated (by Dravidians) assumed the throne. She exacted a terrible revenge for Igor's murder, ordering his actual killers steamed to death and slaughtering hundreds of alleged accessories to the crime. Some years later she traveled to Constantinople, saw the light, and became the first Russian ever to be baptized.

12. THE FEAST OF SAINT JOHN GUALBERT

Tree-planting abbot, 1073

Patron of foresters, park keepers • (emblem: with crucifix, Christ bending toward him)

St JOHN Gualbert

When he met his brother's killer in an alley in Florence, John drew his sword but found himself unable to take his revenge. He proceeded to the nearest monastery, where Jesus (on a crucifix) nodded to him three times. John took this as a sign, cut his hair, and joined a religious order. He soon sensed some irregularity among his superiors (simony? nepotism?) and departed to found an order of his own. He and his monks became the self-appointed monitors of the lax and corrupt clergy, destroying degenerate institutions by fire and thunderstorm. John accused the bishop of Florence of buying his office and brought this charge to the attention of the Pope, the police, and most of Florence. He lit a great bonfire in the town square and challenged the bishop to walk through it, which he declined to do. Our Saint then ordered one of his own monks to submit to trial by fire, praying he be spared only if the bishop "had obtained his episcopal throne by means of money." The monk coolly emerged from the inferno, the crowd went wild, and the bishop was forced to resign. When not walking through fire John's monks busied themselves transforming the desolate lands around their monas-tery into a park of evergreen trees, which explains his Patronage of foresters.

THE FEAST OF SAINT VERONICA

Matron whose veil was imprinted with the face of Christ, 1st century

Patron of laundresses • (emblem: veil with Christ's face)

Veronica (née Seraphia) is the middle-aged woman who took pity on Christ and wiped His bloody and perspiring brow as He was on the way to His Crucifixion. Our Lord left the imprint of His face on her handkerchief, which important relic is known as the Sudarium, or sweat cloth. Veronica in her final years gave it to Pope Saint Clement. Saint Peter's in Rome claims possession of this cloth, which bears the true image of Christ, or *vera icon*—hence her new name. Veronica was not an important figure in the story of the Passion until the fourth century, when her good deed was immortalized in the sixth Station of the Cross. Her veil has had, like the Shroud of Turin, a long and miraculous history. Saint Bridget of Sweden, for one, chided anyone who doubted its authenticity. From time to time it glows with a supernatural light, and the Holy face printed on it assumes a tinge of lifelike color. In its owner's honor the pious Spaniards have named the bullfighting pass in which the toreador draws his cape across the bull's face a veronica.

13. THE FEAST OF SAINT CLELIA BARBIERI

She haunts her former convent, 1870

Patron of those ridiculed for their piety

Although her parents were simple hemp workers, they sensed that Clelia was special after seeing her conversing with invisible friends and levitating. Even as a small child, she expressed her wish to "leave the world" and was interested in the Saint-making process. Clelia became the youngest founder of a religious order (Minims of Our Lady of

Sorrows) and died at the tender age of twenty-three, promising her sisters that she would always be with them. Not long afterward her voice was heard accompanying the nuns in prayer and hymns. Soon nuns in other convents also began to hear her high-pitched voice, singing, praying, and speaking the local dialect, sometimes preceded by a series of knocks.

14. THE FEAST OF SAINT CAMILLUS DE LELLIS
Male nurse and recovered gambling addict, 1614

Patron of nurses, the sick; invoked against compulsive gambling • (emblem: with his Guardian Angel)

Born in Abruzzi in 1550, when his mother was close to sixty—she died, not surprisingly, soon after his birth—Camillus, at six feet six, was a giant by the standards of his day. He led a dissolute youth and after a stint in his father's regiment became a soldier of fortune. Camillus was a compulsive gambler, and, at the age of twenty five, having literally lost the shirt off his back, he began his life as a penitent. Rejected by a monastery because of an ulcerated sore on his leg, he went to work in a hospital nursing incurables. Sometimes, unable to walk because of his rotting extremity, Camillus would crawl from sickbed to sickbed. In 1585, along with Saint Philip Neri, he founded a congregation of male nurses, the Servants of the Sick. He was a pioneer in hospital hygiene and diet, and successfully opposed the prevailing practice of burying patients alive. Camillus often saw his Guardian Angel by his side, and the two are represented together in art.

THE FEAST OF SAINT FRANCIS SOLANO
Shipwrecked missionary, 1610

Patron of Argentina, Bolivia, Paraguay

A flute-playing Spanish priest, Francis sailed for the New World aboard a slave ship, which struck a reef off the coast of Peru; he rushed belowdecks and unchained the eight hundred Africans in the hold, and he preached the Gospel to them as they all drowned. He himself was rescued after three days and proceeded to the interior of the Argentinian rain forest known (to the Spaniards) as the

Green Hell. Father Solano was a gifted linguist and charismatic orator. It is recorded that after one of his sermons, nine thousand natives came forward to be baptized.

THE FEAST OF SAINT PROCOPIUS

Owl-befriending hermit, 1053

Patron of the Czechs • (emblem: stag)

When this priest retreated to a cave near Prague to become a hermit, he first had to clear out the thousand Devils infesting the place. He lived undisturbed except for a few friendly owls, until the duke of Bohemia came hunting. As Procopius relates in his autobiography, a stag sought his cave for sanctuary, and the duke, humbled by the hermit, gave him a grant of land. Procopius soon attracted a following and in his later years founded the monastery of Sazaba.

Also: The Feast of Saint Donald of Ogilvy, a Scottish laird whose seven daughters all became nuns, 8th century.

15. THE FEAST OF THE BLESSED ANNE MARIE JAVOUHEY

Woman with a mission, 1851

Her family hid priests during the French Revolution, and Nanette, as she was called, grew into a pious young woman. Though she nursed her country's soldiers during the Napoleonic Wars, she had, as one biographer put it, "always dreamed of taking care of black men," which was odd, because Anne Marie had never actually seen anyone of color. But Providence intervened when her government asked her to lead a delegation of nuns to Africa. There she established schools, hospitals, and leper colonies. She went on to organize the slaves in French Guiana, buying them their freedom, giving them land, and teaching them how to farm. The former slaves unanimously elected Anne Marie as their delegate to the French parliament, on which occasion King Louis-Philippe called her "that great man."

THE FEAST OF SAINT BONAVENTURE

"The Seraphic Doctor," 1274

Patron of children, load bearers, silk manufacturers • (emblem: cardinal's hat in a tree)

When he was a sickly child Saint Francis of Assisi cured him. When, as a young man, he joined the order, Francis cried out, *"O bona ventura!"*—What good luck!—and the name stuck. Bonaventure eventually became minister general of the Franciscans and wrote books of mystical, Neoplatonic theology (as opposed to the neo-Aristotelian theology of Saint Thomas Aquinas). When a solemn papal delegation showed up to announce his elevation to cardinal, Bonaventure was washing dishes in the kitchen of the friary. He asked the delegates if they'd mind hanging the cardinal's hat on a tree until he finished doing the dishes.

THE FEAST OF SAINT HENRY THE EMPEROR

Made war, not love, 1024

Patron of childless people, dukes, kings, Benedictine Oblates, people rejected by religious orders, physically challenged people; invoked against sterility • (emblem: holding a globe with a dove on it)

The son of Henry the Quarrelsome of Bavaria, Our Saint was as a young man favored with a vision of Saint Wolfgang, who cryptically pointed to a sign with the words "after six." The prince assumed this to be a foretelling of his death, but its true meaning became evident six years later, in 1014, when he was crowned Holy Roman emperor. (Actually in a pre-Napoleonic gesture, Henry took the tiara from the Pope's hands and crowned himself.) He became a staunch advocate of clerical celibacy, once it occurred to him that the lands of childless priests reverted to the Crown, and to set an example he lived in ostentatious chastity with his queen, Saint Cunegund. On his deathbed he returned his bride to her troublesome family with the words "Receive back again the virgin you gave me." By means of many battles (he prayed fervently before each one), Henry succeeded in reuniting the German Empire.

Also: The Feast of Saint Mildred, who found refuge from her relentless suitor in the convent. Her relics were a source of bitter rivalry between France, England, Holland, and Bavaria, too.

THE FEAST OF SAINT SWITHIN

Rain-loving bishop, 862

Invoked for or against rain • (emblem: shower of rain)

Every Britisher knows that if it rains on Saint Swithin's Day, it will keep raining for the next forty days. Swithin (or Swithun) was a bishop of Winchester, renowned for his business acumen and good deeds. His most celebrated miracle was the putting-together-again of a peasant woman's basketful of broken eggs. He is said to have enjoyed the rain and asked to be buried in the churchyard so it would fall upon his grave. In honor of his canonization in 971, his bones were dug up and enshrined inside the cathedral on July 15—whereupon a forty-day deluge ensued, as it may again at the height of any English summer.

THE FEAST OF SAINT VLADIMIR

Lusty, conquering czar, 1015

Patron of large families, murderers, Russia • (emblem: king being baptized)

Vladimir was a pagan prince of Kiev who had five wives and three times that number of mistresses when he converted to Christianity. (The Muslims also courted him, but that religion had little appeal because of his affinity for pork and wine.) Byzantine Christianity and its attendant political advantages caught Vladimir's eye, and he loved the ritual, especially the fluttery white robes of the deacons, which he mistook for Angels' wings. His Christian marriage to Anne, sister of the Byzantine emperor, while hardly a love match, sealed the alliance between the two empires. The new convert forced the entire city of Kiev, starting with the nobles, to be baptized. Thousands shivered in the river while a priest stood on the shore yelling out patronyms in a mass baptism. Vladimir's new religion must have influenced him somewhat, because he stepped up his almsgiving and reduced the number of robbers he sentenced to death.

16. THE FEAST OF OUR LADY OF MOUNT CARMEL

Patron of Bolivia, the Carmelites, Chile, fishermen

Early in the thirteenth century an English baron, while visiting Mount Carmel in the Holy Land, discovered a group of religious hermits living there. He brought them home with him and set them up in his manor house as Carmelites. In 1251 Our Lady of Mount Carmel appeared in England to one of these holy men, Simon Stock. Mary presented him with the brown scapular, a sort of religious dogtag, promising all who wore this scratchy emblem that they would be released from Purgatory on the first Saturday after their death. (N.B.: The scapular should be 100 percent wool, not encased in plastic, and under no circumstances should it be pinned to clothing.) Bernardo O'Higgins, the liberator of Chile, had a particular devotion to the Virgin in this aspect and dedicated first his war of independence from Spain to Her, then placed his new nation under Her protection.

THE FEAST OF SAINT HELIER

Martyr who kept his head, 6th century

Patron of the Isle of Jersey

The capital city of Jersey, largest of the Channel Islands, is named for this Belgian hermit who took up his abode on a sea-bound rock there. When Helier was beheaded by a band of Vikings, he calmly picked up his head and walked away, which caused the marauders to flee in terror, sparing the island.

17. THE FEAST OF SAINT ALEXIS

Ostentatiously destitute hermit, 5th century

Patron of beggars, belt makers • (emblem: beggar under a staircase)

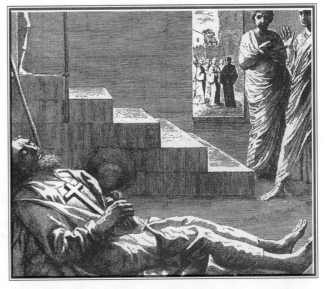

A rich but chaste Syrian, Alexis married but on his wedding night escaped to a distant country, disguised as a beggar. Years later, on the advice of a talking statue of the Blessed Virgin, he returned, still in disguise, and lived under the staircase in his parental home, where he suffered many indignities from his parents and their snooty servants. Just before he died he revealed all and enjoyed a splendid funeral. Saint Alexis staircases are architectural features of many convents.

18. THE FEAST OF SAINT ARNULF OF METZ

Soldier-statesman-bishop, 640

Patron of millers, music; invoked to find lost objects • (emblem: bishop, a coat of mail under his cloak)

A rnulf (in English, Arnold) was a Frankish soldier and statesman, a friend and adviser to King Dagobert. One day, on a whim, he threw a ring into a river. On the day he was proclaimed bishop of Metz a fish was served to him—and inside it was that very ring! His bishopric notwithstanding, Arnulf had two sons, one of whom succeeded him as bishop of Metz; the other became the grandfather of Charlemagne. A drunken lout named Noddo once publicly called into doubt Our Saint's chastity, slandering him as "full lusty and ready to all delices." That night in bed Noddo's pants caught fire.

THE FEAST OF SAINT FELICITY

Proud mother martyred with her seven sons, 165

Invoked to conceive male children • (emblem: seven swords)

Felicity and her sons were martyred after they refused to worship false idols. To compound the cruelty, she was the last to be killed, so she was afforded the added torture of watching all of her beloved sons die, after which the family was buried in seven different cemeteries in Rome. Or so the story goes. In actuality the seven martyrs probably were not Felicity's sons; in fact, it is unlikely that they even knew one another. Felicity's contemporary Saint Symphorosa, whose Feast Day is July 18, has an identical story. The early Christian Church was eager to identify with the Old Testament story of the Seven Maccabees and *their* sainted mother, all of whom were martyred for their (Jewish) faith.

THE FEAST OF SAINT THENEVA

Unmarried mother, 6th century

Patron of Glasgow

Theneva was a princess of the Picts, the aboriginal people of Scotland. Although a heathen, she had taken a vow of virginity and defied her parents by refusing to marry a neighboring prince. Driven from home, Theneva took shelter with a Christian swineherd, who not only respected her vow but also taught her the rudiments of the True Faith. But somehow Theneva turned up pregnant; her seducer, identified in the legend as a "beardless youth," may have been Eugenius, king of the Scots. Berserk with rage, her royal father ordered that she be thrown off a cliff into the sea. Miraculously, she was unharmed and escaped in a waiting boat. Guided by a shoal of fish, she landed at Culross, and there gave birth to her son. A nearby hermit bishop, Saint Servan by name, heard her singing a lullaby and made haste to rescue and baptize both mother and child. Theneva reformed her life and moved to Glasgow. Her son grew up to be Saint Mungo and is co-Patron of the city along with his mother.

19. THE FEAST OF SAINTS JUSTA AND RUFINA

Pot-throwing virgin martyrs, 3rd century

Patrons of potters, Seville • (emblems: broken pots, image of Venus overturned)

During a ferocious electrical storm in the year 1504, the magnificent Moorish tower El Giralda in Seville was *not* struck by lightning. The natives of Seville attribute this miracle to the Divine intercession of Our Saints, who were the virtuous daughters of a third-century Christian potter. Rather than supply their father's wares for use in an idolatrous and lewd ceremony honoring the pagan goddess Venus, they smashed his entire inventory; after a mockery of a trial the sisters were thrown to the lions.

20. THE FEAST OF SAINT ELIJAH (ELIAS)

Fiery Old Testament prophet, 700 B.C.

Invoked when flying, against drought, earthquakes • (emblem: chariot of fire)

Several Old Testament figures, including Enoch and Elijah, are venerated as Saints simply for the reason that they are, the Bible says, in Heaven. Elias, a ninth-century B.C. prophet, traveled there in style, in both a chariot of fire *and* a whirlwind (2 Kings 2:11).

THE FEAST OF SAINT MARGARET

Virgin swallowed by dragon, 1st century

Patron of escape from the Devil, exiles, nurses, peasants, women in childbirth;

invoked against infertility, kidney disease, and loss of milk • (emblems: dragon, pearl)

A princess of Antioch, Margaret was thrown out by her father when he discovered that her nanny (one Theotimus) had made her a Christian; together the maiden and her maid became simple shepherdesses. A stunning beauty and consecrated virgin, Margaret was pursued by an amorous prefect, who, upon her rejection of his advances, threw her into jail. In her cell she was visited by Satan, who assumed the form of a dragon and swallowed her. But in the very belly of the beast a cross she carried grew to such enormous proportions that the dragon was split in two, and Margaret emerged unharmed; for this reason, and her virginity aside, she is the traditional Patron of childbirth. On another occasion the Devil appeared to Our Saint as a man, but Margaret saw through his disguise, knocked him down, and set her foot on his neck, saying, "Lie still, thou fiend, under the foot of a woman." She was eventually beheaded and went directly to Heaven, where she enjoyed enormous popularity throughout the Middle Ages. Hers was one of the voices heard by Saint Joan of Arc.

THE FEAST OF SAINT UNCUMBER

Bearded lady, date unknown

Patron of unhappy wives; invoked against men's lust • (emblem: bearded maiden, crucified)

One of an all-girl set of septuplets, Uncumber was originally named Wilgefortis, "strong virgin," in which state she fervently wished to remain. Her father, the pagan king of Portugal, had other ideas, insisting she marry his ally, the king of Sicily. Desperately she prayed to become ugly, a wish that was miraculously granted when she sprouted, overnight, a formidable beard and mustache. Incensed, her father had her crucified, and from the cross she promised to all who invoked her aid that she would free them from male encumbrances—hence her name in English, Uncumber. (In German she is Ontkommer, and in Latin, Liberatrix.) Unhappy wives would leave sacks of oats at her shrines, intended to inspire horses to carry nasty and troublesome husbands to the Devil.

Also: The Feast of Saint Joseph Barsabbas, surnamed "the Just," who competed with Saint Matthias for the job of twelfth Apostle (replacing Judas) and lost. His emblem in sacred art is said to be "a child blowing soap bubbles," which should be looked into, 1st century.

21. THE FEAST OF SAINT VICTOR OF MARSEILLES

Idol-kicking martyr, 290

Invoked against foot troubles • (emblems: spear, shield, windmill)

A Christian soldier in the Roman army, Victor was captured and subjected to a variety of tortures, including being fed poisoned meat while hanging in chains and spending three days in a furnace. Christ and a host of Angels came to his cell to console him, filling it with light. When asked to worship at a pagan shrine, Victor defiantly kicked over the idols, for which crime the heretic governor ordered his foot chopped off. Victor was finally decapitated and thrown into the sea. In art he is, for some reason, shown with a windmill.

22. THE FEAST OF SAINT MARY MAGDALENE

Redheaded penitent, 1st century

Patron of fallen women, glovers, hairdressers, perfumers • (emblem: ointment box)

History's most famous fallen woman, the glamorous Mary Magdalene washed Christ's feet with her tears and dried them with her long hair before anointing them with perfume. Pope Saint Gregory the Great, after lamenting that beauty was her downfall, promoted her as a composite figure: a notorious harlot, the languorous sister of Martha and Lazarus (aka Mary of Bethany), and the sometime fiancée of John the Divine. Mary Magdalene is venerated as the most ardent

and loyal of Christ's disciples, a member of His inner circle, and one of the women with Him at the Crucifixion, helping Him down from the cross. Christian feminists point to her significant role as the first witness to the Resurrection, announcing the Risen Christ to the Apostles. Indeed, Catholic women's groups in their struggle to win equal rights within the Church have taken her name for their organization. Our Lord took her side against various maligners—Temple elders, angry mobs, Judas, even her own sister. Mary Magdalene inspired His (mostly ignored) teaching against hypocrisy: "Let he who is without sin cast the first stone." It is said that after the Ascension she retreated to France to live as a hermit, being fed and otherwise attended by Angels. Her final home, La Sainte Baume near Marseilles, was visited by every French king and attracts pilgrims to this day. Fittingly, the cookies named after her were immortalized by Proust, for La Madeleine is one of the most beloved Saints of France.

23. THE FEAST OF SAINT APOLLINARIS OF RAVENNA

Martyr, bishop appointed by Saint Peter himself, 75

Patron of needleworkers; invoked against diseases of the sexual organs

*A*pollinaris was the first bishop of Ravenna, appointed by Saint Peter. On four separate occasions he was stoned and driven out of town. All this ill treatment has been forgotten in later years, and magnificent churches in Ravenna are dedicated to him; one contains the famous mosaic depicting Apollinaris as shepherd of his flock.

THE FEAST OF SAINT BRIDGET OF SWEDEN

Queen, pilgrim, mystic, 1373

Patron of scholars, Sweden • (emblem: candle)

*T*his Swedish holy woman, lady-in-waiting to the wife of King Magnus II, was married at thirteen to one Ulf Gudmarsson. One of her first visions inspired her to tell King Magnus to mend his wicked ways, so the repentant and grateful monarch gave Bridget the money to start up an order of nuns and monks, wherein she strictly enforced segregation between the sexes. Bridget's visions compelled her to dispense advice worldwide—to several kings and even the Pope, then in exile at Avignon. Her last pilgrimage was to the Holy Land, where she envisioned all the scenes of the Passion reenacted and was shipwrecked off the coast of Jaffa. This pilgrimage was also the occasion of the romantic entanglement

between Bridget's son (married) and Queen Joanna of Naples (ditto), a state of affairs that caused Our Saint considerable distress, although her daughter did go on to become the remarkably virtuous Saint Catherine of Sweden. Curiously, Saint Bridget was officially canonized a record three times.

Also: The Feast of Saint Liborius, bishop of Le Mans. Pope Clement XI designated him the Patron Saint to be invoked against gallstones—from which His Holiness himself suffered, 390.

24. THE FEAST OF SAINTS BORIS AND GLEB
Assassinated princes, 1015

Patrons of Moscow, princes, Russia • (emblem: holding swords)

Boris and Gleb were Russian princes, sons of the saintly czar Vladimir of Kiev and younger brothers of the villain Svyatopolk, who had them both murdered. Stabbed in the throat by a cook, they met their deaths with Christlike meekness typical of the Eastern Saints known as strastoterptites, meaning "passion-bearers"—innocents accepting death with resignation. A fourth brother, Yaroslav, opposed and overthrew the dreadful Svyatopolk and had the incorrupt bodies of both Saints enshrined in the cathedral of Saint Basil, where their tomb became a place of pilgrimage and miracles.

THE FEAST OF SAINT CHRISTINA THE ASTONISHING
High-strung, levitating, insightful virgin, 1224

Patron of psychiatrists • (emblem: maiden with disheveled hair sitting on a wheel)

Christina, the youngest of three sisters, was born in Belgium and orphaned at fifteen. At twenty-two she suffered a cataleptic fit and was assumed to be dead, but at her funeral Mass she flew out of her coffin and took refuge in the rafters of the church. The mourners fled in horror, leaving behind only one of her sisters and the priest, who finally persuaded her to come down. She had been disturbed, she explained, by the garlicky breath of the congregation. Christina then related the story of her death and out-of-body experiences: She had visited Hell and Purgatory, seen friends in both places, and when she finally arrived in Heaven heard the priest at her funeral Mass intoning the Agnus Dei. She thereupon decided to return to Earth and liberate the souls she had seen suffering in Purgatory. Christina was tormented throughout her life by her acute sense of smell (she found men particularly offensive) and to avoid noxious odors was forced to sit in baptismal fonts, perch on towers, balance herself on weathervanes, and crawl into ovens. Many people were convinced she was "full of Devils," and attempts, usually futile, were made to confine her. She even once escaped after being chained to a pillar—she was suffering from a broken leg at the time. Later in life, however, she achieved respectability, and many notable people sought her inevitably wise advice.

25. THE FEAST OF SAINT CHRISTOPHER

Ferried the Infant Jesus across a river, 3rd century

Patron of bachelors, bus drivers, ferryboat men, fruit dealers, police officers, skiers, soldiers, travelers, truck drivers; invoked against nightmares, sudden death, peril from water, storms • (emblem: giant carrying Christ child on his shoulders)

Christopher was a twenty-four-foot-tall giant from Palestine, a blacksmith's son obsessed with the desire to serve the most powerful king in the world. He joined the mercenary army of a tribal chieftain, but after he witnessed his master tremble before a wicked necromancer, Christopher resolved to follow the mighty Satan. Then the Devil cowered and fled from the crucifix worn by an ancient hermit, so Christopher bound himself in service to that holy old man, whose task it was to ferry travelers across a river. One stormy night a child (usually pictured as a baby) appeared and asked Christopher to carry him on his shoulders across the raging flood. During the crossing the child grew increasingly heavy, so that the giant barely reached the far shore. The "child" then revealed Himself as Christ and told Christopher (Greek for "Christ-bearer") that he had just borne the weight of the world on his shoulders. Christopher planted his staff by the side of the river, where it instantly became a palm tree, and set out on a career of preaching and brothel closing. Christopher's cult was strong throughout the Middle Ages, for it was believed that anyone who looked upon his image before noon would not die that day. His popularity declined during the so-called Enlightenment but has flourished in our own age of dangerous road and air travel; a Saint Christopher medal dangles from the rearview mirror of many an agnostic's automobile. In 1969 the doubtless mythical Christopher's Feast was expunged from the official Roman Catholic liturgical calendar, but Christopher remains the best known and probably most loved of all the Patron Saints.

THE FEAST OF SAINT JAMES THE GREATER

Apostle drafted by Spain, 1st century

Patron of furriers, Guatemala, horsemen, laborers, Nicaragua, soldiers, Spain, veterinarians; invoked against arthritis and rheumatism • (emblem: scallop shell)

One of the original twelve Apostles and the brother of Saint John the Evangelist, James was recruited by Jesus when he was fishing. James and John, called the Sons of Thunder, soon became part of His inner circle. James once brought back to life a boy who had been dead for five weeks. When the boy's father heard of the miracle, he sputtered that his son was no more alive than the roasted fowl on the table. The fowl rose from the plate, refeathered himself, and flew away. Though he was beheaded in Jerusalem—the first Apostle to be martyred by King Herod—a concourse of Angels transported James's body to Spain. Centuries later his relics were taken to Compostela, where miracles took place and the name Sant'Iago became the rallying cry of the Spanish army during its eight-hundred-year struggle with the Moors. The largely ignoble conquistadors who arrived in the New World were energized by stories of Santiago Matamoros, or Saint James the Moor-Killer. James, the gentle fisherman who had centuries before died and gone to Heaven, had now become a bloodthirsty warrior-Saint.

26. THE FEAST OF SAINT ANNE

Mother of the BVM, 1st century

Patron of broom makers, cabinetmakers, carpenters, childless women, grandmothers, housekeepers, housewives, lace makers, miners, old-clothes dealers, seamstresses, stablemen, women in labor; invoked against infertility and poverty • (emblems: door, matron with a child and a book)

The mother of Mary and grandmother of Jesus, Anne somehow contrived to conceive her daughter "immaculately," that is, without the stain of "original sin," which is normally transmitted by the act of sexual intercourse. In the fifteenth century she appeared to Saint Colette in a vision and confirmed the persistent rumors that she had been married three times. In Brittany it is widely believed that Anne was a princess of that country who had emigrated (in a "ship of light" piloted by an Angel) to Judea. In her old age Anne is supposed to have returned to France, where she was visited by her Divine Grandson, Who personally created the fountain at Sainte-Anne-de-la-Palude for her. Saint Anne's entire head, a precious relic, is displayed and venerated (simultaneously) at Lyons, Apt, Aix-la-Chapelle, and Chartres in France; in Bologna; in Sicily; and in Düren, Germany. Martin Luther's decision to become a priest was triggered by a thunderstorm during which he prayed to Saint Anne for protection.

Also: The Feast of Saint Joachim, father of the Blessed Virgin, 1st century B.C.

27. THE FEAST OF SAINT AURELIUS

Foundling pagan raised by Christians, 852

Patron of orphans

alf Moor, half Spaniard, Aurelius and his wife, Natalia, lived as secret Christians in Córdoba while the Moors occupied Spain and had outlawed Christianity. When the couple witnessed a local merchant being mocked and scourged to death for his faith, they blurted out that they too were Christians. The two were immediately beheaded, and their daughters instantly became orphans; thus, presumably, Aurelius's traditional Patronage.

THE FEAST OF SAINT PANTALEON

Physician-martyr, 305

Patron of doctors, Venice; invoked when buying lottery tickets and against consumption • (emblems: lion, nails, sword, vase)

lthough he was raised a Christian, Pantaleon lapsed into apostasy when he became personal physician to Emperor Galerius. After recovering his Faith he took to treating poor patients for free and soon was brutally executed. Because the war cry of Venice was *"Piante lione!"* (Plant the lion!), Pantaleon became the Patron Saint of that city. Its citizens were then known as *pantalons,* and the distinctive trousers they wore were called pantaloons. Thus from the name of a third-century Saint we derive our English words *pants* and *panties.*

THE FEAST OF THE SEVEN SLEEPERS

Slept 208 years, awoke, went back to sleep, 362

Invoked against insomnia • (emblem: poppy)

n this Christian version of Rip van Winkle, seven boys from Ephesus (named Maximian, Malchus, Marcian, Denis, John, Scrapian, and Constantine, if you must know) were escaping persecution by Emperor Decius, when they hid in a cave that was walled up. They then proceeded to sleep for either 208 or 363 years. When they awoke one of the boys furtively entered Ephesus looking to buy bread. The boy paid for the bread with coins that the locals suspected were part of a stolen treasure. They followed him back to the cave and found the rest of the boys stretching and yawning, their complexions quite rosy. Naturally, the sleepers became famous. They are mentioned in the Koran, along with their faithful dog, Katmir, who had stayed with them the whole time and is one of only nine animals permitted to enter Paradise. King Edward the Confessor, who saw them in a vision, divined that when the sleepers turned from their right sides to their left, sorrows—war, pestilence, and famine—fall on the world.

28. THE FEAST OF SAINT SAMSON OF DOL

Dragon-slaying Breton bishop, 565

Invoked for strong children, against eye troubles, insanity, rheumatism • (emblem: dragon)

When he was five (around the year 490—just before Britain degenerated into England), Samson's Celtic parents dedicated him to God. After his ordination at fifteen (a dove perched on his shoulder throughout the ceremony), Samson turned around and dedicated *them*— and his brothers as well—to God. He omitted his little sister, however, allowing her "the world's pomps and pleasures." He then became the prototypical wandering Welsh monk, inspired by visions to travel far and wide, reforming monasteries, intervening in local politics, and naming places after himself. He wound up in Dol, in Celtic France (Brittany), where he became that land's first bishop. (He was ordained such in a dream by Saints Peter, James, and John but recognized by Church authorities.) In sacred art Samson is pictured slaying a dragon, a deed by which he endeared himself to the Bretons.

29. THE FEAST OF SAINT LUPUS OF TROYES

Bishop accused of treason, 478

Invoked against stomachache • (emblem: protecting the city of Troyes from Attila)

This ill-named Frenchman (his name means "wolf") married a sister of Saint Hilary, but after six years they separated (amicably) and donated their estate to the poor. Lupus became bishop of Troyes and in that capacity confronted Attila the Hun in 453. He asked the fearsome invader to spare the province and offered himself as a hostage. Unfortunately, his countrymen misinterpreted his motives and thought him a collaborator, so Lupus was ostracized and ended his days as a solitary hermit.

THE FEAST OF SAINT MARTHA

Christ's robust hostess, 1st century

Patron of dietitians, hemophiliacs, housewives, landlords, waitresses, women workers • (emblem: ladle)

The hardworking sister of Mary and Lazarus and the "hostess of Christ," Martha was the one for whom Jesus raised Lazarus from the dead—although He gently chided her for her household bustling, contrasting it with the contemplative life as exemplified by her beauteous sister, Mary. After the Resurrection, Martha, accompanied by her brother and sister, reportedly landed at Marseilles. She began preaching and working miracles throughout Provence and even vanquished a dragon that was half beast and half fish, longer than a horse, with horns and the tail of a serpent. Martha made the Sign of the Cross over the grotesque creature, tied it up with her girdle, and rallied the crowd to tear it to pieces. She died not long after she saw her sister ascend into Heaven, and in Divine reciprocation Christ served at her funeral Mass and burial. In art she is usually stout, plainly dressed, and holding a ladle or broom but occasionally depicted in her slimmer, more heroic form, conquering the dragon.

THE FEAST OF SAINT OLAF

Wood-whittling Viking king, 1030

Patron of carvers, Norway • (emblem: battle-ax)

After a long career as a Viking pirate, Olaf returned home to Norway and seized power, both as self-appointed king and as a ruthless advocate of Christianity. In his big push to have his subjects baptized in the Faith, he would hack off hands, dig out eyes, and plunder and burn farms of reluctant communicants, afterward justifying his actions by saying, "I had God's honor to defend." Olaf married the illegitimate daughter of the king of Sweden but was ultimately succeeded by his own illegitimate son by a servant girl. Olaf's military victories—described in numerous ballads, some of them two hundred stanzas long—were truly impressive. When coming to the aid of England's King Ethelred the Unready, Olaf actually made London Bridge fall down. By the end

of his bloody twenty-five-year reign, he had managed to alienate all his subjects, who joined forces with King Canute (the Great) of England and Denmark to defeat Olaf in battle, thus earning the Saint his dubious martyrdom. (Although a spring with miraculous healing properties *did* gush forth from his grave.)

30. THE FEAST OF SAINTS ABDON AND SENNEN

Persian coopers, friends, martyrs, 3rd century

Patrons of barrel makers • (emblem: barrels)

Saint Abdon was a Persian cooper, or barrel maker, who, with his friend Sennen, testified in the year 250 or so their Faith in Christ by spitting publicly on pagan idols. They were thrown to the lions and tigers and bears, but the savage creatures declined to harm them, whereupon gladiators hacked them to bits—but "the more their bodies were mangled with wounds, the more were their souls made beautiful by Divine grace." As if to confirm their traditional Patronage, these Saints' holy relics were eventually smuggled to France, concealed in wine barrels.

31. THE FEAST OF SAINT HELEN OF SKÖVDE

Widow who made an ill-timed pilgrimage, 1160

Patron of the falsely accused and those martyred for having moral integrity

A member of Swedish nobility, Helen was noted for her charitable acts and building the church at Skövde. Her daughter married a wicked merchant who was murdered by his disgruntled servants. The victim's family came to investigate his death, and the (guilty) servants fingered Helen as the killer, pointing out that she had left on a pilgrimage suspiciously soon after the murder. It was easy convincing the in-laws of pious Helen's "guilt": they had a long-standing vendetta against Helen's family. They tracked her down and killed her, and miracles were soon reported at her tomb.

Also: The Feast of Saint Abel, slain so long ago by his brother Cain, date unknown; and Saint Hatebrand of Olden-Klooster, a Frisian and a Benedictine monk with a curious name, 1198.

THE FEAST OF SAINT IGNATIUS OF LOYOLA

Author of the original 12-step program, 1556

Patron of the military, religious retreats, spiritual exercises; invoked against scruples • (emblem: two wolves at a hanging cauldron)

T he founder of the Jesuits was raised to be a soldier and a courtier—a knight. He was the youngest of

eleven children, a five-foot-two, swaggering redhead, "a man given to the vanities of the world," as he later wrote of himself. During his wild youth he fathered an illegitimate daughter, Maria de Villarreal, whom he remembered in his will. After a cannonball shattered his shin, Ignatius was confined to bed. He asked for something to read—his tastes ran to romance novels—but his pious sister-in-law gave him a book of Saints' lives. He forthwith dedicated himself to God, dressed as a beggar, and retired to a mountain cave, where he began to practice his original metaphysical-fitness program, the "Spiritual Exercises." He prayed for seven-hour sessions, during which time his hair and fingernails grew to unseemly lengths. Then, at thirty-three years of age, Ignatius went back to school, studying Latin with a class of eleven-year-olds. By age forty-three he was a master of arts in Paris, where he was twice imprisoned (and released) by the Inquisition for his unorthodox evangelical methods. But his disciples remained loyal to his cause, and after being ordained priests they (Bobadilla, Favre, Laynez, Rodriguez, Salmeron, and Xavier) became, in 1540, the first members of the Society of Jesus, the original Jebbies. Our Saint is traditionally invoked by those troubled with scruples, that is, suffering from an overly delicate conscience. Although throughout their glorious history the Jesuits have been accused of many faults, having scruples has never been among them.

THE FEAST OF SAINT NEOT

Dwarf who lived in a well, 877

Patron of fish • (emblem: fish)

A descendant of Anglo-Saxon royalty, Neot was so vertically challenged that he had to stand on a stool to say Mass. His reported height of fifteen inches has caused him to be labeled, irreverently, the Pygmy Saint. He preferred to pray and meditate in a well, saying the cold water helped him focus. Celts claim Neot as one of their tribe, since he possessed that gift, unique to Irish Saints, of multiplying fish until everyone was fed—but Neot enjoyed playing with fish as well as working miracles with them. His relics, including an arm, a cloak, a comb, and a cheekbone, were dispersed all around Britain, arousing much veneration.

Also: The Venerable Solanus Casey, priest, who in his youth became friends with members of the Jesse James gang. He was renowned for his work with the poor and his penchant for playing the fiddle in front of the Blessed Sacrament, 1857.

❧ August ☙

1. LAMMAS DAY

Today, the first loaf from the new harvested wheat is offered in church.

THE FEAST OF SAINT ALPHONSUS MARY DE LIGOURI
Sin expert, 1787

Patron of confessors, moral theologians • (emblem: bishop with a wreath of roses)

Born in Naples in 1696, Alphonsus became a lawyer at the age of sixteen but, upon losing his first case, became a priest and in 1732 founded the missionary Redemptorist Order. In his extremely detailed handbooks for confessors, Alphonsus took a moderate position between the extremes of "all sex is evil" and "some sex is good": he concluded that *almost* all sex is evil. So he considered marital intercourse and unmarried handholding only venial sins—provided, of course, that no pleasure was taken or given.

THE FEAST OF SAINT FRIARD
Pious French peasant, 577

Invoked against wasps

Some nasty fellows were jeering at Friard, a hermit who lived with Saint Secundel. But as they mocked his piety they were set upon by a swarm of wasps. Friard, forgiving all, prayed for the louts, and the wasps soon took off.

2. THE FEAST OF THE VIRGIN OF THE ANGELS

Marian statue called La Negrita

Patron of Costa Rica

The Franciscans of Assisi have long celebrated the Feast of Our Lady of the Angels today, and by something more than a coincidence it was on this very day, in 1636, near the village of Cartago, that an old Indian found an image of the Virgin and Child carved in stone. However often he tried to move it, it moved back again—so the people built a church around it, and in the fullness of time the government of the newly independent Costa Rica declared it their national Patron.

THE FEAST OF SAINT SIDWELL

Rustic virgin martyr, date unknown

Patron of farmers • (emblem: maiden holding a scythe at a well)

The name Sidwell combines the words *scythe* and *well*—and wouldn't you know it?—this maiden of (pre-Saxon) Exeter is pictured standing beside a well, with a scythe in her hand. In her other hand she holds her head—for this Saint was decapitated by reapers in the pay of her wicked, jealous stepmother. An even worse fate befell Sidwell's equally beautiful and innocent sister, Jutwara. When that virgin complained of chest pains, their stepmother recommended she apply compresses of cream cheese to her breasts—then informed her own dastardly son Bana that Jutwara was pregnant. He confronted the chaste maiden, confirmed his suspicions by observing her moist and swollen condition, and struck off her head.

3. THE FEAST OF SAINT LYDIA

Sometime hostess to Saint Paul, 1st century

Patron of cloth dyers

She is known as Lydia Purpuraria, that is, "the seller of purple," for that was her employment in the city of Thyatira, Turkey, once famous for its dye works. She chanced to be in Philippi at the time of Paul's visit there and had the honor to become the great Apostle's first convert; subsequently he was frequently her houseguest.

4. THE FEAST OF SAINT JOHN BAPTIST MARIE VIANNEY (THE "CURÉ OF ARS")

Simpleminded cleric, 1859

Patron of parish priests

In the year 1859 Charles Darwin published *On the Origin of Species,* Karl Marx issued his *Critique of Political Economy,* and a hundred thousand French pilgrims traveled to the village of Ars-en-Dombes to confess their sins to a pious simpleton known as the Curé of Ars. Young John Baptist Marie, although stupid to a remarkable degree, was studying (with great difficulty) for the priesthood when, at the age of twenty-four, he was conscripted (by mistake) into Napoleon's army. After an amnesty for draft dodgers was declared, Our Saint emerged from the barn where he had been hiding and resumed his studies. Ordained at last, he was posted to Ars, a backwater parish of 250 souls. There, subsisting only on potatoes, he established a miracle-working shrine to the (utterly mythological) Saint Philomena. But it was primarily as a hearer of confessions that he gained worldwide renown. He was gifted, it seems, at "reading hearts"—which meant he knew one's sins without being told. This presumably saved penitents both time and embarrassment. Sinners made appointments months in advance; a special train service was laid on from Paris to Ars. But the Devil wasn't about to stand idly by while all of France was shriven of its sins—the Evil One frequently attacked the tiny parish priest, administering fearful beatings to his body and once going so far as to set the curé's bed on fire. (The twosome did, on occasion, indulge in a friendly game of chess.) John Baptist Marie did not, understandably enough, enjoy his life as an object of intense international and infernal attentions. He yearned to become a cloistered monk and on three separate occasions ran away from his church to do so. Each time his ecclesiastical superiors obliged him to return. Seventy years after his death the Curé of Ars was papally declared the Patron Saint of parish priests.

THE FEAST OF SAINT SITHNEY

Singularly misogynic hermit, 6th century

Patron of mad dogs • (emblem: snarling dog)

A Cornish monk and nephew of Saint David, Sithney was known for his holy misogyny. He once roundly cursed a housewife for doing her wash in his well—and the woman's brat promptly disappeared. It was widely assumed the child had plunged from a nearby cliff, and Sithney heard some sniping about it, but it was he who discovered the toddler quite unharmed, playing on the beach below. For reasons of His own, God once offered Sithney the post of Patron Saint of girls. The Saint objected that the flighty creatures would be forever pestering him to supply them with fine clothes and/or husbands. He protested that he'd rather be Patron of mad dogs. And so he is.

5. THE FEAST OF SAINTS ADDAI AND MARI

Missionary bishops, 2nd century

Patrons of Iran, Syria

King Abgar the Black of Persia, though not of the Faith, was a pen pal of Jesus Christ. In one of his letters Abgar mentioned to Our Lord an excruciating disease from which he was suffering and inquired (tactfully) about a possible cure. The compassionate Savior immediately assigned the case to the Apostle Saint Thomas, who passed it along to a disciple named Addai. Addai set out at once for Abgar's capital city of Edessa, carrying with him the miraculous (but not, alas, autographed) portrait of Jesus known today as the Mandalyion. Addai not only cured King Abgar but also converted him and his subjects to the Faith. Addai then dispatched *his* disciple Mari on a mission to destroy pagan temples and erect monasteries in their stead. Like the Nestorian Christians of old, present-day Catholic Chaldeans venerate both these Saints highly.

THE FEAST OF SAINT AFRA

Reformed madam, martyr, 304

Patron of fallen women, medicinal herbs • (emblem: hands tied to stake, surrounded by flames)

This daughter of Saint Hilaria became a prostitute and a brothel-keeper in Augsburg. During a time of persecution Saint Narcissus, a fugitive bishop, sought shelter in her establishment. She and all her employees were soon converted to the True Faith and arrested along with their holy guest. At the trial Afra cleverly debated the judge (who had once, ironically enough, purchased her favors), but in the end she was burned to death. In Ahalt, reciting the magic spell *"Afra nostra"* makes shotguns malfunction.

THE FEAST OF SAINT OSWALD

King of Northumbria, 642

Patron of English royalty • (emblem: raven)

Baptized on Iona while in Scottish exile, Oswald returned south determined to Christianize the whole of Britain or die trying—which he did, in the Battle of Maserfield, at the hands of the pagan champion Penda of Mercia.

6. THE FEAST OF THE TRANSFIGURATION

Feast Day of cleaners, pork butchers, c. 30

Three Gospels attest that Jesus took Peter, James, and John to a high mountain; there he was transfigured (*transfiguratus est*), "his face did shine as the sun," and on either side of Him appeared Moses and Elias. Saint Gregory the Illuminator, in establishing the calendar, had this Feast replace the sensual pagan festival of Aphrodite, called Vartavarh (roseflame), and in 1456 Pope Callistus III made it a Feast of the Universal Church, to commemorate the defeat of the Turks. Today in Rome the Pope crushes grapes into a chalice and blesses the new wine.

7. THE FEAST OF SAINT ALBERT OF TRAPANI

Severe Sicilian monk, 1306

Invoked against earthquakes, jaundice, stiff neck • (emblem: female Devil with a fish tail)

Like most Saints venerated in earthquake-prone Sicily, Albert is invoked for protection against such disasters; his selfless nursing of plague victims also entitles him to be appealed to by sufferers from many physical ailments. He was a Carmelite friar at Messina, famous for his knack of refuting Jews in debate, as well as for the excessive severity of his self-discipline.

THE FEAST OF SAINT CAJETAN

Poverty-obsessed founder of the Theatine order, 1547

Invoked by gamblers • (emblem: lily)

Cajetan, a nobleman, a lawyer, and a scholar, became a priest in Rome and in 1523 founded the Theatine Order in an attempt to restore dignity to the clergy. Unfortunately his partner in this venture was the most undignified Pietro Caraffa—later Pope Paul IV—of whom it has been said, "If his mother had foreseen his career she would have strangled him at birth." Due to either Paul IV's notoriety or the ascendancy of the Jesuits, the Theatines never really caught on. Cajetan also founded pawnshops in Verona, Venice, and Naples, which explains his Patronage of gamblers.

THE FEAST OF SAINT DOMETIUS

Dragon-taming bishop, 362

Invoked against sciatica

This Persian, who upon his conversion became a holy monk holed up in a cave in Mesopotamia, inspired many in his neighborhood. When Dometius was bishop of Byzantium, Emperor Julian the Apostate, jealous of his popularity, had him stoned to death. His son, Metrophanes, convinced Constantine to make Byzantium the capital of the empire. It was in Syria, long after Dometius' death, that his reputation as a healer of sciatica was promoted.

8. THE FEAST OF SAINT CYRIACUS

Slave, faith healer, martyr, 304

Invoked against demonic possession, eye disease • (emblem: chained Devil)

Cyriacus was an indentured servant building an enormous bathhouse in Rome when he noticed that the emperor's daughter, Artemia, was possessed by a demon. Cyriacus cast out the evil spirit, and in gratitude the emperor granted Our Saint a sabbatical in Persia. There he exorcised a demon from the king's daughter, who had been likewise diabolically afflicted. Cyriacus not only cured the princess but also converted the king and 430 of his courtiers to the Faith. He then returned to Rome, where for thanks he was bound in chains, dipped in boiling pitch, and decapitated. He was invoked throughout the Middle Ages as a specialist in exorcising Devils; as such he is one of the fourteen holy helpers, upon whose collective Feast Day his personal Feast Day falls.

THE FEAST OF SAINT DOMINIC

Heretic-smiting founder of the Dominicans, 1221

Patron of astronomers, the Dominican Republic • (emblems: star, dog with torch in its mouth)

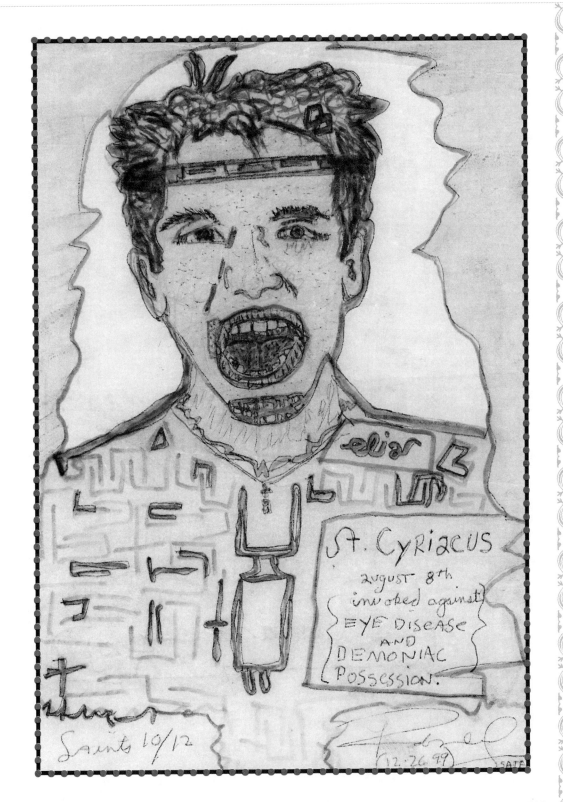

At his baptism Dominic's mother saw a star shining on his breast, which accounts for his Patronage of astronomers. In 1203, Dominic visited Languedoc in the south of France, where he was shocked to see shameless heresy—in this case the Albigensian, or Cathar, heresy—being practiced everywhere with utter impunity. For the next decade he and a small band of like-minded clerics tramped the dusty countryside around Toulouse preaching a return to orthodoxy, with wonderful results. In Dominic's wake marched the great army (financed by the Pope and the king of France) of Simon de Montfort. Whenever an individual or a

community clung stubbornly to Catharism, he, she, or it was put to fire and the sword. Dominic always attributed his success against the Cathars to the power of rosary beads, a device he appears to have invented. In 1216, Dominic founded his religious order, a paramilitary organization of ultraorthodox heretic bashers at first called the Friars Preachers but soon to be known everywhere as the Dominicans. Dominic was famous for his miracles: he raised numerous deserving persons from the dead. To settle doctrinal arguments he would throw books—his own and his opponents'—into a bonfire, where Error would burn, but from which Truth would emerge unscorched. It is also asserted that Dominic met and was admired by the gentle Saint Francis of Assisi, but this strains credulity. Dominic had been dead for ten years when, in 1231, Pope Gregory IX instituted the Inquisition; but we can be certain there was joy in Heaven when Our Saint learned the Dominicans were put in charge of it.

THE FEAST OF THE FOURTEEN HOLY HELPERS

An all-star team of heavenly Patrons

These fourteen worthies are the most powerful of all the miracle-working Saints. Miraculously (for instance), they number nineteen: Acacius, Anthony of Padua, Barbara, Blaise, Catherine of Alexandria, Christopher, Cyriacus, Denis, Elmo, Eustace, George, Giles, Leonard, Margaret of Antioch, Nicholas of Myra, Pantaleon, Rock, Sebastian, and Vitus. Their cult reached its (well-nigh idolatrous) height (understandably enough) during the Black Plague (1347–1351); it was strongly discouraged by the Council of Trent (1545). This Feast itself, like the Feasts of many of the individual Saints, has been officially suppressed in the ecumenical interest of making Roman Catholicism less fun.

THE FEAST OF SAINT HORMISDAS

Persian courtier, martyr, 420

Patron of stable boys • (emblem: camel)

King Varannes of Persia was a pagan tyrant with a live-and-let-live attitude toward his Christian subjects. However, the Christian bishop, Abdas, was a hard-liner, with a policy of destroying wholesale pagan shrines, temples, and stat-ues. Overreacting, perhaps, Varannes ordered Abdas and his flock rounded up and fed live to rats. One of the Christians, the youth Hormisdas, received a re-duced sentence because of his noble birth: his punishment consisted of being made sanitary engineer in the royal camel stables. One day His Majesty chanced to espy young Hormisdas, now reduced to a ragged, begrimed, and malodorous urchin. Moved to pity, the king approached Our Saint, offering him a bath and a clean linen tunic if he would but deny his Savior. The boy refused, in the strongest terms, and Varannes had him executed immediately.

THE FEAST OF THE BLESSED MARY MACKILLOP

Excommunicated nun, 1909

Patron of opposition to Church authorities • (emblem: eucalyptus)

Mary MacKillop and her fel-low sisters were working with aborigines, the homeless, pros-titutes, and alcoholics in Australia when headstrong Mary ran afoul of the local bishop. He had her ex-communicated for disobedience, and even the nuns working under her were stripped of their sacred vows. Mary prevailed and was reinstated, though she continued to battle bishops and priests for the rest of her life. Even when she was into advanced age, Church officials accused her (falsely) of being an alcoholic embezzler. She is the first per-son from Australia to be beatified.

Also: Saint Altman, an outspoken bishop of Passau who supported Pope Gregory VII against King Henry IV, 1091.

9. THE FEAST OF SAINT EDITH STEIN (SISTER TERESA BENEDICTA DE CRUCE)

Jewish convert gassed at Auschwitz, 1942

Patron of Europe • (emblem: nun wearing the star of David on her habit)

Edith Stein was born in Germany to an Orthodox Jewish family on Yom Kippur, 1891. A child prodigy, she was in her teens when she rejected all religion, becoming a fervent atheist, feminist, and professor of philosophy. After nursing victims of World War I, she happened on the autobiography of another intense woman, the mystical Saint Teresa of Ávila. Edith underwent a profound transformation and at the age of twenty-nine converted to Catholicism. Her new religion, however, did not prevent her from losing her teaching job because she was Jewish. Nor did it stop her from praying with her mother in the synagogue. As she said, "My return to God made me feel Jewish again." After she entered the Carmelite convent the politics of the time dictated she wear the Star of David on her habit. In 1933 she tried (unsuccessfully) to see Pope Pius XI and continued to urge him (again, unsuccessfully) to issue an encyclical against the persecution of the Jews. The Carmelites, in an effort to protect her from the Gestapo, shifted her about, finally offering her and her sister Rosa sanctuary in a convent in Holland. It was there that the Nazis arrested them both. A witness who saw the sisters get into the police van said Edith took Rosa's hand and said, "Come, Rosa, we are going for our people." Before she was gassed Edith, never sensing a conflict of interest, offered up her life for the Jewish people, the Carmelites, and the end of war. She was canonized in 1998—the necessary miracle being the recovery of a child from a Tylenol overdose after its parents prayed to Blessed Edith. Her big booster was her fellow phenomenologist Pope John Paul II, but some Catholics and Jews have objected to her canonization, maintaining that she was killed not for her (Catholic) Faith but for her (Jewish) parents. Sadly, this controversy makes Edith, a figure of reconciliation during her life on earth, one of divisiveness now that she's in Heaven.

THE FEAST OF SAINT EMYGDIUS

Idol-smashing German bishop, martyr, 304

Invoked against earthquakes • (emblem: bishop holding up castle wall)

A citizen of Trier, Emygdius was converted to Christianity in the year 300 or so and immediately began rushing about destroying the idols of the locally popular but nevertheless false gods. Then, one step ahead of the enraged pagan clergy, he fled to Rome, where he was made a bishop. His legend is, all authorities agree, historically worthless. But since he is a protector of those in danger from earthquakes, his Feast is to this day vigorously celebrated through Italy, and by Italian Americans living along the earthquake-prone San Andreas Fault in California.

10. THE FEAST OF SAINT BESSE

AWOL Roman soldier, martyr, 300

Patron of draft dodgers

I n the villages of the Italian Alps on the tenth day of August, the people—young men in particular—honor Saint Besse with joyous festivities and invoke his heavenly assistance in staying out of the army. Besse himself was a Roman soldier, a member of the famous Theban Legion commanded by Saint Maurice. Near Lake Geneva in the year 290, all 6,660—or 600, accounts vary—of these brave Christian warriors refused to honor the emperor Maximian as a god and were decimated (one man in ten was beheaded). As they persisted in their Faith, the process was repeated until everyone was slain except Besse, who somehow escaped and made his way to the Soana Valley, where he preached the Gospel to the natives. Ironically, Besse achieved his martyr's crown anyway—he was stabbed and/or thrown from a cliff by unreconstructed pagans—but for his example of resistance to military service he is still venerated by the fiercely independent denizens of the area.

THE FEAST OF SAINT LAWRENCE

Martyred on a gridiron, 258

Patron of archivists, butchers, Ceylon, cooks, librarians, the poor, restaurateurs; invoked against fire, lumbago • (emblem: gridiron)

Each and every Friday since the year 257, Lawrence has been privileged to lead a suffering soul out of Purgatory and into Heaven as a reward for his own heroic martyrdom. He was keeper of the library of sacred books during the holy papacy of Sixtus II and the unholy reign of the emperor Valerian. After Lawrence was arrested the greedy emperor commanded him to surrender the Church's treasures. Lawrence asked for three days to do so—and on the third day he presented, assembled before the prefect's palace, thousands of lepers, orphans, the blind, and the lame, as well as widows and virgins. "Here," he announced, "is all the Church's treasure." Far from enlightening the prefect, this gesture appears to have enraged him. Lawrence was subjected to a sequence of tortures nearly unique in the gory annals of martyrdom: he was scourged, branded, clubbed, stretched on the rack, and torn with hooks before being placed on a gridiron and roasted. After a while Lawrence spoke: "Turn me over, I'm done on this side." His emblem in art is a gridiron, for which reason cooks have taken him as their Patron, but it has recently been suggested that a scribe's error in transcription accounts for his legend: meaning to write *"Passes EST"* (he suffered), the author of Lawrence's *Life* may have written *"Assess EST"* (he was cooked). Be that as it may, the gridiron on which he died is on display in his titular church, San Lorenzo, in Rome: and a jar of his melted fat was donated to the Escorial in Spain. Four hundred years after his burial, when his tomb was opened to receive the newly discovered bones of Saint Stephen, Lawrence moved over to make room for his guest—hence his nickname, the Courteous Spaniard.

11. THE FEAST OF SAINT ALEXANDER "CARBONARIS"

Peasant-bishop, martyr, 275

Patron of charcoal burners • (emblem: as a charcoal burner)

When Saint Gregory the Wonder Worker was in Asia Minor, searching at length and in vain for a candidate worthy to serve as bishop, some wag sarcastically suggested appointing Alexander, a grimy and ragged local character who turned out to be both holy and wise. Alexander was martyred in the year 275, dying—ironically enough—by fire.

THE FEAST OF SAINT CLARE

Saint Francis's female counterpart, 1253

Patron of embroiderers, television; invoked against eye disease • (emblem: monstrance)

Beautiful and kind, lively and rich, the eldest daughter of the Offreduccio family had many noble suitors; but on the night of Palm Sunday, 1212, Clare of Assisi eloped. Clad in her best gown, wearing all her jewels, she slipped away from her father's house to become a bride. Awaiting her at a small church was Saint Francis of Assisi. Clare removed all her finery and put on a sackcloth robe. Francis himself cut off her flowing hair and married her to Christ. In the rules for the order she founded (now called the Poor Clares), Our Saint was a stickler for Franciscan details. Her followers wore no shoes, ate no meat, slept on the ground, and lived in absolute poverty—that is, on alms alone. As individuals and as a community, they were to own *nothing.* This policy in particular scandalized wealthy churchmen—several Popes tried to persuade her of its folly—but Clare had her way. Because she and her sisters stitched vestments and altar cloths, Clare was adopted by embroiderers as their Patron. Her name, which means "light," accounts for her traditional invocation by those with sore eyes. And Pope Pius XII, in 1958, declared her Patron of television. It seems that one Christmas Eve, when she was old and sick, she could not leave her bed to partake in the midnight services. But in her cell she heard the singing and on the wall saw clearly, as if by television, the manger at Bethlehem.

THE FEAST OF SAINT PHILOMENA

Marvelously beautiful, entirely mythical virgin martyr

Patron of children of Mary, destitute mothers, the living rosary, lost causes; invoked in desperate situations • (emblem: anchor)

Philomena's tomb was discovered in the catacombs, where it was determined that she was a fifteen-year-old virgin. Her relics were transported to a church, miracles were reported at her shrine, and sixteen years after her death she was dubbed a wonder worker. Stories evolved about her "life" and her cult spread, due, in no small part, to Saint John Vianney, a devotee of Philomena, who graciously gave her credit for his many phenomena. One Pauline Marie Jaricot advanced her cause: Philomena cured her formidable heart palpitations, which were so noisy they could be heard from a distance. In 1960 scholars visiting her tomb determined it had been tampered with, and Philomena's name was unceremoniously yanked from the Calendar of Saints by the Sacred Congregation of Rites. Her tomb has been likened to that of the Unknown Soldier, and whatever her true identity, a pink candle is suggested in asking favors of her.

12. THE FEAST OF SAINT PORCARIUS

Considerate abbot, 782

On an island off the French Riviera was once a community of more than five hundred monks and novices. It was known as Lérins, and its abbot was Porcarius. One night an Angel appeared to that holy man and warned him that fierce Saracen marauders out of Africa were approaching. The abbot sent away to safety the students and youngest monks on the only available ship, then exhorted the remainder to gather around him and bravely suffer martyrdom, which, upon the arrival of the pirates, they did.

Also: The Feast of Saint James Tam, a Vietnamese priest beheaded for his Faith, 1838; he is one of the 116 Martyrs of Tonkin collectively canonized by Pope John Paul II in 1986, when his "Saint factory" was working to maximum capacity.

13. THE FEAST OF SAINT CASSIAN OF IMOLA

Stabbed with pens, date unknown

Patron of teachers • (emblem: stabbed by pens)

In 1952 the devout Catholic stenographers of Naples petitioned Pope Pius XII to assign them a Patron Saint appropriate to their vocation, and on December 23 of that year His Holiness informed them by Apostolic Letter that Saint Cassian was now and henceforth to be their heavenly example and protector. Imagine their chagrin when they consulted *Lives of the Saints* and discovered that Cassian was a martyr who had been stabbed to death with *pens*! He had been an unpopular schoolteacher, convicted of Christianity and condemned to death, which sentence was carried out by his own pupils, who happily carved, slashed, and punctured him with the sharp steel writing implements of the time. It seemed that Pope Pius XII was playing a cruel joke on those Neapolitan takers of dictation, when in fact the Holy Father had recommended another Cassian, who had been a court stenographer in Tangier, and whose Feast Day is December 3.

THE FEAST OF SAINT CONCORDIA

Saint Lawrence's childhood nurse, martyr, 258

Patron of nannies • (emblem: matron scourged with leaded whips)

The story of the martyrdom of Saint Lawrence was endlessly embellished with gruesome details and secondary characters, included Hippolytus (see next)—the jailer Lawrence converted and baptized—and Concordia, the old lady who had long ago been Hippolytus' childhood nurse. She, too, subscribed to the Faith and suffered for it, being scourged to death with leaden whips.

THE FEAST OF SAINT HIPPOLYTUS

Saint Lawrence's jailer, martyr, 258

Patron of horses, prison guards • (emblem: dragged by horses)

According to legend, when the famous martyr Saint Lawrence was imprisoned, Hippolytus was assigned to guard his cell and was both converted and baptized by the Saint. After Lawrence's ghastly execution Hippolytus managed to gather and preserve many of his charred relics—for which crime he himself was sentenced to death: he was tied by his feet to a team of horses and dragged through thistles and thorns until he joined his mentor in Paradise. In Greek mythology, by a curious coincidence, a son of the hero Theseus, likewise named Hippolytus, died in the same manner.

THE FEAST OF SAINT RADEGUND

Unhappily married Frankish queen, lover of poetry, 587

Patron of Cambridge University, those in difficult marriages • (emblem: chains)

At twelve Radegund was captured by the Franks and at eighteen married to their sordid king, Clotaire. Her husband preferred the company of fast women, killed her brother, and declared that Radegund alone was responsible for their childlessness. After six years of this torment she left the cad and his court to join the convent—who could blame her? She founded the monastery of the Holy Cross at Poitiers, unusual in that its nuns pursued a course of scholarship as well as piety. It may be for this reason that England, most particularly Cambridge University, adopted this French queen as its own.

14. THE FEAST OF SAINT MAXIMILIAN KOLBE

Martyred at Auschwitz by lethal injection, 1941

Patron of drug addicts and their families,
journalists, political prisoners •
(emblem: priest in concentration camp)

This Polish Franciscan priest died of a lethal injection administered to him in a cell in Auschwitz. Father Kolbe had actually *volunteered* to die—that is, he took the place of a condemned prisoner because that man had a family. The family man, having survived the Holocaust, was a witness at Maximilian's beatification; even before he was Pope, John Paul II lobbied long and hard for his countryman's canonization. In his book *Making Saints,* Kenneth Woodward observes that, upon his papal canonization (November 9, 1982), Maximilian Kolbe became a new *kind* of Saint, "a martyr of charity."

THE FEAST OF SAINT WERENFRID

Salad-loving missionary, 760

Patron of vegetable gardeners; invoked against gout • (emblem: ship bearing coffin)

The Christian Anglo-Saxons were tireless in their attempts to save the heathens of Holland; seemingly everyone whose name began with *W* became an English missionary to the (all too appropriately named) Low Countries—Saints Walburga, Werenfrid, Wigbert, Wilfrid, Willehad, Willibald, Willibrord, Winfrith, Winnebald, and Wiro. Werenfrid is venerated in the Netherlands, where he harvested souls and vegetables until his death.

15. THE FEAST OF THE ASSUMPTION INTO HEAVEN OF THE BLESSED VIRGIN MARY

Patron of fish dealers, France, harness makers, Hungary, Jamaica, New Caledonia, Paraguay, South Africa

This day commemorates when the Mother of God, recently deceased, was "assumed," body *and* soul, into Heaven; she is the only human being, besides Her Son, *bodily* present in Heaven—and you'd better believe it, because Pope Pius XII in 1950 defined it, infallibly, ex cathedra, as dogma. At the moment of the actual Assumption, "Doubting" Thomas couldn't believe his own eyes—until Mary, midair, dropped an item of apparel into his hands. In Hungary today Mary is feted as the Great Lady of the Hungarians, as King Saint Stephen of Hungary declared her; in France the season's herbs are blessed today; and Irish tradition has it that anyone who takes a swim today (fortuitously, in the middle of the summer) will never die by drowning.

THE FEAST OF SAINT ARNULF OF SOISSONS

Reluctant bishop, 1087

Patron of bakers, brewers • (emblem: long-handled fork)

Arnulf of Soissons (no relation to Arnulf of Metz) was a French soldier turned clergyman. He unwillingly accepted the position of abbot of his monastery, and even more reluctantly became the bishop of Soissons. Driven from his episcopate by invaders, he moved to Flanders. When a plague broke out he noticed that the water drinkers were dropping like, well, flies, but the beer drinkers were thriving. He hastened to brew up a big batch of beer and saved the town. In art Our Saint is always depicted holding what appears to be a long-handled fork—possibly a utensil for adding hops to his brew—but it was interpreted as a baker's shovel, which accounts for Arnulf's traditional Patronage of bakers.

THE FEAST OF SAINT TARSICIUS

Brave boy martyr, 3rd century

Patron of first communicants • (emblem: kneeling among stones, chalice before him)

The cult of "Little Saint Tarsicius" arose after his appearance in a Victorian historical-romance-Catholic-propaganda novel entitled *Fabiola* (1854). A comely (but manly) lad of noble birth, Tarsicius volunteered to carry the Blessed Sacrament from the hands of Pope Saint Sylvester, then hiding in the catacombs, to imprisoned Christians awaiting martyrdom. Set upon by a gang of street toughs, Tarsicius steadfastly refused to reveal his holy mission, or surrender into their profane hands the sacred Host. So they stoned him to death. His shining example of piety and courage suitably intimidated generations of parochial school first graders.

16. THE FEAST OF SAINT ARMEL

Dragon-taming abbot, 552

Invoked against fever, gout, headache, rheumatism • (emblem: dragon)

The northeast coast of France is, to this day, called Brittany because of the many saintly Celtic-British monks who migrated there at the time of the Anglo-Saxon invasion of their homeland. Armel, a cousin of Samson of Dol, was among them; he was famous as a dragon tamer and worker of miraculous cures, for which reason many French hospitals are named in his honor. In 1485 (933 years after Armel's death), Henry Tudor (soon to be King Henry VII) launched an invasion of England *from* Brittany and claimed to have been saved from shipwreck through this Saint's Divine intercession.

THE FEAST OF SAINT ROCK

Dog-accompanied plague victim, 1378

Patron of bachelors, cattle, doctors, dog lovers, prisoners; invoked against

AIDS, cholera, contagious diseases, plague, problem knees, skin diseases • (emblem: cripple, dog bringing him bread)

This French-born Saint is equally revered in Italy as Rocco (Rocky), in Spain as Roque, and in England as Rock. Though he enjoyed a privileged youth, he gave all his property to the poor and set out on a pilgrimage to Rome. A plague was then ravaging northern Italy, and Rock traveled from town to town nursing its victims. Then he became infected, developing a hideous sore on his thigh. Knowing he was contagious, he selflessly wandered into the forest to die alone—but was soon visited and befriended by a dog. For some time the noble beast daily brought the ailing Saint bread and other food snatched from its master's table. Eventually Rock recovered and made his way back home to Montpellier. Unrecognized because of his emaciated condition, he was cast into a dungeon as a spy. There he languished for five years, ministered to by an Angel. (The jail must have had a "no dogs allowed" policy.) After his death Rock was recognized by a cross-shaped birthmark on his breast, and much mourned by his relatives. The letters *VSR* (*Viva Saint Roch*) were once inscribed over most of the doorways of Europe as surefire protection against pestilence. The Saint's cult, which declined as the Black Death abated, was revived during the cholera epidemics of the nineteenth century.

THE FEAST OF SAINT STEPHEN OF HUNGARY

Civilizing monarch, 1038

Patron of bricklayers, Hungary, kings, stonecutters, those who have lost children • (emblem: banner and cross)

As the first millennium (the year 1000) approached, the end of the world—that is, of Christendom—seemed, verily, to be at hand. From the north heathen Viking raids continued. Infidel Moors from the south occupied Spain. And from the east, from Hungary of all places, came merciless hordes of pagan Magyar horsemen, overrunning Moravia and Burgundy and advancing on Paris. Their very name in French, *ogres,* became a byword for super- (or sub-) human evil. Then, providentially, the Hungarians received the gift of Faith, which happened to include the gift of a splendid crown for King Vaik, sent to him by the Pope in 1001. Vaik was soon baptized, and in a tribute to the first martyr took his name, Stephen.

17. THE FEAST OF SAINT HYACINTH

Crusade-promoting missionary, 1257

Patron of Lithuania • (emblem: curing the bite of a scorpion)

A native of Poland, this Dominican preached both the Gospel's message of peace and his country's bloody crusade against the Prussians. His connection with the flower of the same name is a curious one—his name was Jacob, which the Poles pronounce "Jacko"; this in turn was rendered into Latin as Jacinthus, which means "hyacinth."

THE FEAST OF SAINT MAMAS

Lion-taming martyr, 275

Patron of nurses, shepherds; invoked against colic • (emblem: wild beasts licking him)

amas was a Christian shepherd boy of Caesarea, gifted with a wonderful power over animals both wild and tame. Arrested, he would not deny his Faith and was thrown to the lions in the amphitheater; rather than attack the lad, those ferocious carnivores gathered around him "like a flock of sheep." Soldiers were forthwith commanded to slay Mamas with swords, but one especially large and ferocious jungle cat stood guard over Our Saint. Mamas, eager to achieve the crown of martyrdom, ordered the noble beast to behave himself, and while the pagan soldiers did their duty, the lion stood by, weeping.

18. THE FEAST OF SAINT AGAPITUS

Disemboweled martyr, 274

Invoked against colic • (emblem: hung over flames)

his fifteen-year-old Christian lad was martyred at the Palestrina. He was beaten, jailed, starved, had hot coals dropped on his head, was hung upside down over smoke, and then had boiling water poured on his abdomen (which accounts for the colic connection). When he continued not only to live but to praise the Lord, the governor, Antiochus, fell off his throne in a fit and died. Emperor Aurelian himself then ordered the faithful and courageous boy decapitated. No fewer than five complete skeletons of this Saint are venerated throughout Italy.

THE FEAST OF SAINT HELENA

Empress who found the True Cross, 329

Patron of archaeologists • (emblem: crowned, holding cross, hammer, nails)

elena was either the daughter of that celebrated British monarch Old King Cole or a barmaid in a Turkish saloon. About the year 270 she married Constantius, an officer of the Roman forces then occupying her homeland, whichever it was. She returned with him to Rome and gave birth to a son, Constantine. Then, given the chance of marrying the emperor's daughter and succeeding him as Caesar, her husband divorced Helena and sent her into exile. Remember, these people were pagans. Young Constantine sided with his mother, naturally, and upon his father's death in 306, when he became emperor, recalled her from exile, declared her Augusta, that is, empress, and had coins struck in her honor. A certain General Maxentius disputed Constantine's imperial claims, and the night before the pivotal battle Constantine had a famous vision. He beheld a cross in the sky, surrounded by the words *in hoc signo vinces,* "by this sign you shall conquer." The next day the bridge collapsed under Maxentius' advancing army, and Constantine, while not actually converting to the Christian religion himself, nevertheless legalized it. His middle-aged mother, however, took to the Faith with a passion. As her son continued on his conquering ways to the East (moving the empire's capital to Byzantium, which city he modestly named Constantinople), Helena accompanied him, until, in her eighty-fifth year, she arrived in the Holy Land, where she had a vision of her own: the location of the long-lost True Cross on which Christ died was revealed to her. Under her direction it was duly excavated, along with other priceless relics, such as the Holy Nails and Our Savior's seamless Robe—hence this noble lady's traditional Patronage of archaeologists. A surprising number of pieces of the True Cross are, to this day, commercially available, and the story of the robe was made into *The Robe,* the first movie in CinemaScope.

19. THE FEAST OF SAINT JOAN DELANOUE
Stingy spinster turned holy woman, 1736

Joan owned a religious supply store in Anjou and was such a tightwad that she would refuse credit to the parish priest; she even cried real tears when she put money in the Church collection. However, one day a mysterious stranger called the Widow Souchet visited her, and Joan found herself actually *giving away* a dress. When the widow (who would quote God by saying, "*He* told me . . .") suggested she visit six orphans in a stable, Joan did and took them home with her. Soon other urchins sought refuge with her, and Joan closed her shop, to replace it with Providence House for homeless orphans, an organization that spread throughout France. Though she could heal others, Joan suffered from a lifelong toothache.

THE FEAST OF SAINT SEBALD

Icicle-burning hermit, 760

Patron of Nuremberg; invoked against freezing • (emblem: two oxen)

In the time of Saint Boniface of Mainz, this priest set out to convert the pagan Franconians—that is, Germans—of Nuremberg (of which city he is now the Patron). Once, when preaching to a crowd, Sebald was heckled, and he caused the earth to swallow the mocker. On another famous occasion Sebald sought shelter on a cold winter day in the hut of a peasant couple. He was received with a singular lack of hospitality; the churls refused to add fuel to their low fire, claiming a scarcity of wood. Sebald instructed the stingy hausfrau to gather an armful of icicles from the eaves and dump them into the hearth, which (curiously enough) she did. Needless to say, they burst into roaring flames, which made things nice and cozy.

20. THE FEAST OF SAINT BERNARD OF CLAIRVAUX

"The Honey-Sweet Doctor," 1153

Patron of beekeepers, bees, candle makers, Gibraltar, wax makers • (emblem: beehive)

French poetry first flourished in the twelfth century, when the epic *Song of Roland* was composed and the troubadours of Provence created their immortal verse. Bernard, born in 1090, the scion of Burgundian nobility, showed early promise as a poet. A proto-Romantic, he declared that "we can learn more from the woods, from stones and trees, than from teachers and books." But when his

mother died—he had been her favorite—Bernard changed. He began flinging himself into icy ponds at the sight of young women and before long joined the austere Cistercians, an order of "primitive" Benedictine monks. Afflicted with anemia, gastritis, hypertension, migraine, and an atrophied sense of taste, Bernard had obvious leadership potential; he soon founded his own monastery. His poetic urges poured into voluminous writing and preaching, his "honey-sweet" style earning him the title of Doctor Mellifluus, from which he derived his emblem, a beehive, and his Patronage of the beeswax and honey trades. Our Saint often wrote lengthy commentaries on the biblical Song of Songs, to prove it was not about sex. Certain as he was that the "original sin" was passed on through the sexual act, he argued publicly and vehemently against the then popular notion of Mary's Immaculate Conception. Nevertheless, his personal devotion to the Virgin was most intense. Once when he was afflicted with writer's block, Our Lady appeared in his cell and nursed him from Her own breast.

Also: The Feast of Saint Amadour, who is none other than the biblical Zacchaeus, who married Saint Veronica and moved to France, where his tomb may be visited at Rocamadour, 1st century; and Saint Philibert, an abbot of Gascony in whose honor the tasty nut is named, 685.

21. THE FEAST OF SAINT BERNARD TOLOMEI

Italian abbot, 1348

Patron of olive growers • (emblem: olive branch)

Born in Siena in 1272, Bernard became both a wealthy attorney and a successful politician—some accounts say he was mayor of his city. A partisan speech he was giving one day turned, much to his surprise, into a sermon on the vanity of vanities, and he resigned to found a religious order known as the Oliventines because their abbey was located on the slopes of Monte Oliveto.

Also: The Feast of Saint Pius X, pontiff from 1903 to 1914, the last Pope to be canonized and a rigid reactionary whose policies kept the Church firmly in the Middle Ages as the twentieth century began.

22. THE FEAST OF SAINT SYMPHORIAN

Mother-encouraged martyr, 2nd century

Patron of children, students; invoked against syphilis • (emblem: youth kneeling, bound)

In the town of Autun, France (then the Roman province of Gaul), this Christian schoolboy staunchly refused to participate in the pagan rites honoring the harvest goddess Cybele. Symphorian carried on an edifying theological debate with the local magistrate while being flogged and was then escorted outside the town and beheaded while his proud mother stood on the walls and shouted encouragement to her son.

23. THE FEAST OF SAINT ROSE OF LIMA

Earthquake-preventing virgin, 1617

Patron of the Americas, florists, gardeners, Peru; invoked against vanity • (emblem: crown of roses)

Isabel de Santa Maria de Flores y del Oliva, who preferred to be addressed by her confirmation name of Rose, was the first native of the New World to be declared a Roman Catholic Saint. She was born in Lima, Peru, in 1586, a mere fifty years after the Spanish conquest. As befitted her mixed Hispanic and Incan descent, she liked her religion on the flamboyant side, with a good helping of gore—her role model was the devotionally extravagant Saint Catherine of Siena. Rose's legendary facial beauty distressed her; she found that rubbing her cheeks with pepper and her lips with quicklime helped. In public she invariably wore a crown of roses—with sixty-nine brow-piercing spikes. She lived in a shack in her family garden, whence she was wont to emerge dragging a heavy cross. The Ideal of Catholic Girlhood, Rose slept on a pile of bricks, wore gloves full of nettles, whipped herself with chains, and gouged hunks out of her flesh with broken glass. She was generally assumed to be loco in the coco until the day she announced that through her fervid prayers Lima had been saved from an earthquake. Since there had, indeed, been no earthquake, the populace came to hold her in the highest regard and rejoiced wildly when she was canonized—in 1671, fifty-four years after her death.

24. THE FEAST OF SAINT BARTHOLOMEW

Apostle who was skinned alive, 18th century

Patron of Armenia, bookbinders, butchers, cheese merchants, plasterers, tanners; invoked against nervous tics • (emblem: curved butcher's knife)

artholomew was one of the twelve original Apostles, known in John's Gospel, for some reason, as Nathanael. (This is another example why it is even harder to name the twelve Apostles than it is to name the Seven Dwarfs.) It is believed Bartholomew-Nathanael traveled as far as India and Turkey before being martyred in Armenia, where he was skinned alive by heathens; thus he is usually pictured holding a tanner's knife, with his own hide draped over his arm. This arm has been venerated at England's Canterbury Cathedral since the eleventh century. The curved knife accounts for his Patronage of medieval cheese merchants, who apparently took it for a cheese cutter.

THE FEAST OF SAINT OWEN OF ROUEN

Amiable bishop, 684

Patron of innkeepers; invoked against deafness • (emblem: shipwreck)

his Saint, known to the French as Ouen or Dado, remains popular among them—in the city of Saint-Malo an annual fair is held on his Feast Day. It features the curious custom of eating periwinkles and blowing whistles. Owen was a Frankish courtier until his fortieth year, when he was ordained a priest and made bishop of Rouen. His holy remains may be found in either that city's cathedral or at Canterbury Cathedral in England—miraculous cures of deafness regularly occur at both sites.

25. THE FEAST OF SAINT GENESIUS

Roman comedy star, martyr, c. 303

Patron of actors, comedians, lawyers, mountebanks, secretaries; invoked against epilepsy, freezing • (emblem: clown)

or the sake of amusing the wicked emperor Diocletian, a blasphemous "comic" play was once staged in Rome. In it Christians and their practices were to be parodied and ridiculed. But one performer, Genesius, was—in midact—suddenly converted to the very Faith he was mocking! Forsaking his foolish role, he stepped forward and proudly proclaimed himself a believer. He was forthwith dragged from the stage, stretched on the rack, burned with torches, and beheaded. His heroism is the subject of a play by the great Spanish dramatist Lope de Vega; Saint Genesius medals have been worn, devoutly or superstitiously, by any number of movie stars and other beloved entertainers.

THE FEAST OF SAINT JOSEPH CALASANCTIUS

Free school founder, 1648

Patron of Christian schools

A Spanish lawyer and priest, Joseph founded a free school for the poor children of Rome in 1597; it attracted first hundreds and, by 1621, thousands of pupils. The teachers he gathered were recognized as a religious order, the Clerks Regular of Religious Schools, with Joseph their superior general. Professional jealousy, political back stabbing, scandalous tale-telling, and all the usual features of faculty-lounge life saddened the later years of this idealistic educator, who was assigned his present Patronage by Pius XII exactly three centuries after his death.

THE FEAST OF SAINT LOUIS

French Crusader king, 1270

Patron of bridegrooms, button makers, distillers, marble workers, masons, sculptors, wig makers • (emblem: Crown of Thorns)

King Louis IX of France (ruled 1226–1270) was the very model of a Catholic monarch—he was just, honorable, benevolent, would not abide foul language, and in every way deserved to have a city in Missouri named after him. He waged relentless and successful campaigns against heretics, rebellious nobles, and English invaders (he might be said to have won the

Hundred Years' War). He was a loving husband to his queen, Margaret of Provence, with whom he had eleven children. He caused the magnificent church of Sainte-Chapelle to be built as a shrine for his most precious possession, the original Crown of Thorns. As a Crusader, however, Louis was a flop. He was taken prisoner on his first calamitous expedition against the infidels and died of dysentery on his catastrophic second trip. Historians have assumed he embarked on these lengthy, pointless overseas wars to get away from his mother, the remarkably obnoxious Blanche of Castile.

26. THE FEAST OF SAINT TERESA JORNET E IBARS

Caretaker to the elderly, 1897

Patron of pensioners, senior citizens, people rejected by religious orders

Teresa was born into a peasant farm family, and her piety led her to join the Poor Clares. She soon, however, found herself terminated from the convent after her superiors noted her delicate health. The frail but zealous ex-nun founded a secular order, the Little Sisters of the (Aged) Poor, which, thanks to Our Saint, expanded to fifty-eight houses in Spain and spread worldwide.

Also: The Feast of Saint Elizabeth aiz de Bichier des Anges, who served as a de facto town priest after the French Revolution, 1838; and Saint Zephyrinus, an ineffectual Pope whose two sons gave him no end of trouble, 217.

27. THE FEAST OF SAINT MARGARET THE BAREFOOTED

Defiant rich lady, 1395

Patron of abuse victims, brides, people in difficult marriages

A beautiful pauper, Margaret at fifteen married a wealthy man who mocked her devotion to the needy. It surely must have irritated him when she eschewed shoes and other finery of her class to better identify with the poor. It was only after her husband died that she could perform her good deeds unmolested.

THE FEAST OF SAINT MONICA

Saint Augustine's nagging mother, 387

Patron of alcoholics, married women, mothers; invoked against disappointing children • (emblem: tears)

E verything we know about this Saint we learn from the testimony of her devoted son Saint Augustine of Hippo, in his autobiographical *Confessions*. Monica was a member of the Roman Christian community in Carthage, North Africa, and married a heathen with the unlikely name of Patrick. Her race, and that of her celebrated son, is a matter of some dispute, though the Internet puts her in the pantheon of black Saints. How did she convert her husband from bad-tempered pagan patriarch to True Believer, and her son from a lusty heretic to a Doctor of the Church? She ruthlessly employed a simple mother's method. She wept. She sobbed. She sniveled. She bawled. Until, in self-defense, Patrick was baptized and died, and Augustine abandoned his mistress to become a priest. In Southern California the Spanish explorers found a rock spring that dripped and dribbled ceaselessly. They called it, and the town they founded nearby, Santa Monica.

THE FEAST OF SAINT PHANURIUS

Cretan martyr, date unknown

Patron of lost causes; invoked in desperate situations • (emblem: in armor, holding cross with lit candle on top)

T he primary thing we know about Phanurius, the Eastern Orthodox answer to Saint Anthony of Padua, is that he spent the greater part of his life despairing over his mother's refusal to convert to Christianity. Greeks have been turning to him for centuries to retrieve lost articles and have devised a ritual: bake a cake called a *phanouropita;* before you put it in the oven say a prayer for Phanurius' apostate mother, and after it's baked share it with seven people.

ST. PHANURIUS CAKE

1 cup orange juice

¾ cup brandy

2 tablespoons unsalted butter

2 cups golden raisins

¾ cup sugar

½ cup honey

½ teaspoon salt

1 tablespoon ground cinnamon

¼ teaspoon ground cloves

2 cups all-purpose flour

2 teaspoons double-acting baking powder

½ teaspoon baking soda

2 tablespoons grated orange peel

½ cup sesame seeds (optional)

Preheat the oven to 325 degrees. Combine the orange juice, ½ cup brandy, butter, raisins, sugar, honey, salt, cinnamon, and cloves in a large, heavy-bottomed saucepan. Bring to a boil, reduce the heat, and simmer for 10 minutes, or until thick and syrupy. Set the pot in cold water to cool the mixture completely. Sift the flour, baking powder, and baking soda into the cooled syrup. Beat vigorously for 8 to 10 minutes, or until the batter is smooth and bubbly. Stir in the grated orange peel. Turn into a well-buttered 7-inch fluted tube pan or 8-inch loaf pan. Sprinkle with the sesame seeds. Bake for 1 to 1½ hours, or until a knife inserted in the center comes out clean. Sprinkle with the remaining brandy and cool in the pan. Say a prayer.

28. THE FEAST OF SAINT AUGUSTINE OF HIPPO

African-born Doctor of the Church, 430

Patron of brewers, printers • (emblem: arrow in flaming heart)

It would be difficult to overstate the role of Augustine of Hippo in shaping our Christian way of life; it is to his wisdom that every Pope still defers when making pronouncements about birth control, and it was from his philosophy that John Calvin learned the awful truth of predestination. Augustine was born rather far inland in North Africa—his race remains a subject of speculation. In his famous *Confessions* he claims to have been a naughty young man. "Like water I boiled over, heated by my fornications" is the picturesque way he put it. With his mistress and their son he joined a local mumbo-jumbo sect, the Manichaeans, much to the dismay of his relentlessly pious mother, Saint Monica. After moving to Milan he was converted to the True Faith by her tearful entreaties and the sermons of Saint Ambrose. He returned to Africa as bishop of Hippo and devoted the rest of his life to writing hundreds of books proving that all the unbaptized—including infants—go straight to Hell for eternity, and that, furthermore, the God of Love had, for all eternity, planned that they do so. He was also the first to make the all-important connection between the "original sin" of Adam and Eve and sexual pleasure, which, he argued, was how it was passed along. Like herpes.

THE FEAST OF SAINT HERMES

Mythical martyr, 2nd century

Invoked against insanity • (emblem: Devil issuing from a child's mouth)

There was, no doubt, a Roman martyr with this name, but we know nothing certain about his life and death. Many of his surprisingly abundant relics wound up in Renaix, Belgium, to which site lunatics have long made pilgrimages. Possibly Hermes' curative powers arise from a confusion of this Saint with the Greek god Hermes, whose name he shares.

THE FEAST OF SAINT MOSES THE BLACK

Reformed gangster, hermit, 405

Patron of Africans • (emblem: knife)

Something of a sacred stereotype, unfortunately, Moses is said to have been very large, very strong, and a thief. An unsatisfactory Ethiopian servant in an Egyptian household, he was fired for any number of reasons and became the leader of a dreadful robber gang. How and why he became a monk in the desert at Skete remains a mystery, but he did; though robed in white he insisted, "God knows I am still black within." So complete was his conversion to Christian nonviolence that he offered no resistance when marauding Berbers attacked his monastery, and he was sent to the Green Pastures by their swords in the year 405.

29. THE FEAST OF SAINT SABINA

Roman matron, martyr, 2nd century

Patron of housewives • (emblem: crown and palm)

There are several Saints by this name, all of them models of domesticity; the lady whose Feast is celebrated today was a wealthy Roman widow in whose honor—and at whose expense—a basilica was erected on the Aventine Hill. She was converted to the outlawed Faith by her serving girl Serapia, and thanks to her lofty social position might well have gone unprosecuted, but she practiced her religion so flagrantly the authorities had no choice but to put her (rejoicing) to the sword.

Also: The Feast of Saint Richard Herst, an English martyr who stepped down from the scaffold to give the hangman a hand with the rope, 1628.

30. THE FEAST OF SAINT JOHN ROCHE

Feckless English martyr, 1588

Patron of boatmen

Although the Spanish Armada (July 1588) failed in its noble mission to rescue the England of Elizabeth I and return it to the True Faith, the persecution of English Catholics continued. That very August a half-mad priest, Richard Watson, was arrested and thrown into London's Bridewell Prison. Margaret Ward, the devout Catholic servant girl, took it upon herself to visit Father Watson: she brought him, hidden in a basket of food, a clean shirt and a length of rope. The young Irishman John Roche (aka Neale), a friend of Margaret's, was in on the plot. He was a waterman, one of the many who plied their aquatic taxicabs along the river Thames, and he waited to aid the escaping prisoner. But halfway down the wall Watson slipped and fell, not only creating a hellish racket but breaking an arm and a leg. Thinking fast, Roche exchanged clothes with the priest, who managed to get away. Roche and Margaret were not so lucky—the rope she had taken to Watson was easily traced. They were, naturally, both tortured but offered a royal pardon if they would renounce their religion. They declined, and were duly hanged by order of Good Queen Bess.

31. THE FEAST OF SAINT AIDAN OF LINDISFARNE

Died standing up, 651 • (emblem: stag)

Though his cult was promoted by the perennially venerable Venerable Bede, this Irish monk has never been properly credited for his contribution to England's conversion (that honor goes to Augustine of Canterbury). A disciple of the splendid Saint Columba, Aidan became a bishop beloved for his disdain of pomp. He died leaning against the wall of a church he had built. Famous for his kindness to children and animals, Aidan once saw a stag being hunted, pitied him, and made him invisible on the spot.

THE FEAST OF SAINT RAYMOND NONNATUS

Cesarean-born cardinal, 1240

Patron of Catalonia, childbirth, midwives, obstetricians, pregnant women; invoked against perjury • (emblem: chains)

Raymond's surname means "not born," for surgeons delivered him after his mother's death in labor—thus his eternal compassion for the pregnant. He became a monk in Barcelona and succeeded Saint Peter Nolasco as a ransomer of Christian hostages from their Moorish captors. He proceeded to Algeria with a great deal of money for the purpose, and when it was spent offered himself as a prisoner in exchange for the freedom of another. The wily pagan authorities, assuming they could demand a high price for the return of this man of God, agreed. Although it was against Islamic law, Raymond persisted in preaching to and even converting the Muslim infidels of Tunis. The penalty for this crime—to which he was duly sentenced—was death by impalement, but Raymond was granted a reduced sentence. After he "ran the gauntlet" his lips were pierced with a red-hot iron and a padlock was installed on his mouth. For eight months he languished in a Tunisian dungeon, fed by a jailer who held the key to his lip lock. Finally, his costly ransom was raised by Saint Peter Nolasco himself, and Raymond, who had been looking forward to martyrdom, was obliged to return home, where he was promoted to cardinal just before his death.

❧ September ❧

1. THE FEAST OF SAINT FIACRE

Grimly misogynist horticulturalist hermit, 670

Patron of cabdrivers, gardeners, hosiers, tile makers; invoked against hemorrhoids, venereal disease • (emblem: spade)

Because a hackney stand in Paris was located in front of a hotel named in honor of this Saint, French taxis are called *fiacres*. Thus, Fiacre is the Patron of cabbies. By a lucky coincidence, *fic* (meaning "fig") is a French slang term for hemorrhoids—a common complaint of taxi drivers—against which Fiacre's aid is invoked. He was an Irish hermit who resettled in Brittany and a gifted horticulturalist. When the local bishop offered him as much land as he could plow in a day, Fiacre, using only his staff, cleared several acres, on which he erected a church and hermitage, and planted an extensive vegetable garden. A neighboring shrew complained to the bishop about this land deal, then harangued Fiacre to his face. Her tirade left the Saint so downhearted that he sat heavily upon a stone, leaving thereon the imprint of his buttocks. This stone was later moved to the Church of Saint-Fiacre-en-Brie, where generations of pilgrims have sat on it to be cured of the piles.

THE FEAST OF SAINT GILES

Deer-nourished abbot, 7th century

Patron of beggars, cripples, nursing mothers, spur makers; invoked against breast-feeding problems, insanity, lameness, leprosy, night terrors, sterility • (emblem: deer pierced with arrow)

A doe fed milk daily to this gentle hermit, who lived in the depths of the forest. When a famous king—Charlemagne, Chilbert, Wamba, or Flavius, depending on the version you read—was hunting Giles's deer, he shot the white-haired Saint instead. Filled with remorse, the king built Giles a monastery that became a popular pilgrimage site. Charlemagne once went to Giles for confession but couldn't articulate one particularly intimate offense—so an Angel revealed the sin to Giles, enabling him to absolve the emperor. His healing power was so strong that one fatally ill man was cured simply by wearing the Saint's coat. Numerous churches and hospitals are dedicated to Giles, and he is known as the chief Patron of poor folk (except in Poland, where, for some reason, he is the Saint of the princely elite). In Normandy, on the other hand, women who have difficulty becoming pregnant sleep with a picture or, better still, a statue of the Saint. It works.

2. THE FEAST OF SAINT AGRICOLUS OF AVIGNON

Farm-country bishop, 700

Patron of Avignon; invoked against rainstorms and plagues of storks • (emblem: storks)

Agricolus' father was Magnus, a senator of Gaul who, upon the death of his wife, became bishop of Avignon. When Agricolus was only thirty years of age, he was summoned from a nearby abbey and elected co-bishop of the see; together they formed one of the few father-and-son-team bishoprics in Church history. Agricolus' most celebrated miracle was banishing, by power of his blessing, an infestation of storks, and since his name means "farmer" in Latin, he takes an ongoing interest in crops and weather.

3. THE FEAST OF SAINT GREGORY THE GREAT

Organizer-Pope, Doctor of the Church, 604

Patron of music, Popes, scholars, schoolchildren, singers, teachers; invoked against plague • (emblem: Pope, a dove at his ear)

Gregory, who is generally credited with ushering in the glorious Middle Ages, was born to a wealthy patrician family and quickly climbed the ranks to prefect of Rome. Soon after his mother became a nun, he turned to a life of piety and contemplation, becoming a monk and using his considerable fortune to build monasteries. He emerged, after several years in the cloister, to be made cardinal and, in 590, Pope—a role he resisted and termed "the height of embarrassment." He inherited a Rome in ruins but reformed the clergy and strengthened the papacy, asserting its right to intervene in secular affairs—within ten years he had deposed both an emperor and a king! Gregory suffered lifelong indigestion and gout, as a result of drinking, in his youth, resin-flavored

wine. Perhaps best known as the ultimate music lover, he is credited with promoting plainsong, Gregorian chant, which subjected ancient Church melodies to the rules of harmony. His heightened aesthetic sense was in sharp contrast to the rigidity of his moral teachings: he held that sex is *always* evil ("pleasure can never be without sin"), even when it produces children, and forbade married intercourse during menstruation, pregnancy, and lactation. Gregory was known in his lifetime for his huge, bald head, which today many cities, including Constance, Lisbon, Prague, and Ses, claim to possess as a precious relic.

Also: The Feast of Saint Phoebe, who was definitely *not* Saint Paul's wife! She was a deaconess, possibly even a bishop, of the fledgling Christian Church, an example of the power women held back then. Even the misogynistic Paul, in a letter of reference to the Romans, enthusiastically called Phoebe his "sister in the Lord," 1st century; and Saint Simeon Stylites the Younger, a Syrian who from the age of seven perched either on top of a column or on a series of pointed rocks and worked miracles galore, 592.

4. THE FEAST OF SAINT MARINUS

Beleaguered mason, 4th century

Patron of San Marino • (emblem: mason's hammer and tools)

Marinus was working at a quarry with his chum, Saint Leo, when the two, impressed by their Christian co-workers, converted to the Faith. For the next twelve years Marinus was a cheerful, tireless worker devoted to his family, a paragon of Christian behavior. One day a besotted Dalmatian woman turned up at the quarry, screaming that Marinus was her long-lost husband! What choice had he, really, but to hide in a cave? The Dalmatian dame stood outside the cave shouting obscenities, but when she left for food, Marinus quite literally headed for the hills. There he spent the rest of his life, a holy hermit and suspected bigamist.

THE FEAST OF SAINT ROSALIA

Particularly beauteous virgin, 1160

Patron of Palermo, Sicily • (emblem: crown of white roses)

This noble maiden left her family to reside in solitude in the caves of southern Italy. When she wasn't praying or meditating, Rosalia engraved her name in rocks and wood ("*Ego Rosalia*"), declaring her existence to future hikers. Angels took her to a cave on Monte Pellegrino, where she lay down in a bed of water and lime and died; stalagmites formed around her. Five hundred years later, in the middle of a terrible plague in Palermo, Rosalia appeared to one victim, promising help. A search party went to her cave to obtain bones but instead found her body, encased in Pellegrino water. Her body was paraded through the town, putting an end to the pestilence.

THE FEAST OF SAINT ROSE OF VITERBO

Precociously pious virgin, 1252

Patron of florists • (emblem: nun with roses in her apron)

A child prodigy of sorts, Rose had her first vision at eight, when the Blessed Virgin told her to start wearing the habit of Saint Francis of Assisi. Dressed as a little male monk, the nine-year-old girl hit the streets of Viterbo preaching in her childish voice against the excommunicated emperor Frederick. When she was ten Rose challenged an opponent to trial by fire. She jumped into a bonfire, emerged unharmed, and won the debate. On a less heroic note, Rose became hysterical when the nuns from the convent of Saint Mary of the Roses refused her admission because of her lack of dowry. She threatened, "You will not have me now, but perhaps you will be more willing when I'm dead!" After her death at seventeen, Rose appeared to Pope Alexander IV in a vision and asked him to have her body moved to that elitist convent, which he immediately did.

5. THE FEAST OF SAINT LAURENCE JUSTIANI

Austere but generous bishop, 1455

Patron of Venice • (emblem: distributing church vessels)

When he was a child Laurence told his mother of his ambition to be a Saint. Toward that end he underwent such fearful mortification that his desperate mother arranged a marriage in the hope of distracting him. Instead, the Saint fled in horror to the nearby monastery of Saint George, never to return to his mother's opulent house except as a beggar. As a priest Laurence experienced rapture during prayer and shed copious tears at Mass. He also cried tears of protestation when he was appointed bishop of Venice, in which office he continued to eat from earthenware dishes and sleep on straw. He founded parishes and churches and banned stage entertainment. When he knew he was dying, Laurence embarked on a prolonged deathbed farewell, crying, "Behold, the bridegroom cometh!" while the entire population of Venice visited him, asking for his blessing and last-minute advice.

6. THE FEAST OF SAINT BEE

Beneficent English virgin, 698

Patron of laborers • (emblem: hen with seven chicks)

Bee was a beautiful Irish princess who was betrothed to Christ from infancy. She received, via some Angels, an engagement bracelet marked with the Sign of the Cross, and this enabled her to escape her arranged marriage to a prince of Norway. On the eve of her wedding, she slipped out from the drunken revels and sailed from Ireland on a piece of sod wearing nothing but the bracelet. She washed up on the coast of Cumberland, where she was sustained by food delivered by sea gulls and gannets. Bee eventually became a nun who laundered and mended the clothes of the workers who built her monastery.

THE FEAST OF SAINT MAGNUS OF FÜSSEN

Bear-befriending abbot, 772

Patron of crops; invoked against caterpillars, hail, lightning, reptiles, vermin • (emblem: dragon)

Magnus was a disciple of Saint Columban. Working out of Kempten, Germany, he freed the neighborhood of serpents before proceeding to Füssen, where he expelled a dragon and founded an abbey. On a walk he once encountered a bear who showed him a vein of iron ore. Magnus rewarded the bear with a piece of cake. The pair went back to the abbey, and the bear led Magnus, now carrying his tools and accompanied by his fellow monks, to the mountains. They discovered other veins of iron ore, thus founding the most profitable industry of that region. Magnus' cult, however, remains popular among the local farmers.

7. THE FEAST OF SAINT ANASTASIUS THE FULLER

Working-class martyr, 304

Patron of fullers • (emblem: fuller's club)

Fullers were craftsmen who soaked and pressed newly woven and bulky wool into fine cloth. Anastasius, a nobleman of Aquillia, took literally Saint Paul's epistolary admonition to the Thessalonians to "work with your own hands" and journeyed to Dalmatia to labor at the fullers' trade. In a time of persecution he boldly inscribed a cross on his front door and shortly thereafter was cast into the sea with a millstone around his neck.

THE FEAST OF SAINT CLOUD

Deposed French prince, bishop, 560

Patron of nail makers; invoked against carbuncles • (emblem: abbot giving a hood to a poor man)

The grandson of Clovis, the first Christian king of the Franks, Cloud, with his two brothers, was raised by their holy grandmother, Saint Clothilde. Greedy for the throne, Cloud's uncles tricked the old lady into sending the boys to visit them. The uncles greeted them by stabbing Cloud's brothers in the armpits, but Cloud (only eight) managed to escape to Provence. As an adult Cloud made no attempt to recover his kingdom and instead hid himself in a hermit's cell, venturing out only to do some occasional preaching. Once a beggar came to his cell and Cloud gave him his only worldly possession, his hood. Later, when the beggar was walking in the dark, the hood gave off a heavenly light, indicating to the neighborhood that there was a Saint in their midst. Cloud is the Patron Saint of nail makers because of a crude pun on his name, *clou* being French for "nail."

THE FEAST OF SAINT REGINA

Savagely tormented virgin martyr, 2nd century

Patron of shepherdesses; invoked against ringworm • (emblem: dove bringing her a crown)

A pious nanny converted Regina to Christianity, and when her father found out he disowned her, forcing her to support herself as a shepherdess. A lascivious prefect, Olybrius, keen on the comely Regina *and* finding that she was of noble birth, insisted on marrying her. Meanwhile her father, now impressed by her prominent suitor, dis-disowned her—but Regina rejected them both, preferring to remain chaste. In a fit of pique the prefect had her chained to the wall of a dungeon, tore out her fingernails, and racked her body with iron combs, while her evil father cheered him on. When Regina was finally beheaded, a dove hovered over her, converting no fewer than eight hundred onlookers. Visitors to her tomb are cured of ringworm.

Also: The Feast of Saint Gratus of Aosta, bishop of that city until 479 and now its Patron. He is invoked against insects.

8. THE FEAST OF THE NATIVITY OF MARY

The Blessed Virgin as Birthday Girl

Patron of Cuba, distillers, drapers, fishmongers, needlemakers, pin makers, restaurateurs

In the Indian village of El Cobre, Oriente Province, Cuba, on this day they venerate with much vigor a small statue of the Voodoo/Santeria goddess Oshun, who is known publicly as La Virgen de la Caridad—by which name she was officially recognized by the Vatican, in 1917, as Cuba's national Patron. In Genesis (3:15) Mary's birth was predicted: God promised the wicked serpent that He would one day send a woman whose foot would crush his head—which is why Mary is often pictured standing barefoot on a snake. Many of the details in the apocryphal Gospel of the Birth of the Virgin are of dubious historical value. But we may be certain that she was conceived—immaculately—by her parents, Saints Anne and Joachim, and born either in Jerusalem or in Nazareth, c. 20 B.C. In the East her nativity was long celebrated on September 8, which is allegedly the anniversary of the dedication of Solomon's temple. But the date was not officially recognized by the Roman Church as Mary's birthday until the late seventh century. Fittingly, it makes her a Virgo, born under the sign of the Virgin.

THE FEAST OF SAINT ADRIAN

Dismembered martyr, 304

Patron of arms dealers, butchers, prison guards • (emblems: anvil and armless, legless torso)

A Roman officer in Nicomedia, Adrian was so impressed by the bravery of his Christian captives that he asked to be jailed with them. His wife, Natalia, was delighted and shaved her head in order to disguise her sex and be able to visit him in prison, where she kissed his chains and urged him to endure martyrdom. When his legs were cut off, she prayed that his hands might be removed as well, as befit a true Saint. After his death a miraculous rainstorm extinguished the flames to which his body had been consigned, and Natalia got away with at least one hand—a precious relic. Adrian's sword is still venerated in Walbech, Germany.

9. THE FEAST OF SAINT PETER CLAVER

Slave-saving priest, 1654

Patron of African Americans, Colombia, race relations, slaves • (emblem: with a black child in his arms)

B orn into Spanish nobility in 1580, Peter fell under the influence of one Alphonsus, the porter at his Jesuit seminary. The porter persuaded him to go to the Americas to succor the slaves in the burgeoning New World slave trade. Peter set out to Colombia, clearinghouse of the slave industry, where ten thousand Africans arrived (one-third having died on the way over) every year from Angola and the Congo. Working with the holy Father Alfonse de Sandovel (whose writings on the evils of the slave trade were the first systematic attack on the system), Peter daily visited the slaves, bringing food and clothing to the disease-infested holds of the ships. He learned the slaves' dialects and, using pictures, taught them Christianity. On a mission into the jungle he contracted the plague, but strapped to his horse he continued ministering to lepers and slaves. In the final years of his illness everyone forgot about him, and he was even neglected by his nurse, Manuel, who ate most of his food and would throw the remainder into the Saint's mouth. When he died he had two funerals, one held by the white hierarchy and the other by slaves and Indians.

Also: The Feast of Saint Bettelin, an English monk who impregnated and eloped with an Irish princess, who was fortunately then eaten by wolves, allowing him to get back to his life of prayer, 8th century.

10. THE FEAST OF SAINT NICHOLAS OF TOLENTINO

Compassionate priest, 1305

Patron of babies, Córdoba, the dying, Lima, mothers, sick animals; invoked against fire, thunderstorms • (emblem: star over his head)

In Europe and America, Nicholas was, from the sixteenth to eighteenth centuries, the most venerated of all the Saints. He was born to middle-aged parents after they had made a pilgrimage to the shrine of Saint Nicholas of Myra. In gratitude they named their son after the Saint. At eighteen Nicholas joined a friary in his hometown of Sant' Angelo, Pontano, but soon (while wearing an iron girdle and praying) he beheld a chorus of Angels in white robes chanting "To Tolentino, to Tolentino!" Naturally, Nicholas took off for the town that eventually gave him his surname and stayed there until his death. Once when Nicholas was ill the Blessed Virgin, accompanied by Saint Augustine and his mother, Saint Monica, appeared and assured him he would recover if he ate bread dipped in water. Thus began the custom of Saint Nicholas bread—rolls soaked in water and blessed on his Feast Day, which are wonderfully effective when eaten by the sick and/or by women in labor, and, when thrown, for extinguishing fires. A year before his death a star preceded Nicholas wherever he went; the same star continued to appear on the anniversary of his death. In 1348 a German monk seeking relics for his country broke into Nicholas's tomb and hacked off the Saint's arms. The monk fled into the night, only to find himself the next morning back at the tomb—running in place and holding the two bloody arms. Since this incident the two arms are said to bleed whenever any misfortune befalls the city. Although the rest of Nicholas's body has decomposed, the arms remain fresh, residing in the aptly named Chapel of the Holy Arms.

THE FEAST OF SAINT PULCHERIA

Outlawed Byzantine empress, 453

Patron of betrayal victims, empresses, exiles, orphans; invoked against in-law problems • (emblem: bearing scepter and lily)

Her parents were the Byzantine emperor and empress, and Pulcheria briefly served as regent until her younger brother Theodosius, a gifted calligrapher, was able to ascend the throne. Pulcheria instructed Theodosius on the basics of church and state, secretly realizing that he was too weak and, yes, too artsy-fartsy, to be an effective emperor. Giving nary a thought to herself, Pulcheria took a vow of chastity and stayed active in public life until her brother took a bride, Eudocia. The doughty Saint then departed for a life of solitary prayer—only to be recalled after Eudocia fell from favor because of a liaison with a gouty officer. Theodosius died, and Pulcheria married—it was a celibate, or Josephite, union, of course—an upstanding general named Marcian. They reigned together over Byzantium, building churches, hospitals, and a university.

THE FEAST OF SAINT THEODARD

Assassinated Frankish abbot, 669

Patron of cattle dealers

Theodard, head of a large monastery in the bishopric of Flanders, set out to complain to the king about Church land being appropriated by nobles. On his return he was waylaid by robbers, to whom he addressed a long speech. They countered with a philosophical speech of their own, quoting Horace to the effect that death is common to all, and finishing with a fatal hatchet blow.

11. THE FEAST OF SAINT VERAN

French monk, reluctant bishop, 480

Invoked against insanity • (emblem: in a ship on fire)

This humble fifth-century monk has lent his name to an upscale ski resort in the French Alps and a Chardonnay with a fruity aftertaste that lingers on the palate.

Also: The Feast of the Blessed Louis of Thuringia,✝ who has been elevated to this status solely because he endured the saintly excesses of his wife, Saint Elizabeth of Hungary, who once put a leper in his bed and depleted the palace treasury. Louis sighed that all would be well, "so long as she leaves me Wartburg and Neuenburg," 1227.

✝ *Pictured at right*

12. THE FEAST OF SAINT AILBHE

Irish bishop raised by wolves, 526

Patron of wolves • (emblem: wolf)

Ailbhe's birth mother was a serving girl and his father an Irish chieftain who was so disgusted by the child's birth that he threw the infant to the wolves. A she-wolf suckled Ailbhe until a hunter discovered him in the wolves' den and adopted him. Many years later, after he had become a disciple of Saint Patrick and a bishop, Ailbhe was tearfully reconciled with his aged foster parent. Promising "I will protect thee, Old Mother," he had the old wolf spend her last years in his hall.

THE FEAST OF SAINT GUY

Pauper, pilgrim, 1012

Patron of horses • (emblem: horses lying near him)

On the outskirts of Brussels there is a field of wheat that Saint Wyden, as the Flemish call him, once caused to grow overnight. This holy simpleton was known and revered as the Poor Man of Anderlecht. Saint Guidon (in English, Guy) was a wandering rustic peasant who found employment as a church sacristan in Laeken, near Brussels, and shared the pittance he earned with those less fortunate than himself. One day Guy was offered a business opportunity—a chance to invest in a commercial venture—and, thinking only of the works of charity he could perform when his (literal) ship came in, gave his all. The ship sank in the harbor, and Guy, dejected, not to mention destitute, set out on foot on a seven-year pilgrimage that took him as far as Rome and Jerusalem, until he staggered back to Anderlecht to die. Conclusive evidence of his sanctity was soon provided by a horse, which profaned Guy's newly dug grave in some vulgar equine manner and was instantly struck dead.

13. THE FEAST OF SAINT JOHN CHRYSOSTOM
Golden-throated Doctor of the Church, 407

Patron of orators, preachers • (emblem: bees)

The son of a Latin father and Greek mother, John set aside his classical education to pursue the life of a monk-hermit. But the dampness of the monastery proved too much for the young holy man, and he turned to preaching, earning his name Chrysostom, meaning "golden mouth." Saint John disapproved of the manner in which God ordained that our species procreate. In one of his sermons he said, "Virginity is as superior to marriage as Heaven is to earth or Angels to men." So one bee in his bonnet was the sex life of Adam and Eve. He theorized that asexual reproduction must have occurred in Eden so that our first parents could remain in that perfect state, virginity. When he became patriarch of Constantinople, then a nest of nooky, John attacked the loose morals of the city and clergy, as well as the behavior and appearance of the women at court and their "ready inclination to sin." His attempts at reform earned him the enmity of the empress, whom John pointedly referred to as Jezebel. Jews weren't spared in his oratory either; he flatly stated, "I hate the Jews. God hates the Jews and always did."

THE FEAST OF SAINT VENERIUS
Solitary hermit, 600

Patron of lighthouse keepers • (emblem: raven brings him food)

Venerius left the monastery seeking a life of greater austerity and became a hermit on the Italian isle of Tino. After his death a strong cult sprang up around him as his body was moved from place to place. In 1962, Pope John XXIII declared Venerius the Patron of lighthouse keepers, "because the radiance of his life shone out."

14. THE FEAST OF SAINT NOTBURGA

Virgin hired hand, 1313

Patron of peasants, servants, women in labor; invoked for rest from hard work, against sickness in cattle • (emblem: sickle)

Her Tyrolean childhood ended when Notburga was placed as a servant in the castle of the nasty count and countess of Rattenberg, who shamelessly used her as a drudge, mocking her for having only one eye. Still, Notburga grew fat, making "a feast of the affronts heaped on her." When the cruel countess discovered Notburga giving food to the poor instead of to the pigs, she fired her, and the Saint went to work for a farmer. Notburga became upset when the farmer wanted her to work Saturday evening—technically the Sabbath—because he feared the weather would change. She threw her sickle in the air, where it hung suspended, looking like the harvest moon, the sign of good weather to come. Meanwhile at the Rattenbergs', the mean countess had died and her ghost was haunting the pigsties, terrifying the pigs. An exorcist had to be called in. Since the ghost lamented her sin of giving the food meant for the poor to the pigs, the count hired Notburga back as housekeeper. Four hundred years after her death, Notburga's body was dug up by local residents who, in a gesture of questionable taste, dressed the skeleton in a red velvet gown with blue bows. They then placed it in a glass case over the altar of a new church erected in her name.

Also: The Feast of Saint Maternus, a Saint who could say Mass in Trier, Tongres, and Cologne simultaneously, 4th century.

15. THE FEAST OF SAINT CATHERINE OF GENOA
Slightly hysterical matron, 1510

Patron of nurses, victims of unfaithfulness

Catherine of Genoa was married at sixteen to the son of a rival family, in the hopes of patching up a blood feud. During the first years of their marriage, her husband, Julian, behaved badly—he was unfaithful, bad-tempered, and an ostentatious dresser. Catherine took to her room and alternated between depression and hysteria. Julian complained loudly of her shrewish behavior, which exacerbated the long-standing feud. Then, after seeing a vision of Christ crucified, blood spouting from His wounds and covering the walls of the house, Catherine understandably underwent a spiritual transformation. Thereafter she kept her eyes downcast, put thistles in her bed and wormwood in her food, and rubbed her tongue along the ground to punish herself if she spoke unnecessarily. She eventually converted the now bankrupt Julian, and they moved to a small house, living in chastity. They ministered to the poor and the sick, especially during the plague of 1493, tending sores and delousing garments. After kissing a plague patient, Catherine suffered a lifelong sickness. When Julian died she cared for his former mistress and his illegitimate daughter. Catherine spent her final years writing (actually dictating) her long and psychedelic *Treatise on Purgatory* and undergoing visionary experiences.

16. THE FEAST OF SAINT CORNELIUS
Anti-antipope, 252

Patron of cattle; invoked against earache, epilepsy, fever, twitching • (emblem: cow's horn)

When Cornelius was elected Pope he beat out several rivals, including the controversial Novatus. Novatus enlisted some bishops, "heated them up with wine," and succeeded in having them declare him the first formal antipope.

In the persecutions that followed Cornelius was banished, his sufferings in exile earning him the title of martyr. He is generally depicted in art wearing papal robes and with a cow's horn, *cornus* being Latin for "horn."

THE FEAST OF SAINT CYPRIAN

Carthaginian bishop, martyr, 258

Patron of Algeria, North Africa • (emblem: burning books at his feet)

Cyprian was an orator and advocate who led such a dissolute life that when he converted at the age of fifty and took a vow of chastity, an onlooker exclaimed, "Whoever saw such a miracle!" He then devoted himself to Christian studies, preceding Saint Augustine of Hippo as a great teacher in North Africa. He became a priest and then bishop of Carthage, using his oratorical skills to preach of Heaven and Hell. Borrowing from Greek mythology, he vividly described the horrors of Hell, the "murmuring and groaning of souls bewailing, and with flames belching forth through the horrid darkness of the thick night." Cyprian retreated during a persecution but returned to set an example to his flock. When his death sentence was announced, he said, "Thanks be to God." He was beheaded after giving his executioner twenty-five gold pieces and snapping, "Hurry up and get it over with."

THE FEAST OF SAINT LUDMILA

Duchess strangled by her daughter-in-law, 921

Patron of Bohemia, converts, duchesses, widows; invoked for bodily purity • (emblem: strangled with a veil)

Ludmila and her husband, Borivoy, the duke of Bohemia, converted to Christianity after Saint Methodius told the ambitious duke that if he converted, "his enemies would be made his footstool." Ludmila's eldest son, Wratislaus, married a pagan, "the disheveled one"—Drahomira, mother of Saint Wenceslaus. Before he died Wratislaus entrusted Wenceslaus to Ludmila. In time Ludmila exerted her influence over her grandson to seize the government from his pagan mother. Too late, Drahomira tried to separate her son and mother-in-law, then ordered Ludmila strangled with her own veil. The wicked queen, in a hypocritical attempt to expiate her crime and fooling no one, dedicated the murder site to Saint Michael and made it a church.

Also: The Feast of Saint Edith of Wilton, daughter of King Edgar, who was offered the throne of England but refused, preferring convent life, 984.

17. THE FEAST OF SAINT HILDEGARD OF BINGEN

Abbess, musician, poet, 1179

Patron of philologists • (emblem: flames around her head)

At present a feminist favorite, Hildegard was dedicated to the Church at birth and at the age of eight shipped off to the care of that peculiar German recluse Saint Jutta. The two became anchorites together—their lives were so ascetic that the only link they had to the world was a tiny window in their tiny room. (Before becoming anchorites they had received the Last Rites, since they were henceforth considered dead to the world.) Then, at age forty-two, Hildegard experienced a vision of God that changed her life; despite her lack of formal education, she now completely understood even the most complicated theological texts. After this experience she left her hermitage to become a respected adviser to kings and Popes, an abbess, a poet, a playwright—even to invent New Age music! Among her compositions, much in favor with modern feminist music lovers, is a sort-of opera, *Ordo Virtutum,* in which women portray the Virtues and a single male is cast as the Devil. Hildegard also found time to become an expert on homeopathic medicine and wrote a medical book covering topics from blood circulation to obsessive/compulsive behavior. (She recommends wild lettuce to stifle lust in both sexes.)

THE FEAST OF SAINT LAMBERT

Scandalously flatulent bishop, 705

Patron of children, dentists, nannies, truss makers • (emblem: kneeling bishop, pierced by spears)

No sooner had Lambert succeeded the recently assassinated Theodard as bishop of Maastricht, Flanders, in 668 than he was sent into exile. He retired to join a monastic order remarkable for its austerity—Our Saint once spent an entire night in the snow, clad only in a hair shirt, as penance for having broken the Rule of Silence by breaking wind. Pepin of Herstal restored Lambert to his episcopate, then promptly ordered his murder. He wept in his chambers while a henchman climbed on the roof and hurled a spear through Lambert's heart. The Pope got word of the crime from a visiting Angel, who instructed him to replace Bishop Lambert with a man called Hubert; and who should His Holiness meet the very next day but a pilgrim of that name.

THE FEAST OF SAINT ROBERT BELLARMINE

Pillar of the Counter-Reformation, 1621

Patron of catechists and canonists
• (emblem: cardinal's hat)

A Jesuit and Doctor of the Church whose writings, especially *The Controversies,* were the most influential of their day, Bellarmine had an intellect so great that his work was once thought to be that of a team of scholars and his name an anagram. He revised the Vulgate, created a catechism, and as cardinal was prefect of the Vatican Library. He became the supreme defender of the papacy (even though he once called Pope John XII "the dregs") and fought against heresies, Protestant theologies, and anticlericals. He disputed Galileo's theory that the earth revolves around the sun, staunchly asserting that the sun "revolves around the earth with great speed," but he was sympathetic to the astronomer (who had dedicated books to him). In his later years he withdrew from controversy and wrote books of devotion. His disagreements with Pope Sixtus V, who put one of his books about the temporal power of the papacy on the Index, as well as his assertion that early lives of the Saints were full of incredible embellishments, may explain why Bellarmine's canonization was delayed for three hundred years.

18. THE FEAST OF SAINT FERREOLUS

Martyr drowned in a sewer, 304

Invoked against sick poultry, rheumatism • (emblem: chains falling off him)

Ferreolus was a tribune and secret Christian who was exposed when he refused to arrest Christians or worship idols. He was placed in chains in the prison cesspool, aptly called the *barathrum*. On the third day he slipped from his chains and made a daredevil escape through the sewer, only to be recaptured and beheaded. What any of this has to do with chickens—sick or healthy—is anybody's guess.

THE FEAST OF SAINT JOSEPH OF CUPERTINO

"The Flying Monk," 1663

Patron of the air force, astronauts, pilots • (emblem: monk levitating in ecstasy)

The famous "Flying Monk" was born in a garden shed because his father, who died soon after his birth, had sold the house to pay off debts. His widowed mother resented her slow, pigeon-toed son, and other children called him Boccaperta (the Gaper) because his mouth always hung open. Bad-tempered and a failed shoemaker, Joseph was dismissed by the Capuchins and joined the Franciscans as a servant. A lucky break enabled him to become a novice—the exam he was given was based on the only text he was able to read. He became more devout and was so happy to be a priest that he mailed his underwear back to his mother because his habit was all he needed (he didn't remove it for two years). Soon after he became a priest his famous levitation began; according to his biographers, Joseph levitated over a hundred times. He was able to fly high above the altar and once helped workmen by lifting a huge cross thirty-six feet, then stayed perched on the cross for several hours. Fellow friars soon took to flying around on his back. During his flights Joseph would issue shrill cries and afterward dissolve into fits of laughter. Church authorities, disturbed by this phenomenon and accusing him of "drawing crowds after him like a new Messiah," placed Joseph in seclusion, actually making him a prisoner. But pilgrims kept finding him, so Joseph was moved from place to place, his notoriety preceding him. The controversy around the Saint, who could also predict the future, caused him to slip into deep melancholia. His last flight was, appropriately enough, on the Feast of the Assumption a month before his death.

19. THE FEAST OF SAINT JANUARIUS

Blood-boiling martyr, 305

Patron of blood banks, nail makers, Naples; invoked against the evil eye and volcanic eruptions • (emblem: praying in flames)

Bishop Januarius was beheaded after wild lions refused to touch him and he had emerged from a burning furnace unharmed. (A curious aside: Saint Augustine probated his will.) In the fifth century Naples inherited his relics, including two vials of his blood, which had been collected by followers. In 1389, over a thousand years after Januarius' death, a priest holding the flasks of his coagulated blood noticed the contents beginning to bubble and liquefy. Since then the blood boils whenever it is in close proximity to the bust containing part of Januarius' skull. This "standing miracle" repeats itself on various Feast Days eighteen times a year, except during times of strife, famine, oppression, or the election of a Communist mayor in Naples. The liquefication is inconsistent—sometimes bubbling furiously, sometimes sluggish—and the color varies from dull rust to vivid crimson. If the blood does nothing during the ceremony, the spectators, particularly a group of excited women known as the aunts of San Gennaro, have been known to shout, "Boil! Boil! Boil, damn you!"

Also: The Feast of Saint Emily de Rodat, a French foundress who called herself "the scum of the earth," 1852; and Saint Lucy of Scotland, a princess who fled the licentious Scottish court to become a simple shepherdess in France. In Lorraine both a mountain and a church bear her name, and thither hasten erstwhile sterile wives—as did Queen Anne of Austria, in order to conceive King Louis XIV in 1638.

20. THE FEAST OF SAINT EUSTACE

Bereft martyr, 118

Patron of hunters, veterinarians; invoked in difficult situations, against family problems • (emblem: stag, shining cross between its antlers)

The story of this Saint, now demoted from the official Church Calendar, was enormously popular throughout the Middle Ages. Eustace was, it seems, a wealthy and powerful Roman general—a captain of the guards under the emperor Trajan—who, while hunting one day in the woods near Tivoli, Italy, encountered a stag with a luminous crucifix between its antlers while a heavenly Voice prophesied, "Thou shalt suffer many things for My sake." Eustace immediately converted to Christianity, as did his wife and their two sons. The prophecy came true with a vengeance: Eustace was drummed out of the army and reduced to abject poverty. Pirates kidnapped his wife. Wild beasts carried off his sons. Years later, in a time of need, the emperor recalled his trusted officer. Back in Rome, Eustace was overjoyed to discover that his sons had miraculously survived and were actually serving under his command! And by a greater miracle his wife reappeared, alive and not much the worse for wear. But the family's celebration was short-lived. Ordered to worship idols, they refused. They survived exposure to lions in the amphitheater, only to be roasted to death in the belly of a brass bull. Something in the tale touched the heart of medieval man—the Happy Ending?—and churches in Spain, Italy, Switzerland, and France (most notably the spectacular church in the Les Halles section of Paris) are named after him.

21. THE FEAST OF SAINT MATTHEW

Tax collector, Apostle, evangelist, 1st century

Patron of accountants, bankers, CFOs, security guards, money managers, customs officials, stockbrokers, tax collectors • (emblem: winged man)

No one knows how or where Matthew died—some legends tell of a mission to a faraway cannibal isle that ended badly for the evangelist. Matthew (also called Levi) had been an exile even among his own people, a Jewish tax collector, despised by Jews as an agent of the occupying Romans and by gentiles as an extortionist. Christ thus challenged public opinion when he gave Matthew the call to "follow me," as recounted in Matthew's own Gospel. When Matthew describes Jesus dining with "people of ill repute," he is talking about himself. His Patronage of unpopular but necessary revenue agents was reiterated as recently as December 2000 by the Russian Orthodox Church. He undertook the writing of his Gospel under special instructions from the Holy Ghost, composing it particularly for Jewish Christians and employing his wide knowledge of Jewish customs. His is the most "popular" Gospel, the one that tells the story of the

Star of Bethlehem, the flight into Egypt, the Sermon on the Mount, and the Passion. It was made into a movie in 1964 by the avant-garde filmmaker Pier Paolo Pasolini. In his great novel *The Last Temptation of Christ,* Nikos Kazantzakis, rather irreverently, persisted in describing Our Saint as "hairy-eared."

22. THE FEAST OF SAINT MAURICE

Brave soldier-martyr, 286

Patron of Austria, dyers, hatters, the infantry, knife grinders, Sardinia, weavers; invoked against arthritis, cramps, gout • (emblems: banner, lance, shield)

Maurice was a (possibly black) officer at the head of the exclusive Theban Legion, stationed in Agaunum (Switzerland). The legion included in its ranks such famous Christian soldiers as Besse, Gereon, and Victor. Before the emperor Maximian marched against the Gauls, he ordered the legion to sacrifice to the gods. Maurice, as spokesman, refused and led the army in retreat to what is now Saint-Maurice-en-Valais. The emperor ordered a decimation—the killing of every tenth man—until the entire legion of 6,660 soldiers was chopped to bits. Later accounts maintain it was only a cohort (600 men) that was massacred, and even deny that the more famous Saints were part of Maurice's legion and legend. Although Maurice has suffered from revisionist history, his ring and blood are preserved at Saint-Maurice, as is the slab of stone on which he knelt to receive the final blow.

THE FEAST OF SAINT PHOCAS

Martyr who dug his own grave, date unknown

Patron farmworkers, gardeners, and sailors • (emblem: spade)

Phocas was a Christian, a gardener by profession, who provided a hospice for travelers on the Black Sea. Soldiers, seeking to execute him during a Christian persecution, unwittingly arrived at his house and were welcomed with his famous hospitality. When the soldiers announced who they were looking for, the Saint promised to show them Phocas the following morning. That night he busied himself digging his grave in the garden, and the following morning he told them, "I myself am the man." The soldiers overcame a momentary attack of scruples, cut off his head, and buried him in the grave he had prepared. He became the Patron of sailors primarily because his name resembles the Breton word for seal, *phoc.*

23. THE FEAST OF THE BLESSED PADRE PIO

Modern-day stigmatic, 1968

Padre Pio (né Francesco Forgione), a hairy Italian friar, was praying intensely before a crucifix one morning when he noticed his hands were bloody. Though he had already enjoyed frequent conversations with Christ, Mary, and his own Guardian Angel, he was stunned to realize that, at age thirty-one, he had just received the Stigmata! Not only that, he was the first priest to be so honored. (Saint Francis of Assisi had never been ordained.) American soldiers occupying Italy sent word of the bleeding friar back to the United States, and soon Padre Pio was world famous. He was called a Living Saint, and the image of the humble friar praying at the altar in a pair of bloody mittens (he would sometimes lose as much as a pint of blood while saying Mass) appeared throughout the world; a global network of Padre Pio prayer groups sprang up. He frequently graced the pages of the *National Enquirer* and thus became an icon of modern (albeit gory) Catholicism. But in reality, Padre Pio was a throwback to earlier, simpler times. Like ancient Saints and mystics, Padre Pio could be in two places at the same time, levitate, and heal by touch—once even curing a shattered eyeball. Like the desert fathers he indulged in fisticuffs with Satan, and he shared many a legendary hermit's gift of "reading hearts," which enabled them to know people's sins (sparing the sinners the mess of an actual confession). Like an ancient prophet he could predict the future—most famously when, in the anonymity of the confessional, he foretold the papacy of a recently ordained priest (Karol Wojtyla, later Pope John Paul II). Padre Pio had many and vocal detractors: in his lifetime he was accused of being a coarse bumpkin, a fake (his Stigmata, it was claimed, were self-induced), and even a skirt chaser—his confessional was once bugged in an attempt to catch him flirting. All the accusations, save the bumpkin slur, were proved false. His cause for sainthood was stalled soon after his death, when stuffy elements in the Church hierarchy deemed him more sensationalist than spiritual. But Pope John Paul II, a lifelong supporter, advanced his cause, and Padre Pio was beatified on May 2, 1999.

THE FEAST OF SAINT THECLA

Close personal friend of Saint Paul, 1st century

Invoked for the protection of newborns; against fire • (emblem: palm)

In the 1969 revision of the Calendar of Saints, this Feast Day was officially suppressed. Here's why: in her hometown of Iconomium, Thecla fell under the influence of the dynamic Saint Paul and rebuffed her politically connected pagan fiancé. She then began, in today's parlance, to stalk the Saint. Paul refused to baptize her, on the grounds that she was too attractive. Her rejected suitor got huffy and had them both arrested. Thecla was ordered burned alive, but a storm from Heaven put out the fire. She then followed Paul to Antioch, where he continued to deny her the sacrament of baptism, and she rejected yet another pagan swain. Once again Thecla and Paul were arrested. This time, after the lions in the arena would not consume her but were content to lick her feet, Thecla jumped into a large vat of water, thereby baptizing herself but killing the seals that were swimming in it. Winning a big thumbs-up from the crowd, Thecla was released. She tracked Paul down, joined him on his missionary travels, and lived to be ninety—attributing her longevity and healing abilities to her virginity.

24. THE FEAST OF SAINT GERARD

Oenophile bishop, martyr, 1046

Patron of Hungary, tutors • (emblem: lance)

Gerard walked from Venice to Hungary wearing only a pair of wooden clogs. There he befriended Saint Stephen, the king, who appointed this intellectual monk tutor to his son. Gerard became bishop, renowned for such acts of charity as taking lepers into his own bed. At the same time he was a noted wine connoisseur who carefully selected the wines used at Mass. After Stephen's death pagan factions claimed the throne of Hungary. The evil Duke Vatha, an avowed enemy of Our Saint, ordered his soldiers to pelt Gerard's carriage with stones. The Saint stood up, made the Sign of the Cross, and the stones remained suspended in midair. He was then dragged from the carriage and killed, his body stuffed into a barrel and rolled into a river.

25. THE FEAST OF SAINT CADOC
Whimsical, miracle-working monk, 577

Invoked against cramps, deafness, glandular disorders • (emblem: bishop on bridge giving a cat to the Devil)

Cadoc's dashing father, a Welsh king, abducted the daughter of a rival and after a fierce battle escaped with the princess. The Saint was born soon afterward. On the night of Cadoc's birth, an Irish monk came to retrieve a stolen cow, and the king somehow saw this as a sign to entrust his newborn son to the old monk. Animals continued to figure prominently in the Saint's life, even after he himself became a monk. A white mouse once led him to a stash of corn (after he had tied a spool of thread to its leg) that enabled him to feed the starving monks in his monastery. And a white boar cut a swath in the fields, showing Cadoc what would be the site of his future monastery and church, the Church of the Stags.

THE FEAST OF SAINT FINBAR (AKA BARRY)
Fair-haired abbot, 633

Patron of Cork

Originally named Lochan, Finbar was the illegitimate son of a metalworker and a royal lady. He was the shame of the court until a group of hermits spirited him off. While cutting the boy's hair one day, a hermit exclaimed, "*Finbar! Shining hair!*" thus changing his name. Finbar in his youth rescued a small town being terrorized by a serpent as large as a hill. He sprinkled the beast with holy oil, causing it to flee, roaring, into the sea, tearing up the land in its wake and forming a river. It was there that Finbar built his monastery, which attracted a large following and created what is now the city of Cork. When the Pope wanted to travel to Ireland and consecrate Finbar as bishop, the Saint pointedly refused him, explaining that Heaven itself wished to perform the ceremony. Which Heaven did—during it Finbar was lifted by Angels high above the altar, and oil poured forth, covering the feet of those nearby. Then Christ appeared and took Finbar by the hand—after which the Saint's right hand always emitted rays of light. Sometime later, crossing the English Channel in Saint David's boat, the *Horse,* Finbar hailed Saint Brendan, who was heading in the other direction on his way to discover America. When Finbar died the sun didn't set for two weeks.

26. THE FEAST OF SAINTS COSMAS AND DAMIAN

Barber-surgeon martyrs, 300

Patrons of barbers, candy makers, chemical workers, doctors, druggists, hairstylists, surgeons; invoked against bladder disease, blindness, hernia, pestilence • (emblem: mortar and pestle)

Twin brothers born in Arabia, Cosmas and Damian were doctors who never charged a fee and subsequently became known as the "moneyless ones." When a grateful patient forced three eggs on Damian as payment, Cosmas became indignant and announced that he would not be buried with his greedy twin. After their martyrdom their followers, complying with Cosmas's request, started to bury the twins separately. A camel (the Saints were veterinarians as well) trotted over and begged the mourners, in the name of all four-legged creatures, to bury them together. The Saints' most famous feat was transplanting a healthy white leg onto a black patient (or vice versa). At their martyrdom Cosmas and Damian caused arrows and stones to boomerang back to the executioners until they succumbed to the usually fail-safe method of beheading. In Rome the Medicis (whose name means "doctors" in Italian) were devotees of these Saints and named a number of their offspring Cosmo. Saint Damian, on his own, cures bladder problems.

THE FEAST OF SAINT ELZEAR

Chivalrous, married diplomat, 1323

Patron of Christian gentlemen • (emblems: knotted cord, lily)

Elzear's mother consecrated him to God when he was an infant, and even as a child he mortified himself by wearing a knotted cord around his waist. He was married at sixteen to the heiress Delphina, an equally devout lady who shared his passion for Holy Communion and had only slight difficulty convincing Elzear to agree to a virgin union. The holy couple set up housekeeping in Delphina's castle, following a strict moral code that forbade backbiting, dice, and oppression, and included daily Holy Communion services. When Elzear was sent on a mission to Paris, Delphina voiced concern about his virtue, but Elzear pointed out that if he hadn't fallen into evil ways in Naples (where he had served as tutor to the king's son), he wasn't likely to in Paris. But he did, in fact, fall sick there. He made his last confession—no mortal sins—and died. Fifty-one years later he was canonized by his nephew and godson, Pope Urban V.

27. THE FEAST OF SAINT VINCENT DE PAUL

Humanitarian and founder, 1660

Patron of charitable societies, horses, hospital workers, lepers, Madagascar, prisoners, Vietnam; invoked to find lost objects • (emblem: child in his arms)

The son of a swineherd, Vincent was ordained a priest in 1600, when he was just nineteen. He landed a cushy job as chaplain to a noble family at Folleville and began to visit the impoverished peasants of the countryside. Realizing the deplorable physical and moral state of the poor (he heard some shocking confessions), he founded the Vincentians, an order of priests dedicated to ministering to the oppressed. With the help of Saint Louise de Marillac, he next established the Sisters of Charity. The compassion of "Monsieur Vincent" was legendary—he set up a sort of welfare system for the French proletariat; like their founder the Vincentians were devoted to invalids, orphans, war victims, convicts, and galley slaves. Vincent himself once traded places with a convict in the galleys, having heard the man despair of ever again seeing his wife and children. The Saint slaved for weeks until his followers bought his freedom; his ankles were permanently swollen from the shackles he had worn. Vincent had a gift for persuading the wealthy, especially women, to be charitable. He was an influential adviser to Queen Anne of Austria but could never convince her to fire the infamous Cardinal Mazarin (who enjoyed ridiculing Vincent's homely face and frumpy dress).

28. THE FEAST OF SAINT BERNARDINO OF FELTRE

Usury-smiting preacher, 1494

Patron of bankers, pawnbrokers • (emblem: pawnbrokers' three balls)

This Saint changed his name from Martin, in the belief that Bernardino of Siena had foretold his coming: "After me will come another Bernardino." Around the same time he gave up music, maintaining that "chants are not pleasing to the Lord." He overcame his stage fright and self-consciousness about his *piccolino* (minuscule) height to become a firebrand preacher, once breaking a blood vessel during a zealous sermon. Bernardino, unsparing of either clergy or nobility, railed against fast living and its trappings—finery, hairpieces, dice—and ended each of his missions with a "bonfire of the vanities." He directed his wrath in particular at moneylenders and established his own *mons pietatis* (Church-sponsored pawnshops). Shortly before his death he predicted the invasion of Italy, saying he could "hear the French shoeing their horses."

THE FEAST OF SAINT THIEMO

Bavarian nobleman, monk, graphic artist, 1101

Patron of engravers

A Benedictine monk of Salzburg, Thiemo won great renown for his skill as an artist working in metal and became archbishop of the city. Loyal to Pope Gregory VII in the Pope's ongoing feud with the German emperor Henry IV, Thiemo was imprisoned and exiled. He joined a Crusade, was captured by the Saracens at Ascalon, and was martyred for refusing to apostatize to Islam.

THE FEAST OF SAINT WENCESLAUS

Militantly Christian king, martyr, 929

Patron of Bohemia, brewers, sheep • (emblem: banner with eagle)

Wenceslaus was taken from his pagan mother, Drahomira (the "disheveled one"), and given to his saintly grandmother Saint Ludmila for upbringing. Ludmila urged Wenceslaus to seize the throne from his mother and enforce Christianity, but in 921 the evil queen had the old lady killed. At twenty Wenceslaus was recognized as king and set out to enforce his own boorish brand of Christianity. During royal banquets he would pressure guests to recite the Our Father, unmercifully beating those who refused. Indifferent to the animosity of his mother and brother, he concentrated on his devotion to the Holy Mass, personally making the wine and wafers for the ceremony. He built churches, did good deeds at night, and worked tirelessly for the conversion of his subjects. To the horror of his enemies, Wenceslaus established relations with the rest of the Christian world, allying his country with Emperor Henry of Germany (who gave him the arm of Saint Vitus in a goodwill gesture). He ignored warnings of treason, and when he was murdered by his brother, Boleslaus, he died crying out, "God forgive thee, brother." His mother flung herself on the dead body of her son but hastened away when she learned Boleslaus was planning to kill her as well. Wenceslaus' relics became the site of a pilgrimage, and his face on coins a symbol of Czech nationalism. He was unknown in Britain, a country he never visited, until it was discovered his name scanned with a traditional melody. So, centuries after his death, he became the subject of a Christmas carol, "Good King Wenceslaus," and eventually an English folk hero.

29. THE FEAST OF SAINT MICHAEL (MICHAELMAS)

Prince of Heaven and Archangel

Patron of ambulance drivers, bankers, the Basques, Brussels, coopers, EMTs, Germany, grocers, hatters, mountaintops, Papua New Guinea, paramedics, paratroopers, police officers, radiologists; invoked against peril at sea • (emblem: in armor, standing on dragon)

After Pope Leo XII had an out-of-body experience in which he saw Michael victorious over the horrors of Hell, he wrote the prayer to the Angel-Saint that is still recited at the end of every Sunday Mass. But Michael figures prominently in Judaism and Islam as well as in Christianity. He appeared to Moses in the burning bush and discoursed with Abraham, and the Koran states that his tears formed the cherubim. Majestic in appearance, with a tremendous wingspan, Michael is described by Mohammed as having "wings the color of green emeralds covered with saffron hairs, each of them containing a million faces." Before the creation of the world, he was God's commander in chief in the war against Lucifer/Satan and defeated an army of 133 million fallen Angels before hurling the Devil into Hell, bellowing, "I am Michael, Who is like God!" As Guardian Angel of Israel, he single-handedly wiped out an Assyrian army of 185,000 men, was responsible for the victory of Judas Maccabaeus, and wrested Moses' dead body from the Devil (who maintained that the prophet belonged in Hell for killing an Egyptian). In modern times, Michael defended a convent of nuns in England during the Reformation, protected a party of schoolgirls from robbers, and vanquished the enemies of an Italian town by his use of lightning. Once the Devil, seeking revenge on his old enemy, flew up to earth, terrifying the workers of the Church of Saint Michael in Cornhill, England, where he left his claw marks on the bells. Michael enjoyed renewed popularity after he appeared on battlefields in Italy, France, and England during the two world wars, even commandeering a plane during World War II. At the end of the world he will return to earth for his final battle with the Antichrist, after which he will assist with the judging on Judgment Day—for this reason he is depicted in art ready to fight or to judge, wearing his shield and carrying his scales. Those scales account for his traditional Patronage of grocers.

THE FEAST OF SAINT RAPHAEL

Archangel from the Old Testament Book of Tobit

Patron of druggists, Guardian Angels, health inspectors, the mentally ill, travelers; invoked when leaving home, for happy meetings, against blindness and nightmares • (emblems: pilgrim's staff and purse)

In Hebrew the name of this Archangel (described by the poet Milton as "affable") means "the shining one who heals." According to the Old Testament Book of Tobit (which is considered noncanonical, or apocryphal, by Protestants, who like to take the fun out of everything), Raphael, calling himself Azarias, was of great assistance to the hero Tobias. Together they caught the magic fish that cured the blindness of Tobias's old father, Tobit, and drove out the evil spirit from the beautiful but five times widowed Sara. Raphael is also believed to be the Angel who "troubles the waters" of the curative pool Bethesda in Jerusalem.

30. THE FEAST OF SAINT JEROME

Stern Vulgate translator, Doctor of the Church, 419

Patron of librarians, students • (emblem: skull)

The most learned of the Latin fathers, Saint Jerome, who was actually named Hieronymus, was born in Yugoslavia. He traveled with the smart patrician set in Rome and was known for his sarcastic wit and aggressiveness. Once, however, after reading Cicero, Jerome dreamed that it was Judgment Day and that he was standing before God, pleading that he was a Christian. But the Deity huffed, "Thou liest! Thou are a Ciceronian!" Transformed by the dream, Jerome moved his library to the desert and lived there as a hermit, writing books and learning Hebrew, but often tormented by impure thoughts of his former life. After four years, emaciated and burned black by the sun, he returned to Rome, there to join the priesthood. He worked as the Pope's secretary and became an adviser on celibacy to a group of wealthy Roman women. Jerome befriended Saint Paula, treating her daughters as his own. His relationship with Paula lent itself to scandalous gossip and contributed to his already immense unpopularity. In later years he and Paula—and Paula's fortune—founded a monastic settlement in Bethlehem, and it was there that Jerome did most of his writing, including his most famous work, the Latin version of the Bible that came to be known as the Vulgate. His genuine devotion to Paula aside—he was inconsolable at her death—Jerome deplored women, marriage, and sex. He even argued that any man who loved his wife too much was guilty of adultery, on the first principle that "it *must* be bad to touch a woman." When it was pointed out to him that Saint Peter himself was married, Jerome replied that the first Pope had "washed away the dirt of his marriage with his martyrdom." Some theologians of the time maintained, based on Scripture, that Mary had other children after Jesus. Jerome vigorously denied this, asserting, moreover, that Her hymen had remained intact even after the Virgin Birth. A gentler side of this fierce Saint is revealed in the story of the lion with the thorn in its paw, which came limping to Jerome for aid. Our Saint removed the thorn, domesticated the lion, and put it in charge of his donkey.

THE FEAST OF SAINT SOPHIA
Allegorical figure, 2nd century

Patron of widows • (emblem: carrying her three daughters)

Sophia is an extremely popular Eastern saint whose legend has it that during the persecution of Hadrian, her three daughters, Faith, Hope, and Charity (ages, respectively, twelve, ten, and nine), were martyred with unusual cruelty. A magnificent four-steepled mosque in Istanbul was once known as the Church of Hagia Sophia—that is, of Holy Wisdom—and the vulgar seem to have thought it was dedicated to a Saint by that name. The Greek American movie producers Spyros and George Skouras—both devoted to this Saint—financed the building of a large cathedral in her honor in Hollywood. It was there that the sad funeral of Telly Savalas (who is not yet beatified) took place.

❧ October ❧

1. THE FEAST OF SAINT REMI

Bishop, Apostle of the Franks, 530

Patron of France • (emblem: vessel of oil)

Remigius demonstrated his sanctity at an early age—as a babe at the breast he cured a blind man with a squirt of his mother's milk. He was appointed the first bishop of Rheims when he was only twenty-two and ministered to the pagan Franks for seventy years. Clothilda, queen of the Franks, was a devout Christian. Her husband, King Clovis, was anything but. At the queen's urging her husband invoked Christ's aid before his battle with the neighboring Alemanni and won a great victory. Forthwith Clovis and three thousand of his subjects were baptized by Bishop Remi on Christmas Day 496. On that memorable occasion Angels descended and replaced the heraldic toads on the Frankish flag with the fleur-de-lis of France.

THE FEAST OF SAINT THÉRÈSE OF LISIEUX ("THE LITTLE FLOWER")

Pious sickly nun, 1897

Patron of AIDS patients, Alabama, foreign missions, France, pilots, religious freedom in Russia, Vietnam; invoked against tuberculosis • (emblem: roses entwining crucifix)

The youngest of five sisters, all Sisters—that is to say, all nuns—this member of an obscure French Carmelite cloister became, soon after her early demise, the center of a worldwide cult. Their sacred text is her artless, not to say simpleminded, autobiography, titled in English *The Story of a Soul.* So sheltered and uneventful was her life that the Vatican, with an irony approaching sarcasm, appointed her Patron of airline pilots as well as foreign missions. (She had, in fact, once expressed a desire to be sent as a missionary to French Indochina, i.e., Vietnam—but her delicate health precluded travel.) The secret of her sanctity was what she called her "little way." Forbidden because of her fragility to starve, whip, or mutilate herself as the Great Virgin-Martyr-Saints of the past had done, Thérèse discovered she could make herself beatifically miserable by enduring the *little* things. She would not brush away a fly or scratch an itch. She would sleep under a heavy blanket in the summer heat and without it in winter. She would piously and smilingly endure the irritating faults of others (while keeping careful count). Imagine her delight—and that of all who knew her—when she came down with a lethal, blood-spitting case of tuberculosis.

2. THE FEAST OF THE GUARDIAN ANGELS

Patrons of police officers • (emblem: barefoot four-winged Angels on a wheel)

Every person who has ever lived or will ever live is assigned one. Though often ignored, being invisible, they try to help their charges be moral and make the virtuous decision. They are not recognized as an "article of Faith" by the Church, although Pope Leo X, in 1518, issued a bull assigning this date as their annual Feast. Generations of Catholic youth were reminded, when dancing, to "leave room for your Guardian Angel."

THE FEAST OF SAINT LEGER

Betrayed and blinded bishop, 679

Invoked against blindness • (emblem: pincers holding an eyeball)

This bishop involved himself perhaps overmuch with Frankish politics and was found guilty, on purely circumstantial evidence, of murdering Childeric, heir to the throne. Leger's eyes were removed, as were his lips and tongue. Some years later he was executed, "still protesting his innocence"—which cannot have been easy to do thus handicapped.

3. THE FEAST OF SAINT GERARD OF BROGNE
Reforming abbot, 959

Invoked against jaundice, scrofula • (emblem: Saint Peter appearing to him)

The marquis of Flanders chanced, while attending a Mass said by this military man turned Benedictine, to pass an enormous and painful kidney stone. Understandably grateful, he assigned Gerard the task of traveling from abbey to abbey throughout his realm to enforce much-needed monastic reforms and to restore, miraculously if need be, the sickly monks therein to holy vigor.

Also: The Feast of Saints Ewald the Dark and Ewald the Fair, Northumbrian brothers martyred near Dortmund, 695; and Saint Thomas Cantelupe, contentious bishop of Hereford, banished to France, 1282.

4. THE FEAST OF SAINT FRANCIS OF ASSISI
Nature lover, 1226

Patron of animals, ecology, Italy, merchants, needleworkers, tapestry makers; invoked against fire • (emblem: preaching to birds, deer, wolf)

Francis of Assisi's great popularity, even among unbelievers, has never waned— he remains a subject for garden statuary and Hollywood movies, and pets of all faiths wear his medal. The son of a wealthy cloth merchant, Francis was, in his youth, extravagant and carefree, a troubadour and knight at arms. But on a pilgrimage to Rome he impulsively exchanged his rich attire for a beggar's grimy garb. And on his return to Assisi he took to dismounting from his horse and passionately kissing lepers. When he was twenty-six, while praying in a ruined chapel, he heard an image of the Crucified say to him, "Repair My falling house." Taking Him literally, Francis immediately began restoring the building. In need of funds, he sold bolts of cloth taken from his father's warehouse. His angry parent hauled him before the bishop and disinherited his apparently mad son. Francis happily removed the clothes he was wearing at the time and gave them back. The bishop clad the naked Saint in the rough brown tunic of his gardener; this is the origin of the distinctive Franciscan habit. Francis departed, singing, and was immediately beaten and thrown into a ditch by a band of ruffians. But the knight-troubadour had found his True Love: "My Lady Poverty," he called her. With a few like-minded companions (friars), he wandered the countryside, begging and preaching. Francis wrote a very strict rule for them to live by, emphasizing absolute poverty, humility, and discipline. During his life, and in the following centuries, that rule has been (acrimoniously) liberalized, conserved, reformed, and modified many times. But Francis himself was not so much a religious organizer as a charismatic example—a hero. He preached a sermon to the birds; he made a peace treaty with a wolf; he instituted the tradition of the Christmas crib. And in 1224, while praying, he was granted the Stigmata—the marks of Christ's five wounds on his own body. In 1226, nearly blind and very ill, he composed and sang his "Canticle of Brother Sun" and joyfully went to meet his "sister death." He had wished to be buried in paupers' field but instead was enshrined in the lavish basilica in Assisi that bears his name.

Also: The Feast of Saint Petronius, who was so moved by a journey to the Holy Land that when he returned home he strove to make his city, Bologna, "Little Jerusalem" down to the most minor detail. He succeeded in this devout endeavor, but the city was destroyed by the Huns anyhow, 445.

5. THE FEAST OF SAINT PLACID

Water-walking monk, martyr, 540

Invoked against chills, drowning • (emblem: hung by his heels over smoke)

A young monk beloved of Saint Benedict, Placid was saved from drowning by Saint Maurus when, on Benedict's instructions, Maurus dashed across the surface of the lake to rescue Our Drowning Saint. Placid's grateful father made a land grant to the Benedictine Order—and there the great abbey of Monte Cassino was erected in A.D. 529. According to a bogus legend, Placid later founded a monastery in Sicily, where he, with his brothers and a sister, was massacred by African pirates.

Also: The Feast of Saint Flora of Beaulieu, an unpopular, cranky nun with the gift of second sight, 1347.

6. THE FEAST OF SAINT BRUNO

Considerate abbot, 1101

Patron of Ruthenia; invoked against demonic possession • (motto: *O Bonitas!*)

The founder of the Carthusians, Bruno was born in Cologne in 1030. He became a scholar and teacher at Rheims, where he ran afoul of the scandalously corrupt and worldly archbishop Manasses. When a dead man whose funeral Our Saint was conducting sat up and spoke emotionally about God's strict judgment, Bruno resolved to become an old-fashioned desert-style hermit and, with six companions, set out for the mountain wilderness of the Grande Chartreuse, near Grenoble. There they were welcomed by Saint Hugh, the local bishop, who had recently received a vision of seven stars—clearly prophesying their arrival. Bishop Hugh once heard that an order of beef had been delivered to Bruno and his holy hermits during Lent and arrived to find the men in their dining hall, sitting in a trance before the offending carnal joint. Hugh made the Sign of the Cross over it, transformed it into a turtle, and awakened the monks, who ate sinlessly.

THE FEAST OF SAINT FAITH OF AGEN

Crusader-inspiring virgin martyr, 3rd century

Patron of the military, pilgrims, prisoners • (emblem: grate)

The charred remains of this virgin martyr, stored in an ornate reliquary at Conques, France, were long an object of pilgrimages, especially by Crusaders on their way to holy war. Her cult remains strong in Bogotá, Colombia. Her impregnable virtue was rewarded by her being immolated on a brazen bed during the persecutions conducted by the Roman governor of Aquitaine, the notorious Dacian. The English call her Saint Foy—and her legend is sometimes confused with that of an earlier Greek martyr of the same name.

7. THE FEAST OF SAINT JUSTINA

Sword-slain virgin martyr, 4th century

Patron of Padua, Venice • (emblem: with a sword through her breasts)

The beautiful daughter of a pagan king, Justina was baptized by a (miraculously long-lived) disciple of Saint Peter himself and went to live with the bishop of Padua. While crossing a bridge over the river Po, she was arrested by soldiers and knelt to pray for courage—her knees left dents in the stone bridge that remain there to this day, providing a tourist attraction. One of her emblems is a unicorn, symbolizing her treasured virginity.

THE FEAST OF SAINTS SERGIUS AND BACCHUS

Military deserters, 303

Patrons of desert nomads and (unofficially) gay men • (emblem: in ill-fitting frocks, bearing palms)

Sergius and Bacchus were Roman army officers stationed in Syria, and the favorites of Emperor Maximian, until he noticed the two weren't anywhere to be found during his daily sacrifices to Jupiter. He confronted Sergius and Bacchus; they admitted their Christianity, and the furious emperor not only stripped them of their rank but ordered them to parade through the streets of Arabissus dressed in women's clothes. Bacchus (no relation to the Roman god) was scourged to death, and Sergius was beheaded, after walking all the way to Rosafa in shoes with nails in them. So great was the fame of these martyrs at one time that the emperor Justinian renamed Rosafa Sergiopolis. But the image of these two husky centurions sashaying around in drag started giving people the wrong idea, and their Feast Day has been removed from the Calendar of Saints.

Also: The Feast of Saint Osyth, an Englishwoman whose husband preferred hunting to her embrace, so she became a nun, 675.

8. THE FEAST OF SAINT DEMETRIUS

Serbian warrior-martyr, 300

Patron of Bulgaria, Macedonia, Serbia • (emblem: warrior in armor, leaning on a sword)

As a matter of historical fact, Demetrius appears to have been a simple missionary deacon who was martyred at Mitrovica in Serbia around the year 300. In legend he is a great warrior-Saint, a knight similar to Saint George, invoked by his Balkan clients in their endless wars against the Austrians, Avars, Hungarians, Slavs, Turks, and each other.

THE FEAST OF SAINT PELAGIA

Exotic dancer, penitent, 304

Patron of actresses • (emblem: kneeling, her jewels on the ground)

This Pelagia (there are many others) was, in fact, a performer—a glamorous singer-dancer-stripper in decadent Old Antioch. Her stage name was Pearl. Bishop Nonnus of Edessa chanced (we know not how) to catch her act and in a sermon the next day proclaimed, "This girl is a lesson to us bishops! She takes more trouble over her beauty and her dancing than we do about our souls and flocks." Pelagia chanced (again, we know not how) to hear this sermon. She confessed her sins to the bishop, was baptized by him, gave him all her money, and departed for Jerusalem. There, in male-hermit drag, she lived until her death as Pelagius, the beardless monk.

THE FEAST OF SAINT REPARATA

Fireproof virgin martyr, 3rd century

Patron of Florence • (emblem: dove flying from her mouth)

When she was thrown into a furnace of fire, Reparata sang out joyfully and emerged unharmed. The prefect—unmoved by her performance—called her "horrid and talkative." He ordered her beheaded instantly, and Reparata was led away, loudly singing and chatting about God. Once her head was off, her soul was observed rising to Heaven in the form of a dove.

THE FEAST OF SAINT THAÏS

Upscale penitent prostitute, 4th century

Patron of fallen women • (emblem: burning her jewels)

A beautiful and wealthy harlot of Alexandria, Thaïs had been raised as a Christian, and when reminded of this fact by Saint Paphnutius, a visiting desert monk, she burned her wardrobe, gave away her jewelry, and entered the convent. To help her atone for her sins, her superiors lodged Thaïs in a low, narrow room furnished with a small hole, through which she was occasionally fed bread and water. When she inquired about waste disposal, she was assured that conditions would surely be worse in Hell.

THE FEAST OF SAINT TRIDUANA

Self-mutilating abbess, date unknown

Invoked against eye troubles

This holy Benedictine abbess accompanied the treasured relics of Saint Andrew to Scotland. The abbey she founded at Restalrig, together with its miraculous well, was destroyed by devout Presbyterians in 1560. Triduana is invoked against eye troubles in honor of an edifying incident from her life—after a local clan chieftain fell in love with her because of her beautiful eyes, Our Saint plucked out the offending organs and sent them to him on a plate.

9. THE FEAST OF SAINT ANDRONICUS

Married desert hermit, 5th century

Patron of silversmiths

Andronicus' traditional Patronage of the silversmith's craft derives, reasonably enough, from the fact that this Saint was himself a silversmith, who practiced his trade in Antioch. He was for many years happily married to a woman named Athanasia but, devastated by the sudden death of their two beloved children, the couple resolved to separate and become desert hermits. Years later Andronicus happened to meet upon the road a beardless monk called Athanasius. The two became fast friends and lived contentedly in neighboring hovels, fasting and praying together until Athanasius died, leaving behind a note for Andronicus, revealing in it a secret that you, dear reader, surely have already guessed.

THE FEAST OF SAINT DENIS

Survived his own beheading, 258

Patron of France, Paris, possessed people; invoked against frenzy, headaches, strife • (emblem: bishop carrying his head)

Denis was the first bishop of Paris, one of the original seven missionaries sent from Rome to minister to the pagan Gauls, in the year 250. He might have been a Greek philosopher named Dionysius, converted and baptized by Saint Paul himself. And then again, maybe not. Our Saint was decapitated in a somewhat unsavory district of the city, thereafter known as Montmartre—the hill of the martyr. He flummoxed his persecutors by picking up his head and carrying it six miles to the present site of the great cathedral that bears his name. "The first step," said the Saint's head, "was the difficult one."

THE FEAST OF SAINT GHISLAIN

Bear-befriended abbot, 680

Invoked against twitching • (emblem: bear)

This Frankish monk once hung his cloak on a tree while gardening, and a she-bear, escaping from hunters, hid herself in it. The danger past, the ungrateful brute seized a basket containing Ghislain's Mass vestments and made off with it. Providentially, Our Saint was led to the beast's den by a friendly eagle and recovered the sacred garments. In some mysterious way this tale is said to account for the founding of the city of Mons.

THE FEAST OF SAINT LOUIS BERTRAND

Missionary to the New World, 1581

Patron of Colombia, Panama • (emblem: holding a pistol, a crucifix for its barrel)

This Spanish Dominican friar was among the first Catholic missionaries to the New World, traveling to Colombia, Panama, and many Caribbean islands from 1562 until 1568. Although Louis did not speak the language of the natives, he was granted the "gift of tongues" so that the Indians understood his many passionate sermons, and he is alleged to have personally baptized a hundred thousand of them. To his credit, he was outraged at the soldiers' and colonists' cruel treatment of the natives and loudly protested (in vain) to the authorities upon his return to Spain.

10. THE FEAST OF SAINT FRANCIS BORGIA

Great-grandson of a Pope, 1572

Patron of Portugal; invoked against earthquakes • (emblem: crowned skull)

Alexander VI was, without doubt, the worst of the "Bad Popes" of the Renaissance. Among his children by his various mistresses were the unscrupulous Cesare Borgia—Machiavelli's model for *The Prince*—and Lucretia Borgia, evil incarnate. Among his great-grandchildren was Saint Francis Borgia, the third father general of the Jesuits. He was a Spanish duke, happily married, the father of eight, fabulously wealthy, and enormously fat. Then one day, for reasons of state, he chanced to glance into the coffin of the late Queen Isabella and see the putrefied face of that once beautiful monarch. It made him think. When his own wife died Francis, then forty years old, settled his estate upon his eldest son and, with the permission of Saint Ignatius Loyola himself, joined the Society of Jesus. As a preacher, this duke turned Jesuit was especially popular among the Catholics of Portugal and, to his credit, heartily disliked by the Inquisition.

THE FEAST OF SAINT GEREON

German Roman soldier, martyr, 287

Invoked against headaches • (emblems: lance and shield)

An exquisite mosaic in Cologne Cathedral portrays the heroic martyrdom by beheading of Gereon and 33,318 other brave Christian soldiers, known locally as the Golden Saints. They were (like Saints Maurice and Victor) among the 6,660 newly baptized members of Rome's Theban Legion who, in the year 287, gave up their lives rather than obey an order to worship the "divine" Emperor Maximian.

THE FEAST OF SAINT VICTOR

Late-arriving soldier martyr, 287

Patron of the military • (emblem: in armor with banner)

In hagiographic circles there remains some understandable confusion about this soldier-Saint Victor and the soldier-Saint Victor of Marseilles. Perhaps they were one person. Perhaps he was black. Perhaps he wasn't. In some versions of the legend of the Theban Legion, *this* Saint Victor, a pagan, was delayed en route and arrived to discover 6,659 of his fellow legionnaires being slaughtered for their Faith. Moved by a combination of the Holy Spirit and esprit de corps, he joined them.

11. THE FEAST OF SAINT ALEXANDER SAULI

Counter-Reformation bishop, 1592

Patron of Corsica

While a crowd was enjoying some acrobats, little Sauli, a spoilsport from an early age, started waving his crucifix before the audience to warn them against frivolous amusements. As an adult he was such an inspiring preacher that he moved a future Saint (Charles Borromeo) and a Pope (Gregory XIV) to tears. He was sent to reform Corsica, infested at the time with obese clergy, vendettas, and apostasy. Firm—severe, perhaps—Alexander rebuilt the Faith on that island, making use of his abilities to calm storms and foretell the future to impress the natives.

THE FEAST OF SAINT GOMER

Henpecked hermit, 774

Patron of courtiers, unhappy husbands, woodcutters; invoked against hernia • (emblem: Angel pointing to a cave)

Gomer, or Gummarus, was born in 717 in a castle in Brabant. A knight of King Pepin's court, he was miserably married to a shrew named Guinimaria. When Gomer was away on business his wife was unpleasant to his retainers and employees. Once, for instance, she denied liquid refreshment to the reapers, obliging her husband to create a miraculous well to slake their thirst. During Gomer's yearly festival at Lierre, Belgium, he works wonders for hernia sufferers.

THE FEAST OF SAINT JAMES GRISSINGER

Artisan-monk, 1491

Patron of glass painters

In 1432, at the age of twenty-five, this native of Ulm, Germany, enlisted as a mercenary in the army of Naples. Appalled at "the license of military life" (in the words of Alban Butler), James resigned and found employment as a lawyer's secretary in Capua, where he stayed for five years. After another brief stint in the army, this time in Bologna, he joined, at the age of thirty-four, the Dominican Order, as a lay brother. For fifty years Brother James painted edifying pictures on glass for the fiscal benefit of all, while experiencing ecstasies and performing a miracle here and there.

Also: The Feast of the Maternity of the Blessed Virgin Mary, instituted by Pope Gregory XVI in 1831. The Mother of God, as countless works of art attest, breast-fed her Child. To the shrine of Our Lady of the Milk and Happy Delivery in Saint Augustine, Florida, the pregnant faithful swarm. A vial of Mary's own breast milk may be found at Her shrine in Walsingham, England.

12. THE FEAST OF SAINT EDWIN

Deposed, depressed Anglo-Saxon king, 633

Patron of the homeless, hoboes, kings

Edwin married a Christian, promising to consider conversion. However, being prone to melancholia, he resisted the Faith; he would sit for weeks on end trying to decide whether or not to embrace Christianity, despite the efforts of his wife and Saint Paulinus. After an assassination attempt Edwin, as they say, got religion. He assembled his nobles and, declaring the gods ineffectual, started destroying pagan temples, and was baptized in 627. Edwin built churches and made highway improvements, including putting brass cups and water fountains on the roads for thirsty travelers. It was said that during his reign a woman and her newborn child could walk from sea to sea without being molested. Edwin was slain in the Battle of Hatfield Chase, defending (and losing) his kingdom to a pagan Welsh king.

Also: The Feast of Saint Wilfrid of York, a bishop whose first posthumous miracle was to cure the arthritis of the old lady who was washing his corpse, 709.

13. THE FEAST OF SAINT COLMAN

Wandering Irish hermit, 1012

Patron of Austria, hanged men, livestock, marriage; invoked against headaches, for rain • (emblem: pilgrim holding a rope)

It appears that Colman was once a popular Irish given name, for there are over three hundred official Saints Colman—for the most part holy monks, with a bard or two tossed in for variety. *This* Colman attempted, in the year 1012, to pass through Austria on his pilgrim's progress to the Holy Land. The Austrians, at war (as usual) with the Moravians, arrested the stranger as a spy. His inability to speak German pointed to his guilt, and he was summarily hanged. The resignation with which he went to his death—and the fact that his body would not decompose—convinced his hosts of his sanctity, and they concocted a bogus royal (Scottish) lineage for him. Horses and cattle are blessed in Austria on his Feast Day.

THE FEAST OF SAINT GERALD OF AURILLAC

Malformed nobleman, 909

Patron of bachelors, counts, the handicapped

Delicate and frail his entire life, the titled and wealthy Gerald never presumed to enter the priesthood. Still, he lived in chastity and gave away his possessions to the poor. Gerald would arise at 2:00 A.M. to read the holy office and prepare for his daily Mass—albeit as an altar boy. He also richly endowed a monastery, which act of generosity entitled him to a biography by Saint Odo, and to canonization.

14. THE FEAST OF SAINT CALLISTUS

Ex-convict Pope, martyr, 222

Patron of cemetery workers • (emblem: Pope with a millstone around his neck)

Callistus was born in Rome, the Christian slave of a Christian master. Placed in charge of a Christian bank, he lost or misplaced all the Christian money. He skipped town but was caught and sentenced (by a civil court) to the treadmill. Released by claiming (falsely) that his name had been inadvertently omitted from an amnesty list, he returned to Rome and was hired by Pope Zephyrinus to supervise the papal cemetery. Eighteen years later Callistus succeeded Zephyrinus as pontiff. A man who knew something about guilt and rehabilitation, Callistus ruled that penitent sinners, even murderers, fornicators, and adulterers, were welcome in church. He also formally recognized the many shocking liaisons between Christian widows and their Christian slaves as legal marriages. This led to schism and riot, in the course of which the forgiving slave-convict-Pope was thrown down a well to his heavenly reward.

THE FEAST OF SAINT PARASCEVA

Nobly born virgin who dared to preach, 3rd century

Patron of needleworkers, spinners, weavers • (emblem: holding a cross and a scroll)

Parasceva was the daughter of nobility and a Christian convert. On trial for her Faith, she was asked her name; she replied, defiantly, "Christ!" Actually, her name means "Friday."

15. THE FEAST OF SAINT ANDEOL

Bishop of Lyons, 4th century

Patron of Switzerland • (emblem: club in his hand)

In the year 381, Saint Justus, bishop of Lyons, fled France (then known as Gaul) for Egypt, where he became a desert monk. His deacon, Andeol, was sent to fetch back the beloved bishop but found him unshakable in his resolve and was obliged to return without him, whereupon Andeol was made bishop in Justus's stead. What this all has to do with Switzerland is anybody's guess.

THE FEAST OF SAINT TERESA OF ÁVILA

Mystic author, Doctor of the Church, 1582

Patron of lace makers, Spain; invoked against headache, heart attack, by those who need grace • (emblem: flaming arrow in heart)

The first woman to be honored by the Church with the title Doctor, Teresa was controversial, charming, stubborn, and witty—a practical and energetic reformer as well as a passionate mystic. In her were combined, a poet wrote, "the eagle and the dove." As a very young child in her native Castile, Teresa read the *Lives of the Saints* and ran away from home, resolved to be gloriously martyred by the Moors. As a teenager she enjoyed racy novels and (to her everlasting shame) took an interest in perfume and fashion. At twenty she entered the large and wealthy Carmelite convent at Ávila, which was sort of on an easygoing society nunnery, where an episode of malaria left her virtually paralyzed for three years. It was not until 1555, when she was forty years of age, that Saints Mary Magdalene and Augustine of Hippo appeared to her and granted her a vision of the especially nasty place prepared for her in Hell. When her confessor, Saint Peter of Alcántara, confirmed that the voices she continued to hear and her mystical experiences (which included levitations and ecstasy) were of Divine, not demonic or psychotic, origin, Teresa undertook to save not only her own soul but that of the Carmelite Order, which until the end of her life she strove to restore to its austere and penitential primitive rule. Her efforts at reform got her rather disliked, and ultimately divided the Carmelites into shod (calced) and barefoot (discalced) branches. Teresa founded seventeen small, poor, contemplative convents. ("God preserve us from stupid nuns!" was one of her own prayers.) Influenced by her, Saint John of the Cross undertook to similarly reform the Carmelite friars. Somehow Teresa found time to write her autobiography, as well as a classic of mystical literature, *Interior Castle.* The mental distress her visions caused her— she said to God, "If this is how you treat your friends, no wonder you don't have many!"—entitles Teresa to be invoked against headaches. She experienced God's love "like a lance driven into her heart"—and on that organ, to this day displayed under glass in the convent in Ávila (it wears a little crown), deep wounds may be observed. A slice of this heart is venerated in Milan. Because the Saint's body remained miraculously incorrupt, it, like all her relics—including an arm in Lisbon and a breast at Saint Pancras's Church in Rome—has remained fresh and juicy.

16. THE FEAST OF SAINT GALL

Fierce Alpine hermit, 635

Patron of birds, Switzerland • (emblem: bear)

There are several possible reasons for this Saint's traditional Patronage of our feathered friends. Gall once performed an exorcism on a young girl, and the dispossessed demon flew out her mouth in the form of a black bird. Gall and Saint Columba lived for a while near Lake Zurich on a diet of waterfowl. Furthermore, *gallo* is Italian for "rooster." By destroying their idols and wrecking the vats in which the sacred beer was brewed, this Irish missionary offended the Swiss people and their pagan deities. He did constant battle with the local water sprites (called nixes). Finally, Gall settled in an Alpine cave (which he shared with a bear) near the town of Arbon.

THE FEAST OF SAINT GERARD MAJELLA

Woman-friendly lay brother, 1755

Patron of childbirth, lay brothers, mothers, pregnant women • (emblem: holding a crucifix, lilies near him)

Born near Naples in 1726, Gerard was in his youth properly devoted to his own (widowed) mother, whom he supported by his work as a tailor's apprentice. (He sometimes supplemented the family larder with miraculous loaves of bread donated to the pious lad by a statue of Our Lady.) Because Gerard was both tubercular and simpleminded, the Redemptorists were at first unwilling to accept him. "A useless brother," he was called. But the order's leader and founder, Saint

Alphonsus Mary de Liguori, recognized in Gerard that rare and highly useful thing, a miracle worker—someone who could (for example) cause food and/or money to materialize and/or multiply. There was ample eyewitness testimony at the time of his canonization proceedings that Gerard could heal the sick, be in two places at once, become invisible at will, read minds, fly through the air, and walk on water. All of these abilities are (come to think of it) expected of your average mother—but Gerard's special patronage of them arises from one particular incident. Once, when visiting friends, he left his handkerchief behind. The daughter of the house picked it up to return it to the Saint, but he said, "Keep it, it may be useful to you." Years later the young woman was dying in childbirth when she remembered Gerard's hankie. It was brought to her, she gripped it and prayed—and lived, the mother

of a healthy infant. Although he was a lay brother, not a priest, Gerard was the spiritual director to several communities of nuns. In 1754 an ex-novice, Neria Caggiano, accused Our Saint (the Patron of *mothers*!) of having taken scandalous liberties with her person in the course of his ministry. She was lying, of course.

THE FEAST OF SAINT HEDWIG

Pious duchess, 1243

Patron of Bavaria, bridal pairs, Silesia • (emblem: woman carrying shoes)

At the age of twelve Hedwig was married to the duke of Silesia, Henry I (the Bearded) and bore him six children—a miracle in itself, given her aversion to her husband and to sex in general. It is said that she never spoke to him in private and managed to convince him of the sinfulness of intercourse during Lent, on all Sundays and holy days, and during her pregnancies. Finally, after twenty-five years of wedded grief, Hedwig moved into a nearby convent. There she distinguished herself by habitually kissing the seats of chairs, pews, and stools. She also enjoyed washing the feet of the nuns, then drinking the dirty water. She herself, as she wandered the dukedom doing good deeds, never wore shoes, and her feet were a mess. Her estranged husband sent her a pair of shoes, commanding her never to appear in public without them. Thereafter clever Hedwig✝ carried them everywhere under her arm. On her Feast Day it is traditional to bake Hedwig's bread—a loaf in the form of a shoe.

✝ *Pictured at right*

THE FEAST OF SAINT MARGARET MARY

French nun to whom Christ exposed His Sacred Heart, 1690

Invoked against polio • (emblem: kneeling in her cell before Christ)

In 1654, when she was seven, Margaret Mary was inspired to take a vow of chastity, without (as she later acknowledged in her autobiography) the vaguest idea what the words *vow* and *chastity* meant. From her eighth to her fifteenth year she was bedridden with an illness, possibly poliomyelitis, possibly cured by a miracle. As an adolescent she was tempted to marry, until Christ appeared to her and "made [her] see He was the most handsome, the richest, the most powerful, the most perfect and accomplished of lovers." Thus reminded by the jealous Savior of her childhood engagement to Him, she entered the Visitation convent at Paray-le-Monial in central France. She went to work in the infirmary, where Sister Margaret Mary, clumsy and slow, and the infirmarian, Sister Mary Catherine, brisk and efficient, became spiritually edifying trials to each other. It was on the Feast of Saint John the Divine, December 27, 1673, that Christ again appeared to Our Saint, and invited her out to dinner—in fact, to take the traditional place of Saint John at Our Lord's side, leaning on his breast at the Last Supper. For some time thereafter Jesus continued to appear to Margaret Mary, invariably opening

His shirt to expose a flaming, throbbing, crimson organ—His Sacred Heart—to which she, of all people, had been especially chosen to spread devotion. Her mother superior took an understandably dim view of these revelations, and her fellow nuns were somewhat resentful when Margaret Mary informed them that Jesus had personally asked *her* to expiate *their* sins.

17. THE FEAST OF SAINT RICHARD GWYN

Welshman martyred by Elizabeth I, 1584

Patron of large families, schoolteachers, torture victims

Richard was quite the proper Protestant: a graduate of Cambridge University, a schoolmaster with a large family, and a sometime poet. Then he did the unthinkable—converted to Catholicism. When he stopped attending Protestant services, Richard aroused suspicion. Finally arrested for his refusal to conform, he was dragged to a local church, where he made such a ruckus with his chains that the preacher could not be heard. His seditious behavior, which included mocking the magistrate's red nose, caused Our Saint to be convicted of treason and sentenced to death. In the middle of being disemboweled he understandably screamed out, "*O Duw gwyn, pa beth ydyw hwn?*" which in Welsh meant "Holy God, what is this?"

Also: The Feast of Saint Ignatius of Antioch, bishop of Syria and Doctor of the Church, who as an old man was devoured by lions in the Roman Colosseum, c. 107. The seven letters he wrote to his fellow believers constitute most of what we know about the theory and practice of 1st-century Christianity.

18. THE FEAST OF SAINT LUKE

Portrait painter–physician-evangelist, 1st century

Patron of butchers, doctors, glass industry workers, lace makers, notaries, painters, sculptors • (emblem: winged ox)

The author of the third Gospel and the Acts of the Apostles was a Greek-speaking native of Antioch, Syria. He was Saint Paul's disciple, faithful companion, and personal "beloved" physician (Colossians 4:14). Luke's Gospel, which is the most quotable and "poetic," was obviously written for an audience of gentiles rather than Jews—it emphasizes the universality of Christ's message rather than His fulfilling of Hebrew prophecies. Luke's heavenly interest in graphic artists arises from the legend that he himself painted in oils—his portrait of the Madonna and Child has, alas, been lost. Tradition alleges he never married and was crucified in his eighty-fourth year, alongside Saint Andrew at Patras. Luke's emblem is, inexplicably, a winged ox—which earned him the veneration of butchers.

Also: The Feast of three different Welsh virgin Saints, all named Gwen.

19. THE FEAST OF THE JESUIT MARTYRS

Ingeniously slain by Iroquois, 1649

Patrons of Canada

The first brave missionary priests (known to the natives as Blackrobes) came from old France to New France in 1608 for the purpose of harvesting untold thousands of heathen souls. They began their work among members of the peaceful Huron tribe, and in 1637 the first adult Indian—a Huron—was instructed, converted, and baptized. At that rate, who knows how many souls they might have saved? But by 1650 the entire as-yet-unredeemed Huron nation had been sent to Hell and seven saintly Blackrobes to Heaven by the neighboring Iroquois. Pères Brébeouf, Chabanel, Garnier, Jogues, Lalande, and Lalement, S.J., heroically endured their martyrdom as they were variously flayed, mutilated, scalded, dismembered, decapitated, incinerated, and/or eaten.

ST ISAAC JOGUES

THE FEAST OF SAINT FRIDESWIDE

Blindingly beautiful abbess, 735

Patron of Oxford University • (emblem: nun holding a model of a city)

The very attractive daughter of an Anglian prince, Frideswide spurned the amorous advances of a suitor who pursued her as far as Oxford town and there was struck blind for his troubles.

THE FEAST OF SAINT PHILIP HOWARD

Elizabethan martyr, 1595

Patron of victims of betrayal, difficult marriages, separated spouses • (emblem: nobleman posing with a greyhound)

His father was the duke of Norfolk, a serious suitor to Mary, Queen of Scots; it was said of his family: "The race of Howards could never be made to hide their face from the enemy." Despite his lineage Philip became a foppish Protestant earl, the popinjay darling of Queen Elizabeth, and ignored his wife (whom he married at twelve) most of his adult life. But, after falling under the influence of the valiant Saint Edmund Campion, Philip converted to Catholicism and reconciled with his wife, now also a convert. Arrested, he was placed in the Tower of London, accused (falsely) of praying for the success of the Spanish Armada. He was told he could see his wife if he would attend a Protestant service. He refused and died in the Tower of London, never having seen his only son.

THE FEAST OF SAINT RENÉ GOUPIL

Painfully martyred Jesuit, 1642

Patron of anesthesiologists

Born in France in 1606, René was judged too sickly to join the notoriously robust Jesuit Order. Instead, he became a surgeon and as such joined the Jesuit mission to the colony of New France. He accompanied Isaac Jogues on a trip through Mohawk country (near what is now Albany, New York). Both priest and doctor were captured and brutally tortured: their hair, beards, and fingernails were torn out, their fingers hacked off with clamshells. On September 29, René was tomahawked for making the Sign of the Cross on the head of a child—thereby becoming the first Christian to die for his Faith in the New World.

20. THE FEAST OF SAINT CONTARDO FERRINI

Pious intellectual, 1902

Patron of universities

This modern-day Italian scholar is held up to the Faithful as an example of academic holiness—all too rare in these days of secular humanism. During his college days in Milan, Contardo had a reputation for being something of a nerd—but a pious one, it was agreed. He mastered a dozen languages and earned a Ph.D. In 1880 he (reluctantly) left home for the first time to pursue his studies at the University of Berlin. Shocked by the morals of his fellow students, he made a secret—and possibly quite unnecessary—vow of perpetual virginity. Back in Milan he became a professor of Roman law, concentrating on the Byzantine period. Allegedly, students crowded his lectures, "amazed to discover a professor who believes in God."

THE FEAST OF SAINT WENDELIN

German shepherd turned hermit, 650

Patron of farmers, herdsmen, pastures • (emblem: sheep)

In 1417 a great fire in the German city of Saarbrücken was miraculously extinguished through the intercession of this Saint, who had died eight centuries earlier. According to his legend, Wendel was the son of a Scottish king who, because of his excessive piety, was condemned to herd swine. How he ended up tending sheep in southwest Germany is not known, but he is still venerated there for his simple sanctity and heavenly veterinary skills.

21. THE FEAST OF SAINT HILARION

Miracle-working recluse, 372

Patron of solitude • (emblem: praying in a cave, surrounded by female demons)

Born in Gaza and a convert at age fifteen, Hilarion adopted Saint Antony as a role model, wearing only sackcloth given him by that Saint. And he never changed that garment until it disintegrated, inspiring this apologia from Alban Butler, "It is idle to look for cleanliness in a hair-shirt." Though he openly resented the intrusions on his four-by-five-foot cell, Hilarion still worked miracles, including curing both barren women and drought. His fame caused him to flee, but no matter where he went—Egypt, Sicily, and Cyprus—he always developed a new following. Delicate in his youth, Hilarion is a testament to the efficacy of a vegan diet: he ate only some oil and fifteen figs a day but lived to be past eighty.

THE FEAST OF SAINT JOHN OF BRIDLINGTON

Very ordinary monk, 1379

Invoked against complications in childbirth • (emblem: monk with a crosier)

A native of the town of Thwing in Yorkshire (he is sometimes known as John Thwing), this Augustinian prior led a life "absolutely devoid of a single incident of interest," in the words of the British hagiographer Sabine Baring-Gould. Nevertheless, many pilgrims' prayers have been answered at his tomb, including, one supposes, from his traditionally sanctioned Patronage, those of pregnant women.

THE FEAST OF
SAINT URSULA

Princess martyred with 11,000 other virgins, 4th century

Patron of orphans, schoolgirls, tailors, teachers, universities; invoked against plague • (emblem: queen, maidens kneeling beneath her cloak)

A cryptic inscription on a basilica at Cologne gave rise to the story of the martyrdom of Ursula and her eleven thousand maidens. According to *The Golden Legend,* she was a famously beautiful British (that is to say, Breton) princess engaged against her will to marry a pagan prince of England. Ursula sought to prevent or at least delay the nuptials by insisting that ten English virgins, each accompanied by a thousand chaste handmaids, convert to Christianity and join her on a pilgrimage to Rome. To her astonishment, the prince agreed. Once this holy sorority was gathered and aboard ship, an Angel descended to act as pilot. In one day they had sailed as far as Cologne (where the Angel secretly informed Ursula she would be martyred on the return voyage), and on the second day they reached the Eternal City. There they were warmly greeted by Pope Ciracus. Ursula told the pontiff of their impending martyrdom, and His Holiness decided to join them on the return voyage. Because of this act of impetuosity (says the author) his name was stricken from the official list of Popes. The company was made complete by the sudden arrival of Ursula's English fiancé, newly baptized and eager to die for his Faith. Sure enough, when their vessel docked at Cologne, the city was under siege by the Huns. The Pope, the prince, and all eleven thousand virgins joyously disembarked and were methodically slaughtered. For the beautiful Ursula, however, the Hun chieftain had other plans. When the Saint repulsed his odious advances, he shot her with an arrow.

22. THE FEAST OF SAINTS ALODIA AND NUNILO

Spanish Moorish virgin martyrs, 851

Patrons of child abuse victims and runaways

Alodia and Nunilo were the offspring of a Moorish father and Christian mother. When their father died the mother remarried a brute who ridiculed, imprisoned, and otherwise persecuted the two girls. Worse, in defiance of their vow of chastity, the wicked stepfather insisted they marry and then placed them in bad company (a brothel). They ran away, were found, and were turned over to the Moorish authorities to be beheaded.

THE FEAST OF SAINT MARY SALOME

Ambitious mother, 1st century

Patron of Veroli, Italy

Mary Salome was one of the Three Marys who took Jesus down from the Cross. Earlier she had pressed Our Lord to have her two sons, the Apostles John and James, sit at His right and left sides in Paradise. It has been argued that she was also Christ's midwife and/or the sister of the Blessed Virgin Mary. The last years of her life were spent as a disciple somewhere on the Riviera.

THE FEAST OF SAINT PETER OF ALCÁNTARA

Insomniac abbot, 1562

Patron of Brazil, night watchmen • (emblem: Angels offering him a girdle of nails)

e know on the authority of his friend Saint Teresa of Ávila that this Franciscan reformer, a genius in the art of self-denial, slept no longer than an hour and a half every night for forty years. His cell was too small to lie down in, so he snoozed in a crouch, with the back of his head pressed against a spike. What's more, the nocturnal spiritual ecstasies he often experienced caused him to howl long and loud, which prevented his fellow monks from sleeping as well—hence his Patronage of watchmen. While saying Mass, Our Saint was often observed to rise into the air, curl up in a ball, and fly around the church.

23. THE FEAST OF SAINT JOHN OF CAPISTRANO
Warrior-priest, 1456

Patron of military chaplains • (emblem: setting his foot on a turban)

A man of the world, a lawyer, and the governor of the city of Perugia, John got religion at the age of thirty. How he managed to get rid of his wealthy wife is not known, but since his first pious act was to ride through town on a donkey backward, wearing a paper hat with his sins written on it, perhaps the lady did not object much. He joined the Franciscans and studied holy rabble-rousing under Saint Bernardino of Siena before setting out on his own career—a gaunt, shoeless, withered, doomsday-is-at-hand preacher man. Our Saint could get very testy if his arrival was not celebrated with a parade. According to his official biographer, "His heart blazed with hate against three species of men, to wit, Jews, heretics, and schismatics." Impressed by John's no-nonsense reputation, the Pope appointed him to the Inquisition. In Vienna many a heretical Hussite was brought back to orthodoxy or sent straight to Hell courtesy of Our Saint. Strict he was. Zealous. Then in 1453 the Turks captured Constantinople. John realized that this new peril was worse than the Hebrews and Hussites combined, and with the Holy Father's blessing hastened to Hungary, there to take the field beside the noble Christian general Hunyady. In 1456 they led an army that slew 120,000 infidels, raised the siege of Belgrade, and saved Christendom forever—or at least until 1521, when the city fell to Suleiman the Magnificent. But by then Saint John of Capistrano, a fightin' chaplain if there ever was one, was long dead, of plague he contracted wandering among the corpses on the battlefield.

24. THE FEAST OF SAINT ANTHONY CLARET
Tailor turned archbishop, 1870

Patron of savings banks, weavers

Anthony was the son of a weaver who followed his father's trade before becoming a priest and founder of the Spanish missionary Claretian Order. A man of considerable energy and learning, he preached twenty-five thousand sermons and published two hundred books. In 1850 he was appointed archbishop of Santiago, Cuba. Among his tireless labors for the poor of his see was the founding of savings banks for their use. In 1856 Claret reformed the mistress of a local thug, for which he was nearly assassinated. Upon his return to Spain he became director of the Escorial, where he encouraged the study of natural science. Nevertheless, astonishing supernatural powers were attributed to this sensible man, so that he was popularly identified with reaction and royalism, and as a result was sent into exile during the Spanish revolution of 1868.

25. THE FEAST OF SAINTS CRISPIN AND CRISPINIAN
Companion cobbler martyrs, 285

Patrons of glovers, shoemakers • (emblem: shoe)

So traditional is Crispin and Crispinian's Patronage of the cobbler's trade that *crispin* was long a synonym for "shoemaker," and Monday, the cobblers' day off, was called Saint Crispin's Day. These two were Roman brothers who accompanied Saint Quentin on his mission to the Gaulish pagans of Soissons. There they supported themselves by practicing their craft; they shod the poor for free, with night-visiting Angels (not elves) providing them leather. They were martyred, and their beheaded bodies floated across the Channel to England, where the two shoemaker-Saints are still much revered: see Shakespeare's *Henry V,* act 4, scene 3.

Also: The Feast of Saint Tabitha, a widow raised from the dead by Saint Peter (Acts 9:36–43). She is also known, for some reason, as Dorcas, 1st century.

26. THE FEAST OF SAINT BONAVENTURE OF POTENZA

Flagellant monk, 1711

Invoked against diseases of the bowels • (emblem: monk with scourge)

A Franciscan monk of Amalfi famous for his humility and unquestioning obedience to authority, Bonaventure died (aged sixty) of acute intestinal distress (probably an extreme precursor of today's irritable bowel syndrome)—but also in a state of ecstasy induced by relentless psalm singing. His religious superior ordered, for reasons of his own, the corpse of Bonaventure to bleed from the arm—which it immediately did.

Also: The Feast of the Blessed Bonne d'Armagnac, the beautiful and witty daughter of an ancient line who entered the convent of the Poor Clares with great pomp, "accompanied by a seneschal, seven gentlemen, seven maidens, six guards with muskets on their shoulders, pages and lackeys," 1462.

27. THE FEAST OF SAINT FRUMENTIUS

Tyrian explorer, bishop, 380

Patron of Ethiopia • (emblem: elevating host)

W ith his younger brother, Aedesius, this Syrian Christian philosophy student arrived by ship in Ethiopia in the year 330. While the lads were ashore, sitting under a tree studying and praying, the Ethiopians slaughtered everyone aboard, then fetched the two survivors before the king at Axum. His Majesty was much impressed by the dignity and bearing of the boys and made them members of his court—Aedesius as his cupbearer, Frumentius as his secretary. Upon the king's death some years later, the brothers were set free. The younger returned to Tyre to tell this preposterous tale, while Frumentius journeyed to Alexandria, was anointed bishop, and made his way back to Ethiopia, where he had considerable success Christianizing the natives. Abuna (Our Father), the name by which he was known, remains to this day the honorific title of the Primate of the Ethiopian Orthodox Church.

28. THE FEAST OF SAINT JUDE "THADDEUS"

Neglected Apostle, often confused with Judas, 1st century

Invoked in hopeless cases • (emblem: oar)

This Apostle's traditional miraculous intervention in impossible, desperate, or "hopeless" cases is widely known, even among non-Catholics and pagans. Jude is frequently thanked in the personals sections of all sorts of newspapers Our Saint himself would doubtless have spurned. In the New Testament he is introduced as "Judas, the brother of James" (Luke 6:16) and "Judas, the brother of Jesus" (Mark 6:3). Biblical scholars also identify him with the Apostle Thaddeus, or Lebbaeus. Jude is generally believed to have accompanied Saint Simon to Persia, where they were martyred—beaten to death with clubs. Because his name—Judas—is identical to that of the infamous disciple who betrayed Christ, this Saint was long neglected as an object of veneration. Consequently, he was available to take an interest in even the most impossible, desperate, or hopeless cases. His most public achievement was the unlikely show business success of Danny Thomas, who invoked and received his aid.

THE FEAST OF SAINT SIMON

Apostle known as "the Zealot," 1st century

Patron of henpecked husbands, lumberjacks, tanners • (emblem: fish on book)

cousin of Christ, Simon was, according to legend, the Canaanite bridegroom at whose wedding Jesus turned the water to wine. And so for some reason, on Saint Simon's Day, husbands may not contradict their wives. Some say that Simon succeeded Saint James the Less as bishop of Jerusalem and was crucified there—others that he preached the Gospel throughout Egypt and was martyred in Persia, along with Saint Jude—the latter with a club and Simon with a saw.

29. THE FEAST OF SAINT BALDUS (AKA BOND)

Patricidal penitent, 7th century

Patron of cattle, peace in the family; invoked against colic, gout • (emblem: dead branch blossoming)

As a youth this Spaniard, known to the English as Saint Bond, murdered his parents by accident. Stricken with guilt, he took to the roads, wandering as far as Jerusalem and Rome before arriving in Sens, France. There he confessed his sin to Bishop (and Saint) Artemis, who planted his staff in the ground and commanded Baldus to water it daily. After many years the staff burst into bloom, signifying the parricide's forgiveness. A similar tale concerning the German folk hero Tannhäuser provided Richard Wagner with the climactic scene of a long, loud opera.

Also: The Feast of Saint Narcissus, the bishop of Jerusalem who decided that Easter would be celebrated on Sunday rather than the Jewish Sabbath. It didn't pay to mess with him. He was once accused by three miscreants under oath of some unspeakable crime. Soon thereafter one of the slanderers came down with leprosy, another went blind, and the third, with his entire family, perished in a fire. Narcissus was 116 years old when he died, 222.

30. THE FEAST OF SAINT DOROTHY OF MONTAU

Mother of nine turned recluse, 1394

Patron of Prussia; invoked against the death of children

In 1364, when she was seventeen, Dorothy Swartz married a swordsmith, Albrecht of Danzig. By the constant example of her piety she transformed the surly brute into a Christian gentleman. She also bore him nine children—only one of whom survived to become a Benedictine nun. Upon Albrecht's death Dorothy had herself walled up in a small cell built into a cathedral, where she is said to have experienced many mystical visions.

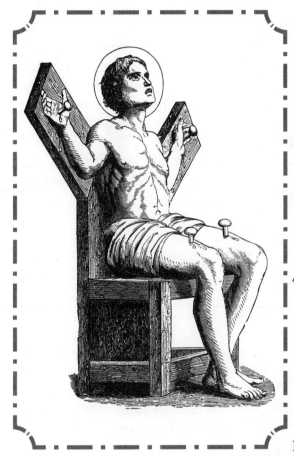

31. THE FEAST OF SAINT QUENTIN

Noose-loosing martyr, 287

Patron of bombardiers, locksmiths, porters, tailors; invoked against coughing, sneezing • (emblem: broken wheel)

An army officer and the son of a Roman senator, Quentin became a Christian and journeyed as a missionary to western Gaul—now Picardy, France. He was martyred with unusual cruelty. Among other tortures, hot nails were driven into his head, he was stretched out on an elaborate machine of pulleys and weights, and his mouth was filled with a mixture of quicklime, vinegar, and mustard. His beheaded body, cast into a river, surfaced half a century later and cured a blind woman who stumbled over it. Gratefully, she founded a church dedicated to the Saint where the city of Saint-Quentin now stands. It is slightly ironic that a famous American penitentiary is named for this Saint: an Angel once descended to the dungeon where he was bound and released him, and one of his first posthumous miracles was to sever the rope by which a penitent horse thief was being hanged.

THE FEAST OF SAINT WOLFGANG

Beloved German bishop, 994

Patron of carpenters, lumberjacks, shepherds; invoked against apoplexy, gout, hemorrhage, paralysis, stomach troubles, wolves; invoked to keep sheep and cattle fat • (emblem: wolf)

Wolfgang was a figure of some importance in the Holy Roman (German) Empire of the tenth century. He founded schools, reformed disorderly nunneries, and served as tutor to Emperor (and Saint) Henry II. His mission to bring the Gospel to the savage Magyars of Pannonia (Hungary) was less than fruitful, but as bishop of Regensburg, Wolfgang was renowned as both just and generous. All his life he had wished to become a simple hermit, and as such he died.

Also: The Feast of Saint Alphonsus Rodriguez, a wealthy businessman of Segovia, who at the age of forty, after the deaths of his wife and children, entered the Jesuits as a simple lay brother and hall porter, 1617.

✣. November .✣

1. THE FEAST OF ALL SAINTS (ALL HALLOWS)

The Celtic calendar year began on November 1, with the festival of Samain, when ghosts and demons were believed to roam the earth. At the turning of the seasons, it seemed, an opening appeared between the worlds of the living and the dead, and the latter were with us for a day and a night. In 835 Christianity instituted on this day a celebration of all the Saints, known and unknown—who, of course, are *always* with us.

THE FEAST OF SAINT MARCEL OF PARIS

Effective exorcist-bishop, 410

Invoked against vampires • (emblem: leading dragon by his stole)

ducated and ordained in Paris, Marcel showed a flair for dramatics even in his youth—holding hot iron bars in his hand and turning water into wine. He was a welcome relief in 400 as bishop of Paris after his strict predecessor, Pudentius. When a rich and dissolute woman was buried in a Christian cemetery, a black serpent wormed its way out of her grave, exposing the corpse and nibbling on the grisly remains, which caused quite a sensation. Marcel, in full bishop's gear and with *le tout Paris* following him, confronted the ghoulish serpent. Ignoring its threatening hisses, the Saint clobbered the fiend with his staff, wrapped it in his robe, and dragged it out of the cemetery.

THE FEAST OF SAINT MATHURIN

Miracle-working French bishop, 4th century

Patron of clowns, fools; invoked against fear, insanity • (emblem: exorcising a girl)

his Saint's Patronage of clowns and idiots is, in French, proverbial—and apparently inexplicable. A precociously religious lad of the city of Sens, in what was then Roman Gaul, Mathurin was baptized at the early age of twelve, then managed the conversion of his pagan parents. Ordained priest (allegedly by the great Saint Polycarp), Mathurin acquired a local reputation as an exorcist and was invited to Rome by the emperor Maximian to expel a Devil possessing his daughter. Mathurin's mission was a success but resulted in the Saint's own death. Buried with great ceremony in Rome, he one day reportedly rose from the grave and returned to his native city to be buried there. Curiously, *mathurin* has long been a French slang term for "sailor."

2. THE FEAST OF ALL SOULS • (emblem: four doves forming a cross)

bviously not all of us are good enough for Heaven or bad enough for Hell. We can anticipate spending some afterlife remedial time atoning for our sins in the fires of Purgatory. Dante visited the place in 1300, and the Council of Florence made its existence a matter of Catholic dogma in 1439. But four centuries earlier a French pilgrim to the Holy Land chanced upon an opening in the

earth through which the howls and moans of the suffering Souls could be heard. He told Abbot Odo of Cluny about it, and that good man immediately instituted the Feast of All Souls—the Day of the Dead, when Catholics the world over remember and pray for the souls of the Faithful departed. The notion of indulgences (which so upsets non-Catholics) simply means that our prayers, good deeds, and financial contributions to the parish here on earth can—if they are "offered up for the intentions" of those souls—shorten their sentences.

3. THE FEAST OF SAINT ALPAIS

Leprous virgin amputee, 1211

Patron of the handicapped

Alpais was a poor peasant with a virulent case of leprosy. While only a teenager she lost both legs from the disease. Though physically challenged, Alphais had the gift of *inedia,* meaning she could subsist on only Holy Communion. Her neighbors, impressed by her holiness and no doubt desirous that she keep her distance, built a church near her hovel and installed a special window so she could view Mass from her solitude.

THE FEAST OF SAINT HUBERT

Popular Belgian hermit-bishop, 727

Patron of furriers, hunters, machinists, mathematicians, metalworkers; invoked against dog bites, insanity, rabies • (emblem: stag with cross between antlers)

Hubert was an affable and shallow hanger-on at the court of King Pepin, content to do little but indulge his passion for hunting, until an event changed his life. (Saint Eustace had a similar paranormal experience.) One Good Friday, after Hubert passed up church for a hunting trip, he encountered a stag in the forest with a crucifix between his antlers. The tiny figure on the crucifix warned

him, "Turn to the Lord, or thou wilt fall into the abyss of Hell!" Soon after this his wife died in childbirth, and the chastened Hubert placed himself and his newborn son in the service of the bishop, Saint Lambert. After Lambert's assassination an Angel appeared to the Pope, proposing Hubert as Lambert's successor. His Holiness concurred. Hubert's traditional Patronage of all things mathematical and mechanical suggest he was a practical, hands-on sort of administrator. After Hubert's death his son succeeded him, while rabies victims came to Hubert's tomb seeking this successful, if complicated, cure: a thread was taken from a stole that the Virgin had given to Hubert and placed in an incision in the forehead of the patient, who, among other things, was forbidden to comb his hair for forty days and ordered to eat only pork and bacon from a boar.

THE FEAST OF SAINT MALACHY O'MORE
Irish bishop famed for his papal prophecies, 1148

Malachy was born into a noble family and became a hermit, a monk, a priest, and a bishop. In the last capacity he was known as a disciplinarian, reforming a church gone soft under lay bishops and Viking usurpers. Acutely sensitive to the complex politics of his country, Malachy was called the Irish of the Irish—but his official biographer was the Frenchman Saint Bernard of Clairvaux, and it was in Bernard's arms that he died. In his time Malachy was known for his

miracles, but he has become celebrated for having the gift (or curse) of second sight. Like the Malachi of the Old Testament, he could make astonishingly accurate prophecies. He said Pope Innocent XI (who reigned 1676–1689, five hundred years after Malachy's death) would be an "insatiable beast." But he was probably referring only to that Pontiff's love of rich food. Malachy termed the ill-fated John Paul I (1978–1978) "of the half-moon" perhaps because that Pope was elected during a half-moon and died (or was killed) shortly afterward—during another half-moon!

In his final, most chilling prophecy, Malachy predicted that the last Pope would call himself Peter the Roman (this should be a tip-off, since even the Bad Borgia Popes never presumed to take the name of the first Pope). Peter the Roman will actually be Satan, the final Antichrist, who will seduce the entire world into thinking he's a good-natured, pious Pontiff, and then . . .

THE FEAST OF SAINT MARTIN DE PORRES

Bilocating mulatto lay brother, 1639

Patron of hairdressers, persons of mixed race, public health workers, race relations, television (in Peru), true love (in Mexico); invoked against rats • (emblem: sweeping with broom)

Born in Lima, Peru, Martin was the illegitimate child of a Spanish knight and a black Panamanian freedwoman. To the distress of his father's family, he resembled his mother, and they refused to acknowledge him. Martin became a Dominican lay brother, working as a barber-hairdresser-surgeon. The rich and poor of Lima flocked to him to be cured by his combination of medicine and miracles (he would heal with a handshake). It was widely known that Martin glowed when he prayed, that he could be in two places at once, and that he was able to fly. He could also resolve marital problems, dispense agricultural advice, and find time to raise a dowry for his niece. He would communicate telepathically with cats and dogs, even giving them scheduled appointments to his clinic. Which they kept. A friend to all creatures, Martin once despaired that the rats scurrying around his friary ("the poor little things") weren't getting enough to eat.

THE FEAST OF SAINT PIRMINUS

Antitoxic abbot, 753

Invoked against poisoning, snakebite • (emblem: driving serpents through a river)

A Spanish bishop who escaped to France from Moorish persecution, Pirminus was sent to the island of Reichenau by King Charles Martel. There he expelled all the serpents and then established the first monastery on German soil. A revisionist theory about his origin suggests that this "shadowy and ubiquitous missionary Saint" may actually have been Irish, and his story about the serpents a mere echo of Saint Patrick.

THE FEAST OF SAINT RUMWALD

Astonishingly pious child prodigy, 7th century

Patron of fishermen

R umwald was born in England, of pagan royalty, and lived for a mere three days. He started his brief life by preaching a sermon to his parents, then addressed the public at large, expounding on the Holy Trinity and virtuous living, freely quoting the Scriptures. The prodigy asked for baptism and Holy

Communion, ceaselessly repeating his mantra, "I am a Christian." On the third day he announced his imminent death and dictated his wish to be buried in three consecutive sites. The infant's holy remains finally rested at Buckingham, and as his cult grew churches, statues, and streets there were dedicated to him.

THE FEAST OF SAINT WINIFRED

Decapitated Welsh virgin, 650

Patron of virgins, Wales • (emblem: carrying her own head, fountain at her feet)

Winifred was living with her parents when she attracted the attention of an ignoble prince who attempted to seduce her. She sought sanctuary in a church, with the prince in hot pursuit. He lopped off her head, which hit the ground and caused a fountain to spring forth. Then Saint Beuno arrived and put her head back on. Kings and pilgrims, Catholics and Protestants have visited her shrine for centuries, and all attest to its success in curing a variety of maladies.

4. THE FEAST OF SAINT AMERICUS

Tragic Hungarian prince, 1032

Patron of America

Americus was groomed by family and clergy to take over the crown from his father and fellow Saint, King Stephen of Hungary. The finishing touches had just been made to Americus' coronation robes when news reached King Stephen that his son had been killed in a hunting accident. The father never recovered from his son's death; the two were buried together, canonized together, and eventually worked miracles from their tombs together. The navigator and mapmaker Amerigo Vespucci was named after this Saint, as, in turn, was the New World.

THE FEAST OF SAINT CHARLES BORROMEO

Counter-Reformation theologian, 1584

Patron of apple orchards, boarding schools, catechists, libraries, starch makers; invoked against stomachache, ulcers • (emblem: kneeling at the altar, a rope around his neck)

Charles, who was born with the proverbial silver spoon in his mouth—his mother was a Medici, and his uncle Pope Pius IV made young Charles a cardinal even before he had joined the priesthood. Charles continued his studies, overcame a speech defect, and assumed the role thrust on him by his uncle. After closing the Council of Trent (which had gone on for nearly twenty years), he set out on a course of pastoral renewal and effectively invented Sunday school. Charles was an avid chess player—asked what he would do if the world was about to end, he responded, "Keep on playing chess." He made enemies (even the good-natured Saint Philip Neri called him a thief) because of his icy demeanor and zeal for reform. Charles's finest hour was during the plague of 1576—he remained in Milan to treat the sick and dying, calling the governor a coward for fleeing the city. He ruined his health and exhausted the remainder of his fortune paying for plague relief, was brought home to Arona on a stretcher, and died in the night. His followers donated jewelry and valuable gems to his shrine, and a large statue, affectionately called Big Charles, was erected in his honor.

5. THE FEAST OF SAINT ELIZABETH

Mary's cousin, mother of John the Baptist, 1st century

Patron of pregnant women • (emblem: presenting Saint John to the infant Jesus)

Elizabeth was a cousin of Our Lady, a barren woman married to the righteous Zachary. Luke, in telling her story, borrows from the Old Testament tradition of hero births: the Angel Gabriel announced to Zachary that the elderly Elizabeth would give birth to her first child, news that naturally struck the old man dumb. The second joyful mystery of the rosary, the Visitation, honors the occasion when the pregnant Blessed Virgin visited her cousin and Our Saint spontaneously authored part of the Hail Mary. Elizabeth's fetus leapt in her womb upon recognizing Christ, also a Fetus and his First Cousin Once Removed. To escape King Herod's persecution of infants, she took her baby into the desert and stayed there to bring him up by herself. After Elizabeth's death her firebrand son emerged from the desert to begin his brief—but memorable—career as John the Baptist.

THE FEAST OF SAINT KAY (AKA KE, KEA, QUAY)

Monk in Brittany, 7th century

Invoked against toothache • (emblem: stag)

He was the son of noble parents (his father may have been a king of Cornwall), and Kay, brainy and with a penchant for the sciences, was quickly made bishop. After a short time he left that position, distributed his considerable wealth to the poor, and took up the hermit's life. One day when he was praying a voice told him to travel, taking with him a bell, and stop only when the bell rang of its own accord. He had a bell made for him—some say by Saint Gildas—and went on the road. In the middle of a forest in Brittany the bell rang, and it was there that Kay built his chapel, and later his monastery. A wicked prince knocked out one of his teeth, and the spring in which Our Saint washed out his mouth has subsequently cured toothaches. This Saint may or may not be the Saint Kea whose name appears on the label of the bottled natural spring water popular in Great Britain.

6. THE FEAST OF SAINT LEONARD

Parole-granting hermit, 559

Patron of childbirth, greengrocers, horses, prisoners of war; invoked against robbery • (emblem: broken chain)

Leonard was a French hermit, the godson of King Clovis. He passed up an opportunity to be made a bishop in order to live in a hut in the forest, eating only fruit and vegetables. Clovis and his pregnant wife visited the Saint while they were out hunting. The queen unexpectedly went into labor, and Leonard successfully delivered the baby. The grateful king told Leonard he could build his abbey on as much land as he could ride around on a donkey in one night, and further granted freedom to every prisoner Leonard visited—many of these prisoners went to live with the Saint once his abbey was built. Presumably Leonard is invoked against robbery because we hold him responsible for those prisoners who returned to a life of crime after being freed. His patronage of prisoners of war began when Crusaders visited his shrine to give thanks for their release from infidel captivity.

THE FEAST OF SAINT WINNOC

Sightless hermit, 717

Invoked against whooping cough • (emblem: grinding corn)

His royal British family fled to Brittany when the godless Saxons invaded England. Winnoc was a monk for many years and in his old age was considered unfit for work. Nonetheless, he continued to grind corn in his cell, always—it is reported—with a look of ecstasy on his face.

7. THE FEAST OF SAINT FLORENTIUS

Wandering Irish bishop, 693

Invoked against gallstones, rupture • (emblem: bear keeping his sheep)

Florentius was a peripatetic Irishman who settled down as a hermit in Alsace. When he reentered society he preached and worked miracles, including healing the king's daughter, who was blind and mute. He set up a monastery for his countrymen, in the Irish tradition, in Strasbourg, Austria. The hard-up monks of Bonneval later sold his relics to the abbot of Peterborough, England.

THE FEAST OF SAINT WILLIBRORD

Missionary to the Frisians, 739

Patron of Holland, Luxembourg; invoked against convulsions, epilepsy, lumbago • (emblem: cross in a barrel)

Willibrord is, not surprisingly, confused with his brothers Willibald and Winebald—fellow English monks and missionaries to western Europe. If it helps, you may think of him as Clement, because when he was made a bishop, the Sicilian Pope, Sergius I, unable to pronounce "Willibrord," changed it to Clement. As a missionary in Denmark, Willibrord earned the enmity of the pagan king, Radbod, who banished the Saint and burned his churches. Willibrord retaliated by desecrating sacred cows and publicly baptizing Danes in a loud voice. The Saint almost succeeded, finally, in converting his old enemy, but when Radbod stepped into his baptismal waters, he asked Our Saint where his own royal Danish ancestors were. Informed they were in Hell, Radbod replied that he would rather be in Hell "with a pack of heroes than in Heaven with a pack of beggars." (Ironically, his grandson and namesake Saint Radbod succeeded Willibrord as bishop of Utrecht.) Willibrord's shrine at Luxembourg became famous because clergy and pilgrims there perform a sacred conga-line dance on his Feast—taking three steps forward and two steps back. The procession jumps and dances until it circles Willibrord's tomb, then snakes out of the church. This queer ritual is supposed to help cure everything from convulsions or epilepsy to lumbago. In art Willibrord is shown with a church in his hand and, because of his ability to multiply wine, a barrel of wine at his feet.

8. THE FEAST OF THE FOUR CROWNED MARTYRS

Executed sculptors, 306

Patrons of carvers, Freemasons, stonemasons • (emblem: mason's tools)

This team of stonemasons in Yugoslavia—traditionally named Claudius, Nicostratus, Symphorian, and Castorius—created a number of ornate carvings for the building-mad Roman emperor Diocletian. But, being Christians, they refused to make an idolatrous statue of Asclepius, the pagan god of healing, and were arrested. When the judge conducting their trial suddenly dropped dead, his influential family blamed the four masons, who were forthwith placed in lead boxes and drowned. (A fifth mason, Simplicius, died along with them but was not granted the crown of martyrdom, for he only pretended to become a Christian in order to improve his carving skills.) Understandably, the four were taken as Patrons by the medieval stonemasons' guild. There is a great church, the Quattro Coronati in Rome, and, ironically, a London lodge of the (militant anti-Catholic) Freemasons with the same name.

9. THE FEAST OF SAINT BENEN

Follower of Saint Patrick, archbishop, 467

Invoked against worms

Benen, the son of an Irish chieftain, was a mere child when he fell in love with the visiting Saint Patrick. He sprinkled flowers on Patrick while the Saint was sleeping and clung to his feet when he tried to leave. Relenting, Patrick took Benen from his family, explaining that "the child shall inherit my kingdom," which he did, captivating everyone with his gentle disposition and lilting voice. Patrick wrote a hymn—"The Deer's Cry"—about how he and his disciples once escaped ambush by the Druids: they transformed themselves into deer and Benen into a fawn. Benen succeeded Patrick as bishop of Armagh and in time went to join his mentor in retirement as a hermit. Before his death Patrick instructed Benen to build a cell wherever his staff burst into leaves. The staff blossomed in the middle of a swamp, and a spring gushed forth. It was there that Benen stayed until his death. At his tomb people miraculously vomit the intestinal worms that have been plaguing them.

THE FEAST OF SAINT THEODORE THE RECRUIT

Soldier-martyr, 306

Patron of the military, Brindisi • (emblem: in armor, with lance and banner)

An enlisted man in the Roman army, Theodore was burned at the stake for his Faith. His martyred body was adopted by the natives of Euchais, a city that eventually changed its name to Theodoropolis, in his honor. In Rome sick children are brought to his church for a cure and affectionately call him Toto.

10. THE FEAST OF SAINT AEDH MAC BREIC

Migraine-afflicted bishop, 589

Invoked against headache

An illiterate farmer, Aedh was bilked of his inheritance by his brothers. Seeking revenge, the future Saint abducted their maid and headed south. A local bishop, after convincing him to return the girl, said he had learned in a vision that the not particularly religious Aedh should start his own monastery. From that time on many miracles were attributed to Aedh, including the ability to fly and the restoration of slit throats; but his signature feat was assuming Saint Brigid's migraine headache as his own. When he knew it was time to die, Aedh asked one of his monks to join him, but the selfish man refused. A convenient peasant volunteered instead, and the two lay down on the Saint's bed and died together.

THE FEAST OF SAINT ANDREW AVELLINO

Ex-lawyer, foe of fallen nuns, 1608

Patron of Naples, Sicily; invoked against apoplexy, sudden death • (emblem: priest dying on altar steps)

Andrew Avellino's mother called her handsome son Lancelot (Lancellotto) and, like his namesake, Andrew fought to remain pure. On vacation from school he recoiled from the effusive welcome of his former nanny and hastened to take his priestly vows. He practiced some ecclesiastical law on the side. His first assignment as a clergyman was to close a convent that the fallen nuns had turned into a brothel. His efforts upset the prosperous ex-nuns as well as their clients, one of whom attacked Andrew with a sword. Andrew is invoked against sudden death because he himself was struck down by apoplexy in the middle of saying Mass. Even as it lay in state, his body remained healthy and rosy-cheeked. His followers, snipping off locks of hair as relics, eventually became more impassioned and made nicks in his flesh, which started to bleed spontaneously—the kind of blood miracle that flourished in the region. (Certain latter-day historians believe that Andrew, supposedly dead, was actually catatonic and in fact had been buried alive.)

THE FEAST OF SAINT LEO THE GREAT

Pope who faced down Attila the Hun, 461

Patron of choirs, musicians • (emblem: Attila kneeling to him)

One of only three Popes called Great, Leo is a Doctor of the Church who consolidated basic Christian doctrine and expanded the influence and prestige of the papacy, emphasizing its divine origin. His most dramatic moment came when he went to confront Attila, the scourge of God, in 452. Dressed in white robes (and flanked by Saints Peter and Paul), Pope Leo identified himself as "Leo, Pope" and managed to dissuade the Hun from ravaging Rome (with the pledge of an annual tribute). He was less successful with the Vandals, who during his papacy sacked Rome for fourteen days, stealing even the candlesticks originally stolen from the Temple at Jerusalem. Leo was a bit of a hard-liner on conjugal affairs, banning intercourse for married subdeacons and in his old age determining that sexual activity of any kind is intrinsically evil.

Also: The Feast of Saint Nympha, a fascinating virgin martyr of Tuscany whose Feast has been, since 1969, suppressed, date unknown.

11. THE FEAST OF SAINT MARTIN OF TOURS (MARTINMAS)

Cloak-sharing soldier, abbot, 397

Patron of beggars, drunkards, equestrians, France, harvests, horses, innkeepers, the military, new wine, tailors • (emblem: goose)

Martin was the first universally popular Saint, and the first Saint who was not also a martyr; more churches are dedicated to him than to anyone else. He was born in Hungary, c. 315, and became a cavalry officer in the Roman army of Constantine. When he was stationed at Amiens, France, he gave half his cloak to a freezing beggar (having slashed it in two with his sword). When Christ appeared to him wearing the very same half garment, Martin went to the local bishop, Saint Hilary, and asked to be baptized. Martin's reputation as the Soldier Saint is somewhat ironic—for his first act as a Christian was to conscientiously object. Although the Church hierarchy complained that Martin never combed his hair, the people of Tours demanded he be made their bishop. Fearful of the honor, Martin hid, until his whereabouts were betrayed by a honking goose. (A goose is among his emblems, and a roast goose is traditionally served on his Feast Day, Martinmas.) As bishop Martin continued his monkish ways, wearing animal skins, riding a donkey, and still not combing his hair. He initiated a method of exorcism whereby the afflicted expelled demons through vomiting and defecation. The Devil himself tormented Our Saint, often appearing to him in the shape of a busty Roman goddess— but reeking of sulfur. Ever the pacifist, Martin defied authorities by preaching against the death penalty, predicting (correctly) that the execution of heretics increased their influence. By chance, Martin died on the day of the pagan feast of Vinalia, when the new wine is tasted—thus he is considered Patron of drunkards. (In England *martin-drunk* means *very* drunk indeed.) His funeral was spectacular. Heavenly music filled the air as two thousand monks followed his coffin. Trees bloomed (in November) as his coffin passed, so that even today a spell of fine weather in November is known throughout Europe as a Saint Martin's summer.

THE FEAST OF SAINT MENNAS

Egyptian martyr with a formidable shrine, 300

Patron of caravans, merchants; invoked to find lost objects • (emblem: camel)

An Egyptian businessman-cum-soldier in the Roman army, Mennas revealed himself to be a Christian and was burned alive. His followers believed he was not in Heaven but in the shrine they had built for him—an elaborate monastery-church-bath complex near Alexandria. A pilgrim visiting the shrine was horribly murdered by a robber—chopped to bits and placed in a sack—but Mennas appeared with some fellow Saints, reassembled the pilgrim, and brought him back to life. Arabs destroyed the shrine in the seventh century, and it wasn't excavated until the twentieth. Restored, it enjoyed renewed popularity, especially during World War II. The Patriarch of Egypt gave Saint Mennas credit for the Allied victory in the Battle of El Alamein, which rescued his country from the Nazis.

THE FEAST OF SAINT ASTERICUS

Missionary and kingmaker, 1040

Patron of Hungary

Astericus was a Benedictine missionary from Bohemia who allied himself with Saint Adalbert, the Saint given credit for converting Hungary and its king, Stephen. But it was King Stephen's ambassador to Rome, Astericus, who obtained the holy crown from Pope Sylvester II, with which he personally (and proudly) crowned King Saint Stephen.

12. THE FEAST OF SAINT EMILIAN

Pastor in Aragon, 574

Patron of Spain; invoked to find lost objects • (emblem: cowled, on horseback, fighting Moors)

ragon and Castile both claim this minor Patron of Spain as native son. Emilian lived a happy hermit's existence for forty years, until a bishop summoned him to serve as parish priest. He was dismissed for being impractical after he gave all the church goods to the poor. The relieved Saint returned to his cell, where he lived to be over one hundred and became known as the Cowled One. In art he is generally represented doing something he never did in real life: fighting the Moors on horseback.

THE FEAST OF SAINT JOSAPHAT

Conciliatory bishop, martyr, 1623

Patron of Ukraine • (emblem: winged deacon)

In the year 1054 the Pope of Rome and the Primate of Byzantium excommunicated each other, formalizing the scandalous Great Schism that divided Catholics of the East and West until 1965. Josaphat (born John Kuncewicz) attempted, in the seventeenth century, to reconcile the Eastern Orthodox and Roman churches. When canonized by the Vatican in 1867, he became the first Eastern Saint to be recognized by Rome.

THE FEAST OF SAINT LEBUIN

Saxon-bashing missionary, 773

Patron of the dying • (emblem: holding cross and book, treading on a spiked club)

An English missionary, Lebuin had labored long and fruitlessly in the dangerous Saxon Netherlands. Dressed in full regalia and brandishing a cross, he determined to gatecrash the annual Saxon assembly at Marklo on the Weser. "Listen to the God who speaks through my mouth!" he howled at the assembled warlords, and disparaged their gods—Odin, Thor, and the rest—as "dead, powerless things." Many Saxons were determined to kill him on the spot, but an ancient chief named Buto granted Lebuin a sort of idiot's diplomatic immunity. Thereafter Our Saint preached and traveled freely until his death. His Patronage of the dying is explained, perhaps, by this stay of execution.

13. THE FEAST OF SAINT AGOSTINA PIETRANTONI

Assaulted Angel of mercy, 1913

Patron of rape victims

A member of the nursing order the Sisters of Charity, Agostina continued to succor the sick even after contracting typhus. While working in the tuberculosis ward, she was stabbed to death by a patient who attempted to deflower her.

THE FEAST OF SAINT BRICE

Demonically possessed bishop, 444

Invoked against diseases of the stomach • (emblem: burning coals in his hand)

While he was serving under Saint Martin of Tours, Brice spread a rumor that the beloved Martin had gotten funny in the head and superstitious in his old age. Martin, resigned to Brice's criticism, nonetheless predicted that he would

succeed him, saying, "If Christ can tolerate Judas, surely I can put up with Brice." Later Brice suffered opprobrium of his own when he was accused of impropriety with a married woman, forcing him to go to Rome to clear his name. He was vindicated by the Pope and spent the rest of his years a chastened figure; his cult spread through Europe, ironically, because he rode on Saint Martin's cloaktails.

THE FEAST OF SAINT DIEGO ALCALÁ

Culinary specialist–monk, 1463

Patron of cooks • (emblem: Angels cooking for him)

Born near Seville, Diego was, as a young man, an apprentice to a solitary hermit—together they grew vegetables and fashioned kitchen utensils for sale. Diego then joined the Franciscans as a lay brother and was sent to a friary in the Canary Islands, where he was employed as cook and doorkeeper. The Saint was raised from obscurity to canonization by the tireless efforts of King Philip I of Spain, who credited the cure of his son to Diego's heavenly intercession.

THE FEAST OF SAINT FRANCES CABRINI

Italian-born first "American" Saint, 1917

Patron of emigrants, hospital administrators, immigrants; invoked to obtain a parking space

Frances Xavier Cabrini was the first American citizen to be canonized, doubtless as much for her business acumen as for her holiness. Frances (she added the Xavier herself) was born in Italy, the youngest of thirteen children. Her lifelong dream was to be a missionary to China, but the Pope, saying, "Go west, not east," sent her to New York. The tiny Frances, who spoke very little

English, came to America in 1889 to tend the fifty thousand Italian immigrants here. She obtained funding from the Countess Cesnola and built her first orphanage on the shores of the Hudson River. By 1917 she had expanded operations into eight countries and built numerous hospitals, schools, and convents. Critics point to her extreme narrow-mindedness—illegitimate Catholic children as well as Protestants were unwelcome in her schools. Controversy raged around her in Italy—a lawsuit was filed against her in the Italian courts, and she was the cause of riots in Milan. Frances died of malaria, and her friend and compatriot Pope Pius XI quickly undertook her canonization process. Her body, originally (and incorrectly) thought to be incorrupt, lies, under

glass, in the Washington Heights section of Manhattan.

THE FEAST OF SAINT HOMOBONUS

Devout dry goods salesman, 1197

Patron of garment workers, tailors • (emblem: Angels sewing garments)

Homobonus, a happily married cloth worker, was, as his name implies, the prototypical "good man"—prudent, diligent, charitable, and devoted to Saint Giles. He even worked the occasional miracle, but he is most noted for his dramatic passing: during the Gloria of the Mass, he stretched out his arms in the shape of the cross and fell flat on his face. It wasn't until Mass was over that people realized he had dropped dead. Pope Innocent III hastened his canonization in an effort to shore up the nonmartyr, nonclergy quota of Saints, describing Homobonus as one who did "ordinary things extraordinarily well."

THE FEAST OF SAINT NICHOLAS I

Pope, theorist of papal power, 867

Patron of Aberdeen, thieves

Nicholas I was a vigorous and active Pope who set many long-reaching precedents. He opposed the divorce of a king and upheld the right of a princess to marry whom she chose. He permitted local clergy to appeal directly to Rome. But, most significant, he laid the grounds for the permanent rift between the Eastern and Western Churches when he decided that confirmation by priests (and not bishops) was invalid, effectively wiping out all the confirmations in the Greek Church. Although he was something of a tyrant, Nicholas's personal integrity was above reproach, so his traditional patronage of thieves is a mystery.

THE FEAST OF SAINT PONTIAN

Slave turned Pope, 236

Pontian converted to Christianity while he was still a slave in his teens. When he was sixty-two, he was made Pope but continued feuding with his lifelong enemy, Hippolytus. The two were engaged in a heated debate on some of the finer points of Church theology when they were both arrested. (The emperor Maximinus Thrax had outlawed Christianity and all its clerics, even the Pope.) Exiled to the mines of Sardinia, Pontian and Hippolytus met and reconciled, falling into each other's arms. Soon afterward both were beaten with sticks, stabbed in the jugular, and their bodies dumped, together, into the sewer.

THE FEAST OF SAINT STANISLAUS KOSTKA

Jesuit "boy Saint," 1568

Patron of Poland, young people • (emblem: lily)

The child of Polish nobility, Stanislaus was tormented by a bullying older brother and a vulgar tutor. Delicate in sensibility as well as health, he was accused of being a prig by his worldly relatives, the standing family joke being

"Don't tell that story in front of Stanislaus, he'd faint." At school in Vienna his brother continued to taunt him, once sending a prostitute to his room, and even forcing him to live with Protestants. When this shabby treatment caused the Saint to fall deathly ill, his Lutheran landlord refused to let a priest bring him Holy Communion. Saint Barbara, ever helpful in these situations, sent two Angels to Stanislaus with the Host; eventually even the Blessed Virgin and the Holy Infant came to visit his sickroom. The Virgin let him play with the Baby and suggested Stan join the Jesuits. The Jesuits of Vienna, afraid of alienating Stanislaus's father, rejected him, forcing the Saint to walk 350 miles to Rome, where he entered the order at the age of seventeen. His poor health returned, because of a combination of fasting, mortification, and the Roman summer, and he died nine months later. Although he went to Heaven on the Feast of the Assumption, his Feast Day was moved to the middle of the school year for the sake of his Patronage of the young.

14. THE FEAST OF SAINT LAWRENCE O'TOOLE
Irish nationalist bishop, 1180

Patron of Dublin • (emblem: light over a church)

Lawrence was canonized in the early thirteenth century, the last person from Ireland (the land of Saints and scholars) to be so honored until the end of the twentieth century, and has come to symbolize his country's subjugation to England and isolation from Rome. Lawrence was the son of a chieftain, taken hostage at the age of ten by his lifelong nemesis, King Dermot. Dermot mistreated Lawrence and killed his father, so when Lawrence became bishop of Dublin he banished the old reprobate to England. The Saint brought order and piety to Dublin, inviting thirty homeless people to dinner each night. Years earlier Pope Adrian IV (a Norman Englishman, the former Nicholas Breakspear) had ceded Ireland to King Henry II of England, effectively giving the most Catholic and Celtic of countries over to the Norman English. The traitorous King Dermot and his new (English) son-in-law, the earl of Pembroke (the infamous Strongbow), invaded Ireland. The Irish rallied around their high king, Rory O'Connor, but were defeated by Strongbow. Lawrence negotiated the treaty between the English king and the Irish high king, and when that treaty failed Ireland's "troubles" began. Henry II arrived on Irish shores, claiming the country given him by one Pope, a claim approved by a subsequent Pope, Alexander III, who went on to demand a Peter's pence from Ireland for Rome. Lawrence continued to work for peace, traveling constantly to England. On his last mission he was snubbed by Henry II, who forbade him to return to Ireland. He died in France, but his last words were in Irish; translated, they say, "Alas! You stupid, foolish people, what will you do now? Who will look after you in your misfortunes?"

15. THE FEAST OF SAINT ALBERT THE GREAT

Albertus Magnus, Doctor of the Church, 1280

Patron of medical technologists, science students, scientists • (emblem: Dominican with pen, book)

After he entered the Dominican Order, Albert's German military family tried to have him kidnapped, but he prevailed and soon distinguished himself as a teacher and a thinker. He rose to bishop but resigned the post, disliking administration, and devoted himself to the natural sciences, as well as to philosophy and metaphysics. Along with his pupil Saint Thomas Aquinas, Albert held the controversial notion that the "scientific" ideas of Aristotle could be integrated into Christian theology. He carried out experiments in his lab and collected plants, insects, and chemical compounds; he was even called upon to design the new cathedral in Cologne. Although his volumes on astronomy, chemistry, and geography (tracing the mountain ranges of Europe) were centuries ahead of his time, Albert failed to grasp some of the basics of biology. He maintained that frequent intercourse (an act, he pointed out, that man "shared with beasts") could lead to sickness, body odor, and baldness, and could cause one's brain to shrink to the size of a pomegranate. He was scientific in his misogyny as well, calling women "misbegotten men" and explaining that the females of the species are less moral, since they "contain more liquid." His liquid theory may explain his supposition that women ejaculated semen during intercourse. In pursuit of knowledge Albert traveled all over Europe wearing clogs and thus was called the clodhopper.

THE FEAST OF SAINT LEOPOLD

Active layman, father of eighteen, 1136

Patron of Austria • (emblem: in armor, holding rosary)

Leopold succeeded his father as margrave of Austria in 1095 and at age twenty-three married the widow Agnes, daughter of Henry IV. The couple had eighteen children and were also active in building monasteries. Leopold resolutely refused the crown when his brother died. He wasn't canonized until 350 years after his death, a Saint by virtue more of his endowments than of his piety.

Also: The Feast of Saint Zachary, husband of Saint Elizabeth, father of John the Baptist. He was a priest in the Temple of Jerusalem and, so the story goes, struck dumb until he agreed to name his son John, 1st century.

16. THE FEAST OF SAINT GERTRUDE THE GREAT

Passionate, mystic nun, 1302

Patron of the West Indies • (emblem: seven rings on right hand)

Gertrude, born in Saxony, was placed with cloistered nuns at the age of five and never left the convent. She had her first mystical experience at twenty-six, when Christ appeared to her, reproached her for studying too hard, gave her the traditional nuptial ring, and introduced her to His Mother. Her biographer, Saint Mechtilde, and other nuns who witnessed her ecstasies often found Gertrude staring at an image of Christ with "greatest ardor," no doubt because He promised her that "my Divine delights shall be as wine to you." Gertrude's writings, which are believed to have been ghosted by Mechtilde, stress the humanity of Jesus; her devotion to the Sacred Heart grew after she placed her head on Christ's chest and listened to the beating of His Heart. Immediately after Gertrude's death a host of souls was released from Purgatory to accompany her to Heaven.

SAINT MARGARET
Queen of Scotland

THE FEAST OF SAINT MARGARET OF SCOTLAND

Royal, loyal spouse, 1093

Patron of learning, Scotland • (emblem: black X-shaped cross)

Margaret, an ancestor of England's current royal family, escaped to Scotland from England after the Norman Conquest. Malcolm, king of Scotland, became enamored of her beauty and style, and they married soon after her arrival. The royal couple transformed the social and cultural life of Scotland—Margaret in particular tried to rid the Church of its Celtic influences. She called a synod to bring Lent, marriage customs, and Holy Communion practices in line with the teachings of the Church of Rome. She succeeded in getting Malcolm to attend Mass, although she failed to teach him how to read. She also organized women's groups to meet, discuss the Scriptures, and embroider—so it can be said that she invented the sewing circle, if not consciousness raising. When her husband was killed by an enemy who put a spear through his eye, Margaret rationalized the tragedy as a form of penance—a purification—for her own youthful sins, whatever they were.

17. THE FEAST OF SAINT ELIZABETH OF HUNGARY

Self-abasing queen, 1231

Patron of bakers, hoboes; invoked against plague • (emblem: bread and roses)

Princess Elizabeth of Hungary was engaged at the age of four to Ludwig (Louis) of Thuringia and went to live with her fiancé and his family as a child. After her marriage and ascension to the throne, her mother-in-law persecuted Elizabeth, but her relationship with Ludwig was said to be one of "mystic ardor." The young queen threw herself into charitable acts, wearing dowdy clothes as she tended the sick—behavior that further isolated her from the worldly court. Elizabeth fell under the influence of a sadistic confessor, Conrad of Marburg, who abused her physically and mentally for the rest of her life. After King Ludwig died—felled by the heat and rancid air on a Crusade—Elizabeth was disconsolate: "Dead! Dead! Dead! The world is dead to me!" she would wail. The melodrama continued when her brother-in-law threw her and her children out of the castle, forcing them to live in a pigsty. Orders were given throughout the country that the former royal family be shunned, and Elizabeth was comforted only by occasional visions of Christ. One Good Friday, Elizabeth renounced the world, her family, and her children, and submitted herself entirely to Father Conrad's authority, causing rumors suggesting their relationship was of a sex-

ual nature. She wore rags, scrubbed floors, and enlisted virgins to follow her. When her father saw her, he cried and begged her to come home, but she refused. It was generally agreed that her confessor's brutal treatment was responsible for Elizabeth's death at the age of twenty-four. Just before she died she heard a heavenly choir—and at her funeral Conrad lost no time in collecting depositions for her sainthood, while the devout, eager for relics, groped in her coffin, cutting off her hair and nipples.

THE FEAST OF SAINT GREGORY THE WONDER WORKER

Magician bishop, 268

Patron of Armenia; invoked in desperate situations • (emblem: driving Devils out of temple)

Gregory preached in the neighborhood of Caesarea (modern-day Turkey), working spectacular miracles that included changing the course of a river, turning himself into a tree, and once even moving a mountain. Gregory was enormously successful in converting Caesarea, although he naively thought that recent converts would enjoy replacing the seasonal pagan festivities with the solemn Feast Days of the martyrs.

THE FEAST OF SAINT HILDA

Ex-princess and most capable abbess, 680

Patron of businesswomen • (emblem: three coiled serpents)

Hilda was baptized a Christian along with her cousin, the king Saint Edwin. She ran a double monastery (nuns and monks), and in the depths of the Dark Ages she stressed learning, the arts, and even personal hygiene. Her order illuminated manuscripts, solved mathematical riddles, and built libraries. Hilda convened the synod that ruled in favor of the Roman liturgy over the Celtic liturgy. Her Patronage of the poet-swineherd Saint Caedmon, the first native English poet, has led many to call her the founder of English literature.

THE FEAST OF SAINT HUGH OF LINCOLN

Carthusian, defender of England's Jews, 1200

Patron of sick children • (emblem: Angels defending him from lightning)

Born in France, this monk attracted the attention of Henry II of England, who asked him to lead one of his monasteries and later made him bishop of Lincoln, the nation's largest diocese. From Lincoln, Hugh defied, in succession, three Plantagenet kings in defense of justice. He helped build the cathedral with his own hands, nursed lepers, and single-handedly defended the Jews against angry mobs. The controversial bishop excommunicated Henry II's foresters for mistreating peasants. He refused to levy money for King Richard's war and reconciled him with a kiss. Bishop Hugh defied King John as well, earning his nickname—Hammerking. Hugh kept a wild swan as a pet: the bird followed him everywhere, attacked anyone who approached, and would "bury its head and long neck in Hugh's wide sleeves." In one of his extant sermons Hugh attests that the virtuous laity have a place in Heaven along with the clergy.

THE FEAST OF SAINT ROSE PHILLIPPINE DUCHESNE

French nun in Missouri's Pioneer Hall of Fame, 1852

Patron of opposition to Church authorities

At the advanced age of seventy-two, this French nun and survivor of the Reign of Terror went to live with the Potawatomi Indians in the Rocky Mountains. She didn't speak their language (actually, she didn't speak English either) but earned the love of the tribe, who called her Quah-kah-ka-num-ad (Woman-Who-Prays-Always). Though she was a leader in social work and Catholic education, Rose's road to sainthood was slow because her order, the Society of the Sacred Heart of Jesus, didn't have enough money to promote her cause. However, in 1987, when Pope John Paul II was about to visit the United States, he wanted to canonize an American Saint on that trip. This revved up Rose's case. Money was found, a miracle was confirmed (a malignant tumor disappeared from the neck of a nun who wore Our Saint's relic), and Rose was soon declared to be among the elect.

18. THE FEAST OF SAINT ODO OF CLUNY

Cultivated abbot, 942

Patron of musicians; invoked for rain • (emblem: stripping himself to clothe the poor)

Odo's family tried to interest the young man in the frivolous life, but hunting and hawking gave him headaches, so he was permitted to enter a religious order. When the intense youth dreamed of serpents in an ancient urn, he interpreted it as a sign from God to give up reading Virgil and the classics. Odo brought this orthodox viewpoint to the abbey at Cluny, and his brand of strict monasticism became the standard for over a century. His Cluniac observance, with its emphasis on poverty, chastity, abstinence—even his arbitrary ruling that underwear must be washed only on Saturdays—seemed odd at the time, and the Saint met with initial resistance. One Friday a monk, defying Odo's rule that chicken and fish were not the same thing, choked on a chicken bone and died.

Also: Blessed Miguel Pro, Jesuit falsely accused of attempting to assassinate the Mexican president. He ripped off his blindfold before being executed by a firing squad, 1927.

19. THE FEAST OF SAINT NERSES I
King basher, 373

After the death of his wife, Nerses became a priest and eventually bishop (*katholikos*) of Armenia. He was obliged to deal with a pair of wicked kings. The first he excommunicated for murdering his wife. The successor, Pap, was worse. Nerses accused him of being possessed by demons. His Majesty, protesting his innocence, invited the bishop to dinner—and poisoned him. Nerses was succeeded as bishop by Isaac, his son and fellow Saint.

Also: The Feast of Saint Anastasius II, a Pope Dante claimed to have seen in Hell, 498.

20. THE FEAST OF SAINT BERNWARD
Contentious bishop, 1022

Patron of architects, artists, goldsmiths, sculptors • (emblem: bishop hammering a chalice) ernward was orphaned at six and raised by his uncle, the bishop of Utrecht. Ordained a priest by his future adversary, Saint Willigis, Bernward took as his avocation ecclesiastical art, especially metalworking: he created the sixteen-foot bronze gate of the cathedral of Hildesheim. When Princess Sofia decided to enter the nunnery of Gandersheim, she insisted that Saint Willigis perform the ceremony, even though the nunnery was out of his jurisdiction. Bernward alone objected to the impropriety: this relatively minor issue eventually involved the emperor and even the Pope. In the meantime Sofia shuttled between convent and castle, inciting nuns and nobility alike against Bernward. (She was living with Willigis on what have been described as "most familiar terms.") A synod eventually decided in Bernward's favor, and Willigis openly repented and went on to sainthood. Bernward became bishop of Utrecht—a post that has produced an unusually high number of Saints.

21. THE FEAST OF MARY, QUEEN OF PEACE

Patron of El Salvador

In 1966 Pope Paul VI declared that Mary, under this title, is the Patron of El Salvador. But, not surprisingly, Mary, Queen of Peace, has lately been focusing her efforts on Eastern Europe. In 1981 she began telling six visionaries in Bosnia-Herzegovina that the world was on the brink of a major catastrophe. They have described her as five feet five inches tall, weighing about 132 pounds, and blue-eyed, with an oval face.

Also: The Feast of Saint Gelasius, an African-born Pope who suggested that babies receive Holy Communion, 496.

22. THE FEAST OF SAINT CECILIA

Vocalist, keyboard artist, virgin martyr, date unknown

Patron of composers, music, musicians, organ builders • (emblems: organ, harp)

She could play any musical instrument, sing any song, hear the Angelic harmonies—and it is said that Cecilia invented the organ, which instrument she played on her wedding night, filled with dread, asking God to help her in her hour of need. "While the musicians played and sang at the nuptials, she sang in her heart to God only." When the awful moment arrived, Cecilia, alone in the bridal chamber with her new husband, Valerian, confessed to him that she had consecrated her virginity to God and that, furthermore, she had a very strict Guardian Angel: "If you touch me in the way of marriage, he will be very angry." Valerian wisely agreed to keep his hands to himself and asked to be baptized. The Angel then appeared and crowned the chaste couple with roses and lilies. Valerian was soon executed, slandering the gods with his dying words. (Jupiter, he swore, was "a libertine.") Cecilia was condemned to die in her own bath, but she survived the boiling steam, so was struck three times in the neck with a sword. She lived for three more days, lying in the tub with her head severed, making the Trinity sign with her fingers. She was buried in gold robes (with her customary hair shirt beneath them). Twelve hundred years later, when her body was exhumed, it was found to be—as the sculptor Maderna, who was present, depicted her—fresh and beautiful, in the languorous pose with which she had met her death. Unfortunately for us, the corpse disintegrated shortly after being exposed to the air.

23. THE FEAST OF SAINT CLEMENT

Drowned convict Pope, 100

Patron of blacksmiths, boatmen, farriers, stonecutters, tanners, teetotalers; invoked against disasters at sea, sickness in children • (emblem: anchor)

he third Pope and a Jew by birth, Clement was converted by Paul and baptized by Peter. Clement witnessed Peter's martyrdom and was himself banished to the marble quarries in Russia by the emperor Trajan. The exiled Pope made many converts in Russia, especially after he miraculously created a spring for the thirsty marble workers. For refusing to sacrifice to idols Clement was thrown into the Black Sea with an anchor around his neck. Angels made him a tomb in the ocean, which was revealed yearly at low tide on the anniversary of his death. The Saints Cyril and Methodius discovered his body seven hundred years later and delivered it to the church of San Clemente in Rome. There is a splendid old church dedicated to Clement in London, and he is the Patron of those who prefer nonalcoholic drinks because, in the famous rhyme, "the bells of Saint Clements" say "oranges and lemons."

THE FEAST OF SAINT COLUMBANUS

Tempestuous Irish missionary abbot, 615

Invoked against depression, floods • (emblem: kneeling among wolves)

lthough sins of the flesh are generally not a problem for Irish monks, Columbanus once found himself taunted by immodest local girls and ran to a female hermit for advice. She reminded him of Adam and Eve, Samson and Delilah, et al., and suggested he leave Ireland for points south, where the women were less beautiful. Columbanus literally stepped over his pleading mother's body ("I will see you no more in this life, Mother") and headed for the Continent. He cut a distinctive figure—he shaved the front of his shoulder-length hair into a half-tonsure, squirrels nested in his cowl, and he wandered around brandishing his staff and felling oak trees with his fist. By the end of the sixth century he had single-handedly revitalized the Faith among the barbarian hordes. The Saint's stubborn orthodoxy, characteristic of the Celtic clergy, put him in conflict with continental Church hierarchy: he berated the French priests for toadying to royalty and distancing themselves from their flock. He gave guff to no fewer than three Popes (Vigilius, Gregory the Great, and Boniface IV), warned them against the potential power of the papacy, and even made jokes about their names—behavior that has caused some historians to suggest Our Saint was daft. The dissolute Visigoth princess Brunhilda, with the grateful approval of Church authorities, banished Columbanus and his monks from the Netherlands. Their subsequent route across Europe—through France, Germany, Switzerland, and Italy—can be traced by the monasteries they founded, centers of learning in the Dark Ages. Not long after an argument with a local bear, Columbanus was alone in the woods talking to himself. He debated which was worse, the savagery of the beasts or the cruelty of men, and just as he had decided on the cruelty of men (they lost their immortal souls), twelve ravenous wolves surrounded him. He stood his ground, reciting "*Deus in adjutorium*" until the wolves dispersed. Columbanus finally settled in Italy, where he founded a monastery and library in Bobbio, building them with his own hands even though he was well into his seventies. He wrote beautiful poems, and even a rowing song with the rousing chorus "Heave, lads, and let the echoes ring!"

24. THE FEAST OF SAINTS FLORA AND MARY

Virgin runaway martyrs, 851

Patrons of the abandoned • (emblem: decapitated, flowers springing from their heads)

Mary was born to Moorish parents, but her mother converted to Christianity and Flora did as well. Her brother remained an infidel and heaped abuse both mental and physical upon Flora for her Faith. She had taken a secret vow of chastity, so when she heard of her impending arranged marriage, Flora ran away, taking her friend Mary with her. Flora's brother betrayed them to the Islamic authorities, and the two runaways—an earlier, holier version of Thelma and Louise, if you will—were imprisoned, scourged, and finally beheaded.

25. THE FEAST OF SAINT CATHERINE OF ALEXANDRIA

Intellectual virgin martyred on a spiked wheel, date unknown

Patron of jurists, knife grinders, librarians, mechanics, millers, philosophers, potters, spinsters, students, wheelwrights • (emblem: spiked wheel)

Although her feast is no longer officially celebrated by the Church, Catherine of Alexandria remains one of the most popular Saints in Christendom. According to her legend, she was a pagan Egyptian queen who, despite her great beauty, preferred the study of philosophy to the prospect of marriage with the Roman emperor Maxentius. Inspired by a visit from the Blessed Virgin, a desert hermit sought Catherine out and showed her a picture of the Madonna and Child. Immediately she not only became a Christian but "mystically married" the Christ Child. (He gave her a ring.) Appalled, the rejected Maxentius summoned a team of fifty pagan philosophers to debate religion with her. Catherine not only confounded them in argument but also converted them to the Faith. The emperor had all of those wise men slaughtered, but he spared Catherine, after whom he continued to lust. Rebuffed once more, he ordered that her chaste body be stretched out on a spiked wheel, the infamous Catherine wheel (after which the firecracker is named). But before her torture could begin, lightning-wielding Angels appeared and shattered the device, causing its blades to hack up bystanders. Catherine was then beheaded, but milk, not blood, flowed from her holy neck. The Angels transported her body to the monastery of Saint Catherine below Mount Sinai. Catherine's Feast falls immediately before the beginning of Advent, during which no weddings can take place. November 25 was, therefore, a sort of deadline for the unmarried women of the Middle Ages, who prayed to her thus:

> A husband, Saint Catherine,
> A good one, Saint Catherine,
> A handsome one, Saint Catherine,
> A rich one, Saint Catherine—
> And *soon*, Saint Catherine!

THE FEAST OF SAINT MERCURY

Warrior Saint, 250

Patron of the military • (emblem: Angel handing him a sword)

A Scythian mercenary soldier in the Roman army, named after a Roman god but a convert to Christianity, Mercury was a favorite of the emperor Decius until he refused to sacrifice to the goddess Artemis and was beheaded. But this warrior-Saint has since reappeared, sword in hand, in times of need. His ghost as-

sassinated the emperor Julian the Apostate and took an active part in the First Crusade.

26. THE FEAST OF SAINT JOHN BERCHMANS

Jesuit "boy Saint," 1621

Patron of altar boys, teenage boys • (emblem: rosary)

John Berchmans was virtuous from early childhood, one of those children who prefer the company of adults to that of other kids. By the time he was nine John was serving Mass twice a day. "If I don't become a Saint when I am young, I never will," he would explain poignantly. Although his father wanted John to join him in his shoe repair business, the boy signed on with the Jesuits. (Curiously enough, his widowed father soon joined the priesthood, too.) As a novice in Rome the young Belgian succumbed to the fever-inducing summer heat and after a short illness fulfilled his childhood wish by dying at the age of twenty-two. Miracles were attributed to him as early as his funeral, and thousands of holy cards bearing his image were distributed in Rome as well as in his native land. His relics rest in an urn alongside those of his role model and fellow Jesuit "Boy Saint," Aloysius Gonzaga.

27. THE FEAST OF SAINT MAXIMUS

Monk and most reluctant bishop, 460

Patron of babies, the dying • (emblem: doe)

Abbot of Lérins, in France, Maximus had a wide reputation for sanctity and miracle working. He is among the numerous holy hermits who abhorred the very idea of becoming a bishop. When offered the job Maximus fled to Italy and hid in a forest during the rainy season. On another such occasion he took off in a rowboat. Obliged in the end to accept the miter, he continued to live as a monk and kept right on wearing his hair shirt. In his own infancy he had been remarkably pious—refusing his mother's breast on fast days and Fridays. As an adult he was especially adept at deathbed healing.

Also: The Feast of Saint Francis Antony Fasani, 1742. Known as Johnny, he was an early and zealous promoter of the Immaculate Conception. Though healthy, he predicted the exact date of his upcoming death, even asking a friend to join him. (The friend refused but died soon after anyhow.) Though Francis died in the eighteenth century (the streets rang out with cries "The Saint is dead! The Saint is dead!"), he wasn't canonized until 1986.

28. THE FEAST OF SAINT JAMES OF THE MARCHES

Itinerant friar, 1476

Patron of Naples • (emblem: cup with serpent in it)

Though he was born in poverty, James's priest uncle helped him become a lawyer, tutor, and judge of accused sorcerers. After he himself joined the priesthood, James took to wandering and preaching around Italy. He served on legations to the rest of Europe as a member of the Friars Minor and supported the occasional Crusade. He was in the center of the unseemly brouhaha over the Precious Blood; James expressed some zany theories about it that upset several theologians. He died in Naples, where his relics are enshrined.

THE FEAST OF SAINT STEPHEN THE YOUNGER

Defiant monk, 764

Patron of coin collectors

As abbot of Mount Saint Auxentius, Stephen opposed the fanatic iconoclasm of Emperor Constantine Copronymus. Hauled before the emperor, Stephen delivered an impassioned defense of holy images, at the climax of which he boldly trampled on a coin with Constantine's picture on it. Saint Stephen and three hundred of his fellow monks were then jailed and executed—the abbot himself was battered to death.

Also: The Feast of Saint Catherine Labouré, to whom the Blessed Virgin Mary personally gave orders for the design and distribution of the miraculous medal. Her body lies under glass in a chapel next to the Bon Marché department store in Paris, 1876.

29. THE FEAST OF DOROTHY DAY
Modern-day Saint who was no Saint, 1980

In her younger days Dorothy was a suffragette, a Communist, a journalist, a free love advocate, and a knockout to boot. She had a series of lovers (including Eugene O'Neill), a divorce, an illegal abortion, and a "punk" hairdo, and she could make wine from dandelions and parsnips. Pregnant with her (out-of-wedlock) daughter, she became interested in Catholicism. Dorothy converted, left her lover, and raised her daughter alone. Because the Catholic Church had brought her to Christ, she put aside her reservations about its bureaucracy and bilious priests—"One must always live in a state of permanent dissatisfaction with the Church," she said. She and her fellow pacifist Peter Maurin founded The Catholic Worker for the poor and disenfranchised of society and personally distributed its newsletter. Dorothy built and lived in a "hospitality house" in the slums of New York, which she established to feed and shelter the homeless. She slept on a cot there and would wear only secondhand clothes. In the words of the *Making*

Saints author Kenneth Woodward, "Dorothy Day did for her era what Saint Francis of Assisi did for his: recall a complacent Christianity to its radical roots." She died penniless, and Abbie Hoffman, Cesar Chavez, and Daniel Berrigan attended her funeral. When Dorothy's expensive canonization process began in March 2000, Father Berrigan, calling her the people's saint, suggested the money be given to the poor instead. She might have agreed: when a reporter, in light of her status as a living Saint, asked if she had holy visions, Dorothy's response was an irritated "Oh shit!"

30. THE FEAST OF SAINT ANDREW

Apostle martyred on X-shaped cross, 1st century

Patron of fish dealers, fishermen, golfers, Greece, Russia, sailors, Scotland, spinsters, women who wish to become mothers; invoked against gout, neck problems
• (emblem: X-shaped cross)

Andrew had been a disciple of John the Baptist but left home to follow Jesus. He enlisted his brother and fellow fisherman Peter, and Jesus offered to make them both "fishers of men." Andrew was present at the wedding in Cana, and in Jerusalem for the Passion and the Crucifixion. He is believed to have founded the Greek Orthodox Church, which seems unlikely, and is the Patron Saint of Russia—a country he never visited. Andrew did, however, spend time in a kingdom ruled over and inhabited by cannibals, where he freed prisoners intended for the king's supper. Andrew was put to death for baptizing Maximilla, the wife of Egaes (the Roman governor of Patras in Achaia); the heathen administrator blamed the Apostle for the fact that his now-Christian wife would no longer sleep with him. There is a story that the governor once arrived home unexpectedly and nearly caught Our Saint and Maximilla—quite innocently, of course—in her bedchamber. But Egaes came down with a Heaven-sent bout of diarrhea, and Andrew made his escape. Perhaps as a result of this Saint Andrew became, in the Middle Ages, the object of a spinster cult. Martin Luther describes certain German maidens stripping naked to sweep their homes on Andrew's Feast Day, a performance guaranteed to provide them with visions of their future husbands; in Poland even today, on Saint Andrew's Eve, girls hold black cats over fires in hopes that this bizarre rite will give them magical glimpses of their future swains. Long after Andrew's death at Patras—he was crucified on an X-shaped cross—an Angel advised Saint Rule to take some of Andrew's relics "to the ends of the earth." Rule, accompanied by Saint Theneva, traveled to Scotland, and there they were joined by (a miraculously revived) Andrew. Together they built Saint Andrew's Church at Fife. This marked the beginning of the Saint's flourishing cult in the West; he became the subject of several early poems and even had a golf course named after him.

❧ December ☙

1. THE FEAST OF SAINT EDMUND CAMPION

Elizabethan prose stylist, martyr, 1581

Patron of printers

History calls the last Catholic monarch of England Bloody Mary and her Protestant successor Good Queen Bess. By order of the latter Edmund Campion was the first of hundreds who were hanged, drawn, and quartered for adhering to their religious beliefs. Campion was born in London in 1540, the son of a printer-bookseller. A brilliant writer and speaker, at age seventeen he became an Oxford fellow, but in the persecutions that followed the queen's excommunication he fled to France, where he joined the Jesuits. In 1580 he returned to his homeland as a sort of secret agent for the Faith. He was the object of a yearlong manhunt, all the while ministering to Catholics in hiding and publishing "underground" pamphlets, including his famous autobiographical *Brag.* Betrayed, captured, tried, and convicted of treason, he was executed. Along with thirty-nine of his fellow martyrs—priests, laymen, and laywomen—Edmund was canonized in 1970.

THE FEAST OF SAINT ELOY

Bishop and shockingly honest artisan, 659

Patron of coin collectors, cutlers, garage and gas station workers, jewelers, jockeys, metalworkers, smiths, toolmakers, veterinarians; invoked for the cure of horses • (emblem: horseshoe)

This popular Patron of "all who work with hammers" was an artisan employed by the Frankish king Dagobert I as master of the mint. Eloy's reputation for honesty was enhanced when he was commissioned to design and fashion a throne for Dagobert's son, Clotaire II. Rather than pocket the excess materials—gold and jewels—Eloy (French, Eloi; Latin, Elequis) constructed for Clotaire a pair of chairs. His most famous deed as a farrier—that is, a shoer of horses—involved an animal possessed by a Devil. Eloy blessed the beast, removed its legs, applied the shoes, and grafted the limbs back on, better than new.

Also: Blessed Sister Maria Clementine Anurite Nengapete. Zaire's answer to Maria Goretti was an African nun murdered after she rejected a drunken colonel, 1964.

2. THE FEAST OF SAINT BIBIANA

Roman virgin martyr, 363

Invoked against hangovers • (emblem: maiden, palm in hand)

Because the Spanish pronounce the letter *V* as the letter *B*, this Saint, whose name means "full of life" (Latin *vivo*), was thought by them to be "full of drink" (Latin *bibo*). Consequently, the Spanish invoked Bibiana's protection against the morning-after ravages of alcoholic indulgence. An ancient church in Rome is dedicated to the virgin martyr Viviana, who was scourged to death for her Faith, during the persecutions by the emperor Julian the Apostate.

3. THE FEAST OF SAINT CASSIAN OF TANGIER

Court stenographer, martyr, 298

Patron of shorthand writers, stenographers

Cassian was a court stenographer in North Africa when Saint Marcellus the Centurion was tried, convicted of Christianity, and sentenced to death. Cassian took exception to this injustice and threw down his pen and tablets, causing the judge to leap from the bench in anger. This unseemly scene is alleged to have moved Saint Marcellus to laughter; Cassian was executed with him.

THE FEAST OF SAINT FRANCIS XAVIER

Jesuit missionary to the Orient, 1552

Patron of Australia, Borneo, China, Goa, India, missionaries, Outer Mongolia, tourism • (emblem: lobster holding crucifix)

Except perhaps for Saint Paul, Francis Xavier was the greatest Christian missionary. A Basque Spaniard, he was born in 1506 into a new, round world, in which rich, untamed lands were known to lie to the east and west of Europe. As a student in Paris, Francis met Ignatius Loyola and, upon being asked by that Saint what it would profit him to gain the world but lose his soul, signed on as one of the seven original Jesuits. By papal command Francis set out for the East Indies. After a ghastly thirteen-month voyage around Africa, he arrived in the Portuguese colony of Goa in May 1542 and labored for seven years to reform the corrupt colonists and to convert the natives in southern India and throughout the Malay Peninsula. There remains some question as to whether Francis mastered the Malabar language, preached through interpreters, or possessed the gift of tongues, but he certainly took his vow of poverty seriously, living on rice and water and sleeping in a hut. Among the Indian poor, therefore, he had great success—but none with sophisticated Hindus of higher caste. When he heard from mariners about the land of Japan (which they had glimpsed but dared not enter), Francis sailed thither, becoming the first European to set foot upon those islands. For two years he preached with astonishing success to the Japanese, establishing a thriving Christian colony among them before setting out for the even more forbidding China. But it was God's will that Francis die on an island within sight of that country, worn out from his labors, an old man at the age of forty-six.

4. THE FEAST OF SAINT BARBARA

Tower-building virgin martyr, 4th century

Patron of architects, armorers, artillerymen, brewers, firemen, fireworks makers, hatters, masons, mathematicians, military engineers, miners, saltpeter workers, smelters; invoked against lightning, sudden death • (emblems: three-windowed tower, lightning)

SANTERÍA 8

SHANGÓ

Dioscorus of Heliopolis was a jealous father. He hid his daughter Barbara away in a tower so that no man should see her great beauty. But a Christian, disguised as a physician, gained access to her and instructed her in the Faith. While Dioscorus was away on business, he commanded that an elaborate bathroom (or swimming pool) be constructed in, or near, his daughter's tower. Because of Barbara's holiness its waters instantly acquired miraculous curative powers. The maiden then asked the reluctant construction workers to add a third window to her tower in honor of the Blessed Trinity—which they did. At the sight of this third window, the newly returned Dioscorus suspected the worst. He drew his sword to slay his child, but she leapt out the new window and fled to a cave in the mountains. An evil shepherd disclosed her refuge to Dioscorus (Our Saint cursed the shepherd, turning his sheep to locusts and him to stone), and the criminal parent dragged his daughter by the hair into the custody of civil authorities. Finally Dioscorus took matters into his own hands, led his difficult daughter up a mountain, and there cut off her head. A mighty clap of thunder was then heard, and a "fire from Heaven" struck Dioscorus, reducing him to ashes. All who handle explosives— miners and gunners and so on—are in Saint Barbara's care. (The French call a powder magazine *une Sainte-Barbe.*) Her patronage of sailors inspired Spanish mariners to name the difficult straits off the California coast Santa Barbara. In the eighteenth century, when the religions of West Africa fused with Roman Catholicism, Shangó, the god of thunderbolts, was transformed into gentle Saint Barbara. So when some slaves claimed to be praying to Saint Barbara, they were actually praying to their fiery, macho god Shangó for deliverance.

THE FEAST OF SAINT MARUTHAS

Relic-collecting Father of the Syrian Church, 415

Patron of Iran

Abishop of the "Christians of the East," Maruthas lived in the city of Maiferkat on the Iran-Iraq border, in the days when Iran was called Persia and Iraq was still Mesopotamia. A diplomat, physician, theologian, and composer of hymns, he was able to persuade the Persian king to cease persecuting his Christian subjects and is to this day revered by members of the Syrian Orthodox Church as their "Father."

5. THE FEAST OF SAINT SABAS

Who kept to himself, 532

In the year 447, when he was eight years old, Sabas ran away from his highly dysfunctional home in Alexandria, Egypt, to join a monastery in Jerusalem. But he longed for the life of a solitary desert hermit and in his fortieth year took up residence in a cave in the mountains near Jericho. (For a while the Saint shared the cave with its original tenant, a lion—but the two quarreled, as roommates will, and the lion left.) Despite his desire for solitude, hundreds of monks came to join Sabas—thereby forming, willy-nilly, a *laura,* that is, a community of hermits. It was called Mar Saba, and to this day Eastern Orthodox monks reside there, making it one of the oldest inhabited monasteries in the world.

Also: The Feast of Saint Crispina, a wealthy Numidian matron who in the course of her martyrdom was forced to undergo many shameful indignities, described in glowing detail by Saint Augustine during his funeral panegyric for her, 304.

6. THE FEAST OF SAINT EMILIAN

Physician martyred by Vandals, 484

Patron of druggists • (emblem: cauldron)

A fourth-century theologian named Arius taught that since there is only one God—God the Father—the Savior Jesus Christ could not have been "God" as well. At the Council of Nicaea in 325, Arianism was debated and condemned as a heresy, and the truth of the Trinity affirmed. But among Arius's disciples were the Vandals, a marauding Germanic tribe. (They were, so to speak, both Aryans and Arians.) The Vandals, after sacking Rome, established a kingdom of their own in, of all places, North Africa. There for a century or so they gave themselves over to rape, pillage, piracy, and the persecution of the indigenous orthodox Christians. On this day in the year 484 the beautiful and chaste Saint Dionysia was tortured in the arena and burned at the stake for her unswerving faith in the divinity of Christ. During the same public entertainment, for the same cause, her cousin Emilian, a physician and pharmacist, was flayed to death.

THE FEAST OF SAINT NICHOLAS

Turkish bishop, jolly old elf, 350

Patron of bakers, barrel makers, boot blacks, brewers, brides, children, dockworkers, fishermen, maritime pilots, pawnbrokers, perfumers, Russia, sailors, Sicily, spinsters, thieves, travelers • (emblem: three balls)

We know him best by his Dutch name, Santa Claus—this Saint so long and universally beloved by Christians of the East and West. He was a bishop of Myra, a city in southwest Turkey, who may (or may not) have attended the Council of Nicaea in 325. If he did, it was after being imprisoned in the Diocletian persecution in 305—but, then, Nicholas was a Wonder Worker. He was a singularly holy child—on holy days and Fridays he would refuse his mother's breast. After his wealthy parents died of plague he set about doing good deeds. Three young women he knew were about to enter lives of prostitution, for their poor father had no money to provide them with dowries. Secretly by night, Nicholas threw three bags of gold into their window. (The "three balls," representing financial aid in time of need, became the emblem of the pawnbrokers' guild.) In a time of famine Nicholas provided the poor with miraculous bread—hence his Patronage of bakers. During that same famine Our Saint (by now a bishop) visited a local butcher and was served—to his surprise—meat. Suspecting the worst, Nicholas proceeded to his host's cellar, there to find three barrels containing three murdered boys preserved in brine. Rest assured, the bishop lost not time in restoring them to life, and he has been a Patron of children in a pickle ever since.

7. THE FEAST OF SAINT AMBROSE

Persuasive preacher, Doctor of the Church, 397

Patron of bees, candlemakers, domestic animals, geese, orators • (emblems: bee hive, scourge)

A swarm of bees settled in Ambrose's mouth when he was in his cradle, foreshadowing his oratorical gifts. Ambrose was a lawyer in Milan who had not yet been baptized when, inspired by the miraculous shouts of a child in the crowd, the people of the city made him their bishop. He insisted that the Church take precedence over the State, declaring, "An emperor is within the Church; he is not above it," and strongly rebuked the emperor Theodosius for being insufficiently anti-Semitic in judging a case of synagogue burning. Ambrose's many "bewitching" sermons are filled with theologically dubious Neoplatonism, yet he preached mightily and successfully against the Arian heresy. Having been raised by his mother and an aunt (a nun), Ambrose was a fierce advocate of celibacy—he is frequently depicted wielding the scourge with which he had his rival Jovian flogged for daring to suggest that marriage was no less pleasing to God than virginity.

8. THE FEAST OF THE IMMACULATE CONCEPTION

Patron of army chaplains, clothworkers, coopers, Inner Mongolia, Tanzania, the USA, upholsterers, Zaire

The Immaculate Conception does *not* refer to the conception of Jesus Christ, which is known as the Incarnation. Teaching nuns in particular become upset if you confuse the two. This major doctrine of the Church and Holy Day of Obligation honors Mary's own conception, in the womb of her mother, Saint Anne. It seems that Mary's parents did not "couple," as it is put, in "human mire," that is to say, they took no pleasure whatsoever in the act; so She was conceived without the hereditary taint of Original Sin, and thus was a fit vessel for God's Only Son to be hatched in. The question of the Immaculate Conception was hotly debated over the centuries—even such Maryolaters as Saint Bernard deemed it blasphemous. It was not made official Church dogma until Pope Pius IX defined it as such, in 1854.

9. THE FEAST OF SAINT GORGONIA

Twice-cured accident victim, 374

Patron of the infirm

Gorgonia's parents were Saints, as were her two brothers, and she brought up her three children to be devout Christians, but misfortune seemed to follow her. She was trampled by a team of mules, suffering broken bones and damage to her internal organs. Miraculously, she recovered, only to be felled by narcolepsy and a fourth-century version of Epstein-Barr disease. Again she prayed, and again she was cured.

THE FEAST OF SAINT LEOCADIA

Teenage virgin martyr, 303

Patron of Toledo; invoked against plague • (emblem: maiden praying in prison)

By means of their devotion to Saint Leocadia's relics in their cathedral, the citizens of the Spanish city of Toledo have been spared many a pestilential epidemic. It is said that this holy maiden was inspired by tales of the exemplary death of Saint Eulalia of Barcelona to bravely undergo her own martyrdom. Perversely, the official Church Calendar suggests that Eulalia died the day *after* Leocadia.

Also: The Feast of Saint Budoc, whose mother was thrown into the sea in a cask, wherein he was born, and both washed up after some months on the coast of Ireland, 6th century.

10. THE FEAST OF OUR LADY OF LORETO

Commemorating the arrival, by air, of Mary's home in Italy

Patron of aircrew and pilots

In 1291 a convoy of Angels moved the Blessed Virgin Mary's house from Palestine to Dalmatia. Three years later Angels moved it again, to its present—and one hopes permanent—place in Loreto, an Italian town on the coast of the Adriatic. The house, only nine yards long, has no standing walls. The stone of which it is made is of Middle Eastern origin. Wherever it came from, and however it got there, it has been the site of many miracles. And the litany of Our Lady of Loreto is the longest and most colorful litany of them all.

THE FEAST OF SAINT EULALIA

Teenage virgin martyr, 304

Patron of Barcelona, childbirth, sailors, travelers; invoked against miscarriage, for calm waters • (emblem: hook)

This devout virgin, beloved through all of Catalonia, was but twelve years old when she decided to denounce the pagan authorities. She was arrested, naturally, and during her trial was so bold as to trample beneath her feet a cake sacred to the heathen Roman idols. She was sentenced to be cruelly executed—but luckily for her a torch held by her would-be tormentors set her long hair on fire and she smothered in the smoke. Thereupon a white dove flew out of her mouth and ascended to Heaven, and a sudden fall of snow covered her innocent ashes. Her aid has been invoked by all who sail the seas off the Costa Brava.

Also: The Feast of Saint John Roberts, English martyr; on the night before he was hanged, he ate his last meal with so much gusto that he won the admiration of his executioners; they made sure he didn't suffer the next day, 1610.

11. THE FEAST OF SAINT DAMASUS

Catacomb-excavating Pope, 384

Patron of archaeologists • (emblem: Pope holding ring)

Like his father before him, Damasus was a simple priest in Rome when at the age of sixty he was elected to succeed Liberius as Supreme Pontiff, in the year of Our Lord 366. His right to the Chair of Peter was contested by a rival, Ursinus, and the armed adherents of Pope and antipope warred in the streets until Damasus' faction negotiated the support of the imperial authorities. Another staunch supporter of Damasus was the learned Saint Jerome, who praised him as "a Virgin Doctor of the Virgin Church." Pope Damasus encouraged devotion to the early martyrs, to which end he ordered that the catacombs in which they were entombed be excavated, drained, adorned, and opened to the public.

THE FEAST OF SAINT GENTIAN

Martyred host, date unknown

Patron of innkeepers

Two Roman missionaries (Fuscian and Victoricus) once traveled to Gaul to visit their friend Saint Quentinus. On their way to his church at Amiens, they took lodgings for the night at Sains, in the home of an aged pagan named Gentian. It was their host's unpleasant duty to inform them that their friend had been most recently, and most cruelly, martyred. The following morning the Roman governor of the province sent a troop of soldiers to arrest Gentian's guests. The hospitable old man stood in his doorway with his sword drawn—and was beheaded on the spot. Fuscian and Victoricus were seized and likewise executed, but the looks on their (decapitated) faces drove the governor stark raving mad.

THE FEAST OF SAINT CURY

Beloved Breton bishop, 6th century

Invoked against blindness, deafness, demonic possession • (emblem: near fountain, holding fish)

The chapel of Corentin, or Cury, at Plomodiern in Brittany is still visited by the Faithful. In the nearby stream once lived a wonderful fish. For his dinner each day Saint Cury would cut a bit off the obliging creature and return it to the water, where it would by the grace of God reconstitute itself overnight. On one occasion good King Gradlon and his attendants dropped by unexpectedly, and Cury's fish fed the entire company. But one wretch returned to steal the miraculous creature and in his greed killed it, forcing Cury to restore it to life and grant its freedom. The people of the neighborhood begged Cury to become their bishop, and he agreed. The Gothic cathedral of Saint Corentin remains the pride of the city of Quimper; below the base of its spires is a statue of the Saint's friend King Gradlon.

12. THE FEAST OF OUR LADY OF GUADALUPE

Marian apparition, 1531

Patron of Central America, Mexico

In the fourteenth century in Guadalupe, Spain, Our Lady appeared on a hillside to a shepherd. A hundred years later she reappeared, on a Mexican hillside, to a peasant named Juan Diego, and this time she left an image of Herself on his *tilma* (his cloth cloak). This garment has been preserved and may be gaped at in the Cathedral of Our Lady of Guadalupe in Mexico City. The shrine is visited by ten million people a year, making it second only to the Vatican as a destination of pilgrimages.

THE FEAST OF SAINT JEAN FRANCES DE CHANTAL

Working widow, 1641

Patron of forgotten people, widows; invoked against in-law problems, separation from children

Her father was the president of Parliament, her husband was the handsome Baron de Chantal, and her four children were healthy. This charmed life came to an end when the baron was killed in a hunting accident, dying in her arms. Jean and her four children were then forced to live with her father-in-law and his hussy "housekeeper," both of whom enjoyed mistreating her. Her only so-lace was helping other widows and, inspired by the sermons of Saint Francis de Sales, Jean decided to become a nun. (Despite her Patronage of separation from children, she stepped over her fifteen-year-old son, who had thrown himself across the doorway to prevent her from joining the convent.) Jean had an episto-lary relationship with Saint Francis de Sales, but upon his death she found and burned all the letters she had sent him. He said of her, "In Madame Chantal I have found the valiant woman whom Solomon had difficulty finding in Jerusalem." Her granddaughter was the risqué Madame de Sévigné, a fixture of Louis XIV's court, who may very well have invented the gossip column.

13. THE FEAST OF SAINT JOSSE

Breton king turned seaside hermit, 668

Patron of harvests, ships; invoked against fever, fire, storms • (emblem: ship)

This Saint of Brittany—whose name is pronounced "Joyce"—was a prince and married man. Upon making a pilgrimage to Rome, Josse decided to renounce his former life and returned home to live as a simple seaside hermit, praying for the mariners. After his death (at the aptly named town Saint-Josse-sur-Mer) his body remained incorrupt, and the Faithful were kept busy trimming his beard and fingernails.

THE FEAST OF SAINT LUCY

Blind, beautiful virgin martyr, 304

Patron of glassworkers, gondoliers, lamplighters, salespeople; invoked against dysentery, eye disease, hemorrhage, throat disease • (emblem: eyes on dish)

Lucy's name, appropriately, means "light"—for her Feast Day fell, in the old cal-endar, on the winter solstice, the shortest, darkest day of the year. She was a wealthy, beautiful, and affianced maiden of Syracuse, Sicily, whose mother was troubled with an internal complaint. Lucy accompanied her to the shrine of the virgin martyr Saint Agnes, where a miraculous cure was effected. Lucy vowed then and there to die a virgin and to give all her worldly goods to the poor. Her acts of charity distressed her fortune-hunting fiancé, who denounced her as a Christian to the authorities. She was condemned to be despoiled in a brothel, but not even a team of oxen could move her from the place where she stood; she survived an attempted burning at the stake; and, praising God all the while, she was dispatched by a sword in the throat. At some juncture in these proceedings she plucked out her eyes and made a present of them to her suitor, who had always admired them. She is, of course, the Santa Lucia about whom the gondoliers of Venice interminably sing.

THE FEAST OF SAINT ODILIA

Sight-restored abbess, 720

Patron of Alsace, the Crosier Fathers; invoked against blindness • (emblem: eyes on a book)

According to her legend, Odilia was born blind. Her father, Adalric, an Alsatian nobleman, wished the child to be "exposed"—that is, left to die (a form of population control often practiced by medieval Christians—see *The Kindness of Strangers* by the historian John Boswell). But her mother gave Odilia into the care of a peasant woman, who in turn assigned her to a convent. At the age of twelve, when she was baptized, Odilia was miraculously granted her sight. Word of this wonder—and of the girl's true identity—reached her brother. He petitioned his father for his sister's return—and was slain for his trouble. Then their father waxed contrite. He welcomed Odilia home, fawned over her, and even arranged her engagement to a neighboring German knight. Odilia, who had vowed to remain a virgin, fled the castle. Once more her dreadful parent made an attempt on her life, but at length he sincerely repented and financed her foundation of two convents. After his death Odilia's constant prayers released him from Purgatory, and father and daughter are now united in Heaven.

14. THE FEAST OF SAINT JOHN OF THE CROSS

Author, "Dark Night of the Soul," 1591

Patron of poets • (emblem: cross, top half red, bottom black)

San Juan de la Cruz's most famous poem, "*Noche obscura del alma*," is *not* about depression but is a description of the soul's mystical marriage to Christ. Born in 1542, this Carmelite priest was a friend of the great mystic and reformer Saint Teresa of Ávila and was himself imprisoned for undertaking to return the (male) Carmelites to their primitive rule of poverty. It was in a jail cell in Toledo that he composed his great poem.

THE FEAST OF SAINT SPIRIDION

Tough-guy bishop, 344

Patron of Corfu, Dalmatia • (emblem: needles for putting out his eyes)

Spiridion, a rough-and-ready sheep farmer, lived on the island of Cyprus with his wife and family. He was also a stalwart Christian and had suffered the loss of an eye rather than take part in an idolatrous ceremony. The Cyprians elected him bishop and sent him as their delegate to the Council of Nicaea in 325. The bishop and deacons from surrounding lands with whom Spiridion set out for the council were all learned and dignified churchmen, and somewhat embarrassed by the company of this one-eyed rustic. One night they conspired to prevent his accompanying them further by cutting off the heads of the two mules—a brown one and a white one—on which he and his servant rode. Before dawn Spiridion awoke and discovered the decapitations. In the dark he restored the animals' heads. And that is why Bishop Spiridion came to Nicaea riding a white mule with a brown head.

Also: Blessed Nimatullah Youssef Kassab, Lebanese friar who supported the rights of his fellow monks to smoke, 1859.

15. THE FEAST OF SAINT NINO

Czar-converting virgin, 4th century

Patron of Georgia

The Georgian Orthodox Church is, says the *Encyclopaedia Britannica,* "one of the most ancient Christian communities in the world. The Georgians adopted Christianity through the ministry of one woman, St. Nino, early in the fourth century." Nino was, according to legend, a beautiful and virtuous Greek (or Italian, or Jewish, or French) girl transported to Georgia as a slave. A child of the household in which she was employed fell sick and was restored to health through Nino's prayers. Word of this miracle reached the ears of the queen, who sought out and befriended the slave girl. Nino explained to Her Majesty, as best she could, the Holy Faith. Not long after the queen shared this information with the king, he found himself lost in the misty forest. He invoked the name of Nino's God, and the fog mysteriously lifted. The king then petitioned Emperor Constantine that bishops and priests be sent into his realm, and all Georgia was soon converted.

THE FEAST OF SAINT VALERIAN

North African martyred by exposure, 457

Invoked against cold • (emblem: old man lying on the ground)

It is somewhat ironic that the Saint traditionally invoked against the vicissitudes of winter was African. Valerian was the eighty-year-old bishop of Tunis who defied Hunneric, king of the Vandals, by refusing to surrender the precious treasures of his Church. The punishment he endured was exile—*within* his own city. The old clergyman was evicted from his home and obliged to wander the streets—to offer him shelter, food, or care was forbidden. And in the streets, on a winter night, he died.

16. THE FEAST OF SAINT ADELAIDE

Stern matriarch and empress, 999

Patron of empresses, stepparents • (emblem: empress near a ship)

The daughter of King Rudolf II of Burgundy, Adelaide was forced by the shockingly degenerate Italian king Hugh to marry his loathsome son, Lothair, at the same ceremony in which he (Hugh) married *her* widowed mother. This incestuous union happily ended with the death of Lothair (he died raving mad), leaving Adelaide free to marry the recently widowed Otto the Great of Germany. In 962 they were crowned Holy Roman emperor and empress by Pope John XII (arguably the worst of the "Bad Popes"—he bragged of worshiping Satan at the altar and having sexual relations with his own mother). Upon Otto's demise in 973, Adelaide quarreled bitterly with her stepchildren; with her own son, Otto II; with her Greek mother-in-law, Theophano; and eventually with her grandson, Otto III. Nevertheless, many clergymen spoke highly of her, because she was exceedingly generous to the Church and even founded a convent.

17. THE FEAST OF SAINT LAZARUS

Raised from the dead by Christ, 1st century

Patron of housewives, lepers, sextons; invoked against smallpox • (emblem: leper on crutches)

Lazarus was, according to the Gospel of John, the brother of Mary and Martha of Bethany, whom Jesus raised from the dead. And because Lazarus was the name of a leper in one of Jesus' parables, it was assumed that the "historical" Lazarus, too, was leprous.

In the lore of the Christians of France, Lazarus, after Christ's Ascension, sailed to Marseilles and was the first bishop of that city; the faithful of the island of Cyprus maintain that he sailed thither and was *their* original bishop. (The Afro-Cuban Santeria religion, fused with Catholicism, and their god Babalu-aye was turned into Saint Lazarus. He, too, is depicted on crutches, but unlike Lazarus, Babalu-aye has a fondness for good cigars and was the subject of Ricky Ricardo's nightclub and theme song.

18. THE FEAST OF THE VIRGIN OF THE LONELY

Statue venerated in Oaxaca, Mexico

Patron of muleteers, sailors

This devotion was instituted to empathize with Our Lady's solitary vigil on Holy Saturday. In 1692 a mule driver found that he had an extra burro carrying a huge box. When officials opened the box they found it contained an image of the Virgin of the Lonely and built Her church on that very spot. There they celebrate Her with colorful paper lanterns; local women top the statue with a jeweled crown, for which local sailors (She's their Patron) provide real pearls.

THE FEAST OF SAINT FLANNAN

Pustular missionary, 648

Invoked against facial boils

The son of an Irish chieftain, Flannan made a pilgrimage to Rome (to which he sailed, Saint that he was, on a floating stone) and, once there, was consecrated bishop by the Pope himself. Flannan returned to Ireland and became a wandering preacher, famous as well in Scotland and in the Western Isles—a group of which desolate rocks still bear his holy name. It had been predicted by Saint Colman that Flannan's father would beget seven kings, all named Brian. (Which, by the way, he did.) Despite *not* being named Brian, Our Saint feared all earthly honors and prayed to be made physically repulsive. Merciful God heard his pleas and afflicted him with rashes, boils, and scars about the face.

19. THE FEAST OF SAINT ADAM

Our sinful-sorrowful forefather, date unknown

Patron of gardeners • (emblem: spade)

The first man, Adam, lived, of course, in a garden—and when expelled from it was obliged to "earn his bread by the sweat of his face"—hence his Patronage of tillers of the soil. Because he (and his wife, Eve) repented their sin, both were presumed to be among the Old Testament Saints who were released from Hell by Christ in the time between His death and Resurrection. Adam's Feast Day (in the Eastern Church) was celebrated on Christmas Eve. So (in the West) was the Feast of any Saint named Adam—including the thirteenth-century British bishop who raised the tithes so high (one handful of butter for every ten cows) that his flock burned down his house, with him in it.

20. THE FEAST OF SAINT DOMINIC OF SILOS

Queen-befriending abbot, 1073

Patron of captives, pregnant women, shepherds; invoked against insects, mad dogs • (emblem: abbot surrounded by the seven virtues)

Dominic, a devout lad, was a shepherd in the Cantabrian Mountains of Spain. He joined the Benedictine Order and became a monk in the abbey at Silos, where he rose to the rank of abbot because of both his piety and his prescient support of the territorial claims of Castile over those of Navarre. His prayers helped a local noblewoman through a difficult pregnancy, and in his honor she named her child Dominic. He, of course, grew up to be the more famous Saint Dominic, heretic smiter and founder of the Dominicans. Following his death, visions of Dominic of Silos often appeared, miraculously freeing Spanish prisoners of war held captive during the long Moorish occupation of the Iberian Peninsula, and for centuries his staff has been brought to the bedside of every Spanish queen during her confinement.

21. THE FEAST OF SAINT PETER CANISIUS

Counter-Reformation preacher, 1597

Patron of Germany • (emblem: holding a book)

When he decided against becoming a lawyer, this Dutch student also took a vow of celibacy. He eventually became a Jesuit, traveling and working closely with Saint Ignatius Loyola. Once when praying Peter saw the poignant image of the Sacred Heart, to which he instantly dedicated his life. The spiritually infused Jesuit then went off to head up the Counter-Reformation in Germany, a serious undertaking in the land where the Reformation had begun. Saint Peter was a major operative at the Council of Trent. His popular catechism was translated into twelve languages, and he was the expert of his day on the Eucharist. Peter was made a Doctor of the Church over three hundred years after his death.

22. THE FEAST OF THE BLESSED GRATIAN

Demon-molested lay brother, 1503

Invoked to find lost objects

Until the age of thirty Gratian was a contented Dalmatian fisherman. But a sermon he chanced to hear while visiting Venice changed his life. He sold his boat and nets and joined a hermitage in Padua, where until his death he was occupied as a tailor, gardener, and all-around handyman. The fasts and austerities he undertook were exceptional (the hair shirt he wore always is still on display in the cathedral of Kodor), and it is said that flames shot out of his breast when he prayed. He was also lame—the consequence of one of the demonic attacks from which he suffered constantly.

Also: The Feast of Saint Jacopone da Todi. His wife, Vanna, called him shallow, and she was right. The two fought about attending a frivolous tournament and he prevailed. While Vanna was in the grandstand, it collapsed and she was killed. Jacopone went mad with grief and became a barefoot Franciscan. It was he who wrote the beautiful hymn "Stabat Mater," 1306.

23. THE FEAST OF SAINT DAGOBERT II

Kidnapped Frankish king, 679

Patron of kidnap victims • (emblem: king with a nail in his hand)

When his father died Dagobert—the last French king from the Merovingian bloodline—was kidnapped and shipped off to an Irish monastery at the tender age of four. Twenty years later, Dagobert was restored to the throne, only to be assassinated by the mayor of the palace three years later. In 2001 there exists an occult organization, Dagobert's Revenge, which is fervently devoted to the Saint, with a magazine, a website, and a convoluted conspiracy theory. Dagobert's Revenge maintains that Our Saint was assassinated by Pepin the Fat, who had conspired with Church authorities to remove the Merovingians from the French throne and replace them with the Carolingian dynasty. The occultists theorize that the Merovingian bloodline was descended from Jesus Christ (!) and the Roman Church had co-opted Jesus with a fictionalized tale of a Virgin Messiah (!!) so it could further its agenda of world domination (!!!). Many members of today's deposed and useless European nobility—delighted, no doubt, to be considered offspring of Jesus Christ—endorse this theory.

THE FEAST OF SAINT JOHN OF KANTI

Generous theologian, 1473

Patron of Lithuania, Poland • (emblem: in a doctor's gown, his arm around a young student)

He was sometimes known as John Cantius, after his Polish birthplace, the town of Kanti. After his ordination to the priesthood and graduation from the

University of Crakow, John became a professor there, but his popularity as a lecturer and preacher inspired envy among his colleagues, and they contrived to have the austere intellectual posted to a simple country parish, where he was as miserable as the members of his congregation. He returned to the university as professor of sacred Scripture, which post he held until his death. John was renowned not only for his academic achievements but also for his boundless charity to the poor and the severity of his personal life.

THE FEAST OF SAINT SERVULUS OF ROME

Devout paralytic beggar, 590

Patron of the handicapped • (emblem: cripple lying in a church doorway)

Afflicted from infancy with palsy, Servulus could not stand or sit, or lift his hand to his mouth. Each day his mother and brother would carry him to the porch outside the doors of Saint Clement's Church in Rome. Although he was himself a beggar, it is said he shared what little he had with the poor. Servulus would constantly entreat passersby to read Scripture or sing hymns to him—so that he learned them all by heart. He died in the year Gregory the Great became Pope; it was Gregory who conducted the paralyzed beggar's funeral Mass, and we have it on papal authority that the corpse "smelled fragrant."

THE FEAST OF SAINT THORLAC

No-nonsense bishop, 1193

Patron of Iceland

This native of Iceland was declared a Saint five years after his death by the Icelandic parliament, the Althing. Rome has yet to officially confirm their decision. As a young man Thorlac went to study in Norway and England—he returned to Iceland as a bishop, full of zeal for such newfangled ideas as clerical celibacy and a Church financially independent of civil authorities. For a while he was heartily disliked, but, wielding bulls of excommunication like a berserker's battle-ax, he soon achieved his reforms.

24. THE FEAST OF SAINT LEVAN

Cornish Breton fisherman-hermit, 6th century

Patron of malformed children

Also known as Levian, Selevan, and Selyv, Levan is venerated in southern Brittany and at Saint Levan, Cornwall, where the ruins of his chapel and his bench may be seen. Why the Bretons invoke his care for children with birth defects is a mystery, but it speaks well of the Saint. In Cornish legend Levan once caught two fish on a single hook. Since he lived in solitude he required only one of them, so he cast one back into the sea. But twice more the fish returned to his hook, so he took both of them home—to discover that his sister and her children had come to dinner.

THE FEAST OF SAINT SHARBEL MAKHLOUF

Lebanese anachronism, 1898

His father was a mule driver in Lebanon. As a youth Sharbel (born Joseph) yearned for the days of the old-time hermit Saints. So he went to live in the desert, wore a hair shirt, vanquished serpents, and rid the land of grasshoppers. He would no doubt have lapsed into obscurity, a Maronite oddity, except that twenty-seven years after his death his corpse began to sweat blood. Reddish goo seeped through his zinc coffin, which was bathed in light, and miracles among Christians and non-Christians alike occur at his tomb.

Also: The Feast of all of Our Lord's ancestors, including King David, the Old Testament musician, warrior, prophet, and adulterer.

25. THE FEAST OF SAINT ANASTASIA

Matron-martyr, 304

Patron of weavers; invoked against
poison • (emblems: loom, star)

Though her official biography claims
she was Roman, she wasn't. Anastasia
was from Yugoslavia, and it was there that
she was martyred for her Faith. A church
near the Circus Maximus in Rome was
named Anastasia, so the legend of a noble
Roman martyr evolved, perhaps to rational-
ize the name of this church and its elaborate
basilica. In reality the church was probably
an *Anastasix* church (that is, one dedicated
to the Resurrection). At any rate, Anastasia
has the unique honor of being commemorated in the second mass on Christmas Day.

THE FEAST OF SAINT EUGENIA/EUGENIUS

Cross-dressing "monk," 258

The thirteenth-century collection of Saints' tales known as *The Golden Legend*
tells us that Eugenia was the beautiful daughter of the pagan duke Philip of
Alexandria. To preserve her chastity she disguised herself as a man—Eugenius—
and fled her father's house to join a desert monastery. Sometime later the young
"monk" was accused of rape by a woman of the neighborhood—at whose motive
we can scarcely guess. "Eugenius" was hauled before the judge—who happened to
be her father!—and sentenced to death. At which point "she rent her coat and
showed to him that she was a woman and his daughter."

Also: The Feast of Saint Fulk, who repented of his youth as a singer-songwriter and
went to work for the killjoy Saint Dominic but is still known as the minstrel
bishop of Toulouse, 1231.

26. THE FEAST OF SAINT STEPHEN

Stoned protomartyr, 33

Patron of bricklayers, builders, casket makers, horses, stonemasons • (emblem: heap of stones)

SAINT STEPHEN
FIRST MARTYR

Stephen is called the Protomartyr, for he was the first Christian to die for the Faith (not including the Holy Innocents and John the Baptist). Although not an Apostle, Stephen was one of seventy-two original disciples and after Pentecost was appointed one of Jerusalem's seven deacons. Accused by pious Jews of preaching blasphemy, he was arrested, tried before the high priest, Caiaphas (again), and condemned to death by stoning. The rocks and bricks employed by his executioners are treasured relics of Christendom; there are an astonishing number of them. In Poland (where his is a popular name), parishioners shower the priest with oats after Mass on Saint Stephen's Day, for the sake of their horses. In England and Ireland children remember the Saint today by hurling rocks at wrens.

27. THE FEAST OF SAINT FABIOLA

Penitent Roman divorcee-convert, 399

Patron of the divorced

This patrician Roman lady was married to a disgusting Roman brute, forcing her to obtain a Roman divorce. She remarried (happily), but when her second husband died Fabiola did public penance for her earlier divorce and was forgiven by the Pope. Welcomed back into the Church, she joined Saint Jerome's inner circle, Jerome having an affinity for rich widows. She donated her vast fortune to religious communities and a hospice for pilgrims, and founded the first hospital in the West—where Fabiola herself tended to the most repulsive patients. She never got to live the hermit's life she desired but did manage to spend time contemplating the Scriptures. The senate and people of Rome attended her splendid funeral.

THE FEAST OF SAINT JOHN THE DIVINE

The Beloved Disciple, Evangelist, 101

Patron of art dealers, mirror makers, paper manufacturers, printers, Turkey, writers; invoked against poison, for forming friendships • (emblem: eagle)

Scholars dispute whether Jesus' "beloved disciple" John, John the Evangelist (author of the Fourth Gospel), and John the Divine (author of the bizarre *Revelation*) were one and the same person. Tradition says that they were indeed, and that his missionary work took Our John first to Ephesus, where he wrote his Gospel. Thence he traveled to Rome, where he survived immersion in a cauldron of boiling oil. Back in Ephesus he was given a cup of poison to drink, but he blessed the beverage and the poison departed it in the form of a serpent. This led, somehow, to his exile on the island of Patmos, where he experienced the psychedelic visions he described in *Revelation*. (Perhaps he hadn't exorcised *all* the poison from that drink.) The youngest of the Apostles, John lived to a very old age on Patmos, boring some of his own disciples by endlessly entreating them to "love one another." He finally dug his own grave, in the shape of a cross, and lay down in it. There was a flash of light . . . and, body and soul, John was gone.

28. THE FEAST OF THE HOLY INNOCENTS (CHILDERMASS)

Infant boys martyred by King Herod, 3 B.C.

Patrons of babies, choirboys • (emblem: two starry crowns, with lilies)

The Bible (Matthew 2:16–18) tells us that, upon hearing from the Magi that a new king had been born in Bethlehem, King Herod took the precaution of ordering the slaughter of all male children under two years of age in that city. (Sacred Scripture aside, there is, remarkably, no historical record of this wholesale infanticide.) The Holy Innocents have long been honored as the first martyrs, and their commemorative feast (Childermass) was celebrated in England, until the seventeenth century, by whipping the children of the household while they lay abed. In continental Europe, December 28 was the Feast of Fools, a day on which a highly satirical sort of anarchy was permitted in the churches; a blasphemous parody of the Mass was sometimes celebrated, in which the congregation brayed the responses like donkeys; the youngest member of any religious community was placed in absolute authority; and a good time was had by all. (An elaborate description of the day's excesses is provided by Victor Hugo in his novel *The Hunchback of Notre Dame*.)

29. THE FEAST OF SAINT THOMAS À BECKET

Murder in the Cathedral archbishop, 1170

Patron of the blind, eunuchs • (emblem: three choughs)

Chaucer's pilgrims, who tell the Canterbury Tales, are on their way to the site of this Saint's martyrdom and tomb; his popularity extends to our own time—the poet T. S. Eliot wrote him up in a verse drama (*Murder in the Cathedral*), and Richard Burton played him in a Hollywood movie (*Becket*). Thomas was a drinking buddy, companion in arms, and lord chancellor to England's King Henry II. But when His Majesty arranged to have him made Archbishop of Canterbury, Thomas, strangely enough, got religion. The ex-friends were equally bad-tempered and stubborn, and commenced to quarrel over the separation of church and state. Finally a group of overzealous soldiers heard Henry mumble something about wishing he were rid of Thomas ("Will no one rid me of this

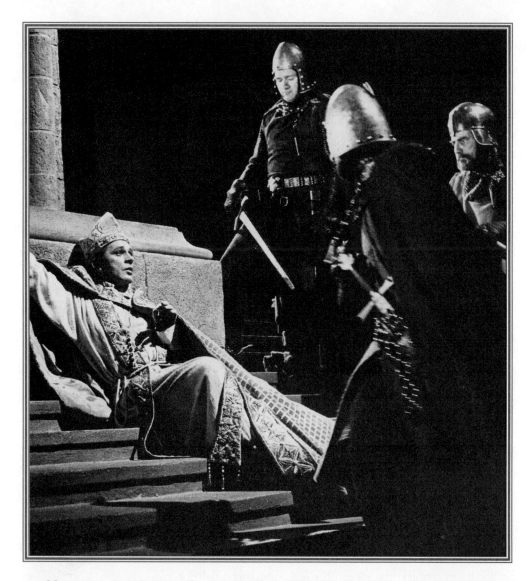

troublesome priest?" or words to that effect). They stormed into the cathedral and bashed out the archbishop's brains. The Pope was appalled at the sort of example this might set, and within three years, even though the king apologized, Thomas was declared a Saint. For centuries the lame, the halt, and particularly the blind were cured in great numbers at Thomas's elaborate tomb in the cathedral, until King Henry VIII, who had his own problems with the Pope, outlawed all veneration—or mention—of Our Saint.

THE FEAST OF SAINT TROPEZ

Legendary bishop of the Riviera, 1st century

Patron of children; invoked against gout • (emblem: boat steered by an Angel)

The notoriously decadent Mediterranean resort city of Saint-Tropez was named for Trophimus, allegedly the first bishop of Arles. The medieval French took great pains to demonstrate that they were Europe's first Christian nation, brought to the True Faith by the missionary labors of Jesus' own disciples, among them Saints Lazarus, Mary Magdalene, and Tropez, the convert and friend of Saint Paul mentioned in Acts 20:4.

30. THE FEAST OF OUR LADY OF LUJÁN

Miraculous statue and basilica

Patron of Argentina, Paraguay, Uruguay

Though Patron of three South American countries, the figurine known as Our Lady of Luján was recently moved from Argentina to Nanjing, China. She resides in the Catholic church there, a symbol of brotherhood between Argentina and China.

31. THE FEAST OF SAINT SYLVESTER

Dragon-slaying Pope, 335

Patron of pets; invoked for a good harvest • (emblem: bull at his feet)

New Year's Eve is Saint Sylvester's Night, and if an east wind blows up, it is said to betoken a calamitous twelve months in the offing. Pope Sylvester cured Emperor Constantine of leprosy and baptized him; in turn, the grateful ruler made Christianity the state religion of the Roman Empire and bestowed upon the bishop of Rome enormous temporal powers. The alliance between Sylvester and Constantine, altar and throne, church and state, was formalized in the Donation of Constantine, 315, a contract by which the emperor granted the papacy unimagined powers and possession, in perpetuity. Shockingly, the Donation of Constantine has turned out to be one of the great forgeries of history, penned, it seems, by a scholarly, sneaky priest in the eighth century. Equally bogus is the story of Constantine's baptism by Pope Sylvester, since Our Saint was long dead when that mighty statesman and murderer succumbed, on his deathbed, to baptism. (The Sacrament was in fact perpetrated by a heretical Aryan bishop who answered to the name of Eusebius.) The good news is that at midnight tonight girls may catch a glimpse of their prospective husbands in a mirror, courtesy of Saint Sylvester.

Also: The Feast of Saint Columba of Sens, a devout Spanish maiden who emigrated to France, where she was rescued from a brothel by a bear, 273.

Appendix

Every year, everybody has a birthday. Big deal. From now on, *you* can have *two*. Unless you are afflicted with a trendy New Age first name, you are officially entitled to a Name Day, a second annual excuse for celebrating the fabulous fact of your very special existence. Throw a party, get cards and presents, and be the center of attention on the Feast of the Saint in whose honor you were christened, or otherwise given your "given" name.

The French all observe both their birthdays (*anniversaires*) and their Name Days (*jours de fête*). In Britain, where they like to use fancy French words, one refers to one's Name Day as one's "fete-day," which is described in the *Oxford English Dictionary* as being observed "in Roman Catholic countries...as the birthday is in England."

But in fact the practice isn't confined to Roman Catholic countries (whatever they may be). Although a majority of Czechs claim to have no religious affiliation, a lot of them are named either Jan or Anna, and the Feast Days of Saints John and Anne are de facto holidays in Prague. In staunchly Lutheran Germany, everyone makes merry on his or her *Namensfeiser.* (You are doubtless familiar with Beethoven's "Namensfeiser" Grand Overture in C major.) Even the secular Swedes do it—a handy calendar of Swedish Name Days is available at ScandinaviUS.com.

The Name Day custom flourishes especially among Eastern Orthodox Christians. (The traditional Greek Name Day greeting is "Chrónìa pollá!") The Russians and Ukrainians think of their namesake Saints as ever-vigilant guardians and refer to their Name Days as their Angel's Days—on which bottle-bearing friends drop by for a drink or three.

Let's suppose you are a Greek, Russian, or Serb named (as is more than likely) Dimitri. Yearly on October 8—the Feast of Saint Demitrius the Megalomartyr—you will be "at home" to your pals not named Dimitri, who will all arrive bearing flowers, candy, and other thoughtful gifts. Lithuanians hang garlands on the door of the Name Day celebrant and sing a rousing tune called "Valio!" Each Latvian celebrates his *vardu dienu*, every Pole her *imieniny.* In fact, just about everybody in the rest of the world has been reveling in two birthdays a year, while you've been making do with one. And when you reach a certain age, you can eliminate birthday festivities and just celebrate your Name Day—on which the subject of how old you are never comes up.

So, send out the invitations and let

the merrymaking in honor of your Saint and yourself begin! (For party games, songs, and recipes appropriate to the festivities, we refer you to Helen McLoughlin's 1962 publication, *My Nameday, Come for Dessert.*)

Listed alphabetically are most of the most common first, or "Christian," names in use in North America and the dates of the Feasts of their appropriate Name Saints.

Now suppose, God bless you, you are called Mary. And you'd rather not share August 15—the Feast of the Assumption of the Blessed Virgin— with all the other Marys of the world. Well, there are a great many other an-nual festivals honoring Our Lady, as well as hundreds of ordinary (so to speak) Saints named Mary, all with their own Feast Days throughout the year. Feel free to choose any one of them for your personal Name Day.

In the interest of conserving paper, we have not included common varia-tions on names but assume that Bess, Beth, Betty, Eliza, Libby, Lisa, and Liz will have the sense to celebrate their Name Day on the Feast of Saint Eliz-abeth. For the same reason, our list is unfortunately ethnocentric—Giovanni, Hansel, Ian, Janek, Jean, Johann, Juan, and Sean are all, for our purposes, Johns.

Aaron—July 3

Abraham—June 15

Adam—December 19

Adrian—September 8

Alan—November 25

Albert—November 15

Alexander—February 26

Alfred—January 6

Allen—January 13

Alphonse—August 2

Andrew—November 30

Angelo—April 12

Anthony—January 17

Arnold (Arnulf)—July 18

Arthur—October 7

Austin (Augustine)—May 27

Barry—September 27

Bartholomew—August 24

Benedict—July 11

Benjamin—March 31

Bernard—August 20

Brandon/Brendan—May 16

Brian—March 22

Bruce (Brice)—November 13

Bruno—October 6

Carl (Charlemagne)—January 28

Chad—March 2

Charles—November 4

Christopher—July 25

Conrad—April 21

Daniel—October 10

David—March 1

Denis—October 9

Dominic—August 8

Donald—July 15

Duncan (Dunchadh)—May 25

Dustin (Dunstan)—May 19

Edmund—November 20

Edward—January 5

Elias/Elijah—July 20

Eric—May 18

Ernest—November 7

Eugene—August 23

Evan—August 18

Francis—October 4

Frederick—July 18

Gabriel—March 24

George—April 23

Gerald—October 13

Gregory—September 3

Guy—September 12

Harold—March 25

Harvey—June 17

Henry—July 13

Herbert—March 16

Herman—March 25

Hugh—November 17

Isaac—September 9

Ivan—June 24

Jacob—February 5

James—July 25

Jan—December 1

Jason—July 12

Jeffrey—November 8

Jeremy—September 15

Jerome—September 30

Joel—January 25

John—June 24

Jordan—February 15

Joseph—March 19

Joshua—September 1

Julian—February 12

Justin—June 1

Kenneth—October 11

Kevin—June 3

Kurt (Constantine)—July 27

Kyle—March 25

Lance (Lancelot, Laszlo)—June 27

Lawrence—August 10

Leo—November 10

Leonard—November 6

Louis—August 25

Luke—October 18

Manuel—June 17

Mario—December 31

Mark—April 25

Martin—November 11

Matthew—September 21

Maximilian—March 12

Michael—September 29

Myron—August 8

Nicholas—December 6

Oliver—July 1

Owen—August 24

Patrick—March 17

Paul—June 29

Peter—June 29

Philip—May 3

Ralph—June 21

Raphael—October 24

Raymond—January 7

Richard—April 3

Robert—September 17

Roger—January 28

Ronald—August 20

Rudolph—June 21

Ryan (Rian)—March 8

Samuel—November 10

Scott (Maurus Scott)—May 30

Simon—October 28

Stanley (Stanislaus)—April 11

Stephen/Steven—December 26

Terence—June 21

Thomas—July 3

Timothy—January 26

Troy (Troyen)—November 30

Victor—October 10

Vincent—January 22

Walter—April 8

Wilfred—January 18

William—June 8

Zachary—November 5

Adele (Adela)—February 24

Agnes—January 21

Alexandra—March 30

Alexis—July 17

Alice—June 15

Amanda (Amandus)—June 18

Amelia (Amalburga)—July 10

Andrea (Andrew)—November 30

Angela—January 27

Ann/Anna/Annette—July 26

Antonia (Antonina)—June 12

Ashley (the Blessed Ralph)—April 7

Audrey—June 23

Barbara—December 4

Beatrice—September 1

Bernadette—April 16

Beverly (John of)—May 7

Bonnie (Pulcheria)—September 10

Brenda (Brendan)—May 16

Bridget—July 23

Brigid—February 1

Brittany (Yves)—May 19

Callista—September 2

Carol/Caroline (Charles)—November 4

Catherine/Katherine—November 25

Cecilia—November 22

Christina/Christine—July 24

Clara/Clare—August 11

Claudia—August 7

Constance—February 18

Danielle (Daniel)—October 10

Dawn (Alba)—June 17

Desiree—February 19

Diana—June 9

Donna (Donata)—December 31

Dorothy—February 6

Elizabeth—November 5

Emily—September 19

Emma—April 19

Eva—May 26

Eve—September 6

Felicia (Felicity)—March 7

Flora—November 24

Florence—June 20

Frances—March 9

Genevieve—January 3

Georgie (Georgette)—February 15

Gertrude—November 16

Goldie (Aurea)—March 11

Grace—July 5

Gwen—June 1

Heidi—July 7

Helen/Helena—August 18

Hope—August 1

Irene—April 3

Isabel—February 26

Jacqueline—February 18

Jane—December 12

Jennifer (Gwen)—June 1

Joan/Jean—May 30

Joanna—May 24

Judith—June 29

Julia—May 22

Kathy/Karen (Catherine)—November 25

Kelly (Cealach)—May 1

Laura—October 19

Leah/Lea—March 22

Lillian—July 27

Lily (the Lily of Quito)—May 26

Louise—March 15

Lucy—December 13

Lydia—August 3

Madeline—May 25

Marcia—June 5

Margarita—June 9

Margaret/Megan—July 20

Maria—April 2

Marianne/Mariana—May 26

Marie—April 16

Martha—July 29

Mary—August 15

Matilda—March 14

Maura/Maureen—November 30

May (Amata)—June 10

Melanie—June 8

Michelle—June 20

Mildred/Milly—July 13

Monica—August 27

Natalie—December 1

Nell (Cornelia)—March 31

Nicole (Colette)—March 6

Olga—July 11

Patricia—March 13

Paula—January 26

Priscilla—January 16

Rachel (Rachildis)—November 23

Rebecca—March 23

Regina—September 7

Rita—May 22

Rosalie—September 4

Rose—August 23

Roseanne—May 22

Samantha (Samuel)—November 10

Sandra (Alexandra)—March 10

Sophia/Sophie—September 30

Stacy (Anastasia)—December 25

Stephanie—January 2

Susan/Susanna—July 25

Tammy (Tammarus)—September 1

Teresa/Tracy—October 15

Theresa—October 1

Tiffany (the Epiphany)—January 6

Valerie (Valeria)—December 10

Veronica—July 12

Victoria—December 23

Vivian (Bibiana)—December 2

Yolanda—June 15

Zoe—July 5

Art Credits

About the Authors

SEAN KELLY left teaching to edit the *National Lampoon*. Going from bad to worse, he now writes books (e.g., *Boom Baby Moon*) and television shows (e.g., *Between the Lions*). He lives in Brooklyn, New York, a loyal Canadian exile and practicing ex-Catholic.

ROSEMARY ROGERS is the coauthor of *Saints Preserve Us!, Who in Hell...*, *How to Be Irish (Even If You Already Are)*, *Boomer Babes,* and the *How to Be Irish 2001 Calendar.* She lives in Manhattan and always wears a Saint medal.